The Poor Are No

Eastern African Studies

Revealing Prophets
Edited by DAVID M.
ANDERSON & DOUGLAS H.
JOHNSON

Religion & Politics in East Africa
Edited by HOLGER BERNT
HANSEN & MICHAEL
TWADDLE

Swahili Origins
JAMES DE VERE ALLEN

Being Maasai
Edited by THOMAS SPEAR
& RICHARD WALLER

*A History of Modern Ethiopia
1855–1974*
BAHRU ZEWDE

*Ethnicity & Conflict
in the Horn of Africa*
Edited by KATSUYOSHI
FUKUI & JOHN MARKAKIS

*Conflict, Age & Power
in North East Africa*
Edited by EISEI KURIMOTO
& SIMON SIMONSE

Jua Kali Keny
KENNETH KING

*Control & Crisis in
Colonial Kenya*
BRUCE BERMAN

Unhappy Valley
Book One: State & Class
Book Two: Violence &
Ethnicity
BRUCE BERMAN
& JOHN LONSDALE

Mau Mau from Below
GREET KERSHAW

*The Mau Mau War in
Perspective*
FRANK FUREDI

*Squatters & the Roots
of Mau Mau 1905–63*
TABITHA KANOGO

*Economic & Social Origins
of Mau Mau 1945–53*
DAVID W. THROUP

Multi-Party Politics in Kenya
DAVID W. THROUP
& CHARLES HORNSBY

*Decolonization & Independence
in Kenya 1940–93*
Edited by B.A. OGOT
& WILLIAM R. OCHIENG'

*Penetration & Protest in
Tanzania*
ISARIA N. KIMAMBO

Custodians of the Land
Edited by GREGORY
MADDOX, JAMES L. GIBLIN
& ISARIA N. KIMAMBO

*Education in the Development
of Tanzania 1919–1990*
LENE BUCHERT

*The Second Economy
in Tanzania*
T.L. MALIYAMKONO
& M.S.D. BAGACHWA

*Ecology Control &
Economic Development in
East African History*
HELGE KJEKSHUS

Siaya
DAVID WILLIAM COHEN
& E.S. ATIENO ODHIAMBO

*Uganda Now
Changing Uganda
Developing Uganda*
From Chaos to Order*
Edited by HOLGER BERNT
HANSEN & MICHAEL
TWADDLE

*Kakungulu & the Creation
of Uganda 1868–1928*
MICHAEL TWADDLE

Controlling Anger
SUZETTE HEALD

Kampala Women Getting By
SANDRA WALLMAN

*Slaves, Spices & Ivory
in Zanzibar*
ABDUL SHERIFF

Zanzibar Under Colonial Rule
Edited by ABDUL SHERIFF
& ED FERGUSON

*The History & Conservation of
Zanzibar Stone Town*
Edited by ABDUL SHERIFF

*East African Expressions
of Christianity*
Edited by THOMAS SPEAR
& ISARIA N. KIMAMBO

The Poor Are Not Us
Edited by DAVID M.
ANDERSON
& VIGDIS BROCH-DUE

*Alice Lakwena & the
Holy Spirits*
HEIKE BEHREND

*Property Rights & Political
Development: The State in
Ethiopia & Eritrea, 1941–74*
SANDRA FULLERTON JOIRE

*Empire State-Building**
JOANNA LEWIS

*Revolution & Religion in
Ethiopia**
ØYVIND M. EIDE

* forthcoming

The Poor Are Not Us

Poverty & Pastoralism
in Eastern Africa

Edited by

DAVID M. ANDERSON &
VIGDIS BROCH-DUE

James Currey
OXFORD

E.A.E.P.
NAIROBI

Ohio University Press
ATHENS

James Currey
www.jamescurrey.com
is an imprint of Boydell & Brewer Ltd
PO Box 9. Woodbridge, Suffolk IP12 3DF, UK
and of Boydell & Brewer Inc.
668 Mt Hope Avenue, Rochester, NY 14620, USA
www.boydellandbrewer.com

East African Educational Publishing
P.O. Box 45314
Nairobi
Kenya

Ohio University Press
19 Circle Drive
The Ridges
Athens, OH 45701-2979

© David M. Anderson and Vigdis Broch-Due 1999
First published 1999

A catalogue record is available from the British Library

ISBN 978-0-85255-266-7 (cased) (James Currey)
ISBN 978-0-85255-265-0 (paper) (James Currey)

Library of Congress Cataloging-in-Publication Data available

ISBN 978-0-8214-1312-8 (cased) (Ohio University Press)
ISBN 978-0-8214-1313-5 (paper) (Ohio University Press)

Typeset in 10/12 pt Baskerville by
Long House, Cumbria, UK

Contents

List of Figures   vii
List of Tables   vii
Preface   ix

I   Introduction: Poverty Past & Present   1

1   *Poverty & the Pastoralist:*   3
Deconstructing Myths, Reconstructing Realities
VIGDIS BROCH-DUE (Nordic Afrika Institute, Uppsala)
& DAVID M. ANDERSON (SOAS, University of London)

2   *Pastoral Poverty*   20
in Historical Perspective
RICHARD D. WALLER (Bucknell University, PA)

3   *Remembered Cattle, Forgotten People:*   50
The Morality of Exchange
& the Exclusion of the Turkana Poor
VIGDIS BROCH-DUE (Nordic Afrika Institute, Uppsala)

II   Metaphors & Meanings   89

4   *Power & Poverty*   91
in Southern Somalia
BERNHARD HELANDER (Uppsala University)

5   *Pastoralists at the Border:*   106
Maasai Poverty
& the Development Discourse in Tanzania
AUD TALLE (University of Oslo)

Contents

6   'We are as Sheep & Goats':   125
    Iraqw & Datooga Discourses
    on Fortune, Failure & the Future
    OLE BJØRN REKDAL & ASTRID BLYSTAD
    (University of Bergen)

III Coins & Calories   147

7   Health Consequences of Pastoral Sedentarization   149
    among Rendille of Northern Kenya
    ELLIOT FRATKIN (Smith College, MA)
    MARTHA A. NATHAN (Holyoke Health Center, MA)
    & ERIC ABELLA ROTH (University of Victoria, BC)

8   Of Markets, Meat, Maize & Milk: 163
    Pastoral Commoditization in Kenya
    FRED ZAAL & TON DIETZ (University of Amsterdam)

9   Mutual Assistance among   199
    the Ngorongoro Maasai
    TOMASZ POTKANSKI (University of Warsaw)

IV Development Dialogues   219

10 Images & Interventions: 221
    The Problems of Pastoralist Development
    DOROTHY L. HODGSON (Rutgers University)

11 Rehabilitation, Resettlement & Restocking   240
    Ideology & Practice in Pastoralist Development
    DAVID M. ANDERSON (SOAS, University of London)

References   257
Index   271

List of Figures

1.1	East Africa showing locations of case studies	2
7.1	Map of Rendille study sites, northern Kenya	153
7.2	Rainfall, 1990 & 1992, Korr Town	156
7.3	Morbidity by location, 1990 & 1992	157
7.4	Diet by location, 1990 & 1992	159
7.5	Child malnourishment by location, 1990 & 1992	160
8.1	West Pokot & Kajiado Districts in Kenya	164
8.2	Cost-of-living index for low-income families, 1975–95	173
8.3	West Pokot District	174
8.4	Kajiado District	182
8.5	Household wealth in TLU	187
8.6	Income in cash & kind, 1980–81 & 1994–5	189
8.7	Expenditure in cash, 1980–81 & 1994–5	191
10.1	Masai District, c. 1970	227

List of Tables

7.1	Immunization data	158
8.1	Average numbers of introduced/cross-breeds of cattle & small stock per wealth class	188
8.2	Average annual household income in cash in Olkarkar, 1994–5	190
8.3	Average annual household cash expenditure in Olkarkar, per household wealth class	192
9.1	Maasai wealth/poverty categories	202
9.2	Wealth distribution of pastoral households in the NCA	205
9.3	Incidence of engalata cases in the NCA, 1985–93	212
9.4	Incidence of engalata cases in Monduli & Simanjiro Districts, 1991–3	214

Preface

The chapters of this anthology come from a larger collection of papers produced for a conference held in 1995 under the auspices of the research programme 'Poverty and Prosperity in Africa: Local and Global Perspectives' at the Nordic Africa Institute (NAI), Uppsala, Sweden. This first conference focused on the contested terrain of poverty and wealth from the perspectives of East African pastoralists – and how these not only change over time, but articulate in complex, often unforeseen ways with more global perspectives on both poverty and pastoralism. To explore these issues, the conveners, Dr. David M. Anderson, Senior Lecturer, School of Oriental and African Studies (SOAS), and Dr. Vigdis Broch-Due, head of the research programme at NAI, gathered several of the leading specialists in their respective fields, drawn from Scandinavia, Europe, the USA and East Africa. The list of participants included anthropologists, historians, sociologists, and ecologists from the academic world, as well as participants who work in the non-governmental organization (NGO) sector and in development consultancy.

The impetus to the conference and for this volume was a growing unease shared by the participants and editors about the ways that images of poverty and East African pastoralism have in recent years become inextricably bound up together in apocalyptic scenes of drought, famine and warfare. Media representations of swollen-bellied children, skeletal figures in drought-stricken landscapes and pitiful refugee camps are so powerful that, rather than stimulating critical examination of the complex causes of the crisis, they have circumvented it and urged upon planners the simplest of diagnoses and cures – pastoralism is not a strategy for survival, it is a recipe for disaster and impoverishment. It must be changed; 'something must be done'. Despite the urgent consensus on these matters, the 'something' that must be done remains far from clear.

The cure for the crisis depends totally on the diagnoses and these are many and contradictory – clearly deriving from different perspectives. There is the profoundest possible opposition between the diagnoses and perceptions of the planners and the perceptions of the pastoralists themselves. While planners see the reduction of livestock and moves towards sedentarization and cultivation as the ways to prosperity, pastoralists tend to see these as the very definition of poverty itself.

This difference brings into sharp focus the leading idea of this volume: that 'poverty' does not come with a single definition that can be easily detected through standardized indicators and measurement. While a lack of key resources is at the core of most local poverty registers, what defines that lack differs widely across societies and over time. It will be clear throughout this book that the essence of being poor in pastoral settings, and elsewhere, is forged from a multiplicity of possible lacks and short-comings: material, moral, social and metaphorical. This is because poverty is produced through processes of social differentiation and the politics of wealth and power as those shape particular communities. In other words, while the end results of poverty-producing processes are scarcity, suffering and social exclusion, poverty is formed within cultural frameworks and has to be examined in its proper social and historical contexts.

This volume explores discourses of poverty and prosperity, along with the social conditions and historical processes that have given rise to them. However, these divergent perspectives do not only manifest themselves as a matter *between* communities, but *within* them too. The ways that access to material and cultural resources, based on gender, generational, class and ethnic differences, within a particular community give rise to different perspectives is an important and little explored avenue of research within pastoral studies. A further aim of this volume is to examine the ways that various poverty discourses interact and influence each other, above all the ways in which the poverty discourse of the international development community has had an impact on understandings and practices at the local level. In short, we want to conceptualize differences in ideas and experiences and the enactments of these in terms of social differentiation; and also to contextualize discursive shifts in relation to socio-economic, ecological, political and institutional changes over the long term. We hope that this volume will highlight the complex interconnectedness of the conceptual and factual in all these areas and stimulate debate and fresh research into the ethnography of poverty and its historical trans-formations.

Much of the material has been considerably changed since the original conference. We are grateful to all the authors who have been so willing to rewrite and reorganize their papers along the theoretical lines suggested by the editors. We would also like to acknowledge the contributions to the discussions at the conference by those participants who, for various reasons, could not be represented by a separate chapter in this book. From this list we are particularly grateful to Gudrun Dahl, Sharon Hutchinson and Paul Spencer, who served as discussants. Thanks are also due to all those who worked so tirelessly to make both the conference and this publication a success, among whom Ulrica Risso, Karin Schiebe Anderson and Abraham Barmichale deserve special mention. Last, but not least, we would like to acknowledge the financial support to the original conference by the NAI and, by extension, all the ministries of foreign affairs in Denmark, Finland, Norway and Sweden, who jointly fund the research activities of the 'Poverty and Prosperity in Africa' research programme.

Vigdis Broch-Due
David M. Anderson

I INTRODUCTION: POVERTY PAST & PRESENT

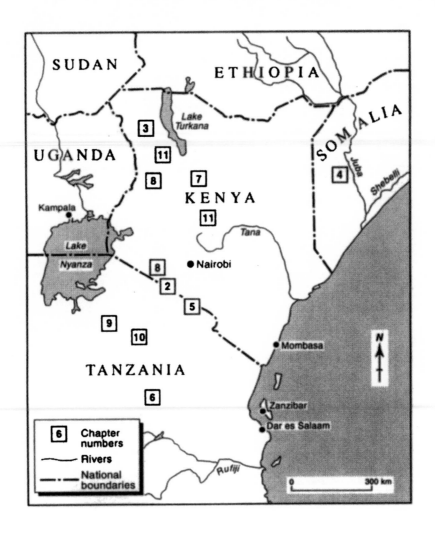

Figure 1.1 East Africa showing locations of case studies (arranged by chapter number)

1 Poverty & the Pastoralist: Deconstructing Myths, Reconstructing Realities

VIGDIS BROCH-DUE & DAVID M. ANDERSON

Taken at face value, the pastoralist peoples of eastern Africa seem to offer an unpromising field for the study of poverty. These are societies which present themselves as ostensibly egalitarian, where the accumulation of wealth is mediated by the need to redistribute livestock as social capital and from which the poor have historically been excluded through their loss of livestock, and hence their inability to sustain the means of pastoral production and reproduction. Unlike other pastoralists, such as the Tuareg of West Africa and the Tswana of southern Africa, who, as John Iliffe has noted, accommodate the poor as dependants within overtly inegalitarian social structures, the herding societies of eastern Africa slough off the poor into non-pastoralist, socially excluded categories (Iliffe, 1987:65). Among eastern Africa's pastoralists, 'the poor are not us'.

To explore the notion that 'the poor are not us' is to discover something of the self-perceptions and community consciousness of pastoralist societies in eastern Africa. It reveals the way in which pastoralist identity has been made in opposition to and as distinct from other modes of production. Above all else, it tells us how pastoralists may want others to see them and how, in an idealized sense, they see themselves (Kituyi, 1990; Spear & Waller, 1993; Fratkin et al., 1994).

But to accept such a statement as a definition of well-being or as an indication that poverty was in no sense a social problem for pastoralists would be to ignore the internal dynamics of pastoral society and economy. The very fact that absolute poverty results in social exclusion necessarily implies the possibility of a decline from prosperity, whether dramatic and rapid or slower and more gradual. Historically, such occurrences have become most visible at times of stress, resulting in the rapid loss of livestock holdings – in the wake of drought and famine or as a consequence of raiding or warfare. The effects of such dramatic events from the late nineteenth century to the present have been well documented, and the mechanisms by which destitute pastoralists have resorted to cultivation or hunting and gathering at times of crisis have been described for a number of cases (Spencer, 1974; Waller, 1985a; Lamphear, 1986; Johnson & Anderson, 1988; Sobania, 1988). These major events illustrate the ways by which the poor become, by definition, non-pastoralists.

Thus, while pastoralists are conscious of the manifestations of poverty in their midst, the terms around which they choose to describe and articulate their attitudes to impoverishment remain incomplete and refractory, tending to obscure the real material and social processes that lead to exclusion from the pastoral economy itself. Instead, pastoralists prefer to highlight the linkages between poverty and more sedentary pursuits and lifestyles. In other words, they readily recognize the end result of exclusion, but not the paths which lead to it.

This muting of the realities of poverty in pastoral societies needs to be scrutinized, but to date the topic has attracted remarkably little scholarly attention. More often the subtle, ideological misrecognition generated by pastoralists themselves has been uncritically reproduced in the scholarly discourse, reinforcing the normative stereotypes of pastoralist egalitarianism. One of the main aims of this volume is to take hold of this issue and clear away some of the confusion that surrounds it.

What, for instance, of the changing patterns of wealth and accumulation that might see one family gradually prosper while its neighbours increasingly struggle? What of the slow, everyday creeping onset of poverty experienced through the dwindling supply of milk to feed your children? What of the effects of compression of rangelands and diminishing resources upon an enlarged pastoral community? What of the impact of external values of land, labour and livestock, upon which some herders have been prepared to capitalize while others have not? To pose such questions is explicitly to reject the premise of pastoral egalitarianism, and to suggest that many pastoralists have in fact experienced poverty without being excluded from pastoralist communities (Schneider, 1979; Galaty, 1981). This is not wholly to dismiss pastoralist self-presentation of their own social order, for the notion that 'the poor are not us' is by no means incompatible with a situation in which the internal definition of poverty has itself been changed by a generally worsening situation in which everyone has less: while we may not be the poor, we may still be getting poorer.

Although the large corpus of general literature on eastern African pastoralism displays little direct awareness of the issue of poverty, much evidence has accumulated in recent years to indicate that a gradual pauperization is currently being experienced among many herding communities (Hogg, 1985, 1986; Little, 1985a&b; Dietz, 1987; Hogg & Baxter, 1990; Broch-Due, 1990b; Rutten, 1992; Campbell, 1993). The reasons for this can be seen in the interaction between a number of dislocating events, which have shaken pastoralist communities over the last decade or so, and

4

underlying socio-economic trends, which have tended to accentuate the gap between wealthier and poorer herders. The political marginalization of pastoralists across much of the region is nothing new, but it has resulted in increasing economic marginalization since the early 1980s, as states, hard-pressed to impose sterner fiscal measures, elect to deliver resources to other sectors of the economy and to areas other than the semi-arid rangelands occupied by herders. Environmental events have also had an adverse impact. The clustering of drought years in the 1980s took a heavy toll of livestock holdings, weakening the productive base of pastoralist society and leaving many herders destitute (Broch-Due, 1986; Hogg, 1986; Fratkin, 1991; Little, 1992). Pastoralists have, of course, recovered from such setbacks in the past, and many have recovered well from the trials of the 1980s. But, for some, environmental adversity in those years was compounded by other factors. In several places, most notably parts of Kenya's Rift Valley, a rapid advance in the commoditization of the rangeland significantly weakened the economic position of a majority of herders, while strengthening that of a minority. This process has seen large acreages of pastureland fall under the plough, especially in the better-watered areas – thereby denying herders some of their most valued grazing. Elsewhere, the shift toward group ranches and individual tenure has made inroads into the commons (Baxter & Hogg, 1990; Rutten, 1992; Galaty, 1994). While these emerging commercial trends have been reshaping pastoralism at different rates in many parts of Kenya and Tanzania, in Somalia, Ethiopia, southern Sudan and northern Uganda the dislocations of war and famine have been the principal factors contributing to an emerging pattern of impoverishment. But even in those pastoralist communities visited by warfare, poverty is to be seen alongside comparative prosperity (De Waal, 1989; Hutchinson, 1996). There are important questions to be asked, therefore, about the factors determining which pastoral households are best placed to survive such trials and which suffer the worst consequences.

The principal purpose of this volume is to probe beyond the myths of pastoral wealth and egalitarianism to consider the present realities of social differentiation among herders that these events and underlying trends have helped to expose. The chapters collected here show that the assumption of egalitarianism has disguised the extent of contestation within pastoral communities over access to material and cultural resources. There is no attempt made to formally define any universal pastoralist measure of poverty in strict material or cultural terms. Rather, the emphasis is placed upon the various meanings of poverty and its material outcomes in different communities. Crucially, we also consider changes in those meanings and thus the social identities of the pastoral poor over time. Poverty is therefore examined in qualitative as well as quantitative terms, and both are set within specified sociological boundaries.

5

In examining the meanings and effects of poverty, the questions raised by our authors fall into two broad categories. The first addresses the issue of impoverishment and asks about the long-term processes behind it. To what extent have pastoral communities cared for their less fortunate members, and can we discern any decline in the utility and effect of such internal welfare provisions? In those communities where a general decline in food security is identifiable, what are its causes and can the effects be evaluated differentially? Within the domestic sphere, have levels of nutrition altered over time and to what extent can such changes be viewed as indicating improvement or decline in economic well-being? And, at the most fundamental level, we shall ask whether pastoral households have lost control over their subsistence production and, if so, in what circumstances this has happened? For many, such a loss of control is associated with the crises of drought or warfare, and we need also to ask how such events affect internal social dynamics. Are the changes provoked by crisis merely temporary, or do they have more permanent consequences? To what extent does the short-term recovery of pastoralist communities disguise a longer-term undermining of the production system?

The second category of questions to be addressed examines the ways in which changing material conditions are experienced and made meaningful by pastoral communities. The last two decades, in particular, have witnessed a profound social transformation in pastoral settings across eastern Africa, as increasing numbers of pastoralists have been dislodged from herding. As destitution has become more widespread, what impact has this had upon internal understandings of poverty and want? How are such matters expressed, and in what ways are new material realities manifested in social behaviour? At the same time, the social topography of the poor and prosperous has changed as cattle have given way to cash as the means of valuation and exchange. To what extent has this wrought a transformation of the key institutions of redistribution in pastoral societies, such as bride-wealth, stock loans and the norms of sharing livestock and their products? Among some communities, this has had a profound impact upon the very fabric of the social order – the mediation and maintenance of gender, generational and kin relationships. How have these dramatic changes affected the moral economy and cultural discourses surrounding ideas of poverty and prosperity – indeed, the very concept of the person? In short, how have pastoralists coped with the gradual realization that, contrary to their own self-image, 'we have become the poor'?

At a more general level, three broader questions form the central concern of this volume. To what extent can we identify new categories of rich and poor among pastoralists? Have these developments been isolated to particular communities, or do they signify a more widespread decline in the resource base of pastoralism across the region? And what changes have occurred in the internal mechanisms by which eastern Africa's pastoralists have in the past coped with the problems of their poor? Our common starting point is an acceptance of the changing patterns of pastoralist poverty and pastoralist prosperity, substantiated by an understanding of the social conditions and historical processes which have given rise to them. The evidence gathered here suggests that there is a quantitative difference in the extent and effects of the poverty being experienced by pastoralists as the twentieth century draws to a close, but in qualitative terms many of the processes involved can be charted through the last century and more of pastoralist history.

Poverty past and present

Our opening two chapters introduce these issues from historical and anthropological perspectives respectively. Richard Waller's survey of historical patterns of poverty among Maasai herders acts as a benchmark against which to assess the nature of more recent interpretations of the changes within pastoralist communities. Although the historical evidence for poverty among eastern African pastoralists is sparse, Waller finds much to indicate that poverty has been an endemic feature of pastoral life over the past century, but that its character has been changing. Taking up Iliffe's approach of distinguishing between structural and conjunctural poverty – that is, between those who are structurally poor because of their long-term personal or social circumstances and those who are conjuncturally poor because of the temporary effects of a crisis – Waller argues that structural poverty only appears to have been absent among pastoralists in eastern Africa because of the social exclusion of persons falling into such a category (Iliffe, 1987). It is therefore important to consider the mechanisms by which pastoralists have marginalized their own poor in the past, and to appreciate the ways in which colonial and postcolonial changes have hampered or transformed the operation of those mechanisms. At one level, then, the poor are now more visible simply because they cannot be so easily excluded, as in the past. This, Waller shows, has led to the emergence of alternative, even 'subversive' internal redefinitions of poverty and wealth among Maasai (see also Spear & Waller, 1993).

Contrary to the widely held assumption that disasters have a 'levelling' effect among pastoralists, Waller suggests that, because the wealthy have greater resources and better-developed social networks, the incremental impact of crises can be to strengthen their relative position and thereby increase differentiation. The 'ratchet effect' of successive environmental crises and the compounding of this by restrictions on access to pastoral resources can be charted historically for Maasailand, demonstrating the manner in which those first struck by conjunctural poverty can come to find themselves in the more serious trap of structural poverty.

7

These processes can be described, but it is more difficult to understand why some families 'bounce back' from conjunctural poverty while others are not so fortunate. The social networks that can sustain the poor within pastoral societies as the dependants of others are more clearly seen in contemporary sociological evidence than in the historical sources. Just as Waller reports some 10 per cent of the Purko Maasai herders surveyed on Laikipia in 1912 holding too few stock to sustain them, Turkana pastoralists in the 1990s include the wealthy and the poor. In her discussion of poverty among Turkana, Vigdis Broch-Due emphasizes that, for Turkana, poverty is 'made' by the choices and decisions of the household. It is the operation of social networks of interdependence constructed by the prudent herder, as Broch-Due shows, that allows for survival and recovery in the face of a decline into poverty (Johnson & Anderson, 1988). 'Flexible and inclusive collaborative arrangements' shield the extent of endemic social inequality among Turkana. In family histories, we hear stories of the construction of relationships that led to prosperity and wealth. These re-affirm the norms of social life in Turkana, demonstrating the achievement of appropriate choices and carefully taken decisions. The poor, marked by failure and inability, tend to be forgotten in these histories and, although it is acknowledged that misfortune may strike anyone, the assumption is that a prudent person will be able to recover, whereas the imprudent will not.

One of the key features of the simultaneous muting and moralizing of the reality of poverty by pastoral Turkana is the way in which livestock become emblems for all the social relations gathered around them. Turkana project all the social dramas surrounding social differentiation into the domain of livestock. The title 'Remembered cattle, forgotten people' draws immediate attention to how social distinctions are reproduced in livestock herds – and, even more than that, how biographies of specific animals come to carry more social and moral weight than the lives of their owners. Given that the domain of livestock thus becomes a kind of mirror for the social processes producing wealth distinctions, Broch-Due explores this domain in great detail, because it gives us privileged access not only to the contemporary poverty scenario, but also to the long-term historical transformations in the topography of wealth and scarcity in Turkanaland.

Recognizing that poverty exists within pastoral communities is not to deny the marginalization and exclusion of the poor, either in the past or in the present. Where in the past stockless Turkana sought refuge in long-established hunting, fishing and cultivating communities on the periphery of the rangelands, whose activities were integrated with the productive cycles of pastoralism and from where the mechanisms for re-entry into herding could be operated, the modern towns to which the poverty-stricken now drift have few points of meaningful articulation with the pastoral system – as Aud Talle makes vividly clear (Chapter 5) in the case of Namanga. Here, again, contemporary anthropological analysis amplifies the historical trends indicated by Waller: while more pastoralists are now being excluded, fewer can find a path back.

To identify underlying trends such as these may suggest a linear progress over time from one type of society to another, but the reality is not quite so simple. Fluctuations intrude as the circumstances of pastoralist communities alter. The commoditization of land and labour in Turkana was accelerated dramatically in the 1980s, fuelled by large-scale aid projects and the development of a stronger market economy. In the 1990s a different economic climate prevails, with a revival in the strength of the local livestock economy, a decline in the availability of cash through a withdrawal of aid and a slump in the market economy, and a general halting of the process of commoditization. The relationship of long-term to short-term change, and the distinctive features of localities are key elements affecting the patterns of social differentiation within pastoralist societies across the region. To comprehend such changes, history and anthropology have to move in tandem.

Metaphors and meanings

Pastoralist poverty is not merely a matter of metaphors, but even where its social manifestations in insufficiency, scarcity and suffering are blatantly evident, its meanings and interpretations must inevitably be culturally and conceptually constructed. Far from being a straightforward condition of deprivation and destitution that is easily defined empirically, poverty is in fact a contentious and complex construct which encapsulates a vast range of social and historical struggles and constantly evolving cultural values (Broch-Due, 1995). The three chapters grouped in Part I of this volume explore the cultural expressions of poverty and the shaping and contestation of their meanings for pastoral communities.

These chapters discuss poverty, sufficiency and wealth in qualitative, culturally specific contexts, avoiding any attempt to quantify or to compare. Any attempt to assess pastoralist poverty at a purely materialist level quickly encounters the difficulty of the various cultural conceptualizations of wealth that are held by eastern Africa's herding societies. As John and Jean Comaroff have written, for the herder, livestock, most particularly cattle, are 'the medium of transformations in a total economy of sign and practices, between a material economy of things and a moral economy of persons' (Comaroff and Comaroff, 1990). Like money, livestock may be currency and capital simultaneously, thereby having the unusual ability to make commensurable different forms of value and to convert one form into another. It is this capacity to equate and transform, to give worth and meaning, that animates both cattle and cash.

It is precisely this extraordinary force of livestock and livestock imagery in the everyday lives of pastoralists that gives the poverty register its

9

particular twist. The 'poor-are-not-us' idiom bears evidence of the existence of blank spots in social consciousness – a lot of forgetting is going on here. How such skewed representations are produced can only be studied through exploring the configuration of specific structures of values and concerns. In her introductory chapter, Broch-Due sensitizes the reader to the ways in which this muting is created by the whole moral and existential universe of pastoralism, which ties together human life and the life of herds in almost every aspect. Poverty is interpreted as a negation of this universe and is seen to be the result of not managing these two vital assets – herds and humans – in a proper way. In short, poverty is given a moral twist.

The 'signs and practices' that give livestock value must therefore be seen in cultural terms, and pastoralists have a rich vocabulary of metaphors with which to express such matters. The concept of 'path', for example, central to Broch-Due's discussions of the conceptualization of things and their values in Turkana, is also employed in this volume by Helander with reference to Somalia. In Turkana thought, the path, visible on the land-scape, is also the metaphor for the construction of networks of real and symbolic capital that will secure the household against the threat of poverty: physical paths are also social pathways along which relationships flow. For Turkana, paths connect cattle and goats, they connect goats and cash, but no path connects cattle and cash. The two are not directly con-vertible, this reflecting cultural views of the domains occupied by different forms of wealth. Goats allow the paths of mundane exchange cycles to intersect with the more enduring and culturally significant cattle cycle.

In the Somali case analysed by Helander, livestock are also used as a crucial signifier in the social landscape that unfolds between the poor and the prosperous. What binds these two ethnographic examples together is the way that livestock are excluded from the poverty equation – and lack of livestock is what defines the poor. However, being poor in Somalia is a stigma attached to a particular position in the social hierarchy – the identity of the *boon* – the commoners, as opposed to the *bilies*, the aristocrats. In other words, Helander gives us a case clearly showing how low social prestige and poverty are phenomena that are parts of the same cultural package. This chapter positions a Somali notion of poverty within the overall fabric of ideas that define groups and the members of groups. Poverty within the Hubeer clan is marked socially in terms of heritage – defined in terms of a cultural mixture of descent and bodily substances – as much as by actual economic standing. Here the trajectories of groups are kept apart by restricting access to political authority. Commoners of inferior status may be thought to have sunk to this through the loss of economic wealth, but the ideology of dominant noble groups among the Hubeer inverts the logic of this: to be a commoner is to be poor, regard-less of the numbers of livestock accumulated. Here, then, a deeply entrenched social discourse about poverty, replete with metaphor and symbol, is conducted without any direct reference to economic resources. Helander alerts us to the ways in which particular poverty definitions can play a more subtle and perhaps malicious role in cementing cultural images of disadvantaged groups.

For many contemporary Somalis, poverty is less a state of economic standing measured in terms of livestock than it is a confining marker of social identity. The fact that lack of livestock – even if merely metaphorical – is still used as the conventional marker of the stigmatized *boon* identity raises the interesting issue of transformations of the poverty scenario and social identities of the poor over time. One should not foreclose the possibility that in the past, real material wealth in domesticated animals was once central to the distinction between poor and prosperous in Somaliland too. The reference to a possible origin of *boon* as hunters indicates that they did not possess livestock in the past. These material conditions have historically been redescribed in terms that relate the poor *boon* identity to other traits and conditions. This redescription is part of political struggles linked to the changes in the topography of wealth and the social identities of the wealthy over time. Each such potential discursive shift may leave its trace – a sort of semantic sediment – in the social conceptualization of poverty (Broch-Due, 1996). As Helander demonstrates, this process generates a vast array of potential cultural and political associations with poverty which can be drawn upon selectively and according to the social context of any situation.

Both Broch-Due and Helander draw upon a far wider African ethnography in which the concept of 'path' features prominantly. The metaphor of the path organizes Ferguson's influential study of 'the topography of wealth' in rural Lesotho (Ferguson, 1992), for example, and is the local summarizing symbol in Jackson's (1989) work on Sierra Leone. More generally, the concept has been deployed as a globalized tool in comparative studies of economies and exchange for theorizing about 'things in motion' and, in this respect, it has particular relevance to our understanding of pastoralist poverty. The idea of 'path' was first abstracted in this way by Appadurai (1986), from the study of Melanesian *kula* exchange, in order to derive a broader model of 'the social life of things'. Appadurai's model tears loose the concept of 'commodity' from its usual grounding in capitalism, and sets it in motion throughout history and across cultural boundaries where the trappings of capitalist development are lacking. This move manages to dismantle a whole set of established dualisms in economic anthropology – between 'gift economy' and 'commodity economy', between 'traditional' and 'modern' and between 'use value' and 'exchange value'. In so doing, Appadurai replaces the vexed definitional question of 'What is a commodity?' with the more promising question, 'Under what circumstances and at what point in time do objects enter into exchange?' This question has very great pertinence to the process of commoditization evident among many eastern African pastoralist societies as both labour and land have become endowed with monetary values and are increasingly being bought and sold (Dietz, 1987; Ensminger, 1992; Little, 1992; Rutten, 1992; Hutchinson, 1996).

The processual perspective of Appadurai's approach allows us to explore the culturally constructed and politically negotiated characteristics of objects that qualify them for exchange in the first place. By tracing objects through specific exchange scenarios, we encounter the conventionally prescribed commodity pathways that constitute a 'regime of value' by promoting the dominant interests in society. Within any system, as Broch-Due describes for Turkana, the enclaving of certain objects protects their status in what Ferguson calls the wider 'topography of wealth' (Ferguson, 1992). The relationships between the status of things and their exchange value is crucial to an understanding of the impact of commoditization (see Guyer, 1995).

It is in the recent work of Sharon Hutchinson (1996) on the Nuer that the potential of this analytical approach has been grasped most firmly with application to pastoralism in eastern Africa. In a close examination of the dilemmas confronting Nuer society as a consequence of the dislocations of war, Hutchinson explores the ways in which social relationships have been redefined and refined in order to articulate older forms of social capital, represented by 'blood', 'cattle' and 'food', with new things, represented by 'money', 'guns' and 'paper' – the cash economy, the weapons needed to defend one's capital and the education that sets some men apart from their fellows. Nuer have entered into the monetary economy in a way that is markedly different from the experience of the Turkana, with a distinctive set of cultural meanings being ascribed to cash and its acquisition and uses. While Nuer cultural expressions attempt to hold the fixity of older, established values, the social reality shows a more significant shift in practice, which their rhetoric (perhaps deliberately) shields. The gap between expression and action may widen as new commodities enter exchange cycles, and this is a feature of Hutchinson's analysis that could usefully be explored in similar ways for other pastoralist groups.

Images and interpretations of success and failure are reflected in notions of wealth and poverty, and the two are often closely bound together. For some pastoralists, their apparent failure to keep control of their own production systems is a consequence of the success of their neighbours in alienating crucial resources for their own use. One such example is found in the long-standing struggle in northern Tanzania between the pastoralist Datooga and their agropastoral Iraqw neighbours, here described by Rekdal and Blystad in Chapter 6. Rekdal and Blystad chart the decline of Datooga prosperity in the face of surreptitious land acquisition by Iraqw. Secrecy, manipulation, conquest and expansion are recurrent themes in

Iraqw discourse on their success, contrasting sharply with the Datooga emphasis on keeping distance, avoidance and withdrawal. Where Iraqw notions and practice are characterized by pragmatism, inventiveness and lack of strong bonds to ancestral spirits, Datooga seem preoccupied with continuity and the reproduction of the eternal order guarded by ancestral spirits. While Iraqw acquire more land to cultivate and more animals to herd, Datooga fear that their lineages may die out. The Datooga decline into relative poverty is powerfully illustrated by the ever more common sight of Datooga labourers at work on Iraqw farms. From this perspective, all Iraqw appear as winners, but the internal tensions and conflicts over rights to land and livestock linger under the surface in the description of both communities. Views of poverty and wealth very much depend upon where you stand.

The internal discourses on pastoralist poverty we have discussed thus far have, of course, their external analogues. How do other eastern Africans view pastoralist societies, and what categories and terms do they invoke to describe the poor in such communities? This aspect is examined in Aud Talle's chapter, the title of which, 'Pastoralists at the border', refers both to the place in which the study is set – Namanga, a multiethnic 'modern' town on the border between Kenya and Tanzania – and to the marginal position of the Maasai within the national context. The border metaphor, associated with peripherality and displacement, captures the essence of the relationship between the Maasai and the encompassing society (see also Talle, 1988). When visiting Namanga town, Maasai become anomalous, their clothing and body ornamentation constituting a stark contrast to 'things modern', setting them apart as people lacking development. Talle emphasizes the importance of smell and the association of poverty with foul odours and perceived uncleanliness in defining the 'difference' of the Maasai who come to town. Viewed by outsiders, all Maasai may thus be thought of as suffering from poverty, as they appear not to accept the 'gift' of development and modernity. It is in town that this 'poverty' is most visible and undermining. This, like Helander's Somali example, reveals pervasive discursive categories of 'the poor' which ignore economic factors. Or, are we rather confronted here with a reinterpretation of the economic in the image of the market – a more narrowly modernist definition in which the economic is reduced to employment income and education? In this version of poverty, cattle wealth is muted and the lack of modern regalia is what defines the pastoralists as poor in the eyes of the 'modernized' residents of the town.

Coins and calories

Quantifiable measures of poverty, defined most usually by incomes or nutrition and, for pastoralists particularly, by the counting of livestock, are often both inadequate and misleading when detached as raw statistics from the context of their cultural moorings. But precisely because such 'thin descriptions' (to borrow Geertz's terminology) model social phenomena in minimal and measurable terms, they give a comforting appearance of objectivity and seem to travel with ease across cultural and historical boundaries. Their attraction as indicators lies precisely in their transferability, and this quality in turn depends upon the assumption of their value-free status. They seem context-free and commonsensical and, for their audiences, apparently also freed from the contamination of authorship and agency. For these reasons, 'thin descriptions' form the basis of most comparative assessments of poverty (Geertz, 1974; Broch-Due, 1995, 1996).

In a wider application, 'thin descriptions' also inform and reinforce the development narratives that permit global prescriptions to be issued to solve identified and 'labelled' problems in pastoral areas and elsewhere (Roe, 1991; Leach & Mearns, 1996). Statistics tell stories: but, for East Africa's pastoralists, the narratives numbers relate can be used to convey dramatically divergent messages. Potential contradictions abound, and the deployment of statistics is often a loaded, political question. In Baringo in the late 1920s, for example, one department of colonial government calculated that the numbers of livestock being herded on the lowland pastures was far in excess of the carrying capacity and that the local Tugen herders should be compelled to destock, while another department interpreted the figures to reveal that the same herders had too few livestock to meet their basic subsistence requirements (Anderson, forthcoming).

'Thin descriptions' of poverty in terms of coins and calories are most meaningful if kept in their cultural context, where apparent contradictions, such as that indicated in the Baringo example, can be explored and analysed. The three chapters in Part II of this volume seek to accomplish this by keeping that which is measurable very firmly within the cultural context that gave rise to it.

In the first chapter, Fratkin, Nathan and Roth set out to assess the impact of sedentarization upon nutritional intake among Rendille camel pastoralists. A nutritional and health survey, utilizing interviews, anthropometric measurements, physical examinations and haemoglobin measurements, was conducted for 105 mothers and their 174 children under six years of age in three Rendille communities, one fully nomadic and two sedentary, in July 1990, a year of above average rainfall, and again in June 1992, a drought year. Results indicate that, while the nomadic Rendille community shares similar morbidity patterns with its sedentary counterparts and had similar numbers of malnourished children during the wet year, the sedentary communities had significantly more malnutrition among children during the dry year. Moreover, the children in the settled town of Korr had significantly higher levels of anaemia. These differences in malnutrition are attributed to distinctive dietary regimes:

during the drought, nomadic children consumed three times as much milk as the sedentary children, while settled children consumed higher concentrations of starches, fats and sugars. This study suggests that the pastoral nomadic diet, particularly one dependent on camels' milk, offers children better resistance to the pressures of drought and is superior to sedentary alternatives, including town diets supplemented by grain-based famine-relief foods. Given that pastoralists struck by stock losses in the wake of drought or dislocation are encouraged by governments and aid agencies to settle, these findings indicate that such a course of action may not be in their best longer-term interests.

The nutritional status of any pastoral household turns upon their access to an adequate number of livestock, the products of which can be directly consumed or exchanged for other foods (see Galvin *et al.*, 1994). In Chapter 8, Fred Zaal and Ton Dietz ask whether commoditization eases the tension that can exist between the limited capacity of pastoral production and household needs. To do this, they develop a caloric production and exchange model to analyse changing pastoral production and consumption patterns, thereby linking nutritional and economic measurements. Their model evaluates shifts in the caloric terms of trade over time, relates this to market risk analysis and assesses the exchange relationship in food energy terms of products bought and sold. In this way, they are able to show for their two Kenyan cases, the Pokot pastoralists of the north-west and the Maasai of Kajiado District, at what points the sale of livestock will bring the pastoralist comparative advantage in caloric terms.

The relatively stable and advantageous terms of trade favouring pastoralists appear to indicate the general value of this strategy, supporting the view that commoditization can improve household food security in the cases studied. But this depends, of course, upon the operation of a functional livestock and cereals market and whether pastoralists are able to choose when to enter into exchange (Ensminger, 1992; Little, 1992). But the way in which commoditization affects individual households in the Zaal and Dietz study very much depends upon their initial economic status. Poor households, whether in Pokot or Kajiado, generally use the market as a means of survival, to be turned to in times of trouble. Wealthier households, better capitalized and more secure in their production, are able to exploit market opportunities in a more structured way. For these pastoralists, increasing commoditization tends to draw them toward commercial livestock production and all that implies. Commoditization can therefore be seen to sharpen the differences between rich and poor in the most fundamental way (Galaty, 1981, 1994; Rutten, 1992; Campbell, 1993).

The comparison of Pokot and Kajiado serves to remind us, once again, that trends in pastoral development are seldom universal. Where in Pokot many pastoralists have been excluded as a consequence of stock losses over the past decade and more and others are evidently still suffering poverty and hardship, in Kajiado pastoralism seems to be thriving in its adaptation to market opportunities. Kajiado's poor would thus appear to be considerably better off than the poor of Pokot. But, of course, any such comparative judgement of relative hardship needs to be rooted in a clear understanding of the social context and support mechanisms operating within each community.

This is the starting-point for Tomasz Potkanski's examination of poverty and its effects among the Ngorongoro Maasai of northern Tanzania. In contrast to the relatively wealthy Maasai of Kajiado, the livestock holdings of Ngorongoro households are, on average, considerably smaller and the process of commoditization is far less advanced (Århem, 1985; Homewood & Rodgers, 1991). Potkanski argues that these herders have been becoming poorer and that many have now reached a critically vulnerable stage. His concern is to examine how they have coped with this reality. To do this, he examines the operation of a clan-based system of mutual assistance, which permits the redistribution of livestock to impoverished families through long-term loans or gifts. The need for mutual assistance is determined, Potkanski argues, by indigenous measures of need. Though difficult to verbalize in quantifiable and comparative terms, these criteria can be seen to function in daily social practice. Maasai views of poverty and the sustainability of households as productive units are derived from their own internal evaluations of the productive capacity of each polygamous household. This allows them to arrive at a quite different assessment of livestock requirements than do externally derived indices. Need, as determined here, has as much to do with the maintenance of expected social norms as with measurements of absolute subsistence requirements, as Potkanski's discussion of the impact of poverty on the payment of bride-price shows. Here, once again, the reality of poverty and its discursive rhetoric stand apart as Maasai maintain expected social norms by negotiating transactions that cannot be fulfilled.

Even though the entire pastoral production system around Ngorongoro is demonstrably under severe pressure, the situation is far worse in some locations than in others. In the most deprived and destocked areas, clansmen are already unable to fulfil their obligations of mutual assistance, and the practical definition of individual entitlement is being modified by the necessity of wider community poverty. In this example we can begin to see the processes by which the erosion of support mechanisms can turn conjunctural poverty into structural poverty.

Development dialogues

Potkanski concludes his analysis of poverty in Ngorongoro with the suggestion that appropriately targeted restocking holds the hope of relaunching some of the area's poorest households back into pastoralism. The two chapters that conclude this volume take a less optimistic view of the prospects for development interventions successfully restoring the productive capacity of pastoral systems.

In eastern Africa, as Aud Talle has reminded us, the rhetoric of development is very much focused upon the need to alleviate poverty. This is a cause that appears neutral and unproblematic, but when applied to pastoralists, it has too often meant the foreclosing of herding as a productive system and the attempt to shift pastoralists into other, alternative and allegedly more secure forms of production (Baxter, 1975; Sandford, 1983; Little, 1985b; Hogg, 1986; Baxter & Hogg, 1990; Galaty, 1992, 1994). As Dorothy Hodgson explains, part of the 'problem' in pastoralist development is the formulation of the 'problem' itself. This is rooted in the continued widespread acceptance of old colonial-era stereotypes, such as Elspeth Huxley's much quoted portrayal of East Africa's pastoralists, dating from half a century ago: 'These obstinately conservative nomads' wrote Huxley, 'wandering with their enormous herds from pasture to pasture, seem like dinosaurs or pterodactyls, survivors from a past age with a dying set of values ... aristocratic, manly, free, doomed' (Huxley, 1948:89). In common with Huxley, the implicit assumption of governments and many agencies involved in bringing development to the pastoral areas is that pastoralism has no future (Anderson, 1993).

The developers' long-standing perspective which views pastoralists, and especially Maasai pastoralists, as 'culturally conservative', stubbornly persistent in their rejection of farming, sedentarization, education and other more 'modern' ways of being, ignores the realities of pastoral adaptation, flexibility and straddling, which are amply illustrated in this volume and elsewhere (Johnson & Anderson, 1988; Spear & Waller, 1993; Fratkin *et al.*, 1994). But is the process of development in any way affected by these other, alternative presentations of pastoralist lifestyle? It would appear not. That development projects have consistently failed to meet their own objectives and yet are repeatedly implemented in almost identical versions has less to do with any inherent Maasai 'conservatism', than with the fixed cultural images nurtured and sustained by a succession of state administrators, non-governmental organizations and other development agents.

The image of Maasai pastoralism as a male-dominated world in which livestock – and only livestock – act as the measure of identity and social acceptability in fact serves to reinforce a now grossly outdated normative Maasai view of their own society. It is a view that overlooks decades of slow change and reform, of adaptation and compromise, processes that have substantially altered what it is to be Maasai (Spear & Waller, 1993). But it is a view that reaffirms the appropriateness of a particular set of interventions, invoking a received narrative of the 'problem' of pastoralist development. To illustrate this more specifically, Hodgson considers the set of development interventions mounted through the US Agency for International Development (USAID) Maasai Livestock and Range Management Project between 1969 and 1979. Shaped by a narrow, ahistorical, gendered image of pastoralism, this project produced interventions considered 'appropriate' and which were designed solely to improve livestock production. All project components, resources and training were directed to Maasai men, not women. The consequences of such interventions were firstly limited by the failure to meet any of the pre-set goals, but Hodgson also demonstrates that the project contributed to the intensification of the economic insecurity of Maasai households, the increased disenfranchisement of Maasai women from their rights in livestock and the further consolidation of state power over Maasai. None of these outcomes were necessarily intended, but all were subsumed within the development package delivered by USAID.

Men and women in pastoralist communities, whether poor or prosperous, accommodate their decisions on production, consumption and exchange to the fact that they occupy gendered structural locations with respect to the control of land, livestock and labour. In many cases, their separate production enterprises have different seasonal rhythms, which correspond in different ways to the family's subsistence needs (Broch-Due, 1983; Guyer, 1993). In daily social practice, there will inevitably be cultural influences that shape who does what and who has access to what kind of resources, but, as we focus more upon gender relations among pastoralists, it becomes increasingly clear that negotiation plays an important role in determining outcomes at a household level (Broch-Due, 1983, 1990a; Talle, 1987, 1988; Kipury, 1989; Kettel, 1992; Hodgson, 1995). Processes of commoditization, for example, will have their effects upon a local economy, as Zaal and Dietz show us, but within households these changes will provoke new internal struggles over livestock, food and services, the terms of which need to be studied more closely if we are to assess the differential impact of such interventions. Indeed, the whole notion of a unified household strategy, shaped to adapt and adjust to externally produced structural change, which has for so long dominated the assumptions underpinning pastoralist development projects, needs to be seriously questioned (Yanagisako, 1979; Harris, 1981; Broch-Due, 1983, 1986, 1987, Broch-Due & Rudie, 1993; Guyer, 1984; Folbre, 1984; Moore, 1987).

Despite the evident failure of development projects in pastoral areas to achieve their stated aims over many years, there remains an implicit assumption that developers learn from their mistakes and that, despite everything, somehow development interventions are improving – becoming better focused, more sympathetic to local participation and less damaging to indigenous institutions. In our concluding chapter, David Anderson rejects such a view as naïve and counter-factual. Like the dissonance between the discourse that asserts that 'the poor are not us' and the social realities of poverty among pastoralist communities, the rhetoric of development fulfils its own images better than its realities. Looking back over the history of some seven decades of development initiatives aimed at the pastoralists of the region, Anderson finds no fundamental move away from a reforming agenda, which seeks to drive pastoralists towards commercial production or into agriculture (cf. Migot-Adholla & Little, 1981).

Three categories of schemes are examined in turn in Anderson's survey. Rehabilitation schemes were the earliest of colonial development interventions in the pastoral sector in eastern Africa, and they remain an important element today. Typically, such programmes invest in improving the productive resource of pastureland or the provision of water points. These schemes have been commonly presented as a means of preserving the carrying capacities necessary to sustain pastoralism, but they have in fact been the vehicles for the commoditization of land through the introduction of controlled grazing and tenure reforms (Roe, 1994; Anderson, forthcoming). The earliest resettlement schemes began as a means of accommodating pastoralists excluded from rehabilitated lands by the limits of newly imposed carrying capacities, but more recently resettlement schemes have been a reaction to the dislocations of drought, famine and war. Resettlement is a response to pastoral disaster which essentially sees all pastoral poverty as structural and therefore terminal (Hogg, 1992). The restocking schemes that have become more popular with development agencies over the past decade appear to be more sympathetic to the maintenance of pastoralism, but in practice even these schemes are often operated on terms set by the priorities of external agencies and not of the pastoralists themselves (Hogg, 1985; Kelly, 1993). Agencies inevitably wish to target the poor as the beneficiaries of such schemes, but in doing so they impose their own measurements of need and their own priorities for the distribution of livestock. Who the poor are is defined by external reference, not internal definition. The poor have needs which development agencies seek to address, but they also have rights and interests, which derive from the social and cultural context in which they live.

As the chapters that follow make clear, pastoralist communities throughout eastern Africa are aware of the changing nature of poverty, and there is lively and robust indigenous discourse about how poverty should be understood and how it can be ameliorated. Pastoralists increasingly recognize that the poor are now among themselves. But, although the alleviation of poverty is also a central tenet of the development dialogue in eastern Africa, there is still much to be done to engage pastoralists themselves in that dialogue.

2 Pastoral Poverty in Historical Perspective[1]

RICHARD D. WALLER

In recent times, East African pastoralists have suffered something of a reversal of fortune in popular imagination and official estimation, and perhaps also in fact. Pastoralism once seemed to be the very store and source of wealth: now it often appears as the dead end of immiseration and rural poverty. Pastoralists themselves have moved from centre stage within regional networks to the periphery of new states, which seem both threatened and surprised by their continued survival. Contemporary development thinking is often tinged with the same mixture of despair and exasperation once found in colonial reports.

Fewer people are now able to make a living out of subsistence pastoralism, which itself is increasingly hard to pursue. While some have been able to escape by widening their options, shifting their assets, making use of access to external political and economic resources or simply coming to the attention of aid agencies through complete destitution – a survival strategy in itself; others have not. New strategies have created new forms of differentiation and exclusion, and the accumulation of wealth now seems to threaten rather than support pastoralism. The 'new pastoralist' is generally a poor pastoralist: the wealthy have left and gone to town, figuratively and often literally (Little, 1985a; Hogg, 1986).

It was not always so. In the past, pastoralists did not see themselves, nor were they seen, as 'poor'. Most expected, and were able, to achieve and maintain a level of sufficiency. Those who could not did not remain pastoralists. They had to seek survival elsewhere. The dynamic of movement into and out of pastoralism linked communities together and created social and economic pathways within regions. In the nineteenth century, Maasai seemed vastly wealthy to their neighbours. The prospect of acquiring some of that wealth and of deploying it at home impelled enterprising outsiders to journey to Maasailand and perhaps to live there for a period (e.g. Marris & Somerset, 1971:31; Waller, 1985b:95–6, 125–7).

The earliest travel accounts confirmed this assessment, noting the large herds they met with and hinting at untapped potential (e.g. Thomson, 1885:177; von Hohnel, 1894:279, 286; Hobley, 1929:61).

Despite the disasters of the 1890s, when the herds were cut down by disease and warfare, this perception survived, partly because the herds were rebuilt relatively quickly and partly because the imagery of wealth in flocks and herds was deeply embedded in regional thought. Incoming white settlers and colonial governments accepted the equation of pastoralism with wealth, although they often did so more in irritation than in admiration. Aspiring white ranchers saw Maasai as rival accumulators and the government once taxed them at a rate almost double that of other communities (Cranworth, 1919:57–8; McGregor Ross, 1927:135, 440–41; Sorrenson, 1968:192–5). Several abortive plans were proposed to institute a graduated cattle tax, to supplement or replace the flat hut and poll tax, on the assumptions that Maasai, and perhaps other pastoralists, such as the Samburu, could afford to pay more than other Africans and that the substance of their wealth lay in the sheer number of animals that they owned.[2]

This decidedly punitive attitude to African stock wealth generally, was prompted by another assumption: that 'native' herds were essentially unproductive and that pastoralists were using their wealth as a shield against 'progress' – in this case, engagement in the market economy and in productive (wage) labour for others. Colonial thinking held that pastoralists were idle because they were rich. If they wished to opt out of the colonial economy, then they could and should pay for the privilege.[3] Such allegations of idleness and lack of productivity would have shocked both pastoralists and their agricultural neighbours profoundly. For they believed that stock wealth was productive, in the most fundamental sense that it both reproduced itself and was the means through which family and community were reproduced. Stock-owners were, in their own estimation, anything but idle. Indeed, (stock) wealth accrued only to those who deserved it through their industry and careful husbandry.

Pastoralists and colonialists alike thus understood stock wealth in moral as well as economic terms. While for the former large herds and a growing household were the accompaniment and reward of virtue, for the latter the unfettered enjoyment of stock wealth was an encouragement to sloth and a hindrance to the civilizing effect of honest labour and commerce. However, with the realization that pastoralists might not be infinitely and effortlessly rich, the basis of colonial thinking and exhortation shifted. It was now argued that the difficulties that pastoralism was experiencing constituted a moral and economic judgement, for pastoralists were being destroyed by their own (unproductive) wealth. Overstocking was ruining the pastures, and the pride, indolence and ignorance of the owners were inhibiting the development which alone could turn the herds into a

21

productive asset for both community and state.[4] The imposition of organized stock sales, linked to the provision of water and other resources, was intended to make the point about surplus and idle wealth and its transformation into productive investment through the market by demonstrating that a reduction of the herds could be accompanied by improvement in their productivity and in the conditions of pastoral life.[5] But pastoral communities themselves did not believe that they were too wealthy. Indeed, their increasing difficulties as pastoralists suggested that their margin of safety was being steadily eroded. To cope, they needed more stock, not less, and their response to colonial admonition and exhortation was to demand access to more grazing and water resources.[6] These contrasting notions of industry and idleness, productive and unproductive wealth have continued to run deep in the attitudes of both pastoralists and those who would change them (e.g. Hodgson, in this volume; comments quoted in Fratkin, 1991:ch. 6; Galaty & Bonte, 1991a: 3–10, 267–91).[7]

This introduction suggests three things: that estimations of wealth and poverty are reflections of a single reality and can be fully studied only in relation to each other; that both are as much subjective and disputed constructions – although starvation is hardly a figment of the imagination – as objective material states; and that, in studies of poverty and its causes, unexamined assumptions have too often substituted for evidence. The topic is large and complex; our concern here is necessarily more limited. Using the Maasai in the first half of the present century as the main example, we examine sources and strategies for uncovering a history of pastoral poverty, focusing on the larger aspects of economic and social change and leaving a consideration of the social and moral imagination of wealth and poverty for another place.

The task is a difficult one, for the poor are seldom seen and almost never heard in the historical record. It is also important. Although there is an established body of scholarship on modern poverty in Africa, including pastoral poverty, far less has been written on poverty in the past and much of that has examined it within the specific context of famine (e.g. Watts, 1983; Vaughan, 1987; Iliffe, 1990). The poverty of communities is best studied in the long term. Yet current debates, while accepting that poverty is a process, commonly fail to situate themselves in time. The result is a distorted and foreshortened perspective, which sees the present poverty of pastoralists only in relation to recent and often externally induced stresses. Partly this is a product of the odd demonologies of development, but it also arises from the dearth of quantitative evidence with which historians of even the relatively recent African past have to work and which contrasts with the easy availability of contemporary field and statistical data.

In his pioneering comparative study of African poverty, John Iliffe sets out what he sees as the three main obstacles to any serious historical study of the African poor (Iliffe, 1987:ch. 1). The first is the lack of a usable definition of poverty. He argues that, given the variety of poverty in Africa and the lack of quantitative data for the past, precise definitions of either absolute or relative poverty are impossible. Iliffe then distinguishes between 'the poor' and 'the very poor' or destitute. The former, he argues, comprised perhaps the majority of Africans, who struggled and survived in an uncertain world. The latter, a much smaller group, lacked resources in even the best of times and were in a state of chronic want. While, in Iliffe's view, historians can say little about the generalized poverty of the many, they can begin to study the specific destitution of the few.

The second obstacle is the assertion that endemic poverty, as opposed to the epidemic poverty caused by crisis, simply did not exist in precolonial Africa. There are three substantive, but debatable, reasons for such a claim. The first emphasizes the strength and cohesiveness of 'family' in Africa, which allegedly provided an almost universal 'safety net'. Destitution could then only be the result of the unusual social isolation of individuals. The second derives from the argument that African societies lacked both the means to create great disparities in wealth and stratified classes to enforce and maintain them.

One of the difficulties facing any study of poverty is the simple invisibility of the poor, the third reason for claiming that endemic poverty was not widely present in Africa before the present century. Indeed, Iliffe's third obstacle is lack of evidence. Since references to poverty in both oral traditions and outsiders' accounts are often stereotyped, overgeneralized or otherwise misleading, 'the subject can be studied seriously only where [local] written [contemporary] sources survive' (Iliffe, 1987:2).[8] If so, the historian's task in much of pastoral East Africa is almost impossible. For even oral, let alone written, sources for poverty are undeniably thin and difficult to interpret. Furthermore, they deal almost exclusively with times of crisis, which can reduce even the otherwise self-sufficient to desperate straits.

While Iliffe does devote a chapter to pastoralists, his main focus is on agricultural societies, where the causes and experiences of poverty are different. Yet his important and perceptive attempt to identify and overcome the conceptual and evidential problems inherent in the study of African poverty raises serious questions for pastoralism as well. Problems of definition and evidence, especially the latter, shape the structure of this chapter, while the question of whether poverty was endemic in pastoral societies lies at the heart of its argument.

We must begin by attempting to define what we mean by poverty, bearing in mind that the perception and experience of poverty is always inflected by age, gender and past and present social standing. In East African pastoral societies, the idea of wealth is conventionally situated in stock and its imagery. Conversely, poverty is closely associated with stocklessness, as the use of the word 'Dorobo' in Maasai to imply both indicates.[9] Thus, 'the very poor' would be those who neither owned nor had clear access to livestock.

This absolute definition, though simple, is clearly insufficient in itself. Livestock are the main subsistence resource as well as the measure of value within the community. Those without stock could not survive as pastoralists. Thus 'very poor' Maasai would be either ex-Maasai or dead Maasai. A more fruitful approach is to focus on relative poverty within the pastoral community, that is, on those who have insufficient stock, for, as Iliffe points out, the true opposite of poverty is not wealth but sufficiency.

It is possible to determine rough levels of sufficiency, based on the number of animals required to sustain a family unit under a variety of conditions.[10] A sufficient or viable household herd will be one large enough to reproduce itself and to support the household members with milk. The larger the household, the larger the sufficient herd will have to be. The calculation is a difficult one because of the seasonal fluctuation in milk production and the wide possible variation in climatic conditions and because diet can be adjusted to fit available resources. If sufficient milk is not available, families may turn to other food sources, including traded vegetable foods.[11] Under extreme drought conditions, it will be virtually impossible for any herd to produce enough for subsistence, but, under normal conditions and taking into account alternative food sources within pastoral society, an 'average' household of five or six adult equivalents will require a herd of 60 to 70 head of cattle or their equivalent. We can use this figure as a baseline. Those below will experience varying degrees of food insecurity and will be 'poor', if not stockless; those above will be cushioned to a greater or lesser extent against the fluctuations of the environment.[12] It should be noted, however, that food insecurity and poverty, though obviously related, are not the same. Poverty is as much concerned with standing as with feeding. Even if a household has a herd just sufficient to survive, it may still be at a disadvantage in social transactions, such as marriage, which require further outlays of stock. During the colonial period, such households might additionally have been particularly vulnerable to the impact of stock levies for tax and communal fines and of fixed quotas for compulsory stock marketing schemes.[13]

Moreover, as the Maasai definition of a rich man (*ol karsis*) – one who has many children – tells us, real wealth resides in (control over) people, including their labour and reproductive power. An elder must have sons to herd and daughters to marry off. Our notion of sufficiency must then include labour as well as stock, since the two are interdependent. Herd and household ideally grow together, but what if one should grow (or decline) faster than the other? Imbalances could be adjusted by 'internal migration' and the redistribution of labour between households, with the poor giving labour to the rich in return for subsistence and perhaps the promise of future accumulation (Borgerhoff Mulder & Sellen, 1994:

218–24; Fratkin & Smith, 1994:100–8). Such exchanges were probably at least as common in the past as they are today, the differentiation they imply being masked by adoption, 'neighbourliness' and the social dynamics of multi-household cattle camps. This suggests a seeming paradox and a twist to Iliffe's argument about poverty. Large families could be a liability as well as an asset, despite the notion of wealth-in-people; although this might be alleviated by the redistribution of the surplus labour to those with more stock.

How might poverty be categorized? Iliffe argues that much of the history of African poverty turns on changes in the relationship between two different types: structural and conjunctural. Structural poverty is 'the long-term poverty of individuals due to their personal or social circum- stances'; conjunctural poverty is 'the temporary poverty into which ordinarily self-sufficient people may be thrown by crisis'. In contrast to Europe, extreme poverty in Africa arose, not from lack of access to land, but from lack of labour, one's own or other people's, by reason of some personal or social incapacity. The destitute might then include the old, the handicapped, orphans, widows and so on. Such people suffered from chronic want (structural poverty), but their ranks might be temporarily swelled by those hit by catastrophes, such as famine and political upheaval, when resources suddenly became scarce or difficult to protect (Iliffe, 1987:4–5).

Iliffe's conceptualization, based on the distinction between 'land-rich' African and 'land-poor' European societies, requires modification in the case of pastoralists. For livestock, unlike land, were always in limited supply.[14] Unlike land, too, animals were mobile. They could be individ- ually owned, shared or disposed of, and they were vulnerable to disease, drought and raid. Moreover, while it was only in a debatable minority of cases that ordinary people could be deprived of land, livestock was a resource to which access could more easily be restricted or denied. Although East African pastoral societies were not stratified to the extent characteristic of, say, the Tuareg, their livestock resources were far from equally distributed within the community, and access and control were often determined by the hierarchies of age and gender.

Possession of livestock or its lack could also be a mark of inclusion or exclusion. A constant theme running through Maasai accounts of the precolonial past involves conflicts over control of stock and the drawing of sharp distinctions between those who had such control and those who did not. Stock ownership has thus had important implications for the construction and maintenance of social and ethnic boundaries. Ownership of cattle has been a differentiating marker between Maasai and others since at least the middle of the last century. Maasai have seen themselves as 'people of cattle': to be properly a Maasai one must own or at least have secure access to cattle (Berntsen, 1980:1–21; Galaty, 1982a:1–20; Waller,

1985b:106–8, 114–18). The earliest recorded exchange on the subject makes the link between stock loss, poverty, identity and status very clear. In 1884, Johnston was told by a Kisongo elder at Taveta that, when he returned, 'you will find us all *Embarawuio* [Baraguyu (here derogatory)] like these people of Kikoro [the Maa-speaking settlement near Taveta]... All our cattle are dying ... and I have to come here to buy food from these *Es-Singa* [*isingan* – menials, slaves]...' (Johnston, 1886:401). The encapsulation of pastoral societies within the colonial state failed to alter this perception of the relation between cattle, wealth and identity, and it is only recently that alternative forms of wealth – in land, for example – have begun to challenge it (Campbell, 1993:258–71).[15]

We might then expect to find a kind of structural poverty of exclusion in addition to the poverties created by individual long-term incapacity and temporary crisis.[16] The rest of the chapter examines these three sorts of poverty and the relations between them.

If signs of structural poverty seem at first to be lacking in East African pastoral societies, there is abundant evidence for conjunctural poverty. This may have struck pastoralists harder and more often than it did others. It came in the form of drought, disease and warfare, and it is from periods of massive (and exceptional) crisis and dislocation that the most vivid descriptions of destitution come. Baumann's oft-quoted description of his encounter with starving Serengeti Maasai refugees at Ngorongoro in March 1892 – 'walking skeletons out of whose sunken eyes looked the madness of hunger' (Baumann, 1894:33ff) – is only the most extreme of many.[17] At the same time, British officials were coping with an influx of starving refugees, stealing crops from their neighbours' fields to survive or haunting railway labour camps (Waller, 1988:94–101). Similar experiences can be recovered in accounts and traditions drawn from most areas of pastoral East Africa at the same period (Lamphear, 1976:223–7; Robinson, 1979; Sobania, 1980:134ff). These were the characteristic expedients of the destitute, but they were destitute only because they had suddenly lost their stock on a scale too massive for their communities to sustain. Many were 'starving and in misery' (Baumann, 1894:19), but their poverty might be temporary.

The crises of the 1890s offer particularly striking evidence of conjunctural poverty because its manifestations were so widespread and because newly established government posts and missions, by offering a limited refuge, drew the destitute into view.[18] In terms of contemporary documentation and observation, this time of disaster in the pastoral world had no parallel until the crises of the past two decades brought poverty once more into the headlines. Yet the very vividness and detail of the sources pose problems. They highlight very unusual circumstances and extreme responses, thus distorting our view of poverty and its expedients. Outside observers may also have misrepresented or misconstrued what they reported, either because they focused on one dramatic instant in a continuing strategy of survival – Maasai women 'abandoning' or 'selling children for food' is an example – or because they were unfamiliar with the historical and cultural context and meaning of what they saw or heard.[19]

Crisis may also blind us to three important points. First, although the 1890s and the 1980s are uniquely documented, they may not have been uniquely devastating. There is no reason to suppose that similar episodes have not occurred in the more distant past (Waller & Sobania, 1994: 60–1). Second, the very magnitude of conjunctural poverty may be both concealing the prior existence of structural poverty and also contributing to its spread. Especially if crises are sequential or prolonged, a 'ratchet effect' will steadily undermine sufficiency and turn one kind of poverty into the other (Shipton, 1990:368–72). Moreover, despite the dramatic and traumatic appearance of destitution in times of crisis, structural poverty may be far more insidious and far-reaching in its effects on pastoral society. While conjunctural poverty may destroy pastoralists, it does not erode the basis of pastoralism, which re-emerges as a viable option after crisis has passed. Indeed, the moral basis and rationale for wealth and poverty is confirmed as the poor die and the rich survive. The growth of structural poverty, however, may transform pastoralism itself by creating new exclusions which challenge the basis of wealth and poverty by suggesting alternative and even subversive definitions of both. This is what has happened in pastoral societies.

The third point concerns the difference between the conjunctural poverty of communities, dramatically exemplified by general disasters such as *'emutai'* ('wipe out'), as the rinderpest pandemic of the 1890s is known to the Maasai, and that of individuals and families. Disease was a major cause of private as well as public loss. A survey of the veterinary record between 1914 and 1940, for example, reveals outbreaks of stock disease in Maasailand almost every year. Few of these were 'disasters', but each was a 'wipe out' for someone. Jacobs, for example, noted that one household in Loliondo lost its entire herd of 57 head in three weeks (Jacobs, 1963:8). Telelia Chieni recalled how her husband's herds had been cut down and rebuilt more than once (Chieni & Spencer, 1993:157– 73). Sudden and often unforeseen dearth would almost inevitably touch everyone at some point and poverty lurked beyond every cattle camp fence.

It is here that the 'poverty ratchet' works most effectively to differentiate and exclude. Telelia and her family survived their losses and remained Maasai; others were not so fortunate. Dahl and Hjort show how families hit by drought may have to disperse when their herd can no longer support them, to become dependants in the households of others (Dahl & Hjort, 1979:25–7). Again, some may recover and prosper – ole Galishu rose from Laikipiak orphan to famous Purko spokesman – but others will remain impoverished, always intensely vulnerable to further misfortune.[20]

Poverty could be concealed in different ways: by silence,[21] by death and migration, by absorbing the poor as dependants of the rich, and by 'defining the poor out', that is, by drawing ethnic boundaries against them and by relegating them to the spatial margins in a way similar to the modern export of rural poverty to towns. In societies where poverty has highly negative connotations, the memory of past poverty is likely to be concealed, except when it encompassed the entire community and not just individuals. Present poverty will be noticed only when it is drawn into the open by the promise of relief.

Poverty, then, may not be easily identifiable within functioning pastoral communities. The influence of an 'egalitarian ethos',[22] however problematic, conceals real inequalities, and we may have to look for poverty on the margins, already redefined as 'non-pastoral', or hidden within household, age and gender structures. We can examine the record for references to groups identified, either by themselves or others, as poor, ask why they were so characterized and consider what is distinctive about their behaviour or circumstances. We can also consider access to resources, especially stock; for those whom we might identify as poor will have either less access or fewer resources.

Evidence for poverty on the margins can be found in the agricultural enclaves that existed within and on the edges of the Rift Valley, from Ngabotok and Baringo in the north to Taveta and Arusha Chini in the south. While these settlements often had an autonomous existence and a history of their own, they and neighbouring agricultural communities acted as havens where dispossessed pastoralists could take refuge and as springboards from which those who had regained stock could re-enter pastoralism. This reminds us that the migration of ruined pastoralists is not new, and we should not assume that all such refugees were the product of great disasters. Enclave communities were not 'pastoral', but neither did they lack resources. Many of them were nodes in the web of interregional and long-distance trade. What defined their inhabitants as 'poor' in the eyes of pastoralists was their lack of stock and the expedients they followed in order to compensate: cultivating, hunting, fishing, trading (Waller, 1985b:92–4; Lamphear, 1986:247; Anderson, 1988:244–51; Sobania, 1988:41–56; Spear, 1993b:120–36).

During the colonial period, there were also people who cultivated at or near their camps. They are usually described in the record as poor and sometimes as marginals or 'aliens'. Some probably were; others were not. Several influential elders had *shambas* worked by others.[23] Settled around Ngong were educated Maasai who had invested wages in land and employed labour to cultivate maize and vegetables and to produce milk for the Nairobi market. They had small herds, but they were hardly indigent.[24] On the other hand, some of the Christian converts who settled and cultivated around the mission station at Siyabei were, and their obvious poverty was one reason why the mission was shunned by ordinary Maasai (Waller, 1999). Again, the facts that marginal cultivation is a long-standing, if not 'traditional', phenomenon inside Maasailand and that it did not always betoken actual poverty should caution us against drawing conclusions from modern appearances. Cultivation in itself has always been less important as a material indicator than who is doing it and why.

Some specific groups inside Maasailand were socially, if not always spatially, marginal and were also defined as 'poor'. They included bands of hunter-gatherers ('Dorobo'), blacksmiths and *il makati*, impoverished Maasai who made a living digging and selling soda from Magadi (Waller, 1979:80–85, 290–302). Dependent herders *(il chekut)* offer an example of less obvious poverty. Having no stock of their own, they worked for others, occupying a niche created by the different labour and subsistence require-ments of particular households. They were noted by Krapf in the middle of the last century (in an account which otherwise made no mention of poverty) and by subsequent observers (Krapf, 1854:20). On Laikipia, at a time when many were still recovering from the disasters, 'every [elder] who can afford to do so keeps at least one *chokut*; many have as many as three or four'.[25] Their identity and status were ambiguous and may have changed over time. They included aliens, war captives, orphans and boys whose families had lost stock, as well as adult men. Ostensibly, they represented the 'worthy poor', young men seeking to better themselves by service with a patron who might be expected to give them a share in the increase of the herd and perhaps a wife to marry. Viewed in this light, their position was clearly different from, and even opposed to, the lazy and feckless paupers and deviants on the margins. In fact, however, they were lesser beings. Their prospects were uncertain and at the whim of another. Ole Galishu thought that they were all potential thieves and should have their throats cut, and they were sometimes referred to as *isingan* ('menials'), the word also used by Johnston's Kisongo elder quoted above. It was the dependence – the lack of autonomy and control – that poverty brought, as much as the want itself, that was despised. This explains something of poverty's social and moral construction.[26]

These, then, were the variously visible poor, but their importance lies less in the fact of their poverty, real or otherwise, than in how others saw them. What they have in common is that their circumstances and behaviour defined them as 'poor'. Here we must allow for the particular lens through which poverty was viewed by others. Colonial officials believed that Maasai were self-sufficient pastoralists, almost by definition. Those who were not herding, therefore, could not be Maasai, or, if they were Maasai, they must be driven by dire poverty. 'Deviant' occupations of all kinds – cultivating, taking employment, even education – were seen as strategies of the poor, and it was only when general crisis hit the community that 'real Maasai' were allowed to be 'impoverished'. Many Maasai agreed, and the claim that men could choose to 'leave herding' and still remain Maasai was deeply contentious within the community. Such individuals retained the stigma of poverty even if their material success belied it.[27]

The presence of 'the (evidently) poor' in Maasailand itself in the present century has further significance. It may suggest two kinds of change: either that there has been a real increase in levels of poverty or that the community is becoming unable to export its existing poverty, although it continues to define it as deviance. In time, the development of pockets of visible poverty will challenge the notion, once sustained by the invisibility of the poor and the absorptive capacity of an expanding community, that poverty is simply an aberration.

But what of the hidden poor in Maasailand: those whose behaviour did not single them out, who were not incapacitated in Iliffe's sense but whose circumstances were none the less precarious, who lacked sufficiency but were not in permanent want? Let us first scrutinise the evidence for data on households and their cattle herds.[28] Maasai did not count their stock, and neither, on the whole, did their colonial rulers. There are no pre-colonial figures and the reported annual estimations of stock in colonial reports are hardly more than notional, at least up to the 1940s when more systematic stock censuses were undertaken by the Veterinary Department. At the end of the First World War, the official number was over 700,000 *in toto*, but this figure was reduced without explanation to 500,000 in 1920. Twenty years later, a probably more accurate count reached roughly the same figure, and this general level is again confirmed by the figure of 650,000+ that Jacobs extracted from the district veterinary files around 1960.[29] The total cattle population thus seems to have remained more or less stable over a period of half a century. Taken with other indications, including high average *per capita* cattle holdings (15 in 1920; 25 in 1930; 11 in 1948) and data from nutrition surveys,[30] this suggests an overall level of sufficiency. But there were considerable fluctuations over shorter periods. Between 1942 and 1962, for example, the cattle population of Kajiado District doubled from about 350,000 to over 700,000 and then dropped abruptly back to 200,000 in the drought years of 1960–62, the characteristic 'sawtooth' pattern of pastoral growth and collapse (Anon, *c.* 1962; Spencer, 1974: 419–21). It is in the troughs that we might look for poverty, not just because downturns in the stock economy squeezed the poor out, but also because they might force numbers of households with barely sufficient herds over the edge into insolvency.

However, these are no more than aggregate figures. Without access to more detailed data on ownership, no statistically informed picture of shifts in the distributional structure of stock wealth over time can be presented. The shortcomings in official estimates of the stock population are matched by the rough estimates of the human population, based, theoretically, on annual hut counts adjusted in various ways.[31] Moreover, since neither stock nor human figures are broken down, it is impossible to say with any comprehensiveness and accuracy how large households and their herds were and, therefore, how many had sufficient stock. Such information as we have emerges randomly from the files. The detail of individual stock holdings, and even more rarely of household size and composition, was recorded only when the stock-owner or a member of his family attracted official attention – generally in connection with unlawful activities. Thus criminal investigations and distress warrants occasionally shed light on particular localities or households at a specific point in time, but the circumstances under which the information was generated make it difficult to assess and dangerous to generalize.[32]

One surviving set of figures, however, is worth closer examination. Between June 1912 and March 1913, the (mostly Purko) households that were being removed from the Northern (Maasai) Reserve on Laikipia were enumerated with some care. The figures for the stock count survive, arranged under what appear to be the names of household heads. Of 490 separate herds recorded and included in this sample, a total of nearly 173,000 head of cattle, 24 (5%) were larger than 1000 head and a further 77 (16%) had more than 500 head. The wealthiest fifth of the sample (101 herds) between them accounted for just over half the stock enumerated (54%). At the other end of the spectrum, one quarter of the sample (123) had herds smaller than 100 head and 61 (12% of the sample) had less than 50 head each. While the top fifth comprised half the cattle, the bottom quarter had just 4%.[33] These figures give us a rough idea of how Purko stock was distributed in 1912–13. The terrain revealed here is uneven: a middle ground that was large and solid, flanked by some very large concentrations of stock wealth, and a minority of definitely subeconomic holdings. This distribution is important in terms of both attitude and subsistence. Faced with highly visible concentrations of stock on this scale, it would not be difficult for colonial officials (and other outsiders) to conclude that the Maasai as a community were unusually wealthy. The view from inside might look different, depending on where one stood, but it did foster the hope that the achievement of wealth was as much a possibility as the descent into poverty. This structure of stock holding may help to explain why many Maasai men, not rich themselves, subscribed to an expansive ideal of wealth and accumulation. However, one tenth of the owners had herds too small for independent survival and, if we add those whose herds were barely adequate (less than 100 head), up to a quarter of the herd-owners and their households might be at risk in a 'trough'. This suggests the possibility of poverty hidden in the midst of evident wealth.[34] It would be unwise to speculate further. We cannot know how representative of Maasai as a whole these Laikipia camps were. The Purko were a large and powerful section, perhaps richer than average, and we have no comparable figures for any other section.

This is as far as we can reasonably go in trying to quantify pastoral poverty. Whatever the record may tell us about the overall structure of stock wealth, it reveals nothing of the identity of the poor and of how their poverty might have changed over time. We can, however, approach these questions indirectly by looking at changes over time in two areas: in the structure of access and opportunity, and in the position of pastoral communities relative to their agricultural neighbours and the state. It may then be possible not only to suggest how patterns of poverty may have altered but also to indicate some of the historical roots of present crises. Accumulation and its opposite are embedded in and facilitated and defined by social processes. Questions about who was able to accumulate stock and by what means and about how access and opportunity changed or became redefined therefore require social, not simply statistical, answers which consider the variables of age and gender within household and community.[35]

Throughout our period, the main mode of accumulation was through the reproduction of herd and household. Under normal conditions, accumulation would be determined primarily by the growth rate of the herd. This has been most closely studied by Dahl & Hjort, using models derived from a wide survey of available data and covering a range of possible conditions and herd structures. There are no comparable statistics that would enable us to test whether the models they propose held good in the past, although, equally, there is no obvious reason to assume that basic reproductive rates changed much before the 1970s, given the low levels of veterinary intervention. They suggest growth rates for 'typical' cattle herds of around 3.5% per annum, which would double a herd of 100 head (more than sufficient for an average household) in 20 years. It would take three or four years longer to double the number of fertile cows, the main productive and reproductive unit in the herd. However, given the uncertainties of disease, drought and warfare in the past, a lower rate of 3% might be preferable. This would double the same herd in 24 years. In either case, accumulation would not be very rapid (Dahl & Hjort, 1976). However, as Spencer's comparison between the cattle-keeping Samburu and camel-keeping Rendille indicates, a cattle herd is thought to increase more rapidly than a family. This fosters a 'capitalist' belief in the possibility of accumulation which has an important bearing on attitudes to wealth and its opposite, and is in contrast to camel wealth, which appears to increase more slowly than the human population, if at all, and which fosters a 'mercantilist' belief in stock wealth as a finite quantity (Spencer, 1965:293; 1973:75–80).

Such impressionistic evidence as we have for the past suggests that pastoralists were probably correct in their thinking about growth. Herds recovered fairly rapidly after the huge natural setbacks of the early 1890s. By the end of the decade, many formerly pauperized men had accumulated enough stock (admittedly in part through raiding and purchase) to return to their former grazing grounds as independent herd-owners (Waller, 1988: 102–3). The concentrations of wealth on Laikipia revealed by the 1912–13 census had largely been built up over a 20-year period. Herds ravaged by drought in 1933–4 had recovered two or three years later, and the survey of herd fluctuations in Kajiado between 1948 and 1962 suggests that the teeth in the sawtooth profile could be quite sharp. After the disastrous losses to drought in 1960–61, which reduced its estimated cattle population by perhaps two-thirds, the surviving stock were expected to double in number by 1966.[36] Herd recovery and growth – accumulation through reproduction – was thus at least as likely as its opposite.

Given the fundamental importance of the herd for the continuation of the household, we must consider who had access to it and was in a position to benefit from its growth, and how opportunities to do so changed. Management decisions were the prerogative of the household head, who exercised undivided control (*enkitoria* – 'rule') over his family and its herd, however much in practice his authority might be tempered by consultation with adult sons and senior wives. The fruits of reproduction accrued to him, although it might be argued that he managed the herd on behalf of a continuing 'family enterprise' or trust (Spencer, 1988:11–14). Wives and sons had access to and rights in the herd, but in different ways. On marriage, women were provided with a milking herd of their own, from which they fed their children and in which their sons had rights of inheritance. Wives were entitled to expect that an adequate herd would remain theirs as long as they had children to support, but they did not own the stock in their own right. Their rights were derived from those of the 'house' which they established (Hakansson, 1989:117–34; Oboler, 1994: 342–57). Ownership remained with their husband, or possibly father-in-law, the household head.[37] While under their father's authority, even after graduation to junior elderhood, sons did not themselves own or control stock either, but they did have both the opportunity and indeed the obligation to acquire it for the household herd, and therefore for their fathers, and ultimately for themselves as the heirs. Their rights were predicated on the future, when they would become independent household heads themselves. However, while the effective rights of men increased with age and maturity, those of women diminished as their children grew up, their milking herd shrank and their relations with husband and sons shifted in focus. Ultimately, as widows, they, like their animals, would be 'inherited' (and provided for) by a son.

For stock owners, the range of opportunity widened with the spread of the colonial economy.[38] Maasai sold stock, both compulsorily and voluntarily, in increasingly large numbers. They did so partly in order to reinvest the proceeds in more stock via Somali traders and border markets, despite the government's intention of using sales to reduce the stock population. There was also a market for hides and milk (for ghee-making)

(Waller, 1975:10–14, 23; 1984:267-72; Tignor, 1976:324-9).[39] As a source of wealth in itself, the market had a minor impact before the late 1940s: first because the majority of transactions continued to take place outside the formal market; second because much of the cash that came into Maasailand was mopped up by taxation; and third, because the formal economy was unstable and offered few opportunities for investment apart from the herds themselves. Moreover, the value of trade was not large. When it peaked in the late 1920s, officially recorded exports were valued at just under £100,000.[40] At a notional sh.40 per head of the population (a bit less than the market price of an ox), this was hardly a cash bonanza; nor did access to the market provide the opportunities for private enrichment at public expense which came later, first with land sales and then with the break-up of group ranches (Rutten, 1992; Campbell, 1993).

However, the penetration of the market may have had an influence on the structure of wealth and poverty, although it confirmed rather than challenged the advantageous position of larger herd-owners. They had more 'disposable' beasts and were therefore better placed to take advantage of the market than those whose herds were more closely tied to subsistence needs. The sale of a couple of slaughter oxen a year, quite possible in a herd of over 100 head but difficult for those with less than 50, would keep the taxman away: any further sales would pay for veterinary services or more stock and thus build and improve the herd. Moreover, an astute herder might take advantage of better market opportunities through managing the sex ratio of the herd so as to maintain a higher proportion of male animals, allowing disposal without adversely affecting the reproductive capacity or recovery rate of the herd. From the late 1940s, grazing and marketing schemes were encouraging a more commercially orientated pastoralism of this kind. The formal establishment of sectional boundaries and grazing zones, tied to the provision of permanent water supplies, was already redefining space and community resources within Maasailand. In part, this was a continuation of an old policy of pinning down pastoralists; in part, a newer development initiative designed to control and remodel land use and to usher in the beginnings of group and private ownership. Some herd-owners began to invest in water and pasture improvement and, later, to develop private ranches.[41]

It was in this way that the community came to confront the implications of individual landholding and private access. 'Improvers' were then in a minority, but the potential for a divergence between commercial and subsistence pastoral production within the community and, therefore, for a new kind of exclusion and inequality based on the privatization of common resources, existed well before differentiation based on access to the market became a pervasive reality. The colonial economy did not create inequality – still less 'the poor' – but it did offer new ways in which wealth could be individually expanded and entrenched.[42]

Accumulation through the market might differentiate between house-holds; monetization differentiated within them, by raising questions of ownership. What development schemes threatened to do for natural resources, the market did for the herd and its product. While the disposal of individual animals, cattle especially, had probably always been potentially open to dispute between fathers and adult sons and husbands and wives, the market now embraced other items – milk and hides especially – whose disposal had previously not been at issue. Hodgson has argued that the colonial period saw the weakening of women's rights in stock and the subordination of their previously semi-autonomous domestic economy. She emphasizes the gender bias of 'development' schemes, but the impact of cash sales was also important (Hodgson, 1995:ch. 7).[43] At the beginning of this century, women clearly had the right to dispose of milk, hides and possibly small stock from their own herds, and trade with caravans and non-Maasai was largely in their hands (Merker, 1910:30; Waller, 1979:26–7, 347–8). Money, however, came to be seen as belonging to men. The sale of hides and milk might thus remove these items from women's control, if men received the payment.[44] In fact, hides were largely bartered against credit at local shops. Allegedly, this was at the insistence of the traders, who thus profited twice over, but it may also have been in the interest of women, who were responsible for food purchases, to avoid cash transactions.[45] Milk, however, was paid for in cash – to household heads (Waller, 1975:14–15).[46] While the cash value of trade to a household may have been small, its significance lay in two things. First, pastoral products were now potentially saleable and could, in a sense, be privatized. While this would not create poverty in itself, it is not hard to imagine – though impossible to demonstrate – its effect on poorer dependents who had been supported by the surplus production of larger households. Ultimately, it might no longer be possible for 'nearly one half of the tribe [to live] on the other half', as John Stauffacher had found on Laikipia before 1910.[47] Second, money threatened to dissolve distinctions between rights of use and disposal in different areas of pastoral production, to place control more firmly in the hands of the household head and, thereby, to reduce women's entitlements. Again, this would not make women necessarily poor, but it would make them more vulnerable to the vagaries of men.

Colonial markets facilitated changes in gender relations: relations between elders and *murran* were affected by another aspect of colonial control. Up to the end of the First World War, the main opportunity for *murran* to accumulate came through raiding, latterly including service with colonial punitive expeditions on what were perceived as government-sanctioned and organized raids against familiar targets (Waller, 1976:536). There has been an intermittent and somewhat futile debate over the nature of raiding, its frequency and its place within an ideal of pastoralism.

But, whatever else they may have been doing, raiders intended to acquire stock, and this was of particular importance to *murran* from poorer households (Fischer, 1885:27; Waller, 1988:100).[48] At the turn of the century, colonial officials worried that banning raiding, at a time of particular stress in the pastoral economy, might drive younger men into permanent poverty and alienation since they would not be able to accumulate enough to marry and become adults.[49]

In fact, as a strictly economic proposition, raiding had its limits. For obvious reasons, hard data on stock capture are very sparse. Contemporary accounts of raiding around the turn of the century give a possibly misleading impression of well-organized and purposeful operations which swept up large numbers of animals (e.g. Dundas, 1893:114–15; Merker, 1910:88–104; and generally, Berntsen, 1979:ch. 5). We know less about raids that failed. But even for successful raiders, it would have taken a huge amount of continuous effort (and luck) to acquire a herd by capture or to equal the peaceful mathematics of natural growth.[50] In colonial punitive expeditions, where stock capture was a prime objective and where numbers are recorded, individual *murran* who took home more than a couple of animals from the haul could count themselves lucky – although reminiscence suggests that private enterprise added more (Waller, 1976:549–50, 552). Moreover, captured stock joined the herd under the father's control and their progeny would be inherited by the raider himself only if the animals were assigned to his mother's herd (Merker, 1910:100).[51] Thus raiding was more of an investment in the future for *murran*, although it might be a significant boost in the present for their families.

After 1913, formal raiding gradually came to an end, to be partly replaced by stock theft. To some extent, the transition from one to the other was a matter of official definition within the context of a colonial legal system, but stock theft was not just raiding criminalized. The two were distinguished in 'Maasai thinking and in their mode of operation. Unlike raids (*injorin*), which had been openly planned, sanctioned and carried out, stock theft (*empurore*) was a surreptitious and unauthorized business, which created private complicities and deliberately excluded the wider community. It was increasingly construed, at least by ruling elders, as irresponsible or even anti-social.[52] Whereas *murran* had had a clear right to raid, stealing was far more ambiguous, especially as regards theft within the community and when collective fines placed the burden of crime on stock-owning elders. Raiders themselves increasingly risked prosecution and heavy gaol sentences, as well as armed and dangerous opponents.[53]

While formal raiding acknowledged the emergence of an age-set, as well as the beginnings of collective accumulation by its members, stock theft might be more closely associated with individual poverty.[54] Rises in the levels of reported theft generally seem to be connected with crises in the stock economy, although colonial wisdom also held that raids were more likely when a new age-set was forming or when an established set was being promoted.[55] There were also certain features which might have made theft an attractive option, whatever its actual profitability.[56] Individual shares in stolen stock may have been larger, since fewer shared; and the need to conceal or 'launder' stolen stock may have incidentally made it easier for individuals to evade family obligations. Stock thieves might also hope to escape detection and arrest. If they were caught, the law might work in their favour for, since *murran* technically had no property, they could not themselves be fined.[57] Ultimately, however, the significance of the transition from 'raiding' to 'stealing' depends first on who was doing it and why, but second on what it suggests about the narrowing and channelling of opportunities during the colonial era – in this case, through the criminalization and punishment of certain kinds of accumulation.

Some Maasai draw a connection between the end of raiding and the beginning of wage labour. *Il Derito* (formed in the later 1920s) is sometimes seen as the first age-set 'never to have raided [properly]'; and the first to go out in search of employment. Wage labour was now an alternative way in which young men might legitimately contribute to the household herd and accumulate sufficient to become independent adults in their turn.[58] Leaving aside the experience of the small group of Western-educated Maasai, who went into government and mission employment, there was one main external outlet for labour: herding on white farms.[59] Maasai herders enjoyed high status and, as skilled labour, commanded high wages – roughly double that of ordinary farm labour. They were primarily interested in acquiring stock and were often paid directly in grade culls from the estate herds, which they were either allowed to herd separately on the farm or required to remove back to the Reserve. The majority were sons seeking cattle for their fathers' herds or junior elders who were attempting to build viable herds of their own. In many cases, wage cattle were sent into Maasailand to be herded by kin or associates until they could be recovered when the herdsman himself returned (Waller, 1975: 20–2). The comparison with raiding, or perhaps better with service on punitive expeditions, is an apposite one since resources were being acquired through a temporary foray into the outside.

We cannot assume that wage labour invariably indicated poverty, given the paucity of the evidence and the particular constructions of social and economic deviance in which pastoral poverty is embedded. It is also important to distinguish between temporary expedients and long-term strategies. Without more detailed data on individual herders and their households, we cannot tell whether the flow of labour did more than follow the fluctuations of the pastoral economy and whether farm employment, with its relatively high returns, might not also have been a good investment of surplus labour.[60] Some herders, however, did remain semi-permanently on the farms, building up herds and sometimes retiring back to Maasailand in old age as relatively wealthy men.[61] For such men, wage labour may have been a necessity as well as an opportunity. White farms were the colonial equivalent of the marginal settlements to which impoverished pastoralists had once retired in order to rebuild their fortunes.

We may now set changes in access and opportunity in a wider historical and social context. Within pastoral society, there was a close but ambivalent relation between two potentially opposed modes of accumulation: the 'predatory' and the 'pastoral', as Spencer has called them (Spencer, 1988:20–21). The latter is the domain of household heads and elders, the former that of the *murran*. The 'pastoral' mode offers the more secure route to growth and is at the centre of the ideal of elderhood. Raiding challenges this, threatening a loss of control and the disruption of patterns of peaceful accumulation and exchange. But *murran* are crucial to the defence of the community and its resources and to the rapid replenishment of the herds after loss, and the solidarity of *murran*hood forms the basis of consensus on which elders rely for their authority.[62] During the nineteenth century, there seems to have been continuous negotiation and contestation between the two modes, with the young often able to assert their right to autonomous action. The crises at the end of the century capture the ambiguity perfectly. Raiding both destroyed the social cohesion of the community and provided it with the means of its economic regeneration. In the process raiders soon became rulers (Waller, 1979:181–5; 1988:109–11).

Once firmly established, colonial rule did little to spread resources more widely, but, indirectly, it began to change their distribution. By simultaneously invading the domain of the *murran* and suppressing raiding and sponsoring commercial development, however imperfectly in both cases, the colonial administration intervened decisively in the internal debate between the generations (Tignor, 1976:75–87).[63] Having presided over the shift from raiding to ruling, it then supported and even extended the accumulation of herd-owners and household heads, while all but eliminating the independent opportunities of their juniors. The struggle was as much over the control of time, both the social time of *murran*hood and the labour time of the young, as it was over material resources. In both cases, the elders and the state largely won, for the latter too demanded access to *murran* labour.[64] In a similar way, colonial marketing and perhaps assumptions about 'pastoral man' intervened between the sexes. Patterns of growth and opportunity were narrowing, and control over the disposal of resources, which included labour and marketable assets, was becoming more concentrated in the hands of household heads. In a sense, colonial rule and commercialzation threatened to make all young men *chekut* and all wives children.

To suggest differentiation and the vulnerability of particular groups is not to demonstrate poverty. However, to see how one might lead to the next, we can return to households and the community. The new opportunities of the colonial economy accrued largely to households that were already well-off. In contrast, there were fewer ways in which less secure households could improve their position. Neither large-scale raiding nor movement beyond the confines of the Reserve were now possible. At the same time, privatization and the internal division of territory threatened to reduce the mobility and wide access to common resources on which poorer households depended. They were thus being forced into a position of double vulnerability, being unable either to exploit what opportunities the colonial economy offered or to find alternative avenues of growth and accumulation. With increasing levels of attrition within the pastoral economy, which made recovery from a 'trough' more difficult, they – or perhaps their successors – would become visibly poor (Kituyi, 1990:178–93).

These changes did not take place in isolation, however. Pastoral communities have always operated within a regional context which included non-pastoralists. Indeed, it can be argued that the existence of neighbouring communities of cultivators and the development of regional networks of exchange played a crucial role in the emergence of the particular kind of 'pure' subsistence pastoralism now regarded as 'traditional'. Recognition of this puts the present pastoral predicament in perspective. The relationship between pastoralists and their neighbours in the region has been changing, to the detriment of the former, over the last century. Conventionally, the beginnings of 'decline' in Maasailand are located in the last decades of the nineteenth century, with the end of the '*Iloikop*' wars, followed by the devastating epidemics and the imposition of colonial rule. However, signs of a regional shift were present earlier, in the conflicts over resources within Maasailand itself and in the growth of mixed pastoral communities on its fringes. At the height of its power and prosperity, Maasai pastoralism had already begun to change and to be superseded by other forms of subsistence (Waller, 1979:319–20). What we are seeing now is not the 'end of pastoralism', but a further transformation, again created by a combination of internal shifts and external factors.

During the colonial period, the process of marginalization continued steadily, although the community and its stock economy had sufficient flexibility and resilience to make some internal adjustments. But there were three major changes over which the community had no control. These altered their relations with outsiders, limited their access to resources and changed the material context in which people thought about growth and accumulation.

The first was the imposition and maintenance of colonial boundaries. Maasai territorial expansion had largely ceased by 1880. The creation of Reserves in both German and British territories not only confirmed this halt but even reversed previous gains by depriving the Maasai of large areas of grazing and important water resources.[65] Maasai would now have to live within the constraints of a resource base which could not be expanded and which, indeed, diminished under the ecological pressures of overstocking and increasing aridity. The division of colonial territory into ethnically defined and legally bounded Reserve units also had an impact on intraregional relations, although it neither entirely interrupted nor immediately transformed them. Kikuyu traders still travelled regularly in Maasailand and the establishment of official border markets in Trans-Mara and Loitokitok acknowledged an existing and flourishing trade in stock (Waller, 1975:14, 17, 1984:270–72). However, colonial ethnic categorization and the restriction on free movement between Reserves made both the 'export' of poverty and the option of escape and economic recovery through migration far more difficult.[66]

Maasai were still part of a wider world, but their position within it was changing. In his survey of the development of capitalist relations in Kenya, Kitching pointed to a decisive shift in the 'terms of trade' between agriculture and pastoralism. He located the shift in the interwar years of drought and depression and in relation both to changes in the relative prices and costs of stock and grain and to the expansion of cultivation relative to grazing land. At this point, he argued, resources began to flow out of, instead of into, pastoral areas and livestock ceased to be the main store of value and medium of exchange (Kitching, 1980:ch. 8). One can conceive of the same shift in broader terms and over a longer period by looking not so much at 'terms of trade' but at 'terms of interaction' or even of 'dependence'. Previously, neighbours who wished to convert their agricultural surplus into an investment in family growth or into authority within the community did so by tapping into the Maasai stock economy, using the stock wealth of Maasailand as a regional 'bank', as Lonsdale puts it (Lonsdale, 1992: 19–20). Both ends of the exchange networks benefited, since Maasai in turn received food to tide them over shortfalls in pastoral production, herding labour and wives (Waller, 1979:362–6, 1985a:359–63). With the development of the colonial state, however, alternative paths to investment and growth were opened which led not through Maasailand but through the colonial market. This was the second major change. Increasingly, outsiders could exploit Maasailand as a source of cheap resources and a place to dump surplus people and goods. This can be seen in a variety of instances: in the changing attitudes and objectives of alien settlers in Maasailand, who had once sought stock but now came for land; in government-sponsored settlement to relieve land pressures elsewhere; in the growth of the trade in slaughter stock for butcheries in neighbouring districts; and even in a reversal of the direction of stock theft and border encroachment, with Maasai becoming the target of others (Waller, 1984: 267–72, 280–2, 1993a: 228–37; Kjerland, 1995:239–46). Whereas in the past, Maasai had used their dominant position to underwrite their accumulation and perhaps 'subsidize' their poor at the expense of others, now the position was reversed.

Of greatest long-term significance, however, was the fact that development and diversification in the larger pastoral economy of Kenya were increasingly taking place outside Maasailand and the north. Both Central Province and Nyanza were developing smallholder dairying with grade cattle and mixed farming, while the export economy in pastoral areas was still largely focused on slaughter stock, with the returns being reinvested in the herds (see Kitching, 1980:ch. 11, but also Cowan, 1974). Just as rapidly expanding mixed subsistence economies had begun to cut into Maasai resources before 1880, only to be halted by the imposition of colonial rule, now the same process was occurring again, this time linked to the development of the state. While the reconfiguration and rearticulation of agropastoral relations by the end of the 1940s did not in itself bring poverty to pastoralists, it meshed with internal changes and the constant attrition of environmental uncertainty to further narrow opportunities for accumulation – and perhaps to direct them down a cul-de-sac. Given that the future now lay clearly with commercial mixed farming – and, perhaps, also with specialized dairying and beef ranching – 'becoming Kenyan' would mean, for those trapped in declining subsistence pastoralism, becoming poorer, both structurally, in relation to the state, and conjuncturally, in terms of their increased vulnerability to crisis.

One important question remains: could poverty (or wealth) in the past ever have been permanent states in pastoral society? This brings us back to the question of endemic poverty in precolonial Africa which troubled Iliffe. Merker, writing at the end of *emutai*, thought that long-term want was rare, because family and community networks supported the less fortunate. Stauffacher agreed: 'A Masai with no property has nothing to fear except the disgrace of being poor. Masai will always offer food and shelter to one another.'[67] Half a century later, others have argued that mechanisms of redistribution and reciprocity between households, combined with the 'positive, egalitarian effect' of disease and drought, work to ensure a relatively even spread of resources over time (see esp. Baxter, 1975; Dahl, 1979a; Schneider, 1979; Dyson-Hudson, 1980; but compare more recent and critical chapters in Fratkin *et al.*, 1994). Where this levelling process has 'broken down', it has been attributed to the incorporation of local communities within the state. The penetration of capital and the intervention of outsiders have encouraged new forms of wealth and poverty – notably those connected with the emergence of property in land – and the development of permanent class divisions (see, for example, Hedlund, 1979:15–34; Rutten, 1992:ch. 10; but also Rigby, 1992:163–5).

Such arguments evidently owe something to an enduring fascination with the ideal of pastoral egalitarianism, part of an 'ethnographic pastoral[e]', now projected conveniently back into the past (Gulliver, 1969:234–41; Clifford, 1986:110–12). While they are helpful in placing modern pastoral societies in a wider context and in explaining why they are now apparently in transition towards more deeply and permanently stratified forms, they lack historical depth. Levelling arguments are concerned with explaining inequalities in the present, using assumptions about past equality as a foil. These assumptions may not be correct, or at least not invariably so.

Redistribution of access, though not necessarily of control, is one way of managing resources which are both essential and relatively scarce so as to keep the largest number of households 'solvent'. Inheritance patterns, systems of stock loans and exchanges, fostering and bride-wealth transfers may all do this in different ways. The rich acquire influence and security by giving to the poor, and the use of resources available within the community is effectively maximized. An alternative, however, is to concentrate rather than disperse resources, so that large units are created and maintained under the control of a single owner or joint owners. These large units then act as nodes around which others cluster. Arguably, this is the historical pattern of Maasai settlement, made possible by their movement southwards into the central Rift Valley where ecological conditions in some areas permitted the concentration of people and stock over longer periods than in the north (Waller, 1979:43–54, 99–104).[68] The structure of Maasai cattle camps often reveals considerable inequalities in household size and wealth, with poorer households contributing labour and gaining access to stock in return.[69] Maasai do not disperse stock readily. Even as adults, sons remain under their father's tutelage, with the household herd undivided, and even, after the father's death, brothers should remain together for as long as they can without strain. Access and inheritance follow the lines of the 'house–property complex', being unequally distributed through the mother's herd at the discretion of the father. The father's 'overlordship' thus maintains the unity of household and herd and prevents the dissipation of resources. Here the commitment to growth seems to imply a commitment to inequality, thus neatly reversing Schneider's contention (Schneider, 1979: ch.8; Spencer, 1988: ch. 13; Oboler, 1994:342–7).

As well as ignoring the logic of concentration, levelling arguments often fail to take into account the greater potential of larger herds. As pastoralists have always known, bigger herds survive crisis better than smaller and they recover faster. During drought, for example, wealthy stock-owners will have greater initial resources to draw on and they may be able to delay or avoid liquidating their holdings to buy food. Unless stock loss is total, they will also be left with a larger number of beasts when conditions improve (Fratkin & Roth, 1990:385–402; Borgerhoff Mulder & Sellen, 1994:220–2).[70] Moreover, beyond the simple numerical advantage of having many animals, there is the no less important one of having many friends. The widely ramifying social networks that prior investment of surplus stock in marriage alliances, bond friendships, patronage, hospitality and the like create spread risk and foster reciprocity. Provided that a crisis is local rather than regional, wealthier pastoralists can call in their lines of credit to help them weather the immediate impact and rebuild afterwards. Poorer households, lacking this resource, may have to disperse or join the wealthy (Almagor, 1978:139–58; Turton, 1980:67–90; Sobania, 1991:118–42).[71]

Thus disaster may actually increase rather than decrease differentiation. Studies of crises in the past bear this out. Although the rinderpest pandemic in Maasailand is portrayed in tradition as an all-encompassing public calamity, private experiences sometimes tell a different story. They show, for instance, that those who already had established trading networks beyond the community did better in the search for refuge than those who were forced to go searching for any household that would take them in. They demonstrate the cumulative effects of several different crises within a short period, and they suggest not only that the wealthy may have recovered faster than the poor but that the former were able to expand their influence by acting as patrons to the latter. For a short time in, say, 1892, there may have been a rough equality of misery, but this was quickly replaced by the inequalities of patronage and protection (Waller, 1988:74–5).

This is not to say that levelling does not take place. There is abundant proverbial wisdom and anecdotal evidence to show that stock wealth is highly volatile and that families and individuals rise and fall through luck and misfortune, good and bad management and so forth. Ole Galishu, the very model of disciplined achievement, died in relative poverty and obscurity, his herd having been cut down more than once by disease. However, the uncertainties of pastoral subsistence and even the redistributive mechanisms to which levelling arguments have been tied can have a more subtly differentiating effect. Levelling does not mean that every player remains in the game. Given the greater resilience of larger households and herds, it is possible for a wealthy stratum of stock-owning families, albeit with a changing membership, to maintain itself for long periods, alongside an equally enduring stratum of poverty. While the condition of individuals may not be permanent, sharp differentiations persist within the community. We need not invoke the spectre of development to explain the roots of poverty.

Poverty, wealth and the practical and moral issues they raise are at the centre of pastoral history. More than temporary poverty has probably always existed in Maasailand, and the antecedents of its contemporary forms can be found in the continuous process of change since at least the end of the last century. Reviewing more than a century of gradual change and 'remarkable continuity' in African poverty, Iliffe concluded that its different types were now both growing and converging. Old forms of structural poverty continue and have been joined by new kinds of want. The old, the weak and the isolated have been joined by the able-bodied landless and by the unemployed and underemployed. At the same time, conjunctural poverty, whose worst effects had been ameliorated by late colonial welfare, has returned in the form of drought, disease and warfare beyond the capacity of the African state to contain (Iliffe, 1987:81 and, generally, ch. 13).

Pastoral societies appear to be taking a similar path. Conjunctural poverty has returned in drought and warfare from the Sahel to Somalia – if, indeed, it ever left, for pastoral societies, especially in the north, were hardly touched by colonial welfare. Yet sudden, universal, crashes have occurred before – the herds in Maasailand dropped by perhaps 90% in 1892 and by 70% in 1962 – and pastoralists have survived. More significant in the long term is the constant attrition of particular loss on smaller and less wealthy households as the bottom of the pastoral heap is gradually eaten away. This erosion is accelerating, as the structures of opportunity and access are simultaneously being narrowed and reshaped to the disadvantage of the poor. Structural poverty has always included more than the incapacitated in pastoral societies, but the poverty of exclusion and dependence is gaining new force and new ground – often literally, since land itself is now at issue.

Yet, despite its increasing salience, poverty itself is still stigmatized and shunned (Talle, 1988:138–40). This returns us to the constructions placed on poverty and its causes, the aspects of impoverishment which have perhaps changed least among both pastoralists themselves and their rulers. That widespread long-term poverty has been recognized so comparatively late in societies like Maasai is, ironically, a result partly of the myth of the rich and conservative pastoralist and partly of earlier stages of differentiation, which created a controlling oligarchy of wealthy householders able to marginalize the poor while denying, through a hegemonic ideology of growth, the very existence of permanent poverty. Present myths of wealth and poverty still derive from the exercise of power, whether by the state, by development agencies or by the newly rich themselves, and are no less obscuring and distancing than in the past (e.g. Hodgson, in this volume; Ferguson, 1990:esp. ch. 5). The poor are always with us, but, of course, they never are us.

Notes

1. My thanks to the participants at the original workshop for their comments, and especially to David Anderson, Elliot Fratkin, John Lonsdale, Tom Spear and Paul Spencer, whose influences are very evident in what follows.
2. Partington to Bagge, 11 Sept. 1908, encl. in Sadler to Crewe, 23 Sept. 1908, Public Record Office, London [PRO]: CO 533/47; Sandford, 1919:82–9; Byrne to Bottomley, 25 Sept. 1931, CO 533/412/1; Government of Great Britain (1932:14–15). A stock tax was strongly advocated by settlers in search of labour and was incorporated in the recommendations of the 1912 *Labour Commission – East Africa Protectorate* (NLC) (Govern-

ment of Kenya Colony, 1913: 319–36).

3. See, for example, the forthright comments by Cranworth and in evidence to the Labour Commission – Cranworth, 1919:154–9; *NLC*, 114. For official attitudes, see for example, Eliot to Lansdowne, 9 April 1904, PRO: FO 2/835; Spencer, 1983:113–40.

4. See, for example, Government of Great Britain (1934a: ch. 10; 1955; 73, 280–2, 293–312.) Both reports summarize colonial wisdom on the subject in very similar ways. The Kenya Land Comission (KLC) was the first major enquiry to accept that 'in the midst of plenty, [pastoralists] are, in fact, living under conditions of extreme poverty' (Government of Great Britain, 1934a: 495) – although its definition of poverty was market-orientated. One of the members of the Commission was R.W. Hemsted, who had served as Senior Commissioner in both Maasailand and the north. The assumed connection between decline and greed/ignorance had in fact been challenged as early as 1930 by a British consultant, who pointed instead to government neglect and the loss of grazing lands; but this inconvenient opinion was ignored, as was a government statistician's warning that calculations of wealth based on conversions into monetary units were unsound – C. Speller, 'Native Livestock as an Economic Asset', n.d., in Speller to Shiels, 15 July 1931, CO 533/415/9; memo by Walter, n.d. 1932, in CO 533/421/1.

5. This idea gained currency after drought and depression had revealed the fragility of the stock economy, and was continued under wartime and postwar regulation – Masai Province, *Annual Reports* [MPAR] (1936, 1939), Kenya National Archives [KNA]: PC/SP 1/2/2 and *idem* (1945) PC/SP 1/2/3. The muddled thinking behind the policy was exposed in the comment that 'it cannot permanently be true that the best way of teaching a man the uses of money is to take it from him', Masai Province, *Handing-Over Report*, Jan. 1936, PC/SP 2/1/1.

6. See, for example, Government of Great Britain (1934a:195–6). Demands for more grazing were sometimes supported by sympathetic local administrators – see, for example, exchanges over the Leroki Plateau and the 'Mile Zone' along the railway – correspondence and memoranda in files CO 533/329, 658, 377/19, 389/7 (Leroki) and 533/416/12 (Mile Zone). Margery Perham, on tour in south-east Kajiado in September 1930, was taken by the DC to visit a camp of eight households with about 1000 head of cattle. This herd, she was told, was insufficient to meet subsistence needs (Perham, 1976:165, 180).

7. Colonial discourse on pastoral wealth can perhaps be seen as an early example of the 'development narrative', with pastoralist views as a kind of 'counter-narrative' of poverty and constraint (Roe, 1991:287–96).

8. Iliffe may be too sweeping in his dismissal of oral sources, although scepticism is justified. Despite their distortions, they may convey important information about dominant attitudes towards and constructions of poverty (Iliffe, 1987: 48–9).

9. The gloss is widespread among pastoralists and appears early in the literature. Von Hohnel recorded that the word in Maa meant 'poor folk without cattle or other possessions' (Von Hohnel, 1894:260; see also Waller, 1985b:127–33).

10. It will be useful here to clarify my use of 'household' and 'family'. The latter is a particularly slippery concept, with many possible definitions, and I use it only in a general way. For our purposes, it is convenient to link the social unit to the herd. What I here call 'household' is the unit dependent on a single household herd, under the overall control of a husband/father. The household herd is managed as a unit, but, if large enough, it is divided into separate milking herds for wives/children, with a residual herd left un-allocated. Each wife and her children therefore form a separate sub-unit with stock, and there may be additional sub-units, composed of married sons and their wives, while these remain under the father's aegis. Family and household structures, of course, change over time. The usage I have adopted here reflects the past of large cattle camps and 'extended families' – and also the impossibility of 'family reconstitution' – perhaps better than the present trend towards 'nuclear families' living separately. For an overview, see Guyer (1981).

11. The precolonial trade in foodstuffs is well attested. It continued into the colonial period and was supplemented by shop-bought *posho* from at least 1914 onwards (Waller, 1975:11, 14–15; 1985b:101, 125; Narok District, *Annual Reports* [NDAR] (1942, 1943), KNA: DC/NRK 1/1/3).

12. Derived mainly from Jacobs (1965:157) and Dahl & Hjort, (1976:ch. 7). I use these sources in preference to more recent studies, because they predate major recent changes in diet and economy.

13. See, for example, Goldfinch, 'The Masai Scandal', n.d., ms. in Anti-Slavery Society papers, file G137, Rhodes House, Oxford; PC Rift Valley to Resident Magistrate, Nakuru, 31 Jan. 1934, KNA: PC/RVP 6A/15/17. In theory, levies for communal fines were apportioned by the communities concerned, according to ability to pay, but this is qualified by local memories of arbitrary seizure. Correspondence over the organization of compulsory sales is also suggestive – see Officer-in-Charge, Masai Reserve [OiC] to DCs, 2 Oct. 1938, KNA: DC/KAJ 9/2/1; OiC to Chief Secretary, 14 Aug. 1939, Headmaster, Loitokitok to OiC, 16 Aug. 1939 and reply, 18 Sept. 1939, all in KNA: PC/Ngong 1/2/4.

14. There were degrees of scarcity, related to breeding rates and capacities. Camels were the scarcest resource, cattle second and sheep and goats, the 'small change' of the pastoral economy, far less scarce.

15. This is not to argue, however, that the possibility of acquiring new forms of wealth – through permanent wage employment, for example – did not exist before.

16. The most striking example of exclusion is still in Lovejoy & Baier (1975). Iliffe mentions the possibility, but his examples, apart from Maasai and Tuareg, are drawn from southern African cattle-keeping societies, whose economic and social structures are significantly different from those of East African pastoralists (Iliffe, 1987:ch. 5; Brown, 1994:259–72).

17. These were refugees. Less often quoted are Baumann's references to people who were not starving (Baumann, 1894:31).

18. For example, at Fort Smith, Kikuyu — see Hall's Diaries, entries for 20, 31 Jan. 1894, *Hall Papers*, Rhodes House; Ainsworth to Hardinge, 20 Jan. 1896, encl. in Hardinge to Salisbury, 10 March 1896, FO 107/50.

19. Baumann, 1894:32; Meyer, 1900:187; Hardinge to Salisbury, 27 Feb. and 17 May 1898 and Salisbury to Hardinge, 13 April and 7 July 1898, all in FO 107/91, 93, 88, 89. Chagga also 'sold' children when food was short, reversing the flow – DC Teita to PC Mombasa, 14 Dec. 1904 and 23 Feb. 1909, KNA: Coast Province, Teita Inward 1904 & 1909. Pawning was often interpreted as a sale, but the giving of children as pledges was not necessarily intended to be irrevocable, and it shaded into the equally common practice of fostering.

20. As studies of modern famines have pointed out, it may be particularly difficult for pastoralists to reverse the downward spiral once their main assets have been liquidated (Sen, 1981:104–12, 120–22; Turton, 1985:331–9).

21. I have in mind here an extension and adaptation of Moore's discussion of the 'muting' of women (Moore, 1986:160–71). The generic proverb, 'When the rich man speaks the poor keep silent,' captures the sense. See also Chambers (1983:18); and Spear & Waller (1993:299).

22. 'Egalitarianism' and age in relation to social and economic differentiation are discussed in Waller (1994). It should be noted that equality of opportunity, not equality of resources, is what is implied.

23. For example, MPAR (1917–18, 1928). 'Kikuyu wives' figure prominently as the main cultivators, but some elders employed Kikuyu labourers to cultivate for them (MPAR, 1914–15, 1929).

24. By 1928, they were cultivating 500 acres, and in 1936 they officially sold over 3000 bags of maize – (MPAR, 1928, 1936). The 1948 Ngong census describes this enclave in unusual detail: James Ngatia, a Maasai teacher, had 50 acres and 40 head of cattle at Ololua and employed four workers; Abdallah Kaurai, also a Kaputiei and a prominent Kiserian trader and church elder, had a 20-acre shamba worked by four men, together with a forest concession at Kerarapon with nine more labourers – data in file PC/Ngong 1/1/16. There were similar but smaller developments elsewhere.

25. DC North Masai, 'Memo, on the [Laikipia] Masai', n.d., KNA: Native Affairs Dept. MSS, Vol. III, Part II, 19/iii/48.

26. NDAR (1930) Appendix, DC/NRK 1/1/2; Dundas, 'Masai Organisation', 1906, KNA: DC/MKS 26/2/1. Justin Lemenye referred to '*osinga* which might be translated as

slavery', but distinguished between the voluntary servitude of the dependent herder and slavery as found elsewhere (Fosbrooke, 1954:40; see also Waller 1979:76–9; 1985b:109–11; Talle, 1988:241–2). For ideas of poverty, and virtue in Maasai, see Waller (1994).

27. See, for example, comments on cultivation in MPAR (1934, 1935) and Kajiado District, *Annual Report* [KDAR] (1934), DC, KAJ 2/1/1. For attitudes towards cultivation and ethnicity, see Waller (1993a:237–46).

28. Small stock can also be vitally important in the household economy, and perhaps especially for the poor, but the sheep/goat figures are either non-existent or so vague as to be useless.

29. MPARs, *passim*, PC/SP 1/2/1; Jacobs, 1965:151. More accurate spot counts were made during veterinary campaigns, but these are patchy and incomplete.

30. Surveys were undertaken in 1926–8 (Foster) and 1930–1 (Philip) – Orr & Gilks, 1931; Medical Survey of Masai Reserve, Nov. 1930 – April 1931, cyclo. copy in CO 533/416/3. Neither found malnutrition (an indicator of food insufficiency) in the Maasai population at large, although we need to be aware of biases in sampling and interpretation (see Brantley, 1997).

31. No colonial tax registers for Maasailand seem to have survived. For a sense of the randomness of counting, see explanations of statistics in MPAR (1924, 1934 Appendix) and the insouciant response of the DC when his figures implying a population drop of one-third in two years were queried – OiC to DC Narok, 16 April 1936 and reply in KNA: DC/Ngong 1/13/2.

32. Trespass and stock theft files, where they survive, are especially useful – see, for example, PC/RVP 6A/15/17 and 6A/17/19.

33. Figures in McClellan to Bowring, 21 April 1913, encl. in Belfield to Harcourt, 9 May 1913, CO 533/118. Frustratingly, comparable figures for the household count, which was taken at the same time, were not included, because they were less relevant to government concerns – a reminder that official data were collected for the purposes of governing, not research.

34. There were certainly poor people on Laikipia, including stockless Maasai living as dependents in wealthier households. However, the 5692 persons recorded had an average per capita holding of nearly 34 head, a very high figure if reliable – DC North Masai, 'Memo on the Masai'; 'Memo on the Masai', n.d., in *Ngong Political Record Book*, Part A, DC/KAJ 1/2/1.

35. For the interlocking of social and economic change, see Berry (1993). My argument here draws on recent studies of famine as a social and political process and, loosely, on Sen's notion of entitlement (although entitlement tends to be market-focused) (see Sen, 1981:ch. 5; Watts, 1991:9–26; Devereux, 1993).

36. MPAR (1934–6) PC/SP 1/2/1–2; Anon, *c*. 1962:12.

37. Hodgson has suggested that wives may previously have had a greater share in the herd and its management (Hodgson, 1995:37–42).

38. Analysis of the colonial economy in Maasailand is at a preliminary stage: the findings presented here may need revision. For an important and pioneering attempt to rethink cash and cattle, see Hutchinson (1996:ch. 2).

39. Average annual sales were in excess of 10,000 head between 1923 and 1930, rising to 15,000 for the 1930s and to 20,000 during wartime requisitioning, not counting smuggling and non-cash exchanges – official figures calculated from MPAR.

40. MPAR (1928) PC/SP 1/2/2. The economy rose again to slightly above this level in the late 1930s. An official analysis of the figures for 1934 (a year of serious drought) concluded that the Maasai made little from the market and would remain poor as a result. Of a total export value of £43,000, only £17,000 was received in cash and, of this, £13,000 was due in taxes, leaving only £4000 cash in the Reserve. Additionally, Maasai required food to the value of £12,500 (though not all paid for in cash). Only about £15,000 value *in toto* remained – (MPAR, 1934).

41. The first scheme was at Konza – KDAR (1949) PC/SP 1/5/3. See also Government of Kenya Colony (1962: esp. 68–83, 222–32, ch. 6). Postwar grazing policy in Maasailand is set out in Masai Province *Handing-over Reports* (Dec. 1946 and June 1949), PC/SP 2/1/1, and MPAR (1947, 1948), PC/SP 1/2/3.

42. Waller (1993b) discusses the origins and implications of privatization in Maasailand in the

1930s. For useful discussions of differentiation through the creation of private resources elsewhere, see Peters (1994) and Mazonde (1990:182–90).

43. Talle has argued that women's rights have declined as commercialization reduces the autonomy of the 'house' within the larger unit (Talle, 1988:3–5, 268–9; for an overview, see Kettel, 1992:23–41).

44. Indirect evidence of this comes from the official complaint that Maasai (men) could pay tax without liquidating stock, by using the cash from hides and ghee sales – MPAR (1924) PC/SP 1/2/2. We cannot, of course, know how, if at all, cash was redistributed by the household head.

45. In a good year, a hide might fetch up to sh.18 wholesale; in a bad year, it might fetch a quarter of that, but Maasai suppliers got less than 20% of the traders' price. Both the proportion sold for cash and the money received increased as hide preparation gradually came under official control in the late 1930s.

46. From 1923, local dairies were operated, when milk supplies permitted, by pupils seconded from the government Maasai schools. In 1938, three dairies in Loita processed nearly 6000 gallons of milk, supplied by 86 households. Pay-out (based on the wholesale price of ghee) was sh.2377 at 38c./gal. The largest supplier, a *laibon*, received sh.158 (average pay-out sh.26). By the late 1930s, a few elders had bought ghee separators of their own – see file DC/NRK 2/6/1.

47. Stauffacher letter, 7 Jan. 1907, *Hearing and Doing*, 12:1 (1907), 9–11.

48. It is said that, when Maasai war-leaders were assembling parties of spearmen to join British punitive columns, they deliberately gave preference to poorer *murran*, and poor men who had already retired from *murran*hood sometimes, and rather ignominiously, joined raiding parties to better their fortunes.

49. Government of Great Britain, 1905:6.

50. There is one possible and important exception. During the '*Iloikop*' wars of the mid-nineteenth century, very large numbers of cattle clearly did change hands within the Maa-speaking community. We do not know how these herds were redistributed between households and individuals, but some sections, like Purko and Kisongo, are thought to have become particularly rich and powerful as a result (Waller, 1985b:107).

51. Some informants claim that returning raiders sometimes made arrangements to conceal or divert beasts for their own use.

52. The line between 'stealing' and 'raiding' may always have been a matter of construction and negotiation (Almagor, 1979:138-9; Berntsen, 1979:240–41, 251–2).

53. See, for example, Collective Punishment Enquiry file encl. in Byrne to Cunliffe-Lister, 4 May 1933, CO 533/430/1; MPAR (1921, 1934), PC/SP 1/2/1.

54. This suggestion must be highly tentative. My study of stock theft and its social context in colonial Maasailand is at a preliminary stage and suffers from a dearth of hard evidence which makes it difficult to determine how widespread theft was and whether it was in part a response to poverty. However, in one of the few sympathetic Maasai references to the plight of the poor, Henry Kulet tells the tale of the son of a poverty-stricken father who is pursuaded to go on an unsanctioned and disastrous raid through shame at his family's condition (Kulet, 1972; see also case quoted in Talle, 1988:243).

55. In 1918–19, there were raids into Tanganyika, which the administration attributed in part to recent losses from drought and disease, and the 1930 Loitokitok raids were linked to drought as well as to the promotion ceremony (*Eunoto*) of the senior circumcision of Il Derito *murran* – Northey to Milner, 14 Aug. 1919, CO 533/212; KDAR (1930).

56. Both Anderson and Kjerland suggest that stock theft could be highly profitable, but there is no hard evidence for the existence of professional stock theft 'rings' in Maasailand comparable with those in operation in Kalenjin areas (Anderson, 1986:399–415; Kjerland, 1995:ch.3).

57. DC Narok to Chief Native Commissioner, 18/4/33, PC/RVP 6A/17/31. The reliance placed on crudely deterrent and often collective punishment, together with the returns of unsolved cases and fugitive offenders, supports the point – see, for example, investigation files in DC/Ngong 1/1/21 and 1/8/13.

58. The numbers involved were never large. In 1939, 1356 were registered as in employment, the number having perhaps doubled during the 1930s (figures from MPAR). Initially, Maasai would not work for cash wages, although they were willing to pay non-

Maasai labour for specific tasks, such as well-digging. Stauffacher complained of the difficulty of getting Maasai to work at the Rumuruti mission, despite their willingness to become *chekut* in other households. He attributed this to their fear of losing status and to their intention of resuming raiding as soon as the whites left (Stauffacher letter, 21 July 1906, *Hearing and Doing*, 11:3 (1906), 11–13).

59. Unlike the Samburu, relatively few Maasai enlisted in the KAR. Thirty were recorded in 1937 and wartime recruitment produced a few more, 76 being demobilized in Narok in 1946 (compared with between 350 and 400 Samburu) – MPAR (1937); NDAR (1941, 1946), DC/NRK 1/1/3; Spencer, 1973:163–4.

60. Sperling's distinction between the modern labour strategies of growing and mature/ declining households, the former using wage labour as a way of accelerating growth, the latter as a way of surviving loss, is useful here, as is the concept of 'straddling', through which some households sold labour on the colonial market and replaced it more cheaply by hiring in local labour (Sperling, 1987:174–89).

61. See permit applications in file PC/Ngong 1/7/4.

62. I have argued elsewhere, following Spencer, that *murran* espouse a communal ideal of what might be termed 'virtuous poverty', in contrast to the private 'acquisitiveness' of old age (Waller, 1994).

63. It was, however, ruling elders who urged the 'suppression' of *murran*hood, and their views were largely adopted by the administration – see e.g. NDAR (1929) DC/NRK 1/1/2; Kajiado District, *Local Native Council Minutes*, 12 Aug. 1932, DC/KAJ 5/1/3; Narok District, *Monthly Intelligence Reports*, Feb.–March 1941, PC/Ngong 1/1/1.

64. Communal labour demands imposed by the administration on *murran* from the mid 1930s provoked their deep resentment, as did elders' demands that they 'leave *murran*hood', for *murran* feared that they might never be allowed to become adults – see, for example, file on 'Rotian Riot' (1935) PC/SP 6/2/1A. The young did not quite become a kind of internal proletariat whose labour power was appropriated by the old, but they were being squeezed by the combined pressures of colonial and paternal authority (see Bonte, 1977:189–92; Rigby, 1992:57–77; Brown, 1994:265–7).

65. Details in Sandford, 1919:20–43; Government of Great Britain, 1934b: vol. II, 1224–30.

66. But not impossible. By February 1935, at the height of a major drought, 300 'Maasai destitutes' had taken refuge in the Kikuyu Reserve and 'hundreds' more had moved on to white farms – MPAR (1934).

67. Merker, 1910:119–20; Stauffacher letter, 7 Jan. 1907. Merker's view of the prospects of dependents was equally optimistic. However, it would be unwise to assume *a priori* that lineage or age-set always provided a safety net. Pastoral societies vary in the extent to which the unfortunate can expect relief. Clans in Samburu, for example, appear to be far more generally supportive of their members than their equivalents in Maasai, where aid is more closely tied to reputation and the chances of reciprocity (Spencer, 1973:77–8, 1988:250).

68. For another example that explores ecological as well as political implications of concentration, see Giblin (1992:esp. ch. 2). I am grateful to Tom Spear for this reference.

69. This appears to be the pattern revealed by the 1912–13 Purko figures. A camp is often known by the name of its most prominent household head (Jacobs, 1965:225–35).

70. Levellers usually focus on drought, but the dynamics of infectious disease might better support their point.

71. A wealthy Datooga herd-owner allegedly received 200 head of cattle in 'gifts for hunger' over two years, after having lost over 600 in a raid (Borgerhoff Mulder & Sellen, 1994:218–19). But note Turton's point that extreme and generalized crisis tends to dissolve obligation and credit (Turton, 1985:335–6).

3 Remembered Cattle, Forgotten People: The Morality of Exchange & the Exclusion of the Turkana Poor

VIGDIS BROCH-DUE

Paths to pastoral poverty and prosperity

Turkana pastoral life in northern Kenya moves to natural rhythms, ruled by the ebb and flux of resources. The seasonal cycles between dry and wet, scarcity and plenty, are chronicled in the family herd's patterns of feeding, mating, calving and producing milk. Depending on the nurturing powers of herds for survival, the lives and reproduction cycles of pastoralists and their cattle, camels, sheep, goats and donkeys are inextricably tied together in one essential equation. Weather patterns determine not only everyday routines of work and rest, but also the schedule of most major social events – movements, births, initiation, marriage and burials – for these depend on the processes of growth and change that the rains set in motion. Thus, it is not particularly surprising that Turkana are keen weather watchers, for the arrival of rainfall or its failure potentially means the difference between wealth and want. The peaks of dry seasons are times of waiting, and the month of March, normally bringing the 'long rains' which set the natural growth cycle of grass, calves and children in motion, is the entry point into the local calendar. The advance of the dry season is gradual, containing within it months of growth and ripening, and yet at the same time a constant drying out and dying off. One day the green grass is yellow and still nutritious, the next week it is almost gone. The rainfall tends to come in two peaks but, even so, one area may benefit from soaking downpours and good grass, while another, not too far distant, is passed over. Sometimes the rain fails entirely and famine threatens, forcing humans and herds to range further afield in search of fodder and water. The effects of a widespread drought are highly visible by the animal carcasses littering the ground and the heaps of hides placed by desperate pastoralists along the roads, in the hope that traders will buy.

Since drought, along with the disease and raiding that tend to follow it, is clearly the force which periodically kills off the largest number of livestock and since 'lack of livestock' (*Ngikebootok*) is the literal definition of being poor, one would expect that these calamities would figure high on the local list of factors causing poverty. Yet, in a recent round of interviews with Turkana pastoralists, I was confronted with a very different line of argument. Although the reduction in herd size by drought or raid was acknowledged as a serious setback and source of much suffering, it was none the less vehemently denied as the reason behind anybody becoming permanently poor. Those present, women as well as men, seemed to perceive poverty not as a condition beyond one's control, but rather as the cumulative effect of a person's inability to 'move things his/her way'.

And yet this kind of explanation, which makes each and every one the author of his/her own misfortune, did not sit well with my experiences from fieldwork among people on the periphery of the pastoral system – the settlers in towns and the sites of development projects. The evidence that emerged from the large corpus of surveys and life stories collected among those pushed out of pastoralism, was that events beyond the individual's control – drought, disease and raids, along with different forms of social inequality – were the foremost forces leading to destitution. More to the point, few had managed to recover their former livelihood with resources earned in new occupations – at least in the sense of being able to build a sufficient herd for subsistence. When I brought up this statistical fact in conversations with pastoralists, themselves far from being poor according to dominant Turkana definitions, they remained un-impressed, insisting that my *Ngikebootok* friends had not conducted themselves properly.

'You make poverty or prosperity through the ways you move your livestock!' was the standard statement that ran through these recent interviews. Often the informant would point his or her finger towards the numerous livestock trails that twist over the savannah, creating a web of pathways, connecting the many pastoral camps constructed along migration routes. One obvious interpretation of this effort to situate the argument spatially is that the skills with which one manages herding and husbandry decisions on an everyday basis is crucial in the process of making or breaking pastoral careers. Forced to cope with the destructive forces of their livelihood and landscape, Turkana are intensely concerned with promoting fertility and growth in their herds. They have to be, given that theirs is a volatile economy, in which the main capital is unreliable biological matter, subject to cycles of boom and bust, not so much in terms of money and markets, but in terms of demography and vegetation. The periodicity of nature forces these pastoralists not only to be alert and to take advantage of the fodder when it is there, but also to plan ahead and safeguard against disasters. Given this context, it is not difficult to understand why the proper handling of the reproductive potential of herds is not only a technical question, but one that has wide-ranging social implications.

Yet the significance of 'path', *erot*, which people incessantly invoked in our discussions of survival strategies is multilayered and subtle. Paradoxically, during droughts, when the herds that traverse them are in decline, the contours of paths scarred on the sun-baked surface appear even more sharply – a sort of visual reminder to herders of their importance as a way out of the immediate crisis. This is because the myriad cross-cutting pathways linking corrals and courtyards, camp and countryside, are physical signposts conjuring up a social landscape – a web of relationships and potential transactions that might come along these paths. They are the route to building real and symbolic capital in terms of both human relationships and herds.

Building a successful livestock ledger starts within the compound. Proper and prosperous marriages, most people agree, are those where the minds and material efforts of husbands and wives join in moving 'up the path'. This path wends its way beyond the fence, being the route along which animals are exchanged and, by extension, it connotes the various paths along which participation in exchange leads. Physical paths are also the social pathways along which people, livestock and other assets move, creating a 'roped path', *eropit*, between donor and recipient. The more livestock that have moved between partners, the more solid the relationship and the more likely that resources will flow from that relationship in times of scarcity. Each 'rope' has thus a history, constituted by past transactional sequences, shaping the biographies and social standing of those involved. The metaphor of pathways extends beyond the physical and social worlds to include individual anatomy and physiology. What one eats moves along 'food paths' (*akimuij erot*) and the image of paths and flows goes on to characterize the inner workings of the body, including the essences of human life – breath, knowledge and power. If these vital flows move freely along the interior pathways, the person is healthy, the outward signs being a willingness to move animals along the exterior paths and to participate in food sharing systems. If the person neglects the circuit of reciprocal exchanges of food and livestock, the movement of life-sustaining forces and flows is constrained, resulting in illness, misfortune and poverty. Vitality, well-being and wealth are all linked to movement of a wide range of assets along these multiple paths (Broch-Due, 1990a).

The conceptualization of 'path' is central in the cultural construction of poverty, in the sense that it is the inability to 'make paths', in its manifold layers of meaning, that leads to misfortune. Through many conversations with pastoral people over the years and from the cases they brought up, it has become clear to me that the Turkana vocabulary of poverty is tightly woven into a moral economy, which moves individual responsibility for affairs to the forefront. In local talk about poverty, processual qualities, such as agency and activity, are emphasized, while destiny is entirely eclipsed. If not interrupted, informants inevitably set off along a narrative route of human deeds and acts, which seems to serve as a memorizing device for positioning themselves and their forebears favourably on moral (high) ground. The deeper they go into their own family history, the more the topic of poverty is sidetracked. In its place emerges tales of prosperity and the growth of wealth, in people and animals, and how these multiplied from one generation to the next through a series of successful participations in key social events.

Clearly, this detailed remembering contains a lot of forgetting – a muted list of disasters, mischief, treason, loss and all the vagaries of real life. Lost from the recollection of their living relatives are all the losers of past generations, whose hopes and life's-work were probably shattered by scarcity and lack of support, but whose destinies it is no longer possible to retrieve. Yet, reading through this corpus of interviews, it strikes me that we are faced with a mediated relationship between remembering and forgetting, which is brought to bear on the shaping of subsistence strategies in general. The potentially constructive work of forgetting in the activity of memory in the Turkana context of poverty is the way in which it suppresses individual cases of misfortune, while maintaining an acute sense of the preventive manoeuvres available to avoid impoverishment. In that sense, forgetting foregoes past suffering but works within the mechanisms of memory to preserve the future of the pastoral community itself. Through the productive interaction between remembering and forgetting emerge social recipes for the survival not of all people, but rather of a livelihood based on livestock, and the repertoire of key values and ideas that participate in reproducing it from one generation to the next.

For when I pressed the issue, everybody recognized that anyone, because of being unlucky or victimized, could find themselves without livestock, but the dominant opinion was that this need only be temporary if the person has taken the right moves towards related people in the past. They even had a term for a person in this type of situation, *Ekechodon* – only one among several such definitions of specific poverty scenarios and precise social identities linked to each of these. Another version of transient impoverishment was *Elongait* – a person having lost his family and thus his pool of labour due to raid and disease, but who was expected to recover relationships by using his livestock to marry and build a partnership. *Emetut*, I learnt, was a person falling short in both registers of wealth – livestock and people – a twisted loner, living without family and possessing little knowledge about animal affairs, walking from camp to camp feeding on leftovers from other people's meals. But the poor person proper was the *Ekebotonit*, who, because of mean and deviant social behaviour, never managed to 'make paths', a one-dimensional person who could handle neither people nor animals in ways that create wealth and a supportive following. An *Ekebotonit* is simply a nobody who authors nothing, an empty person off-track, so to speak. This identity is sharply contrasted with *Ebarasit/Ngebaren*, the terms for prosperity, which simply translate as 'livestock' in the plural. Being prosperous refers quite literally to a 'full-filled' person having the profound ability to author all sorts of relations in the world through animals.

One notices how competing discourses about poverty and prosperity implicitly and explicitly evoke each other in these definitions and distinctions. For the prime principle that structures the poverty scenario is, as the local proverb goes: 'Livestock speak louder than sweet words.' The premiss laced into this proverb is that meaning is concretely embedded in the materiality of the things themselves – and it is through the play on this physicality that livestock become central movers within a moral economy of persons. Having herds brings life and death close to everyone's experience, and these dimensions become focal because human and livestock reproduction cycles are so closely interwoven. The key to this moral quality of the pastoral economy is the host of intimate, visceral and emotional experiences which tie human and animal together in Turkana minds – procreation, the birth and death of livestock, the carefully observed pregnancy, the washes of blood and water at birth, the swollen udders, the tiny calf struggling to stand up, the decaying body at death – all unavoidably connote the same essential processes in the human world, the more so in that all major social events in that human world depend completely on these events in the life of their herds.

The development cycle of herds lies at the heart of a web of events which are ecological, physiological, social and symbolic all at once – the seasons, reproduction, herd size and movements, the redistribution of animals in exchanges, marriages and inheritance, and the shared consumption of meat, blood and milk. All aspects of this web – which is the intimate web of their personal universes – are part of their moral universe as well and 'the good' only emerges from the individual's capacity to make the appropriate moves with his/her animals. In other words, 'the good' in the Turkana world is a complex quality, relating to the person's ability to manage a whole range of physical and social processes. On this moral ground, it is not difficult to grasp why the possession of animals is the key to the valuation of personal attributes and the only source of sociality. It is so powerful that it affects claim procedures and the positioning of different people at other levels and in other contexts as well.

This morality woven into the human–herd equation informs the register of social identities of poor people through the ways in which discourse positions people as specific sorts of subjects endowed with specific sorts of capacities. These social distinctions and their subject positions are clearly shaped from conflicting moral orientations: sharing versus selfishness. The hardship of *Ekechodon* and *Elongait* is claimed to be short-lived because people in these situations set their agency, acts and assets towards collective ends: by reproducing their wealth in people and animals in prescribed ways, they reproduce their social relations. The two serious poverty states are put in sharp opposition to the domain of sociality and solidarity. However, the category *Emetut* is a foil for the whole range of displaced subjects, such as the lonely old, widows and widowers, orphans, spinsters, sick, handicapped and eccentric individuals, who, despite being defined as lacking in social skills, can still expect to be fed. The only category defined out of the circles of support altogether – the *Ekebotonit* – contains individuals who, according to pastoral standards, handle their assets in a selfish and amoral manner. Because of such 'poor' social capacities, the dominant discourse places them in a permanent situation of poverty beyond the confines of the (moral) community. In between and in relation to both opposing identities of poor-prosperous (*Ekebotonit–Ebarasit*), one infers the varied struggles of people to value themselves in some publicly demonstrable way.

The turn of topic by my informants from poverty to personalized narratives about prosperity must be understood in this context. To evoke any traces of *Ekebonit* in their own life and that of their forebears would mean to disqualify themselves as persons, as Turkana proper. To project yourself favourably in public depends on personal efficacy in pressing claims within the recognized idioms, combined with your virtuosity in playing the vocabularies attached to these idioms. Clearly, I had inspired this whole interpretative horizon in my queries into poverty. I believe the moral narratives I got in response were parts of the larger canvas of something Fraser (1989) has termed 'the politics of needs interpretation'. One recurrent discursive resource was to involve the agency of ancestors, which, not surprisingly, is focal in the paradigms of argumentation accepted as authoritative. Another discursive resource was to project an unblemished social record. Passing setbacks did sometimes surface in these family fortunes, expressed either as *ekechodon* (lacking livestock) or *elongait* (lacking labour), but these problems were always partially solved within the span of the intergenerational story. This is not to suggest that these narrative solutions were always fictitious. There are plenty of devices available to deal with such imbalances in the human–herd ratio in the factual world – such as the fostering of children or calves, herding and herder cooperation, and a range of transactions, including marriage. Indeed, the very fact that my informants and their relatives have remained pastoralists means, by definition, that they have been able to stave off periods of hardship and maintain a state of sufficiency through successfully activating the means available.

This brings me to another significant feature of the poverty register, which, in addition to specifying the social identities of the poor, also carries a subtext about the wider social landscape. It is possible to read these moralizing scenarios as a kind of social reportage, situated descriptions about the structural relationship between the poor and the prosperous which are part of the everyday dynamics of pastoral inequality. For the three definitions of poverty states that are still on the 'pastoral path', so to speak, all presuppose a set of social relations with more fortunate people. This is organized within a flexible framework of cohabitation and cooperation between units who score differently along the two axes of wealth – in people and in animals. A Turkana herding association, *adakar*, ranging in size from a handful of camps to around a hundred (in areas riven by raiding), reflects in its social composition such disparity in the distribution of assets. Each *adakar* is commonly organized around a few wealthy units, who not only command more material assets but whose words carry more weight through their greater bargaining power and broader networks. They can more easily demand stock debts, attract more labour and have a wider choice of grassland and wells. Linked to the wealthy are smaller holding units; some are self-sufficient in terms of labour and livestock, while others experience imbalances or temporary setbacks, such as the *Echedon* and *Elongait*. Whatever the case, they are all gaining from the fortunes of the prosperous among them through cohabitation, marriage, clientship and exchanges. There is usually room for a few *Emetut* poor as well – marginal relatives who are particularly welcomed in times when more hands are needed, but who are also the first to be put on short rations during lean times in the hope that they will leave and join somebody else.

It is precisely such flexible and inclusive collaborative arrangements between pastoral camps, coupled with an egalitarian ethos, that have tended to screen off the existence of endemic social inequality from much contemporary work. Destitution and dislocation are commonly conceptualized as the effects of crises, such as drought, disease and famine, which, it is imagined, hit the population randomly and also even out wealth differences. In reality, however, despite positive attitudes towards sharing and solidarity, considerable concentrations of cattle wealth occur and sometimes persist from one generation to the next. While the institutional means for exchange of labour and livestock across pastoral units clearly has the effect of redistributing resources more widely and equally, a substantial segment of the real poor is exported to other areas and other economies. They are thus not only out of the way of the remaining pastoralists, but out of the context of observation of most scholars of pastoralism as well. Whatever the case, exclusion and erasure are the harsh reality for most Turkana who are caught up by the stigma connected to the *Ekebotonit* identity.

The term *Ekebotonit/Ngikebootok* has multiple references, morally and socially. It reverberates through Turkana 'high culture' as a troubled signifier for everything falling short of conventional cattle standards. Within the community, we have seen how it connotes a material lack produced by a failing of personal character and sheer incompetence in pastoral pursuits. The distinction also draws elements of externality and difference around itself. For it is also a label attached to a local group depending primarily on agriculture, the *Ngikebootok* community on the banks of River Turkwell. Growing grain is thus seemingly conceived of as a deficient means of producing food. It might come as a surprise to learn that pastoral wives do, in fact, seasonally plant grain, pumpkins and gourds in gardens on river sites along the migration routes. Indeed, sorghum – planted to produce the whole spectrum of possible shapes and colours – is significant both socially and symbolically. Sorghum, boiled with milk into a thick porridge or made into a raw stew of whole grains mixed with butter, figures prominently on the pastoral menu, eaten as part of everyday meals as well as ritual ones.

However, when the act of planting is performed by pastoral women it ceases to be described in the vocabulary of cultivation. Rather, cultivation becomes virtually reinscribed within the pastoral register of acts and labels, causes and effects. For example, the term for garden, *anama*, refers to the entrails enveloped within an animal abdomen. This imagery of an animalistic incorporation of organic matter is not only a play with tropes, but points to a technical and practical tie as well. This is clearly evidenced in the firm belief that the act of scattering chyme from the entrails of goats on the soil is essential for promoting plant growth in gardens and beyond. This idea develops from the empirical observation that fresh grass germinates from animal dung left in the corrals. Pastoral Turkana perceive of animals as mobile 'planters' carrying seeds from one place to another, constantly cultivating the landscape. The diverse types of sorghum seedlings are themselves distinguished by cattle terms. Pastoral women take great care in the choice of names to produce a visual approximation between the specific shape and colour of the sorghum cone to similar configurations on the skins of their favourite cattle. Most significantly, cultivation within a pastoral frame is completely defined by the terms of animal husbandry. Through these mediations, the pastoralists' crossbreeding of the concepts of crops and cattle escapes the moral negativity connoted by the human category of being poor.

Paths to the pastoral periphery: farming, fishing and town-living

The *Ekebotonit/Ngikebootok* pair of terms sets up a distinction (albeit ambiguous) between dominant livelihoods based on livestock versus grain, fish and game, and associates this with the distinction, on the one hand, between 'insiders' and 'outsiders' and, on the other, between prosperity and poverty. The term for 'poor' is the summarizing symbol for everything non-Turkana. The Turkana term is the local version of the 'Dorobos' – a distortion of the Maasai word '*Ndorobo*' – which has come to mean remnants and outcasts of any group who, for various reasons, have turned to hunting, planting and fishing (see Spencer, 1973). A *Ngikebootok* elder explained things as follows:

> The *Ngikebootok* were hungry people who came one by one to settle in this area as hunters. They were just unfortunate people who had no cattle. It is like nowadays: some people in town have money and others do not. It was like that with the Turkana: some had cattle, others did not. When the *Ngikebootok* came here, they found the area vacant; no one lived here. They found the land had many wild animals and was good for growing crops and so they began earning their living in those ways. If a person is troubled by hunger, he can discover many things he did not know before. The *Ngikebootok* had seen sorghum growing along the shores of the lake and the *Ngibochoros*, those who eat fish, there showed them how to cultivate it. They had mixed somewhat with *Merille* (*Dassanetch*) and have learned to grow sorghum ... In those days, people cultivated with wooden digging sticks as iron hoes had not come yet. The *Ngikebootok* were also the only Turkana who made beehives. So they ate three things: (game) meat, sorghum and honey. Other poor people came to join the *Ngikebootok* from time to time and their numbers grew. Eventually, they grew into a community. Even these days, people who become impoverished come here to join the *Ngikebootok*'.[1]

This account is buzzing with all the signs attributed to the poor by the dominant pastoral discourse. The reference to hunting is highly relevant because this activity also carries the stigma of poverty. A few mobile bands of hunters and gatherers (*Ngikirionok*) live in the mountains and in the gallery forests along perennial rivers; their numbers grow during droughts, when pastoral paupers join, but diminish when conditions improve. Seasonally they gather honey, which they bring to pastoral camps in exchange for a goat kept in the host herd. Specialized hunters form uneasy relations with herders and are seldom invited inside a pastoral homestead. If they do enter, they are served poor food by husbands close to the gate and must by no means consume milk or step over the threshold to the yards of pastoral wives. When livestock return from pasture, hunters must hide away. To have one caught in the midst of a herd is a great misfortune, signalling sickness and death. Hunting is often combined with cultivation and fishing – and all these activities may also be performed by pastoralists. Again, it is not so much the activity which stigmatizes those who perform it, but rather their lack of livestock.

For, as long as anything – acts, concepts and substances – is mediated through an animal medium it is incorporated into the morally 'good', as the case of the pastoral appropriation of sorghum planting demonstrates very clearly. These protective and transformative operations are also vital for bodily well-being, extending into the domain of food consumption, the treatment of visiting hunters being an apt case. This is because such acts ensure that the substances embodied will flow freely along the interior pathways of the pastoral person. Food substances and the possibility of food-sharing are also powerful markers of the content of social relationships. Consumption distinguishes between insiders and outsiders, between those who can participate in common meals and those with whom any food relation carries risks of disease and destruction.

Here we have come to the point where it is possible to grasp why it is that the *Ngikebootok* poor are morally condemned by the pastoralists as being 'selfish'. This is linked to the fact that they are not included in the circles of shared consumption, but also to the characteristics of their possessions and produce. In contrast to cattle, which are a highly visible and thus potentially very social form of wealth, crops and cash are both examples of more concealed forms of wealth which can change hands and be consumed in secrecy. The cultivator whose produce can not only be kept exclusively for private consumption, but is also highly perishable and thus does not have the same capacity as cattle to produce enduring social bonds, is comparable to the mean pastoralist who is not willing to participate in reciprocal circles of sharing to (re)produce his community. This is a topic to which we shall return in more detail later.

Calling themselves *Nkiketak* or *Ngikatap*, 'the porridge people', this farmer/hunter community has existed for centuries as an agrarian pocket on pastoral land, serving as a trading centre for goats and grain as well as a shelter for the stockless. In his narration, the *Ngikebootok* elder conjured up a larger canvas of the Lake Turkana region, from precolonial times to the present. We learn that along River Turkwell and the shores of Lake Turkana there were several farming and fishing enclaves through which poor people moved. Clearly these groups did not only recruit Turkana paupers, but included many impoverished foreigners from most of the other 'tribal' groups. Enclaves served as 'halfway houses' helping the needy to adjust their livelihood and identity – building the image of the region as a 'melting-pot'. As elsewhere in East Africa, this account bears evidence that droughts, famine, and epidemics clearly contributed to the reconstruction of societies, binding different economies together through the movement of people and produce between them (Waller, 1985b). The following Turkana account adds to this mosaic:

> The *Ngibosheros* have been fishing here at the lake for a very long time. They have been fishing for generations: at least from the time of our grandfathers and perhaps before ... Those who began fishing were people without livestock and because they lived near the lake, they began catching fish for their food. We don't know what happened to the livestock of those first *Ngibosheros*. After they had been fishing for a long time, people began getting goats ... Also, other people who had livestock joined the *Ngibosheros*. In the past, most people had cattle and so they tended to stay in their own areas, but some Turkana have been migrating to the lake for a long time. Because of recent droughts, many people have now begun coming here. Nowadays especially, people have mixed together ... The *Ngibosheros* also grew sorghum near the lake long ago. The

other Turkana would bring goats here to trade for that sorghum. That was the only trade that went on here. Men also got livestock as bride-wealth for their daughters. People who would acquire many animals would occasionally move away from the lake, but most would remain here fishing, growing crops and tending their animals.[2]

Obviously all the complexity of reconfigurations of livelihoods and redefinition of identities within the larger political economy of the Lake region is outside the scope of this chapter, but it clearly reminds us of the importance of the ways in which herding, farming and fishing are linked, and how these transregional and historical relations have a direct bearing on the present politics of poverty in Turkanaland. We can draw from the two local accounts quoted some of the practical consequences entailed by each economic activity and contrast these.

Fishing has served as a survival strategy for agrarian and pastoral paupers alike, but also as a seasonal activity for those more permanently involved in herding or cultivation elsewhere. This flexibility is due to the fact that the equipment needed to establish oneself in fishing is rather simple; the return on work comes immediately, only limited to the time it takes to trap the fish. Given that the amount of fish landed is rather small, however, growth is only possible by including other activities, which poses particular problems. A good fishing spot along the arid shores of Lake Turkana is seldom close to lands sound for herding and cultivation, and a compromise must be struck between these concerns. The costs, however, are small harvests and a slow growth in flocks. It is unlikely, therefore, that many specialized fisherfolk ever made careers as full-time herders and cultivators, and those who did probably quit fishing in the process. An agrarian enterprise has a different time and investment profile, since land needs to be cleared and there is a considerable time-lag between planting and harvesting. After its establishment, access to fields in farming enclaves becomes more restricted, rights being passed down from one generation to the next through kinship ties. Growth is dependent on accessing the wealth-in-people domain, the best options being to invest in animals and deploy them in marriages to gain access to labour through wives and children. Yet the possibility of working virgin land and combining grain and game gives some room for including newcomers. Although agrarian communities tend to be more stable, there are also movements through these, which was the organizing trope of the *Ngikebootok* narrative.

Both accounts bear evidence that a pastoral enterprise is always faced with the possibility of rapid growth and decline. High growth in herds depends on continuous work by many hands to give each animal optimal care. But the dilemma in pastoralism is the need to balance the number of animals and people with one another and against the pastures. Large herds can feed a larger pool of labour, and these will gain prosperity for the whole unit faster than those who strike the balance between a small herd and a smaller supply of labour. The wealthy have better chances of coping with drought and diseases and continuing their pastoral careers than those who have few animals. Still, small and large herds alike are subject to intermediate setbacks, sometimes even gross decline. Since surplus and shortage are complementary options, there is room for some reshuffling of animals and people between pastoral camps. When these checks fail to correct imbalances, a downward spiral sets in, forcing the unfortunate to go into fishing, foraging and cultivation. A two-way stream into and out of pastoralism is possible, as some leave and others enter. The latter often start as clients before making careers as self-reliant herders. Given the many advantages of having herds, one would expect that the major route of wealth would be set up from cultivation and fishing towards herding, gradually leading to a regional system dominated by pastoralists (Waller, 1985).

It is clear from the two Turkana informants how partnership in trade, transaction, production, and marriages worked historically to weave together the biographies of people across diverse economies, social identities and ethnic groups. The *Ngikebootok* village at Kaputir is the oldest settlement in Turkanaland, visited by coastal caravans well before colonization. The fishing villages in the Kerio delta are old ones too, serving as strongholds during the Turkana resistance to colonial expansion. The British built more solid signposts in the vast landscape, in the form of clusters of barracks linked together by rough roads, which multiplied as the frontier moved. Many old people associate these first towns and roads with misery and impoverishment. Typically, their narratives centre on the ways in which the colonialists' tax demands, coupled with large-scale confiscation of cattle to force the Turkana to accept colonial rule, pushed many into sedentary activities. Since Independence, towns have continued to grow in the wake of major dislocations of pastoral people but have changed their architecture and functions, along with the activities of administration, missionaries and aid agencies. In an effort to curb the flow of clients into the famine relief camps, heavy investment of development funds in irrigation and fisheries has been made. Improved communication has spread settlements from rivers to roadsides. The spread of shops, beer halls, market places and feeding centres linked to these project sites has drawn one-third of the population into the associated villages. Despite their varied background and careers, these settlers have, in effect, all moved in under the *Ngikebootok* label. For some, towns may only be a stage before emigrating, while, for others, they have become poverty traps.

The contemporary exclusion scenario has two empirical dimensions built into it: more pastoralists are being pushed out while fewer manage to recover their herds. This implies that any meaningful analysis must move beyond the boundaries of the pastoral community. Today, as in the past, many pastoral poor change their economy entirely, but their life careers and coping mechanism continue to be influenced by pastoral concerns. The task for the rest of the chapter is to explore in more detail the different domains of wealth that exist, the constraints placed on their convertibility and the different types of social power they encode. Since the relationship between poverty and prosperity is inextricably tied to the pattern of movement between the different economic environs of the region, we need to examine briefly the product profile of each and the pathways exporting people and produce across them.

The crossroads of wealth

The concept of 'path' is not only central in the Turkana conceptualization of things, it has also been abstracted into anthropological analysis by Appadurai (1986) in his effort to model 'the social life of things' more generally. By retaining the core meaning of 'commodity' – notably its 'exchangeability' – past, present and future (1986:13) – as its socially relevant feature, Appadurai extends this concept beyond the bounds of capitalism, and sets it in motion across historical and cultural boundaries. Within any political economy, he tells us, there are conventionally prescribed commodity pathways that participate in constituting a 'regime of value' by promoting the dominant interests in society. Yet there is also typically scope for engineering 'diversions' and enclaving objects, turning the making and breaking of paths into a contested terrain in the wider 'topography of wealth' (Ferguson, 1992). One obvious advantage of this processual approach for the points posed in this chapter, is that it makes it possible analytically to consider livestock, just as the Turkana do, as social beings endowed with lives and careers, and to trace empirically how their meanings become inscribed in their forms, their uses, their trajectories. Likewise, it also makes it possible to understand why the network of pathways livestock traverse tend to promote the political interests of the prosperous, while channelling many poor people out of the pastoral system altogether.

One disadvantage of the model, however, is that it cannot properly account for the complexity, social and semiotic, of the pathways not only of different produce – grain and fish versus cattle – but also of different species of domesticated animals. This is partly because the model completely dispenses with the distinction between 'commodity' and 'gift' not only as contrasting tropes for systemic types (Gregory, 1982) but, more problematically, as different forms of prestations and different aspects of possessions internal to each economy as well. As many critiques have pointed out, erasing the concept of 'gift' from the vocabulary of exchange eclipses many of the important elements which make up 'the social life of things' and which, at times, remove things from circulation. It also makes an analysis of economic systems as totalities more difficult, simply because a series of significant prestation forms, produce and social relations fall outside the scope of the model (Comaroff & Comaroff, 1990; Thomas, 1991; Guyer, 1993).

In order to trace the process and progression of Turkana transactions, we need to borrow concepts and principles from several contemporary vocabularies. Concepts like 'currency' and 'alienation' from the 'commodity' register are as appropriate for our analysis as the attributes associated with the 'gift' – 'inalienability', 'authorship', 'singularity', 'prestation' and 'pathway'. Being sensitive to local constructions, these concepts are central for a cultural analysis of commodity paths and the structure of possessions. However, given that among Turkana poverty is inscribed in a moral idiom, much of the socio-economic dynamics resulting in poverty is distorted or muted. And, although the ways in which the association between producers, their work and their products are culturally represented are themselves a social force, actively shaping the social landscape of poverty, factors falling outside the politics of representation are still at work. In this particular case, the picture is even more complicated, because poverty is a social fact situated at the cross-roads of different domains of wealth production containing different standards for evaluation.

We need to assess briefly the ways in which the objectification of work and the characteristics of capital interact with cultural constructions in deciding the relative value of the products resulting from pastoralism, farming and fishing. The contrast between livestock, crops and fish shapes exchanges across realms. Livestock and fish occupy the top and bottom steps on the value ladder, while crops range somewhere in between. The returns from herds are threefold: calves, which replenish the herds; milk, blood, meat and hides, which supply nutrition and utensils; and surplus livestock, which are used to set up social relationships. In contrast, crops and fish are dependent on avenues to transform them into economic and social assets. This typically involves middlemen, who, in return for a share of the surplus, act as brokers in the conversion process. While the conversion chain from crops to livestock contains one or two stages, the one from fish to livestock involves several. To this we can add that animal investment, in contrast to investments in land and fishing equipment, is self-operating through calving. In our setting, the value gap is even wider, since livestock are the only means of building marriage and partnership, while attitudes towards fish as food further prejudice this produce as against crops.

Let us discuss the effects of commercialization on these dynamics and on the structure of property. Commoditization has penetrated some fields of production more thoroughly than others. The first thing to note is that land does not circulate with other forms of property. Traditional claim structures exist on the commons, centred on small pockets of critical resources, which are typically fenced in, such as sorghum gardens, the groves of trees producing pods for goats and the fresh grass grown inside the animal corrals of an abandoned pastoral camp. Wells and the breeding grounds for *Tilapia* fish are also subject to specific protection. Rights are acquired through inheritance or membership in territorial sections. Although temporary access to these resources are assets that circulate between relatives and friends, they do not move against money. It is possible to obtain commercial plots in town for cash, and there also exist government plans for the privatization of the commons in Turkana, but so far they have not been implemented. Titles to irrigated fields are allocated to the tenants by a committee, according to criteria decided by the donors. There is a market for labour in town, dating back to colonial times, but few jobs are at hand. Mobilization of labour, not only in pastoralism but even in irrigated farming and fishery, has not moved much beyond the bonds of kinship and partnership.

Neither natural resources nor labour has been extensively commoditized. However, a market in certain things has had important effects. Privileged access to fields, browse or fishing grounds may produce a marketable surplus of crops, goats and fish, which can be exchanged for cash. While herds and harvests can be increased by more hands at work on the same holding, higher catches per fisherman/woman requires an upgrading of equipment to reach the fish over a wider area. Provision of nets and boats has produced this effect, but the income earned from fishing is still very low. The same can be said about irrigated cotton production, which, like the fish, is also destined for export. Thus, commoditization tempers to some extent the regime of value outlined earlier. Grain (sorghum and maize) in particular, has improved its rank and value within the conversion hierarchy. With commercialization, grain generates cash not only by itself, but by its convertibility into the sphere of consumer goods through an assortment of processed food-products currently in high demand among settlers, such as beers, pancakes and porridges. Beer brewing is particularly profitable. The surplus generated from the grain–beer–cash–goat conversions potentially results in more animal assets than can be gained from the more restricted grain–goat or grain–cash–goat chains. Female farmers in particular have been able to reap the profit from the commoditization of grain. Local markets for milk, meat and fish cannot compare with that of grain, and are further hampered by a series of state regulations.

Indeed, the most booming trade in Turkana towns belongs to a black-market economy, encompassing a wide range of items, many of which reflect the district's heavy reliance on famine relief and development dollars. Firewood, small stock and dairy products brought in by the pastoralists are sold or bartered in return for maize rations, medicine, tobacco, crushed palm nuts and fish oil provided by relief recipients, traders and fisherwomen. These 'bush markets' offer fresh fish sold outside monopoly regulations, the meat of donkeys and goats not being inspected by the public health officer. Other illegal products include sacks of charcoal together with unknown quantities of local brews. Typically, the surplus earned is either re-invested in fishing tackle, seeds and fertilizers, thus being channelled back into the production cycle, used to buy consumer goods, such as clothing, crockery, watches and radios, or invested in goats.

While goats and money are interchangeable, cattle and money are not. This is a very important point. The avenues available between the domains of cash and livestock are either the cash–goats–cash circuit or the cash–goats–cattle pathway. There is no direct avenue between cattle and cash. Cattle wealth and wealth-in-people are enclaved together in a semi-discrete domain. This has vast implications. For, in a situation where labour is not commoditized, most economic enterprises have to be formed around a family of sorts. Given that, in the Turkana context, building a family of a cooperative kind can only be accomplished through the medium of cattle, it follows that those closed off from the dominant domains of wealth are caught up in a vicious circle. In fact, this hits men harder than women. For a woman can access the wealth-in-people domain directly through procreation. Children will always be an asset to a mother, even when she is without animals. A man, on the other hand, can only gain access to children through marriage. Without cattle, however, he cannot provide the bride-wealth necessary to marry and build a prosperous career for himself. The effect of these dramatic reconfigurations of the domestic scene is twofold: not only has it proved difficult for most settlers to stage a comeback to pastoralism, but aid recipients have experienced that it is difficult to keep a foothold in the new economic environments as well. Consequently, many recently recruited fisherfolk and farmers have left their nets and hoes in favour of food rations (Broch-Due, 1986, 1987).

Underlying the picture painted of Turkana trade is the fragility of these monetary bonds and how much they depend on huge subsidies being injected into the regional economy through aid investments. This is by no means a modern phenomenon. One thing that becomes clear from reading colonial reports is that the local government, by and large, was the local economy also. Administrators created cash-generating and regulated markets, bought from them and then forced Turkana to return much of the cash as taxes. In contrast to their policy in most other pastoral areas, however, the colonial government was against setting up a marketing structure locally that would promote the export of Turkana cattle. This prohibition on the movement of cattle was part of the protective measures against rinderpest and other destructive influences erected around the European-run commercial ranches in the so-called White Highlands, which happened to be close to the Turkana district. Ever since, cattle have been exempted from general commodity exchange. While taxation of ordinary Turkana has ceased and aid agencies operate under more benign banners, the devastating effects of the recent withdrawal of development dollars from the district compare with some of the upheavals created by the colonialists (Lamphear, 1992).

For the Turkana, the mid-1980s were the heyday of high spending by NORAD (the major donor), a time when the district headquarters, Lodwar, even got a roundabout and the town was veiled in the fumes and noise of lorries and Land Rovers. In a matter of five years from the opening of the highway connecting Kenya and Sudan, Lodwar changed from having a few dusty offices, shops and bars to becoming a thriving town with a great variety of retail shops and services. Daily bus routes and weekly flights to the capital Nairobi attracted tourists, traders and agents of change who in great numbers tried to imprint their own ways on the local lifestyles. However, this (bygone) boom in town life had corresponded with a bust in livestock holdings and a loss of pastoralist control of their pastureland. Returning to Lodwar in the mid-1990s, the situation had completely turned around. A recent breakdown in diplomatic relations had forced the donor to close down all activities and stop all funding of projects. Back in Lodwar, a few non-governmental organizations (NGOs) and the Catholic Mission were left with limited resources to buttress the devastating effects of the recently implemented World Bank's structural adjustment programmes.

During this recent field-trip I was struck by the ways in which well-being seemed to prevail in most pastoral camps. Amidst old rusty machines on the sites of closed-down irrigation and fishing facilities, there were now animals in abundance, the herders clearly in the process of claiming back old paths and pastures from which they had been expelled by 'modernization'. In contrast, the situation among most town people was one of desperate poverty and despair. Ethnic clashes on a national scale had the effect of ending all external marketing of small stock, simply because the traders were not willing to take the risk of transporting live animals on trucks through these troubled zones. This loss of a significant source of cash, coming on top of the regular restrictions placed on cattle sales from Turkana, had spreading effects, curtailing other types of local trading. Among the settled population, all this contributed to severe economic depression. While the pastoralists could subsist directly from the nurturing powers of their milk herds, few townspeople had any cash left to spend on food and even less to cover the increased fees for schooling and hospital treatment.

One result is that the commoditization process has been put in reverse. Most movement of commodities and people between Turkana and the outside world had ended. Inflationary processes, acting on the domains of both livestock and cash, produce a pattern where more goats are needed in exchange for a cow and more money is needed to buy a goat. Typically, at each end of this troubled chain is a Turkana person who has, in every sense, less. Clearly, the problem with livestock and the problem with labour are intimately linked with the problems of commoditization. In the eyes of many Turkana, the value has simply been stripped from money in the wake of these traumatic experiences, caused by the sudden exit of cash from most exchange scenarios. This recent disenchantment with money has enhanced cattle even more, fuelling a drive towards violent forms of acquisition, with spreading effects throughout the social fabric.

To sum up the points of this section: one significant feature of the regional economy is the existence of different kinds of wealth and valuables which cannot easily be converted into one another or compared, as is common in a more fully commoditized system. Money has not achieved the status of a medium of exchange in all domains of the transactional system, and the other major 'currency' – livestock – consists of a complex domain of wealth, in which goats and cattle move along distinctive pathways of value and exchange. Through the specific combination of general and specific attributes of animals and people we get a regime of value based on quality as well as quantity. When transacted locally, the values of Turkana produce – livestock, crops, fish, etc. – are not fixed, but are variously assessed against a flexibly intervalued receptor – something Guyer calls a 'continuous value register' (1993:246). What characterizes a continuous value register is its capacity for incorporating and valuing new dimensions and relating them to the old. This is because measurements grow out of socially constructed concepts, which change their meanings through political struggles. The mix of composite wealth and a continuous value register results in a hybrid transactional system, which lies halfway between the fixed ranking of the 'gift' economy and the complete exchangeability of a commoditized market economy. It also opens the way for a very active politics of interpretation and negotiation, which, among Turkana centres on animal assets.

A Turkana herd itself represents a composite form of wealth: diversity – in terms of species, sex and age – is as foundational of the pastoral production profile as it is for the construction of pathways in exchange. Earlier I emphasized that livestock exchanges are deeply entrenched in a moral economy among the Turkana. This is because, in contrast to other forms of wealth which are fixed objects fabricated by human hands, animals are living wealth, which reproduce by themselves and respond eagerly to human contact. Most pastoralists manage mixed herds, combining 'large stock', such as cattle and camels, with 'small stock', such as goats and sheep. Not only are the demographic dynamics and behaviour different across these species, they also represent different domains of wealth. Moreover, at different stages in their life cycle and in different contexts, the attribution of a single beast can alternate between the 'commodity' form and the 'gift' form. In other words, domesticated animals are true 'assets', in the precise definition of the term – that is, anything (human, animal, artefact, abstract) accorded a 'powerful multiplicity of meanings and applications' (Guyer, 1993:252). This multiplicity has implications for the ways in which each species is valued, more generally and in specific situations.

There is a basic discrimination between small stock and large stock, visually expressed in the marking etched on their skins. Turkana burn the clan brand on the forehead of sheep and goats, but leave their torso unmarked by human hand. This restrained marking is in sharp contrast to the lavishly decorated bodies of cattle and camels. This contrast in tattoos signals a significant distinction of the kinds of social relations they create and the pathways they traverse. Exchange partners are conceptually divided between those of small stock – the 'friends of butter' (*epey akidet*), and those of large stock – the 'friends of ripe oil' (*epey akimet akinom*). The choice of dairy products as labels is highly motivated: in the conversion of milk–butter–oil, the end-product, oil, is an apt metaphor for the most mature relationship. While adults transact with both kinds of exchange partners, a social youngster is restricted to those of small stock. Initiation is the turning point, opening up the pathways of cattle and camels. Most profoundly, the initiation ritual, *asapan*, plays out this change of affairs. Towards the end of this transformation from child to adult, the novice has to gaze into the oil container, *akitam* ('to give knowledge') – an act which 'matures' (*asapan*) the candidate both mentally and materially. This move from goats to cattle as exchange medium is a necessary pre-stage for marriage. For proper bride-wealth must contain a large share of large stock to bind the two camps and clans in a firm web. Thus, while most goats are transacted within 'a short-term cycle', characterized by the self-interested acquisitive activity of individuals, cattle, in particular, circulate in a 'long-term cycle', concerned with the broader reproduction of the social and cosmic orders (Parry & Bloch, 1989:2). This differentiation between cattle and goats reverberates throughout the Turkana world.

Cattle, community and cosmos

Among large stock, cattle occupy a special position. Men and women spend a lot of time in the cattle corral decorating their favourite beasts. Few people show the same fondness for camels. There are endless tokens of the intimate connections between humans and cattle (Broch-Due, 1990a, 1991). The most primordial is the profound ways in which calf and child, cow and mother are equated. The preference for cattle in this culture is not only because oxen embody and project the force associated with warriors – which is the conventional explanation. What tends to be overlooked is the ways in which cows are equally cherished, because they illuminate various aspects of exemplary human fertility, nurturance and care. Cows commonly conceive with calm and ease, but rarely deliver more than one calf. Cows and women are matched both in the length of their pregnancies and in the quality of the care they give to their young. Cows are seen as good mothers, who show much affection towards their calves and train them to walk – and the pair is often referred to in human terms as 'mother', *ito*, and 'child', *ikoku*. A woman who mothers in similar caring manner is politely addressed *aitee nakidala*, 'milking cow', imagery clearly moulded on the parallel feeding relationships evinced in the milk flows from udder and breast.

Once human and cattle reproduction is interwoven, these physiological metaphors reverse themselves – as figure to ground – expanding into ever larger frames of reference. It is elaborated further through the idiom of kinship and the internal division of polygamous homesteads *(awi)* into maternal houses *(ekol)*. A cow is the founder of a specific house line, *ekol*, within the herd, named and organized just like that of the wife to whose house herd the cow belongs. After it is weaned, the human mother will feed her child with milk from a specific cow, and the child will continue to build specific affectionate bonds with the calves born from its milk-cow. In early childhood, boys and girls are given a young animal to tend and close identification between person and beast will continue throughout life. Like humans, livestock are perceived as individuated subjects, who are nursed, named, trained, adorned and mourned when they die.

The play of biological metaphors is matched with minute attention to the physical appearance of the animal. On the belly of cows and oxen are made transient drawings in dung and clay, and sometimes the skins are scarred with lasting marks, which express the experiences in love and combat of the individual to whom the animal is attached. Each and every large stock animal in camp is different from the others, individuated through the specific design of colour, shape and drawings etched on their skins. The capacity of a cow/oxen to carry the biographies of its care-takers on its back and accumulate its own history of exchange depends on this specificity. Animals, like people, are diversely 'singularized' (Munn, 1986; Strathern, 1988). By investing their social identities in the bodies of cattle, Turkana also seek to project the image of the person and his/her exchanges spatially, the token beast serving as a physical reminder in the recipient's camp of the relationship with the donor. This 'oneness' of person and beast is elaborated to emphasize the personality of exchange partners and the quality of their relationship. For example, the 'milk cow' label in the cattle vocabulary is also used for close friends, who frequently exchange gifts of stock. *Aite namojong*, an old cow, is postmenopausal, but has a long, fertile career behind her and is therefore treated with respect.

'Old cow' is used as a polite term for an old couple who have had a proper and prosperous marriage, in which wife and husband have jointly enacted the role of 'good' parents to the satisfaction of everybody. In contrast, a dry cow, *aite nakaonikinom*, is used in the third person to refer to a relationship held in suspension, as it were: not as good as was hoped, but which may, in the end, prove to be either 'pregnant' or completely 'barren'.

The intertwining of cattle and people moves cattle into the 'long-term cycle' of exchange concerned with the creation and confirmation of the enduring web of community and cosmos (Parry & Bloch, 1989). Together with the emphasis on 'authorship', which the enhanced tattooing of Turkana cattle evidences, these Turkana ties to cattle provide a pathway into the contemporary discussion of 'gifts' – the phenomenon of 'inalienable possession' and the principle of 'keeping-while-giving' (Weiner, 1992) that surrounds it. At first sight, animals do not sit well with the defining characteristics of 'inalienable possessions'. For these are typically precious things made of more lasting matter, such as heirlooms or landed property, which can be passed down from one generation to another, carrying with them a vision of permanence and a rare, emblematic value in a world of flux. Occasionally, such iconic objects do change hands and will enrich and enlarge the social space of new owners, but their ongoing fame hinges on the associations to the original source being kept alive.

Thus it is not the portability which is the potential problem in our context, but the permanence of the things themselves. Being alive, animals have a finite lifespan and thus represent a highly perishable form of possessions. If left to live until old age, the normal lifespan of cattle is around two decades, but usually it is shorter, particularly in the case of a male animal, which carries a greater risk than a milk-cow of being prematurely disposed of, as a sacrifice or during regular slaughter for meat consumption. If we add transactions, thefts and mortality due to drought and diseases, it follows that the turnover of individual beasts in Turkana herds is high. However, even when cattle move between people, the aspects of inalienability, which still survive even after usufruct rights have been alienated by the transfer, are precisely the collection of memories and social identities carried by its mark – both the collective and the individual ones.

The collective marks, enduringly etched into the skin, conjure up clanship and cattle genealogy. These social identities are not linked so much to the life of a single cow, but to the 'line of cows', so to speak. The paternal clan is perceived to be the ultimate holder of all animals attached to its constituent camps that carry its particular brand. In practice, this principle is expressed in the expectation that a request for an animal from a clan member should morally be redeemed, while the active engagement of senior people of the clan is required in all cases of major events involving animals, such as marriage deals and the range of rituals linked to birth, initiation and death. In addition to this clan identification, the calves born to a camp belong to members of one of its maternal houses, to whose sub-herd the animal pedigree is attached. While such practices bind together cattle and people in one intimate physical and social equation, as explained earlier, the forging of genealogies in dams can also be inter-preted as efforts to counteract the perishability of life more generally by creating a vision of continuity between past, present and future genera-tions of people and cattle.

It is exactly the multiple ways in which cattle evoke widespread, common symbolism associated with human reproduction and the cultural reproduction of the kin groups that qualify Turkana cattle for the position of inalienable possession. Cultural reproduction also includes what Weiner calls 'cosmological authentication' (1992). Turkana express this in a cosmic vision of their world as the silhouette of a containing maternal body by day, dissolving its contours into a dark surface spotted with red by night, which simultaneously represents the fires of the dead and the most auspicious skin configuration of Turkana cattle. Through such authenti-cating images, the central divinity – the androgynous *Akuij* – legitimizes the social powers vested in clans and agnates, in senior people and the cattle-rich – but also the powers of procreation and the principle of matrifiliation, which permeates the patrilineal system of the Turkana people (Broch-Due, 1990a, 1993). These encompassing ideologies are both moral and economic forces, actively validating the absolute value of cattle in this culture while verifying social distinctions and social differences created through the circulation of cattle.

The other series of marks carried on the backs of cattle are more transient and idiosyncratic. Given that these relate to the exploits of an individual and will be erased by the death of the animal, they signify a time dimension locked into the biographical frames of a specific pair of person and beast. Sometimes the text of tattoos will have multiple authors, because the token animal has moved between many hands in the course of its life. But there are also particular beasts in the herd, favourite oxen and cows, which the persons who have chosen them as their counterpart will never part with. The name(s) of such a special beast, the shape of its horns, the colour configuration, the design imprinted on its skin, the songs composed to its honour are all attributes of identification, well advertised in the larger community. To multiply the effect of this fame, one strategy is to breed calves that have many of the same characteristics as the favourite beast and to channel these duplicates into the pathways that are the most rewarding for the reputation of the focal person. Again, the token beasts that enter into exchange are closely associated with the personal attributes and agency of their author, the deeds and acts that make up a life career. This intimate linkage of destiny is forcefully enacted during the memorial rituals that follow the death of adult men and

71

women, when the large stock most closely associated with the personal attributes of the deceased are destroyed. This sacrificial killing takes place in a funerary rite after one year has lapsed and involves about 20 stock from the focal camp, together with eight stock brought by agnatic kin.

Through its close association with humans, each cow, ox or camel builds up a social biography of its own. The pathways it has traversed, the relationships it has created, the fate of those relationships all become attached to the beast through marking and labelling. Indeed, each of these animals carries the weight and imprint of the human relations in which it has been involved, to the point where they are seen as moral actors themselves in those relations. By the same token, their past life history influences the transactions and pathways in which they will participate in the future and determines the pace of movement. A beautifully decorated cow in a herd I surveyed had participated in marrying five wives, having obtained the honourable title *Erereng* ('the blessed one'). Through its smooth and speedy exchange trajectory, the cow had linked together in a circular chain four clans, being cited in the community as a proper example of an *erochit* ('to bind strongly'). In contrast, a beast given in bride-wealth, and thus put on a pathway where it is supposed to bind together many people, but which then, due to divorce or other disturbances, breaks out of the chain to return to the original holder, is labelled *elakit* ('waste'). Thus an animal's life history also influences its future pace of movement along these pathways.

Labelling serves as a memorizing device and a mechanism for selection. An individual beast that has been involved in a divorce, has not been properly purified after a period of mourning in its camp or has been part of compensation for homicide, etc., should simply not be given in bride-wealth or participate in other life-generating processes. The present owner will seek to dispose of it in exchange for goats, give it away or, if the reputation is really disagreeable, simply set it aside for slaughter and feasting. And conversely, a beast equipped with an exceptionally successful exchange career, formed along those paths that promote wealth and fertility in the community, should continue to be reserved for those tracks. Moreover, at the beginning of the migration season and during the year between the burial and the last funerary rite, there is a ban on all transactions in large stock. Because of their social record, many large stock are either taken out of circulation, temporarily or permanently, or enclaved in discrete circuits. This reinforces the exclusivity of cattle wealth and contributes to the slowing down of their movement in the transactional world. It also reinforces the moral qualities attributed to cattle wealth and the ways it is interwoven with the wealth-in-people domain.

Thus cattle, as prime exemplars of inalienable possessions, participate in the constitution and reconstitution of social identities and social relations over time. These reconstructions are effected through the cattle exchanges that are linked to reproductive events. These are controlled by senior people and occur in connection with death, marriage, birth, inheritance and the transmission of ancestral authority. Clearly, through cattle and the communitarian values vested in them, the pastoral Turkana have a profound sense of an expanded selfhood and participation in a social world in which solidarity and sharing are prime concerns. In the footsteps of cattle flow all significant relationships that build a successful biography – male and female – through initiation, marriage, procreation, partnership and elderhood. It is not surprising that Turkana take a keen interest in the reproductive career of their cows. Most pastoral wives I met could account for the pathways of all the calves born to a particular cow while in their care. In the eyes of the Turkana beholder, the social power encoded in cattle seems to emanate directly from their bodies and their particular exchange trajectories. To see a large herd of cattle on the move, to watch the myriad signs of social identities, individual and collective, tattooed on the gleaming skins and knowing that they embody not only wealth and values, but the whole history of transactions that frame Turkana lives, is to understand them as 'total social phenomenon', in the sense implied by Mauss (1954:1).

The ways in which pastoralists objectify their social institutions in the beasts they breed and circulate among themselves turn livestock into highly 'fetishized commodities', but with a particular twist. Far from disguising human agency in the Marxist sense, Turkana animals are adorned to reveal their social origin. A herd projects a unified image of the social group as a whole, of the joint capacity of the members of a camp or clan to create a series of social relationships. However, this image masks the long series of specific labour relations which produced it over time and the differential access of humans to each animal in the herd. Similarly, the varying ability of those it represents to put these animals on the path is hidden. The cloud of sentiments and moral concerns that surrounds Turkana herds tends to remove from public consciousness the ambiguous fact that cattle, in particular, make some careers while breaking others, being the source of disparity and social distinctions as much as the means of reciprocity and wealth redistribution. This form of possession, in the words of the Comaroffs, has 'the tautological quality of all political currency: it (is) taken to be an expression of the very power it serves to create' (1992:144).

Goats, equality and externality

In contrast to cattle, wealth in goats moves in different ways and with different purposes and effects. A detailed recall of the web of pathways that animals traverse is easier to accomplish with cattle and camels than with goats and sheep, not only because of the personal identification with large stock and the ways they are individuated, but also because they reproduce more slowly and live longer. To keep detailed records of the reproductive events and the whereabouts of the numerous offspring resulting from the mixed flocks of goats and sheep would be an exacting enterprise. Small stock multiply with a speed not matched by any other species raised by the Turkana. They often breed twice a year and have a high number of twin births. Of the pair, the goat is by far the most significant symbolically and socially.

The goat is conceived of as the 'clever' leader of the 'confused' sheep – indeed, the two are often lumped together in one flock called 'goats'. Apart from extreme fertility and virility, traits that are uniquely 'goat-like', Turkana also pay attention to mortality in sheep and goats. This is not only a reflection of the high turnover in these flocks, due to regular meat slaughter and exchange, but, more importantly, because the small-stock pen is so closely associated with giving birth and dying. This is the place where human placentas are thrown to be consumed by goats, where other domesticated stock are speared in sacrifice and where the corpse of the husband is buried, after which the goats are let in to trample on the grave. Turkana pastoralists visualize the central role of small stock in the passage of life by constructing the pen in the centre of the compound, in intimate closeness to the small thorn-bush hedge that is the personal space of the husband. The corrals of cattle and camels, in contrast, are constructed close to the courtyard of each wife, just inside the outer, encompassing fence of the compound.

The Turkana are keenly aware of how the small bodies of goats and sheep generate an exceptional fertility, vitality and growth – far beyond the natural capacity, not only of humans, but also of other livestock. The overlapping cycles of life–death–life in humans, livestock and landscape, are embodied to excess in these flocks, turning goats into summarizing symbols for growth, transformation and decay across all domains and species. It is this profusion embodied in small stock that Turkana pastoralists seek to harness and exploit for their own ends through a series of practices – from using goat chyme to promote plant growth in gardens to the recycling of human placentas through the bellies of goats. While these fertile acts are wealth-generating, there are matching death-linked acts of wealth destruction, which, as we shall discuss, are vital for the whole dynamic of the exchange system. The liquidation of the favourite cattle of the deceased in the goat pen has the effect of erasing the records, imprinted in perishable animal flesh and memorized as long as the marks last, of an individual life's-work. This has been embodied and graphically locked into the domain of wealth represented by large stock. Likewise, if the deceased is a man, the act of flattening the grave by the feet of goats obliterates the individuality of the person and returns him to the diffuse class of ancestral spirits. As a purification of the mourners at the end of

74

the funerary rites, goat chyme is smeared on the bodies of people and cattle, after which normal life resumes.

Most interestingly, the Turkana label for goats, *akine*, literally means 'gift', which gives this animal the mixed role of a mover and transformer. However, the form of gift goats represent is very different from the form of gift that cattle represent. More correctly the two types signify different forms of prestations. The giving of a goat is an act that initiates a relationship and/or introduces a series of transactions in other types of livestock. Thus goats provide bonds with outsiders and, through the potent contents of goat bellies, bind human growth to growths in nature. The important thing about these kinds of gifts and prestations is that they should be 'many' and 'multiply' to foster relationships between sets of donors and recipients, traits which goats, through their rapid breeding, fit better than any other livestock. In contrast to cattle, the significant characteristic of goats is not their singularity and individual identity, but their multiplicity of attributes and applications. And it is precisely this generic multiplicity that makes small stock particularly well fit to be cast as 'alienable possessions' within the local transactional world. The branding of the clan mark only on their heads, leaving the bodies of smal stock free of any personal signatures, is the ultimate sign of their alienability – and thus relative anonymity.

Multiplicity, alienability and anonymity are the qualities that symbolically move goats into the short-term cycle of transactions, characterized by acquisition, accumulation and consumption. Goats are exchanged for a heifer to adjust herd composition, or a bullock is bartered for goats which are then brought to the market and exchanged for money. The small size and the abundance of goats make them equally fitted to be served as a family meal and to bolster individual reputation by being given out as tokens of generosity. In contrast to the cattle cycle, which ensures the continuity of the community over time, the arena of the goat cycle is the satisfaction of the more immediate needs, desires and interests of individuals. Despite the somewhat disapproving aura that surrounds the notion of 'alienability' in Western thought, in Turkana thinking it is the positive purpose and great value of certain kinds of assets, like goats, to be alienated, to move against aspects of kinship, debt and other forms of asset (including fruitfulness, grain and money). Turkana seem to share with many other peoples the perception that the disposal of such valuables represents an accomplishment, rather than being a loss (Thomas, 1991). Indeed, small stock are immensely appreciated among pastoral people precisely for the ways in which they mediate all sorts of external relations and domains in which the pastoral world is entangled – with an animated nature, with ancestral spirits, with affines, with other economic activities and with a long list of external agents – explorers, traders, government officials and aid personnel.

These intimate associations between goats, fertility and growth in humans and nature clearly motivate the metaphorical association between goats, aspects of femininity and anything foreign. This is reinforced by the social practice of exogamy, in which femininity and foreignness are brought together in the bride, who, as outsider to the new clan, moves against their livestock given in bride-wealth. The goat is the first gift to the affinal clan, while the marriage ox that seals the deal is speared in the goat pen. The placing of goats in camp in the close vicinity of the senior man also conjures this 'feminizing' of goats. As the senior agnate proper, he is structurally in charge, on behalf of the clan, of exchanging for livestock this fertile aspect among the multiple attributes of femininity. As an introductory gesture, he presents the goat to get a wife, and his wife will be presented with a goat in return for his promise to give their daughter away.

Clearly, this equation between goats and elements of externality is an old one. It is elaborated most actively through the pathways that lead to the periphery of the pastoral exchange system, into the enclaves of the *Ngikebootok* 'poor', where animals move against other kinds of produce and valuables. In situations of barter between pastoralists, cultivators and fisherfolk, goats and sheep are the only livestock available for conversions across these productive realms. From the perspective of pastoralists, the most valued form of barter is goats against grain. To exchange goats for grain has the obvious advantage for the consumption profile of a pastoral household that a bag of cereal lasts for many meals, while a slaughter must be eaten immediately, because of the perishable nature of meat. Yet these bartering links are mutually beneficial to the extent that the exchange of low-value grain with goats enables agriculturalists to take advantage of the growth capacity of small stock, and later to enter the more socially profitable pathways by converting small stock into cattle wealth. Fish, in contrast, cannot move against goats directly, but have first to be converted either into grain or other precious items, such as tobacco, cloth, etc.

Besides serving almost as an all-purpose currency in these conversion scenarios, the central role of the goats is to cultivate these 'foreign' products for pastoral consumption. The goat mediates between these more mundane exchange cycles and the more enduring cattle cycle, having an equalizing effect within the diversified economic system as a whole. As emphasized by both Turkana narrators in their ethnographic accounts of the enclave economies, the goat is also in close proximity to the 'poor'. The huge potential for accumulation embodied in goats provides the impoverished with a highly convertible form of capital – food, cash, production inputs, consumer goods, as well as being the entry ticket into the prestigious pathway of cattle. The desire of the poor man is to exchange the anonymous hide of the goat for cattle skin, which can be carved and adorned to launch authorship and potential fame, leading in turn to more cattle, marriage, and maturity. For without a dance ox to project your personal influence more widely, without another ox which is sacrificed in your name at initiation and without a third ox speared during your wedding, an adult man is simply considered a 'child', whose words will be muted in public. For the cattle-rich, these oxen come from kin; for the poor, they come from goat barter.

By being a medium through which it is possible both to temper instabilities in the realm of goods and inequalities in the realm of people, the goat is a liberating force in the Turkana transactional world. The many pathways pivoting on the bartering of goats make room for personal freedom and individual choice, but not without ambiguity. For in as much as barter does not entangle the parties in further obligations, it appears as a relatively neutral phenomenon that reduces the costs of social trans-actions (Appadurai, 1986). Yet, in our context, this is highly questionable. This is because, through the hierarchy of valuables bartered, one endur-able social effect of these exchanges across productive realms is the definition and confirmation of ethnic difference and distance (see also Humphrey & Hugh-Jones, 1992). Culturally, these are also the defining features of the social identities spun around the Turkana poor. These conversion chains of commodities from different production regimes in the region, and the ways in which the act of bartering not only differen-tiates between produce but simultaneously reproduces social differentia-tion between producers are among the historical keys to processes producing poverty for some and prosperity for others. From this perspective, the goat appears as 'gatekeeper', maintaining the distinctions within the moral economy that reproduce patterns of inequality. In the form of currency, goats have contradictory effects. Like money, they are an ambivalent medium of exchange.

Through specific historical developments the equation between goats and the whole register of external qualities seems, through time, to have taken on added significance and application through the actions of colonialists and contemporary aid workers. In their effort to extract revenues from the region, the colonialists imposed taxation – the so-called 'hut tax' – which had first to be paid in goats collected in the camp. Initially each maternal house within the homestead was the tax unit – probably because visually each wife's courtyard presented itself to the eyes of the ignorant colonial beholder as a separate 'hut' and thus a household. Later, in an effort to connect the Turkana closer to the market and civilization, the annual tax had to be paid in coins. In order to facilitate this conversion, auction grounds for small stock were set up by the administration and the taxpayer had to bring his goats to this site, sell it for coins and pay the tax. The surplus, it was hoped, would be used to buy other goods from the stalls erected around the auction ground. This change in taxation policy was followed by a change in what was considered

77

as the unit of account and in who was held accountable. The whole camp was now the focus and senior men were defined as 'heads of household' and registered in the roll-books.

The (unintended) effect of all this was to reinforce the cultural construction of goats as the mediator with outsiders. This has continued up to the present situation of development efforts through which all restocking programmes, for example, have focused on goats. The quarantine on cattle is still in place, which means that the movement of cattle (and camels) against money has never had the chance to develop – except for a few internal sales. Most significantly, the spread of colonialism and capitalistic relations in Turkanaland did not change the general contrast within the Turkana culture itself between the domains of long and short transaction cycles. The increased convertibility of goats and cash only brought to fruition features which were already there (a degree of autonomy, anonymity, transmutability and leeway for individual gratification). Commoditization of goats did nothing to rupture the cattle/human equation, so central to maintaining the exclusivity of the long-term exchange cycle. If anything, it only empowered the existing division of 'inalienable cattle wealth' and 'alienable goat wealth', by making it even more important to command cattle to be able to contract those relationships that carry social power.

Alienation and the problem of acquisitive wealth

What is particularly interesting is that all this highly valued alienability vested in the bodies of goats has rubbed off on local conceptualizations of the market and the role of money in livestock transactions. The market-place and the goats pen seem to be closely connected spaces, symbolically and socially. Analogous to the ways in which the goat pen is an arena for diverse acts of purification and erasure, an animal moving against money in the market-place is similarly cleansed of its marks and memories, and thus also of its identification with the biographies and conduct of particular people. In a recent round of interviews with buyers and sellers at the small-stock market in Lodwar, I was very struck by this parallel drawn by informants between the two major sites for goats, the pen in the camp and the market in town. Having worked quite a lot with Turkana symbolizing strategies, it was not the juxtaposition of sites that surprised me, but rather the very positive way in which my informants spoke about the role of the market. The whole 'goat' vocabulary of purification, fertility and growth was invoked to stress the advantages of purchased stock and the potential freedom this provided in terms of the choice of pathways. Indeed, many lamented the lack of auction grounds and traders, the lid put on the sales of cattle and the recent scarcity of coins in circulation.

These statements did not resonate well either with what I recalled other Turkana people having expressed to me earlier or with the relevant literature on the linkages between livestock, money and markets in comparable settings. These sources stress the eroding effects of commercialization in the (moral) economy, locally referred to in constructions like the Luo 'bitter money' (Shipton, 1989) and the 'legless cattle' of the Tswana (Comaroff & Comeroff, 1990). Many Turkana elders, men and women, would agree with this condemnation of money, as browsing through my notebooks and transcripts confirms. In the words of a senior man, who, after having first spoken at length about the admirable traits of animals as the yardstick against which money had to be assessed, continued:

> Money is a foreign property. It is detached from Turkana people. One piece of a shilling coin in my pocket is just the same as in everyone else's pocket. Money does not multiply, money does not change its colour, money does not change its sound. Money lives hidden in pockets inside wallets, unlike livestock, who graze in the open and display their admirable characteristics. Money promotes laziness and serfdom. People do not sing about or praise money, they are scorned as *ngalemukejen* ['round legs']. Money was brought into the district by *Soroi* – the *emoit* [Europeans/enemy]. Money does not help during marriages or mourning. It is only used as a distant relation's property. Those who get enough use it to buy livestock and food. The important thing is not to get money itself but to buy food. In the old days, people preferred direct barter to getting coins or paper in exchange for an animal. Not many people knew how to use it [money], but everybody knew how to use the animals on the hoof. Money promotes theft and other bad behaviour, like alcoholism and prostitution. It is the coming of money which is spreading bad diseases, which were not there when people only related to their livestock. People who have money, even the *Wazungus* [Swahili for the White], do not eat money, they eat livestock and edible plants. So even the owners do not have any close relationship with their property. It is just a means of acquisition which has no relationship with the community.

Yet this moral statement is as situated as the ones I recorded in the market-place. It was voiced by a senior and wealthy person who has all the reasons in the Turkana world to keep money out of the transaction system. In contrast, of the people I met in the market-place, the majority were socially in junior positions. For them, the market was one important escape route from the major paths, which were controlled by senior people and effectively excluded them. From the juniors' perspective and in a world buzzing with 'inalienable possessions' – the beautifully decorated cattle which they desire but cannot get hold of in sufficient numbers – the market is a welcome refuge. Here one can obtain goats whose skins are not already clogged up with the marks of specific histories, identities and claim structures that would slow down their movements or remove them from circulation altogether. Indeed, to possess some animals that are anonymous and alienable is an attractive possibility for most people – for some more than for others. If goats are combined with plenty of coins, it is even better, precisely for the added anonymity these two valuables provide. Given that money is an avenue for accessing the livestock circuits – first, through small stock, which can later be converted into cattle and camels, and, secondly, through the large stock, through which one gets into the prestigious arena of marriage and partnerships – it is not surprising that its value is contested.

Reflecting more on the specific moral implications involved in the money–goat conversion, a young man explained it as follows:

> When I bring home to my mother's house a beautiful billy goat I got as a present from my bond-friend, or even raided cattle, my mother will be very happy and give us a warm welcome. She will run towards us, take hold of the tethers and lead the animals into the corral. When I bring back these goats I bought tonight, she will just be standing there silent and without smiling, watching me penning them on my own.

These contrasting scenes about a mother's reaction towards her son and the different kinds of animals that accompany him home succinctly conjure up the tension between selfishness and sharing, which the commercialization of livestock intensifies. This mother seemingly acted according to the common expectation that all animals that arrive along the established paths constitute a shared resource, subject to more or less overlapping and inclusive claims, rights and interests. Animals obtained with coins, on the other hand, are treated more exclusively as the possession of the purchaser.

These different statements about the morality of money demonstrate a large degree of ambivalence in contemporary Turkana attitudes towards the monetization of the livestock economy. The contrast between animals as private property and animals as bearers of a wide range of social relations brings us to the heart of the whole political, contested terrain of paths and diversions. The battles waged over exorbitant bride-wealth (among the wealthy it may be driven up to 300 head of stock) are particularly fierce. This is because this is the only avenue that accesses the semi-discrete domain in which cattle wealth and wealth in people are enclaved together in the interest of the senior generation and the cattle-rich. The political instrument for circumventing the conventional path to marriage is to exploit the avenues that exist to newly acquired wealth. Indeed, the juxtaposition of purchased animals and raided animals in the statement by the young man happens to be a very appropriate one. This is because animals stemming from these two sources of acquisition – capture and purchase – are the ways to transcend the barriers which operate in the transactional system. Both the destruction of wealth in funerary rituals and other slaughters and acquiring of new wealth play active parts in the cultural process of alienation, which, as Gregory (1982) wrote, is 'the only way of accumulating assets without accumulating liabilities'. The competitive process involved here is that, while the destruction of animal assets works to maintain the exclusivity of cattle and the social power of the seniors, animal assets that flow into the hands of the junior through raiding and purchase enhance individual possibilities for autonomy, by weakening their dependence on a whole range of social relationships. Despite social inequalities inherent in the pastoral economy, the sundering of the strong bonds created through cattle carries its own social costs in a commoditized context – hence the ambivalent attitudes towards both cattle and cash. To get a grasp of what is at stake here it is worthwhile to begin deconstructing this drama by briefly examining the wider, entangled property relations that exist around marriage.

A survey I did in the late 1980s of pastoralist herds comprising 3325 livestock evidenced that purchased animals were somewhat anomalous, making up only 2 per cent (Broch-Due, 1990b). In contrast, a comparative sample of settlers' animal holdings, which consisted mostly of small stock, gave a comparative figure of 75 per cent obtained through the market. Despite a richly inflected vocabulary of specific exchange histories and share holdings, it is possible to reduce the bulk of beasts held by Turkana pastoralists into two broader categories. The first, *ngibaren nakibuu* ('to hold'), are cattle coming from the ancestral herd of agnates representing the clan (22 per cent). After a wedding, the husband parades some of these in front of his newly-wed wife, who calls out when the right number of heads have passed by. Through this act, those ancestral cattle allocated to his wife are renamed as *anyare t* ('to call'). When the wife 'hears' the sound of these animals, I was told, her heart would grow fond of her new spouse. A husband is not allowed to speak to his bride before the display of these animals. In fact, a married man will always retain a fund of such cattle as political instruments to keep all his maturing sons born to the different wives under his controlling influence. The mother, in contrast, will work to ensure that the ancestral animals in her care are set aside to contribute to the future bridewealth for her sons, as well as the inheritance for the next generation linked to each separate house herd (*ngibaren ekol*). Each child has exclusive milk rights to one such cow as a new member of the agnatic line and homestead (*awi*) from the father. These cattle are regarded with particular affection. The milk flowing from their udders is stored in a beautifully adorned container, *akirum*, which is placed in the night hut where the spouses sleep together. This container is not only closely associated with procreation, but also with the continuation of the agnatic line of people and cattle. Ancestral cattle and their calves are held in trust by the maternal houses and, even though their disposal is a common concern, the senior agnate (the husband or his widow) will have the last word, ensuring that they continue to be put on life-generating pathways.

The second form of livestock are those given in the name of a particular person, as opposed to the clan – the *ngibaren eropit* (38 per cent) – animals that have 'roped' together giver and receiver by opening a 'path' between them through a share of bride-wealth and an assortment of different kinds of gifts. Although such personal beasts are easier to release for individual transactions, they are still part of the aggregate and other members have claims in their milk and produce. The holder will be put under pressure to contribute personal livestock to major social investments or to carry another house over a crisis. Linked to these are those animals that have been part of various types of barter and fines (11 per cent); these are managed either by each house or by the homestead as a whole, depending on the context of the transaction.

A conventional bride-wealth transfer, *akiutun* ('to grow people/to know'), combines these two categories of animals. The ancestral cattle are given in the name of the bride's closest cognates – her father, mother, father's brothers and sisters, mother's brothers and sisters. The bride in turn brings a small dowry from her own mother's house herd, called *inakina* ('suckled-breast'), which is shared among her new co-wives. It is particularly critical that the social lives and pathways of these core beasts exchanged between agnate and affine are unblemished. In the opening section, I stressed the volatile and vulnerable backcloth to pastoral life in Turkana, which brings death and destruction close to everybody's experience. Miscarriages and child mortality are the cause of a huge amount of distress and worry. Fertility events are thus morally and emotionally charged moments – particularly the wedding, which launches a new procreative career. Given the 'oneness' of person and animal, it is not surprising that the peril of life is projected on to the beasts that move against the bride. The largest portion of the bride-wealth consists of *eropit* beasts connected to particular persons. The largest share of the bride-wealth, consisting of specified beasts to specified receivers, is handed over on the spot. A smaller portion is passed on in delayed instalments to the periphery of the wife-givers' exchange trajectory and thus carries more diffuse claims.

While the recipients of bride-wealth are drawn from a rather narrow circle of the bride's cognatic field, a wide range of kin and partners on the groom's side are potential contributors. An analysis of the composition of a collection of bride-wealths, from both the giving and receiving positions, reveals that the senior generation – men as well as women – gets far more than it gives – not only in quantity but also in quality. Most cattle circulate among those socially placed in senior positions. If we move the attention within the camp, however, the record demonstrates that among its constituent houses the relation between contributions and collections is carefully balanced over time. This nicely illustrates a larger point: notably that the ledger of giving and taking is kept on the level of the houses (*ekol*) managed by wives, rather than between entire homesteads (*awi*) as units managed by husbands. On the other hand, the heavy investments a son's marriage entails for a single house are not compensated for in terms of incoming bride-wealth for daughters. Importantly, this imbalance is not shouldered by the members of the house in common. The groom must spend the bulk of his personal animals, as well as hoping for the goodwill of his father in contributing cattle from his own fund of ancestral animals. The groom may have to beg the last beasts from his entire field of close and distant partners. The donations he manages to attract increase his debts and set in motion new series of exchanges.

In the drama surrounding bride-wealth, father and son are put in structural opposition. This generational configuration is quite complex when linked to the gender dynamics and the development cycles of home-steads. The difficulties of amassing the excessive Turkana bride-wealth are such that most men do not marry before they are well into their 30s, if at all. While most pastoral women marry, because of polygamy, they are all married at a much younger age – in fact, when their male age mates are still dependent herd boys. The point of marriage is the point at which a man's career begins to peak, as he starts to gather wives, children and livestock around him. His career is at its height when his young daughters are married away and bride-wealth flows in, which allows him to marry more wives himself. He tries to delay his sons' marriages as long as possible because for him they will signal the beginning of the end. His homestead will start to be broken up into its constituent houses, each headed by one of his wives. As his career and animal capital decline, those of his wives begin to flourish.

Senior wives have a strong interest in promoting their sons' marriages, because this enables them to set up a separate homestead with their sons and daughters-in-law, enjoying the privileged position as the senior person in the new homestead. Given the age gap between Turkana spouses, the husband is becoming an old man while his wives are in their prime, enjoying the material and emotional benefits that come with strong maternal bonds. If they do not leave with their married sons, they do not have long to wait before the husband dies anyway. For whatever reason, it is when a middle-aged woman has been separated from her husband that her wealth, power and influence are at their zenith, while an elderly man, separated from his wife and losing paternal control over sons through the dispersal of the family herd, will often face loneliness and bitterness. Thus, husbands and wives reach the peaks of their careers at about the same age, but they do not get there together – their career cycles are out of sync with each other. This is a very important point and goes to show that, in the determination of these cycles, seniority is even more significant than gender.

The social power encoded in seniority is particularly brought to bear on the battles surrounding bride-wealth. Senior men have an interest in high levels of bride-wealth, because it eases the competition with younger men for brides, as well as keeping the younger generation out of the most prestigious pathways. Marriage is a scarce good, interwoven with the control of labour, livestock, alliances and security, all of which are crucial factors in the political economy of pastoralism. My survey material strongly suggests that the cost of marrying has accelerated since the 1940s, particularly because the proportion of cattle in bride-wealth has increased. The seriousness of this inflation can be seen in that now a cow is worth 20 small stock, whereas it used to be about six. The age gap between spouses is increasing. Men in the late 1980s were older at the time of both initiation and marriage than was the case before the 1960s. Moreover, many men continue to cohabit with their parents after their marriage. Drought years also show up in my statistical material as temporary drops, both in the size of bride-wealth and in the age of brides. This is because families desperately in need of livestock in such situations are willing both to accept a lower bride-wealth and to marry away girls younger than is normal. In the wake of this process of social differentiation, many men have been left in a lasting state of bachelorhood or, if they are lucky, in the company of a concubine, whom they may marry later in life.

Through the medium of money, for example, it is has been possible for entrepreneurial individuals to engineer detours from the conventional cattle paths by embarking on exchange strategies that exploit to breaking-point the cash–goats–cattle conversions. To this effect, I know a few educated Turkana men who have invested their salaries not only in small stock but also in buying some of the 'bad' cattle and/or old camels that are sometimes offered for sale to the slaughter house in Lodwar. By skilful husbanding of these animal assets, they have produced 'clean calves' by matching the 'bad' cow with a 'good' ox and, in order to cultivate pastoral support, have presented the old camel for consumption at a feast in the neighbourhood. One of these men told me how he had managed to persuade his in-laws to accept bride-wealth containing not only a higher proportion of goats than is common, but also more purchased animals, including a few camels formerly involved in a divorce case. He had argued that any 'badness' was erased and the animals purified through their most unusual detour through the market. His argumentation was eased and accepted because of some exceptional circumstances. First, given that the social life of the camels had unfolded in a distant corner of Turkanaland, it was unlikely that anybody within this particular exchange trajectory would be able to read their unfortunate life histories from the marks imprinted on their skin. Thus their records could be kept a secret between the two men. More importantly, the prospective groom was an up-and-coming leader and broker with the government, and to have him in the family was itself such an important asset that the father-in-law was willing to 'swallow a few bad camels', as it were.

While it is possible today to blend a few purchased animals, goats in particular, into bride-wealth, allowing prospective grooms to take advantage of the principle of private property and the limited liability associated with it, money cannot flow directly into the wealth-in-people domain. And, even in the cases involving purchased goats, the numbers have to be negotiated in each case and they are accepted or rejected according to the social record of the partners involved. Having a few purchased cattle parade as bride-wealth stock is clearly possible, although more difficult to get through than goats. However, the volume of cattle put through internal sales is still so low and the attitudes which emphasize the 'oneness' of people and cattle are still so overpowering that this remains the exception that proves the rule. The recent shortage of cash in the district has seriously affected the much more important market in goats which was the most reliable path to cattle for the less advantaged. This has left Turkana with the more violent avenue to cattle wealth – capture.

The developments charted in this last section, not surprisingly, coincide with an escalation in raiding. A striking feature of the pastoral herds I surveyed was the large number of raided animals they contained (17 per cent). Raids and warfare are endemic and are triggered by a complex nexus of social and cultural facts. The desire to marry motivates men, since it links the need for stock for bride-wealth with the attainment of adulthood and autonomy. Captured cattle, *ngibaren iremuno* ('brought through a spear'), from neighbouring pastoral societies allow young men to circumvent the power of fathers and, with the support of their own mothers, embark on a career that takes them through new exchange trajectories that will end in the power of seniority. Clearly, the conditions of this power arena put a premium on assertive qualities in people, fostering alertness and the capacity to manipulate physical force. However, warriors risk their own lives and the lives and livelihood of their community in war, as well as triggering counter-attacks. Raiding promotes personal reputation and vitalizes the military organization, but it also strengthens the development of unequal levels of wealth. Not only do captured cattle have an inflationary effect on the size of bride-wealth, but the fact that raids and counter-raids tend to create a vicious circle means that it has become a major impoverishing force. The life stories of Turkana settlers demonstrate this very clearly.

And here we have come full circle to the problem of acquisitive wealth in contemporary Turkanaland. Whether the settlers are pushed out of pastoralism due to drought, raiding, social inequality or an unfortunate position in marriage or inheritance structures, they are all destitute, according to Turkana cultural standards, in that they all lack livestock. And this very fact gives rise to a host of problems within their new occupations, since claims in critical resources lapse and alliances are forgotten when animals can no longer act as a medium to express and cement social relationships. Sedentarization is therefore a cumulative

85

change process. An unfortunate combination of demographic, social and economic dynamics has turned towns and development projects into poverty traps. Low productivity and low capacity to build herds have eroded kinship, marriage and partnership institutions and put the settlers in increasingly precarious relationships with other people. This strikes at the cultural core of society, notably the relationship between spouses. Concubinage is widespread in settlements and lack of cattle to bind the spheres of men and women together constrains the mutual exchange of work between them. Settlers need to husband carefully scarce assets, and this, combined with an absence of marital ties, decreases the transfers between spouses and thus the very motivation to cooperate. Individuals tend to struggle on their own to make a living, and a vicious circle is created, labour and other assets being insufficient to exploit those opportunities that may exist.

In Turkana, as in most pastoral communities, procreation, marriage and motherhood feature prominently in the complex topography of prosperity and poverty. The only medium that can create and register these vital relationships is that of animals – particularly cattle. For, through the ways the identities of people are entangled with their cattle – which thus become an extension of their caretakers' capacity to act on the world – a large herd on the hoof seems to reflect an inherent ability on the part of the homestead it represents to engage partners in prosperous relationships and to disseminate a personal presence everywhere. In all these ways, livestock are the prime mediators of the Turkana world, between production and exchange, between representation and experience and between memory and morality. It is this multiplicity that generates an endless desire and demand to display livestock publicly. The lack of proper substitutes which carry the same cultural meanings as livestock was succinctly put to me by a fisherman in the following way:

> How can a bundle of fish marry a wife? If I were to marry my wife with fish, maize or money, her parents would be the only persons to receive and I would be the only person to give. The brothers and sisters of the mother and the brothers and sisters of the father would not be given anything since that would indeed need a lot of fish! Anyway, if you came to their homesteads the next day, their bellies would be full of fish and maize and the money finished on beer and they would say that they did not receive anything. What is the use of it?

The muted poor

The great force of animals as a legitimizing device is achieved among the Turkana through the ways in which the linkage of animals, people and their shared paths is endlessly reproduced and represented in different modes: ecological, social and symbolic. 'The path' is the narrative convention which opens origin myths, tales of history and technical instructions for herding alike, as well as being the imagery invoked in all sorts of transactions, both social and symbolic. As a manifestation of the life-sustaining force in the landscape, both a tarmac road and an animal trail are talked about as *erot* – 'path'. None the less, they are the physical sign-posts of different production profiles, as well as mighty metaphors for cross-cutting power fields, social and spiritual. The contrast of roads and trails is a summarizing sign for a whole range of distinctions – between town and plains, settlers and nomads, alienable and inalienable wealth, cash and cattle, selfishness and sharing, centre and periphery – to mention but the dominant ones.

Trails and roads also represent the profoundest possible opposition between the diagnoses and perceptions of the relations between poverty and prosperity held by development planners and those of Turkana pastoralists themselves. For most expatriates, the landscape beyond the tarmac road is shrouded in the imagery of a doomed and primitive wilderness, where vegetation is being devoured by pastoral herds, the land has been baked by a merciless sun and the indigenous nomadic Turkana have been reduced to marginalization and poverty. In contrast, the emerging towns are typically portrayed as hubs of progress, modernity and wealth creation in this otherwise stricken area. For the Turkana it is the towns which are the manifestations of poverty. The relative truth of these claims and counter-claims is not easily assessed, because the reality of poverty, addressed from these divergent perspectives, is in itself so complex and contradictory.

After my last visit to Turkana in 1995, I was inclined to agree with the pastoralists' perspective, which sees the growth of these towns as examples of 'poverty in the making'; oases not of 'development' and 'progress' but of destitution. The contemporary crisis had changed the whole sound-scape around Lodwar town. The dominant sounds of the wild entertain-ment, which used to fill the evenings during the boom in development dollars a decade ago, were now muted by more disturbing sounds of drunkenness, domestic violence and grief. It was clearly not the com-moditization which was at the core of the problem, but rather the con-straints put on it. If markets in cattle and labour had been created, this would probably have eased the social inequalities inherent in the pastoral economy – as experiences from similar settings strongly suggest (Hutchin-son, 1996). However, one obvious destructive factor was the effect of the aid and development discourse about pastoral poverty and the benefits of urbanization. Whatever the case, an unfortunate mixture of local events and external interventions had created a devastating combination of demographic, social and economic dynamics, which had turned these urban environments into poverty traps.

Yet this is not unrelated to the ways in which the pastoral community defines and disposes of their poor. This brings us back to the more subtle meaning conveyed in the contrasting representations of 'trails' and 'roads' – muted in the dominant pastoral discourse, but one which, none the less, has vast implications for the distribution of wealth and want. While (animal) trails evoke in Turkana minds the continued participation in the pastoral regime, roads are the signs of the more concealed counter-fact that they are the way out for the impoverished and the unfortunate, who simply cease being members by moving beyond the moral boundaries of the pastoral community. Although the pastoral Turkana view the town as a site of poverty and destitution, they also use it as the contemporary arena in which to slough off those they consider to be morally deviant and socially different. This dislocation of the destitute, both spatially and economically, results in the identity of the poor person being remade into that of an ethnic 'other' – a non-Turkana.

Notes

1. John Lamphear, 'Report on Historical Research in Turkana District, 1976', quoted from interview T43. Unpublished manuscript, held in library of Kenya National Archives, Nairobi.
2. Ibid., from interview T50.

II ‖ METAPHORS & MEANINGS

4 Power & Poverty in Southern Somalia

BERNHARD HELANDER

Low social prestige and poverty are phenomena that often tend to go hand in hand. What interests me in the context of this chapter is how the two are interlinked, how poverty – and wealth – can indicate the social position of some groups but not that of others. While poverty is, indeed, both ubiquitous and tangible among pastoral and agropastoral groups in north-east Africa, the very notion of poverty can also play a more subtle and perhaps even more malicious role in cementing cultural images of disadvantaged groups. The purpose of this chapter is to position a Somali notion of poverty within the overall fabric of ideas that define groups and the members of groups. Poverty, I shall argue, is for many Somalis less a state of economic standing than it is a confining marker of social identity.[1]

My focus will be on one Somali clan, the Hubeer, who belong to a cluster of some 30 closely related clans, known as the Merifle.[2] The Merifle group of clans speak a dialect of the Somali language which they call Af-Maay.[3] The Hubeer, who consist of some 15,000 members, live in a locality they refer to as Ooflaawe, situated some 80 kilometres west of the regional capital, Baydhabo. Most Hubeer are agropastoralists, combining rain-fed cultivation of sorghum, maize and vegetables with the breeding of small stock, cattle and camels.

While membership in the clan is supposedly based on patrilineal descent from the ancestor, the Hubeer and other Merifle clans also allow people to become 'adopted' by the clan, so that they 'become' members of that clan. As I have shown elsewhere (Helander, 1996), this ability to switch clan membership is an essential tool by which households may gain access to resources that would otherwise be outside their control. However, the consequence of accumulated adoptions over a long period of time is that Merifle clans are rather heterogeneous compositions of people of diverse provenance and clan origin. While clans internally make distinctions between those members who are descended from the clan

founder and those who are merely adopted, these distinctions play little or
no role in their external relations with other clans. Nor do such
distinctions imply any considerable prestige ranking of different clan
members. There is, none the less, one category of adopted members who
never assume the same political or social rights as others, and they are,
among the Hubeer and the neighbouring clans, called *boon* or 'commoners'.
In relation to *boon*, all other members – whether adopted or not – are
called *bilis* or 'nobles'. It is in the distinction between these two endogamous categories that ideas about poverty play a rather particular role,
which I shall highlight in the following pages.

Boon do not constitute a homogeneous population category although
the nobles' attitudes often seem to suggest that. In reality the category
covers descendants of former slaves, immigrant groups from neighbouring
ethnic groups, such as Oromo, and destitute remnants from originally
noble clans, as well as groups claiming original settler status in the area.

The existence of an often vaguely defined category like that of the *boon*
is not unique to the Hubeer. Elsewhere in north-east and East Africa there
are many examples of what are variously called 'remnant peoples',
'outcasts' and 'low-castes'.[4] Such terms are sometimes chosen to depict
groups who display significant cultural, economic, dietary or organizational contrasts to the larger ethnic groups among whom they live. At
other times, such terms are invoked to describe sub-groups with less clear-
cut differences. The question here is how one such group, the *boon* among
the Hubeer, are positioned in their society and what role is played by real
or alleged poverty in carving out that position for them.

The topography of poverty

Ferguson (1992) has stressed that in approaching cultural constructions of
wealth and poverty – what he terms the 'topography of wealth' – it is
essential to direct attention to the 'processes through which such topogra-
phies are created and maintained'. He does so by focusing on the trajectories that different commodities may take through the Basotho economic
universe, for instance in highlighting the exchangeability and non-
exchangeability of different forms of wealth and goods. I believe it must be
equally important to study the social and cultural collaterals of wealth and
poverty, i.e. the culturally moulded assumptions which may sanction
exchange and, above all, to define what wealth is and what poverty
implies.

Poverty has a rather specific set of cultural connotations in the Somali
context. If one may speak of a 'topography of poverty', it is closely
associated with absence of political strength, which, in turn, is seen as
dependent on the numerical strength, and therefore power, of the descent
group to which a person belongs. As Fallers (1964:119) once pointed out,

'the emphasis in African stratification is primarily political' and involves differential access to authority roles, such as lineage elder, chief, etc. Commoners of the Hubeer are effectively excluded from such attractive roles. There are examples of commoners who have actually challenged the Hubeer nobles' monopoly over political offices – and been publicly humiliated because of it.

Yet poverty and the associated political weakness do not necessarily imply a lack of all forms of power, at least not as far as individuals are concerned. There is a rather strongly pronounced idea among Somalis generally that, where apparent political power is scarce, mystical powers abound (Lewis, 1963). The notion of the poor and needy as the special protégés of God, *megen Allah*, is coupled with the idea that such individuals may exploit hidden and dangerous forces to the detriment of those who are better off.

The paradigm of prestige

Distinction between persons and groups of noble descent and those of common descent is one of the most fundamental and far-reaching social distinctions that exist in Hubeer society. It is also widespread among the other Merifle clans, as well as in Somali society at large. Local configurations and terminology may vary, but the essential property of the distinction is the birth-ascribed division of people into one of two hierarchically arranged and endogamous categories. These endogamous categories bear some similarity to Indian 'castes' and there have been discussions about the applicability of that term to African material. One argument for the African applicability of the term is based on the assumption that caste systems 'have a division of labour which is divinely approved, and protected by pollution concepts' (Todd, 1977:411). Luling also adopts the term 'occupational castes' in dealing with southern Somali artisan groups. She contends that the basis for their social position was 'established by diversification of functions within the social group' (Luling, 1984:43). Levine, in attempting to synthesize some similar Ethiopian cases, describes the process by the term 'mutualistic specialization' (1974:169). My reason for eschewing the concept of caste here is that the groups of common descent among the Hubeer are of different demographic and historical origin, a fact that would be obscured by giving them a caste label. Also, as Cassanelli (1987) has shown, the commoners as a category have undergone considerable changes during the twentieth century.

The Hubeer clan as such is seen as *bilis*, but numerous minor groups regarded as *boon* live among them all over Ooflaawe. Most of these groups are associated with or adopted by powerful Hubeer lineages and, similar to other adopted Hubeer members, they will claim Hubeer identity, especially when confronting strangers. In contrast to other adopted members, *boon* are not allowed to marry the *bilis* members of the Hubeer. In effect, they never achieve the same level of assimilation and integration in the clan and their membership is often talked about as *sheegad*, i.e. 'what is only said [but not true]'.

Boon among the Hubeer and Merifle are a wider category than the small scattered groups of bondsmen and artisans found among the northern Somalis and in the Benaadir coastal communities (cf. Cerulli, 1957:53–4). The *boon* include artisans too, but the category is also comprised of groups who lead lives that, in terms of subsistence, are very similar to the *bilis*. In Ooflaawe, it may be estimated that approximately 20–30 per cent of the population belongs to the *boon* category. Estimations such as these are fraught with difficulties, partly because the term itself has derogatory connotations. It is only rarely, and in carefully circumscribed contexts, that a *bilis* can use the term *boon* without it being taken as an insult.[5]

Those with the status of *boon* are subjected to much prejudice and a contempt verging on racism. This, however, does not prevent the development of amicable relations and bonds of friendship between individuals belonging to the two categories. Although such relations are the rule rather than the exception, they do not affect the animosity between the categories.

It should be added that there is no consensus regarding the various features attributed to the *boon*. Rather, *boon* will tend to dispute both their supposed inferiority as well as the social limits it imposes. In the recent history of Ooflaawe, there have been several incidents of minor armed clashes between *bilis* and *boon*. Also, there are geographical areas where the *boon* outnumber the *bilis* and where the former, as a consequence, maintain that *bilis* are less prone to settle. Examples are the grazing zone known as *bilis-kay*, 'kidnapping the *bilis*', and the village *bilis-düd*, 'refusing the *bilis*'. I shall return later to the objections that the *boon* have against *bilis*' characterization of them.

To the *bilis*, the *boon* are second-class citizens who provide cheap labour and beyond that one should have as little as possible to do with them. The *boon/bilis* dichotomy has multifaceted ideological and historical roots. As Cassanelli has shown, the inferior category has not been constant through time. With the manumission of imported East African slaves during the early decades of this century, a merging often took place between the freedmen and indigenous groups of inferior position (Cassanelli, 1987). The *boon* proper will sometimes make a distinction between themselves and those whom they regard as descendants of slaves, for whom they use the term *muddo*. The term *habash*, used closer to the coast, has similar connotations. In the eyes of the *bilis*, however, these various categories are, for all practical purposes, lumped together and the term *boon* is regarded as encompassing them all.

As I have noted above, *boon* is actually not as neatly circumscribed a category as *bilis* ideology would sometimes have it. In particular, the relations between low-prestige, 'short-branch' (*laan gaab*) noble lineages and *boon* are unclear. And it appears that sometimes the distinction is a difficult one to make. Among the *boon* of Hubeer, there is at least one group which is regarded as an original *bilis* low-prestige segment, the Ojayle. There are also some other difficulties with the classification. For instance, the commoners of the Rer Ma'allin lineage have the same name as their noble hosts. It is not always made clear if the commoners of that group represent an originally independent set of people. Another confusion is that the Waanjeele, a commoner section of the Foqaqoonle, a subclan of Hubeer, are said to have been adopted previously by another noble clan, the Hawaadle. For that reason, the commoner section is often referred to as Hawaadle.

These and other examples would suggest two different ways in which the seeming rigidity of the *boon/bilis* distinction is moderated. First, it would appear that one obvious road to becoming *boon* is the gradual decline in prestige that would be the result of an impoverished economic standing. Most *bilis* informants, however, deny that this could ever be the case. In their view, poverty is deplorable but does not create inferiority. It is precisely the other way around: poverty is merely a result of the low social prestige. Second, it would be reasonable to assume that changed economic standing could result in an altered social standing. However, *bilis* claim that, although certainly a wealthy *boon* enjoys more respect than others, the inferior position is not washed away by sudden fortune. Again, the view of *boon*'s poverty seems to be that of an epiphenomenon of more deeply situated causes. The fact that there are groups and individuals whose social standing or background is slightly obfuscated does not alter the image of inferiority as such. A commoner suddenly acquiring a wealth of animals would certainly be regarded as rich – but he would remain classified as *boon*.

Real or putative poverty?

It is important to note that differences do exist in the economic and social standing between the nobles and commoners. While the average size of household property does not vary greatly, there is a marked difference between noble and commoner households in the extent to which they are able to claim shares in the property of relatives living in other localities. I have described elsewhere how the practice of postponing the division of inheritance for, sometimes, several generations creates a geographically dispersed set of resources and property on which most households can fall back in times of crisis (Helander, 1996). However, the extent to which such claims exist and can be utilized by nobles and commoners, respec-

95

tively, is ultimately dependent on the size and strength of a person's lineage. Since commoners' lineages tend to be small and politically subjugated by more powerful noble hosts, it means that the ability of individual members to claim shares of inheritance elsewhere will often be less than that of the nobles. In practice, a commoner pursuing such claims would have to require the assistance of noble-lineage elders in both his own clan and the noble clan to which his commoner relative belongs. While this is by no means impossible, it can often result in time-consuming proceedings, which minimize the value of the property one seeks to claim. The net effect of this difference is most clearly revealed in times of crisis, such as prolonged droughts or armed conflict. Facing such circumstances, the commoners clearly lack some of the securities that the nobles can fall back upon. Almost every such event produces yet another few destitute commoner households, who, in order to survive, are forced to sell some of their livestock and fields and take up work as agricultural labourers on the farms of others.

Curses and complementarity

Bilis argue that the ultimate cause of the inferior position of the *boon* was a curse (*inkaar* or *habaar*) that the prophet Noah (*nabi Nuuh*) put on his son Ham. The *boon*, it is said, are the descendants of this cursed son, whereas *bilis* trace ancestry through the line of another son of *Noah – Sam*.[6] The curse is held to be manifested in a variety of undesirable characteristics displayed by the *boon* category and by *boon* individuals. Poverty of both spirit and means is one such trait held to derive from the curse. Another characteristic is said to be that *boon* lack independence. The alleged curse also has a more local meaning, since the major noble segments of the Hubeer clan claim that they arose from the blessings awarded them by powerful outsiders. The cursed ones, or at least the unblessed ones, became the *boon*.

For their political and military security, the *boon* are dependent upon the goodwill and solidarity shown by the *bilis*. It is the *bilis* clan that stands as the guarantor of their rights in grazing, farming land and water. Without that support, they would, for instance, be an easy prey to a sudden invasion of migrants. On the other hand, the *bilis* admit, the *boon* perform some highly specialized functions, which are often seen as too degrading for a *bilis* to engage in. Such functions include, among other things, slaughtering, tanning, blacksmithing, pot-making and hunting. The *boon* are also seen as being always available to provide a cheap labour force for various tasks at times when family labour is insufficient.

The fact that there is some mutual specialization between *bilis* and *boon* may convey a picture of a complementary or symbiotic relationship between the two categories. For instance, during my stay with the Hubeer, the *boon* were approached on several occasions with direct requests from the elders that they initiate large-scale hunts for hyenas, which were posing a threat to the grazing livestock. A comparable case may be cited from the (neighbouring) Luuq area, where the commoner clan Goobwiin had central ritual functions *vis-à-vis* their noble superiors of the Gassar Gudda clan. No *bilis* marriage could be concluded without the *boon* performing their parts of the ceremony. The commoners also carried out crucial functions whenever a new chief was appointed in some noble clans (Ferrandi 1903:254, 264–5).

The nobles of Hubeer, however, deny that this complementarity of functions would allow the *boon* a status equivalent to their own. The general feeling among *bilis* seems to be that *boon* only engage in such income-generating activities because they lack a sufficient amount of livestock for their subsistence. A standardized way of expressing the perceived difference between oneself and the *boon* is to say that the *bilis* and *boon* are like the right and the left hand. They look alike, they can work together and even assist one another, but subjected to closer scrutiny they reveal unbridgeable signs of incompatibility. The right hand is the hand which Muslims use for greeting and it is therefore said to be morally superior. And, if the hands are held with the palms up and the fingertips pointing to each other, one finds that in the creases of the right hand is inscribed a higher number than in the left: the creases of the right hand normally form the Arabic number '81' (Λ١) whereas the left is only '18' (١Λ).

The meaning of this metaphor emerges when considering the ideal of male numerical strength, which is supposed to underlie any group's ability to govern its own affairs. It refers directly to the commonly held notion that the *boon* as a group, by possessing fewer members than the *bilis*, lack the prerequisites for an agnatic structure and that, instead, they consist of small clusters of families loosely knit together by co-residence but without any knowledge of or reference to genealogical ties. This is wrong, of course: the *boon* do have clans and genealogies. The *bilis*, however, point to the *boon* 'hunting associations' (*hirin*) and claim that they are the closest the *boon* come to having clans of their own. The point made by such allegations is that the *hirin* among the *boon* demonstrably perform some of the functions that descent groups perform among the *bilis*. The different *hirin* groups that exist in Ooflaawe are mythologically structured around concepts of *boon* as hunters appointed as such by the Prophet. *Hirin* have an internal hierarchy of statuses and the highest ranking members, the *harganti*, enjoy considerable respect, even among *bilis*. Advancement through the hierarchy is achieved by proving one's skill as a hunter and is accompanied by gifts of bows and arrows from the previously initiated. Recruitment to a *hirin* is based primarily on locality; it is interesting that there is a high incidence of marriages among families of the same *hirin*. Apart from occasionally assembling a hunting party, the *hirin* organization can also assume important social functions. I have seen *hirin* members support one another in, for example, the settling of disputes and the payment of blood wealth and other legal compensations (*mag*). It is particularly this latter feature of the *hirin* that is upsetting in the eyes of *bilis*, since blood wealth is something that agnates should provide.

Wealth as a vehicle for the construction of descent

A fundamental aspect of the concept of *boon* as hunters is apparent only when seen in relation to how descent is culturally constructed among the *bilis*. The solidarity and cohesion in Merifle clans is to a large extent constituted by common interests in and control of the wealth of the clan. Wealth to the Hubeer is mainly thought of as the livestock, and idiomatically the term livestock, *hoolo*, is also used to mean wealth in general. A very clear example of the close relationship between livestock and wealth was the fact that one of Somalia's largest landowners living in the area, who happened to possess a very tiny herd of animals, was not regarded as wealthy at all.

The animal wealth has very specific functions in the conceptual construction of links between fathers and sons. The ceremonies establishing this include the 'tying' or 'closing' of a piece of the umbilical cord of each newborn son with hair from the tail of an animal from the father's herd. This animal and its offspring become the property of the son and both the animal and the ceremony are called *huddun hir* (lit. 'to tie/close the umbilical cord'). The purpose of the ceremony is said explicitly to be to cut off the tie with the mother and replace it with a bond to the father and his group.

Many of the other postnatal practices may be said to gradually subdue the symbols for maternal ties while emphasizing the paternal links. In this gradual construction of descent ties, the property of the father plays the most essential role. In late adolescence or in connection with their marriage, sons will receive more animals from their fathers. This is a burdensome expense for many men, but popular sayings state that unless the father makes sure that these animals are given, he may not be buried: *gaal duuga galee, kii duduufan ma galeen* ('a camel enters the burial, the frivolous don't enter'). The implication is that a son who has not been given his proper share of the herd will not fulfil his duties as a son, such as performing the burial ceremonies for his father.[7] These gifts are called *wahad*, which means 'unify' in Arabic, a meaning that the term also has in the Maay dialect. The term thus suggests that camels establish ties of unity between a son and his father.

The symbolic importance of livestock and gifts of livestock is not restricted to the father–son relation: it entangles the whole of society in a pattern of constant exchanges and settling of debts. Incoming bride-wealth (*yaraad* or *fad*), for instance, is distributed among a wide circle of the agnates of the bride's father. Similarly, the groom's father will turn to his patrilineal relatives for collecting the requested amount. The principles are the same when it comes to the settling of legal compensations in the form of blood wealth (*mag*). In most of these contexts the amount to be paid is expressed in terms of camels, although it may actually be paid in cash or sorghum. In view of the importance given to camels as vehicles of social relations, it is perhaps not surprising that they are marked with a collective clan brand, regardless of individual ownership.[8] One could say that livestock serves both as material proof of relations of agnation (cf. Lewis, 1961:84) and as one of the very elements that help constitute and define such relations.[9]

Commoners, poverty and the threats to descent

Against the background of this brief outline of the symbolic role of livestock transfers among the *bilis*, some qualities associated with the *boon* assume particular significance. First of all, it is often maintained that 'in the old times' there were restrictions on *boon* ownership of livestock in general and of camels in particular. Today there are still groups of *boon* who do not raise any livestock other than goats, and in general their livestock holdings are smaller than those of *bilis*. These restrictions, if they did exist, could perhaps be viewed as extensions of the *de facto* marriage prohibition. Both would seem to counteract the establishment of institutionalized relations between the two categories.

However, the significance is more subtle than that. Another aspect of livestock in this context is that *boon* social relations are not maintained through links phrased in terms of domestic animals (*hoolo*) but through organizations (i.e. the *hirin*) developed for the pursuit of wild animals (*dugaag*). Corresponding to the *bilis*' gradual transfer of livestock is the *boon*'s gradual transfer of hunting skills and equipment. One also finds that in the myths concerning the origin of many *boon* groups they are described as descendants of some wild animal,[10] while there are noble clans in whose myths of origin descent from domestic livestock is implied. There is a proverb which captures rather well a feeling I think many Hubeer have: *adduun la'aan waa addoonnimmo* ('to be without property/livestock is slavery'). This proverb suggests that the one without property (which is both culturally and linguistically synonymous to livestock in Somalia) will become the slave or dependant of someone else.

Poverty, in the sense of absence of livestock, is, in this *bilis* version of society, the ultimate proof of *boon* inferiority. Without livestock, sons cannot be made into patrilineal descendants and without such there can be no lineages, since it takes livestock to forge agnatic solidarity. In this powerful simulacrum, every action by a commoner, every alleged trait they possess seems to further cement them in their position. Indeed, just as Baudrillard's simulacra (1994) may be described as representations without objects, the *boon* do not have to be poor to be subjected to that image. Once, outside a teashop, a quite wealthy *boon* man explained to me that he preferred to drink his tea without milk. Later on, a *bilis* man who had heard us explained that the man had only made a virtue of necessity: 'How could he like tea with milk? He has no animals.'

The logic of prejudice

One could say that the noble version of the commoners is based on a simple and circular formula, which runs in the following way:

ancestral curse ➡ subjugated by others ➡ small in numbers ➡ poverty ➡ no proper descendants ➡ weak agnatic structure ➡ subjugated by others ➡ etc.

There is no definite end or beginning of this circular imagined state of affairs, but, to most *bilis*, the logic is impeccable and the social confines it implies inescapable. There are also an almost infinite number of attributes which the *bilis* derive from this simulacrum and ascribe to the *boon*. For instance, the *boon* are held to be lacking in *'aqli* (intelligence/reason/ knowledge). There are terms which are sometimes used as synonyms for *boon* that illustrate this. One such term is *'aqli lih sa'*, 'intelligence at midnight'. This ironic expression is said to indicate the fact that the *boon* gain full intellectual competence only when other people are asleep. A variation of this theme is expressed in a commonly cited proverb: *boon dhugoowdi ii kurdo beer galli bilis dhibaasa* ('*boon* getting wisdom and weeds entering a field make trouble for the *bilis*').

This prejudice portrays *boon* as lacking the central substance thought to be inherited patrilineally, since wisdom or knowledge is thought to be part of those traits that come from the father's contribution at conception. Thus, it is basically a variation on arguing that they lack (male) numerical strength. Similarly, they are also believed to lack any substantial form of agnatic framework, and the chief instrument of creating of such relations, livestock, are said to have been prohibited even for them to own. The organization among the *boon* that replaces agnatic groupings may be seen as 'twisted', since it makes use of symbols related to wild animals rather than to domestic animals.

However, the status of *boon* not only features elements that are a negation of male dimensions of society and personhood; it also is ascribed certain qualities that connote female aspects. Above all, this is conveyed by the term *timo jariir* (hard hair) by which they are called. It is a commonly held belief that the hair of *boon* is harder than the hair of *bilis*. In fact, the terms *jariir* (hard) and *jilee'* (soft) are often used in preference to the terms *boon* and *bilis*.[11] As with all those things acquired matrilineally and classified as 'soft', hair should be soft. 'Hardness' is a male attribute describing the quality of elements acquired patrilineally. In view of this it would appear that the attribution of hard hair to the *boon* is slightly paradoxical. However, this paradox fits with a number of other distortions concerning the classification of the socially inferior and it actually serves to stress their 'femaleness' in contrast to their 'male' superiors. Another such distortion is the fact that the *boon* are regarded as excessively muscular (*muruqleh*) and physically strong (*hoogleh*). The strength implied is not the ideal one, which is vested in an agnatic group; instead it is the individual strength of the – matrilineally acquired – muscles. The 'hard' hair of the *boon* and their 'strength' thus represent a transposition of male elements and agnatic ideals to female aspects and parts of their bodies. In the same way, it was previously seen how it is alleged that 'agnatic functions' among the *boon* are performed by non-agnatic structures, such as locally based networks and hunter associations.

The hard hair of the *boon* becomes a way to further deride their lack of agnatic ties by saying that they lack the hard agnatic parts of the body and that it is instead their soft, matrilaterally inherited parts that have grown hard. Similarly, *boon* children are often said not to have had their umbilical cord detached properly and that a large part of it is still visible at their navel.

It could be argued that these stereotypes help nobles to create a certain consistency in their interpretation of the social environment. They see inferior social categories as 'female' and, with the help of the inverted bodily traits of commoners, these, too, can be assigned the female mark.[12] I have also come across statements that expressly linked commoners with various female qualities. It was said that their interest in shameful types of dancing made them 'like women'. Their alleged promiscuity was described in a similar way. In brief, there is little doubt that nobles make the commoners' alleged absence of agnation the reason for ascribing to them a chain of associated and female characteristics. Strength or hardness in itself is a good thing, but in social matters it should be reserved for agnates. As is said in a proverb, everything has its proper place and proper use ('a road is for walking, a kitchen to be worked in [not the other way around]'). The proper place for strength is not in relation to matrilateral or affinal relatives.

Interpretation and resistance

It would be hard for the commoners to argue against the stereotyped notion of their own poverty. Their livestock holdings are often slightly smaller and their social, economic and political opportunities more confined, yet there are other dimensions of the nobles' scheme which are open to attack. In the metaphors that nobles use to degrade the commoners, there remains what Ricœur (1976) has called 'a surplus meaning', a possibility for further interpretations – and the commoners do not let that opportunity slip away unexploited. The commoners maintain that it is really they who are, or rather ought to be, the hierarchically superior. One of their ways of expressing this claim is by taking the insults received at face value and interpreting them literally – as signs of masculinity.

There are several difficulties with the interpretation suggested by the noble perspective. One is that there is nothing in the noble version to account for the fact that the very word *bilis* actually also means 'feminine'.[13] Another difficulty is the fact that commoners loudly dispute the legitimacy of the nobles' classificatory scheme. They object, for instance, to the interpretation by which they are made 'female'. Instead, they very explicitly claim that the nobles are female. As nobles do their best to put the commoners in close relation to the wild, the amoral, the cursed and the ignorant, commoners reply by depicting the nobles as weak, lacking courage, eschewing labour, susceptible to diseases and boastful without reason. These are themes that can be encountered in a variety of circumstances and expressed with varying degrees of seriousness.

Individuals belonging to the two different categories are in constant contact and interaction. In work and leisure, in worship and mourning, persons of noble and commoner descent mingle with one another, discuss with and insult one another. Although both categories to some extent maintain separate religious and secular institutions, members of the other category are free – though perhaps not welcome – to come there as spectators, something which they also frequently do. Although at least the nobles frequently claim ignorance in any matter concerning the commoners, members of both categories have extensive experience of the preconceptions and stereotypes of themselves that prevail among members of the other category.

The nobles' view of commoners can, to some extent, be seen as an explanation for what they see as deviant behaviour. The commoners, however, do not agree that they require any explanation at all. Where nobles seek help in curses and the eating of carcasses for explaining the commoners, the commoners seek to explain the existence and observed weakness of the nobles by, for instance, the following myth:

> Once there lived a man called Binisoow Seymar Bilaad. His last name, Bilaad, comes from *bilis* and means 'the one who takes care of and respects other people and the one who does not damage other people'. Binisoow was indeed a good man. However, Binisoow fell in love with a *jinny* [invisible ugly beings, thought to have their mouth twisted 90 degrees]. That was his mistake. Her name was Aqliimay Derbaan Eelo Derbaan Muuse. They got married and had several children, among them some of the ancestors to Somali *bilis* clans. From that day, the descendants of Binisoow and Aqliimay are sometimes born with their mouths twisted (harelipped, *derbaan*). This defect is never observed among us (the *boon*). From that day, the *bilis* have also misunderstood the meaning (*ma'ne*) of the word *bilis*, they think its meaning is 'superior' (*gob*) but in the times before it did not have that meaning.

This myth both explains the observed weakness of the *bilis* and accounts for how the word came to mean feminine. The latter issue was developed more explicitly – but with less elegance – on another occasion by one of my commoner informants:

> In times of disease all the *bilis* will be ill. We [commoners] just do like this [he blew his nose], and go to our fields. If you want to wrestle with a *bilis* he will run away, he thinks it is a rape. [Turning, jokingly, to a *bilis* man present:] you are like women, you have holes!

What the commoners take issue with is not the existence of hierarchy and I do not think one can say that, in general, they dispute the fact that the nobles have appropriated the superior position of this hierarchy; their point seems to be that the hierarchical superiority was originally awarded to the *bilis* in a different sense from that in which it is used today. It is something meant to depict personal moral qualities and not meant to go hand in hand with political power. This is perhaps most resoundingly amplified by the fact that *bilis* also means 'feminine'. This parallels the status of *bilis* with the many positive traits that are associated with femininity, such as fairness, respectfulness, tenderness, etc. It is traits like these, they seem to argue, that should go with *bilis*hood, not political supremacy.

There are reasons to suspect that the commoners among Merifle clans may find yet other angles for attacking the noble images of them. In several issues of the journal *Demenedung*,[14] feature articles have portrayed crucial social institutions among the *boon*. One example is a penetrating article describing the *harganti*, the leaders of the hunting associations, *hirin*. It is not inconceivable that this attention in an exile-based journal heralds a new conception of the attributes of hunting, which have previously been regarded as stigmatizing and unmentionable. Looking more broadly at post-civil-war Somalia, there are many examples of how low-prestige groups have struggled, more or less successfully, to alter confining images of them, precisely by bringing to the fore the hunting connection in which many of them are trapped. In the north-eastern regions, for instance, the term *Gabooye* (a container for arrows used in hunting) has been widely promulgated by several low-prestige groups to replace pejorative names used for them in the past (Helander, 1998).

Conclusion: poverty and the simulacra of hierarchy

In arguing with Ferguson's influential proposition (1992), I have taken the position that poverty makes sense only when seen against the background of a 'topography of poverty' or a simulated model of ideological constructs used to justify political positions in a prestige hierarchy. Poverty in itself does not 'mean' anything as long as we do not position it in a context of wealthy and poor people, along with their aspirations and assumptions.

This, of course, is not meant to minimize the suffering and hardships that go with poverty regarded as an economic state. Nor should such a perspective make us blind to the exploitation and deprivation of the post-colony and its inhabitants. However, the perspective I have advocated here is that poverty is not just an external assessment of individuals' relative wealth, but a concept that touches upon what society defines as property and what the desirable uses for that property are.

The material I have presented evolves around livestock and the role of livestock transfers in cementing the social ties between fathers and sons. In the admittedly wobbly version of the nobles, commoners are commoners because their allegedly smaller numbers of livestock do not seem to allow for the proper ritual prestations to be performed at the birth of a son. The fact that some commoner families do own large herds does not alter that perception, because, in addition, thére is the idea that commoners build their social ties on transfers of hunting equipment and on the alleged fact that their social relations are centred on the pursuit of wild animals, not on the breeding of domestic ones.

We have penetrated a long series of undesirable characteristics that the nobles are able to derive from these assumed attributes and ascribe to the commoners: bodily traits, intellectual ability, etc. It was seen how all these prejudices in fact emanate from the central tenets regarding the insufficient patrilineal strength of commoners. The economic realities that could potentially contradict such beliefs – such as that there are poor nobles too – do not seem to matter, because the meaning of poverty is like a scrapbook containing bits and pieces of the social position of those whom one wants to be poor. One could even say that social standing defines the meaning of poverty, and not the other way around. The main point, however, is that 'poverty' implies a dimension of social construction that is immensely broader than the economic standing of those regarded as 'poor'.

Notes

1. Most of the material for this chapter is based on my fieldwork in Somalia before the civil war, in 1982, 1983, 1984–5, 1988 and 1989. While I have continued work in Somalia since the war broke out, I have not been able to return to Ooflaawe.
2. They are also known variously as Rahanweyn, Rahanwiin or Reewiin.
3. The spelling of Somali terms in this chapter follows the pronunciation pattern in Af-Maay rather than the standard Somali spelling. Briefly, this means that the voiced pharyngeal fricative, 'c' in standard Somali is pronounced as a glottal stop, ' '', and the unvoiced pharyngeal fricative, 'x' in standard Somali, becomes an ordinary 'h'.
4. Some well-documented such cases include the Watta (Cerulli, 1922) and the Torrobo (Galaty, 1977, 1979, 1986), and are also to be found among the Dizi (Haberland, 1984, 1993), the Dime (Todd, 1977, 1978), the Gurage (Schack, 1964), the Macha Oromo (Lewis, 1970; Hultin, 1987) and the Konso (Hallpike, 1968). Although I am not suggesting that the perspective applied in this chapter is valid in all these cases, at least problems of a similar character can be found among them.
5. The origin of the word *boon* is obscure. Although Zoli (1927:193), Cerulli (1959:284n.) and Stiles (1980, 1981) identify it with the Boni hunters of the Juba area and although a

link between the *boon* and hunting exists, there is, to date, nothing to suggest that the original meaning of the word was 'hunter', as Colucci (1924:69) translates it. Nor is there any evidence, apart from the similarity of name, that links the category of *boon* with the inhabitants of the Boni forest south of Kismaayo. Ferrandi (1903: 301) simply translates it 'inferiors', and that catches the general value given to the word among – nobles of – the Hubeer. Until there is more historical evidence at hand, it seems safer to regard the similarity of the two words as a spread of terminology for talking about inferior groups, rather than a spread of people *per se*.

6. Although this biblical motif is not entirely in agreement with the text versions available (Isaac, 1985; Muhammad, 1985), it is found throughout Africa as part of ideologies sanctioning the position of subordinate and slave groups (Sanders, 1969; Willis, 1985). In the eastern African case, Cerulli has suggested that the myth won repute through the spread of an Arabic textbook called *The Book of Golden Bars* in Koranic schools (Cerulli, 1957:253), probably towards the end of the eighteenth century. However, although this particular version of the myth may be imported, the notion that a curse played a crucial role in the development of an inferior category is inherent in other ideological features and symbols related to the *boon*. For many specific *boon* groups, there are stories in which a recurrent element is that their ancestor at one time consumed prohibited food and that as a result he was cursed and expelled by his *bilis* brothers.

7. For another interpretation, see Massey *et al.* (1984, vol. I:79).

8. This refers to the practice among the Hubeer. One will find, however, that the level of grouping embraced by a camel brand corresponds fairly accurately to the highest effective level of patrilineal ties. See also Colucci (1924:278–9).

9. It is perhaps significant that the Somali (and Af-Maay) verb 'to milk', *maal*, is the same word as wealth or property, although it appears to have been borrowed from Arabic.

10. Cerulli (1957:54) mentions that the Shiidle are held to be descended from a hippopotamus. Similar stories are told about one Eyle section.

11. Closer to the coast and in Mogadishu, a distinction is often made between the *boon* and the *jariir*, and the former are seen as a category superior to the latter. In Ooflaawe and its surrounding areas, this is not the case.

12. I have described more fully elsewhere the way in which male/female traits figure as markers of prestige (Helander, 1988).

13. The two most comprehensive dictionaries of the Somali language leave little room for doubt: '*bilis* … 1 high cast, family of rank. 2 … of high cast, of good family. 3 … women, feminine' (Agostini *et al.*, 1985:58). In Keenadiid (1976:35), the term is said to mean 'a person of good birth' and the words 'women' and 'feminine' are listed as secondary meanings.

14. This is an English-language magazine focused on Merifle issues, published by Mohamed Haji Mukhtar, Department of History, Savannah State University, Georgia. The name *Demenedung* means, approximately, 'The Times'.

5 Pastoralists at the Border: Maasai Poverty & the Development Discourse in Tanzania

AUD TALLE

A problem of traditions

> Change lifestyle, Maasai told ... We cannot accept the current Maasai lifestyle to continue. We must change with time. (*Daily News*, 1994)[1]

In Tanzania, as elsewhere in East Africa, the concept of development is deeply embedded in notions and images of change, modernity and prosperity; in practical terms, for somebody to be developed means, generally speaking, to become educated, go to church, present a properly dressed and well-cared-for body, live in a brick house, eat 'good' food. 'Development' (*maendeleo*, 'going forward') is more or less everything that is associated with the 'modern' (*-a kisasa*) as opposed to the 'traditional' (*-a asili*). During villagization in Tanzania in the mid-1970s it was not uncommon that traditional houses were condemned and demolished with the sole justification that they were 'old-fashioned' and 'backward'. In their zeal to stand out as development-committed, village governments passed by-laws criminalizing the erection of such houses. The distinction between the traditional and modern is frequently invoked in the temporal imagery of a discontinuity between *zamani* ('before') and *sasa* ('now').

Defined primarily as a combat against 'poverty' (*umaskini*), 'development' remains a continuous, daily struggle and is as much a national concern as an obligation of the individual. The message of 'development' is conveyed again and again in political rhetoric, the mass media, government documents and informal encounters among the general public. Within this discourse, 'development', then, embodies practical as well as moral aspects, and 'poverty', being its antithesis, is intimately linked to images of backwardness, primitivity and ignorance.

This chapter focuses on local expressions of the development discourse. It concerns the pastoral Maasai in Tanzania and their positioning as an image of anti-development and primitivity within discursive practices.

106

'Maasai' is used both as a descriptive term of an ethnic group and as a normative concept, depicting a way of life from which, for reasons of conceived ideas of progress, the encompassing society distances itself. The master narrative of the Maasai as economically irrational and forever resistant to change has served to construe them as the 'other' in the modern, development-orientated society (see, for example, Raikes, 1981; Hodgson, 1995). This chapter also discusses how the Maasai themselves, by marking their difference or otherness, negotiate this somehow negative symbolic identity in new contexts of self-presentation.

The title of this chapter has a double meaning, referring both to the site of the study, the border town Namanga between Kenya and Tanzania,[2] and metaphorically to the precarious role of the Maasai as modern citizens and urban dwellers. Towns are not 'natural' settings for the pastoralists. When visiting such places, they become anomalies; their ethnic clothing, body ornamentation and behavioural patterns constitute a stark contrast to 'things modern' (*vitu vya kisasa*).

Field research in Namanga resulted from acquired immune deficiency syndrome (AIDS)-related research done among Maasai living in the villages surrounding the town. From the study in the rural villages, the assumption was made that human immunodeficiency virus (HIV) transmission into the pastoral communities would largely depend upon the kind and frequency of contacts between them and people in places like Namanga (Talle, 1995). Some Maasai, when travelling to town, become involved in sexual relations with the women living there, in particular with female bar attendants. Many of these women routinely engage in commercial sex and the HIV prevalence among them is alarmingly high all over Tanzania (Klepp *et al.*, 1995). Through the field research, it became evident that bar women who entertain Maasai men were in general secretive about these affairs lest they ruin their chances with other men. Similarly, Maasai were reluctant to disclose their personal experiences for fear of being held in contempt by their own community. The sexual encounters between town women and Maasai men, in a subtle way bringing out larger discursive issues of development and poverty, inclusion and exclusion, is a major focus in this chapter.

Namanga residents, not least the bar women, commonly make use of sensory markers in their representations of the pastoral Maasai: Maasai identity is perceived and expressed by negative images of sight, smell and body aesthetics. Conversely, Maasai would express olfactory disapproval of 'town people' (*watu wa mjini*), with whom they contrast themselves by, for example, referring to their soaped and perfumed bodies. The sensory argument, by creating and informing differences and hierarchy, values and preferences, likes and dislikes, appears to make a particularly strong case in 'othering' processes everywhere (Almagor, 1987; Synott 1993; Classen *et al.*, 1994).

Poverty among the Maasai

The Maasai economy, basically orientated towards livestock subsistence production, has, since the colonial era, been considered to generate solely unproductive wealth, which is of little profit to the state and harbours few development potentials. Hence development efforts in the Maasai areas have been orientated largely towards ways of raising productivity, primarily land demarcation and privatization, as well as stock-rate control (Homewood, 1995). Over the last three to four decades, many Maasai have barely survived on their livestock herds and have been forced to seek income from other sources (Århem, 1985; Talle, 1988; Kituyi, 1990). Besides cropping activities, poor Maasai men frequently find employment as night-watchmen in towns, as herdsmen for their more fortunate tribesmen or, less often, as casual labourers; women engage in petty trading, beer brewing and, increasingly, prostitution. Tourism is another employment niche; being represented as the 'noble savage', the image of the Maasai fits well with wildlife and dramatic sceneries.

Marginalization and processes of destitution are particularly severe and rapid among the Maasai in Kenya (Hillman, 1991; Homewood, 1995). Severe droughts and hunger, however, have been documented repeatedly from Maasai areas in both Kenya and Tanzania. More recently, in early 1994, the Tanzanian media reported several people dying from hunger in Monduli District, the very district in which this study was conducted. In February 1997, on a short visit to the Maasai, I witnessed a by now too frequently recurring scenario emerging: the short rains had failed and the long rains were delayed, animals were dying in large numbers, people desperately shifting their animals in search of the deficient pasture resources, and distribution of relief food had been initiated. The situation was as critical in Kenya as in Tanzania.

The Maasai themselves are indeed aware of the losses of livestock and land resources in their communities and they lament and articulate their plight. They claim that institutions of reciprocity and redistribution are less vital than they used to be; that men remain unmarried beyond marriageable age; that food served at weddings is not of the quality it used to be; that people come to circumcision ceremonies 'only for food'; and so on. To a great extent, the pastoral Maasai verbalize poverty in terms of its social effects, evidenced in the saying 'there is no man so clever that he can be generous while poor' (*metii olng'en oidim ataa supat aa aisinani*) (Mol, 1978: 125). A 'poor' man (*olaisinani*) is a person who performs badly in regard to generosity and hospitality – virtues of the highest degree in Maasai society – and who, wanting livestock wealth for distribution and sharing with fellow Maasai, lacks influence (Talle, 1990). Maasai often say that men without cattle are men without words. A man's poverty bears witness to his failure in livestock husbandry and, as he has not been able to

108

advise himself, he has no power to advise others.

In their articulation of poverty, its opposite, prosperity, is implied. While deploring their own lack of resources which keeps many from living up to the standards of being pastoral Maasai, contrasting references are made to the wealthy ones (*olkarsis*), those who are 'blessed' (*mayiana*), indicating both kinds of luck – many children and an abundance in livestock products for allocation and common consumption. The growing economic and social differences within the Maasai communities are there for people to observe and contemplate.

A recent survey among Maasai in the rural communities bordering Namanga found that livestock ownership was highly skewed, with roughly 10 per cent of the households in the sample owning 57 per cent of the cattle (FAO, 1993). Some of them were very wealthy indeed, with livestock herds of several hundred animals. These large herds contributed to a relatively high average of 60 cattle, 75 goats and 28 sheep per household of eight in the area. The median, which was just above 20 for cattle and 20 and 14 for goats and sheep, respectively, may be a more reliable measure for the livestock holdings of the typical Maasai household in the Namanga hinterland. All the households owned some cattle, but a substantial number of them (roughly 30 per cent) possessed fewer than ten animals. According to these figures, a total of 77 per cent of the households fell below the minimum pastoral survival limit of 5.5 livestock units per capita. Another survey of Maasai villages, partly in the same area, found people reporting 'lack of food' as a major concern (World Vision 1991).

The Maasai inhabiting the Namanga border area constitute, in many ways, the representative Maasai pastoralist, often surviving on a very limited number of cattle, sheep and goats (Århem, 1985; Lane, 1996). Despite efforts by various development agencies to boost crop cultivation, only a few of the families grow small acreages of maize and beans for home consumption. Largely for reasons of poor cropping facilities and lack of knowledge and organizational capacity, Maasai agriculture is often of a substandard quality (FAO, 1993). In addition, pastoral Maasai until recently regarded involvement in agriculture as a sign of poverty; cropping activities or settlement among cultivators was a temporary strategy of survival in times of drought and livestock diseases. For cultural as well as practical reasons, cultivation has never been very popular with the pastoralists, the importance of grains in their diet notwithstanding. In the Food and Agriculture Organization (FAO) survey, 90 per cent of the households reported that they bought maize for consumption on a regular basis. Thus there is a heavy dependence on the sale of livestock and livestock products (milk, hides and skins) to meet cash needs.

Pastoral households possessing a minimum number of livestock tend to be extremely vulnerable and have to rely on relatives and friends (e.g. age-mates) for the maintenance of living standards. Lending and borrowing, however, are not as widespread as perhaps expected; according to the cited survey, only about 15 per cent of the herd owners were involved in that kind of transaction. Accounting for reporting errors in survey data, this figure, however, may indicate that people are increasingly less willing to share and redistribute livestock wealth, a claim often made by Maasai of scarce means, in fact.

Although many poor families survive on a subsistence level not dramatically different from their wealthier neighbours, due to a still functioning redistributive system, the fact that they do not control livestock wealth, in particular cattle, makes them none the less feel utterly impoverished. (Poverty, then, as the Maasai see it, is not necessarily lack of housing or lack of food, but primarily lack of transactional goods, namely livestock, to mobilize and commit partners to their personal projects. Concerning communication rather than material survival, poverty is a matter of 'personal dignity' more than destitution (Douglas, 1982:16). Within their conceptualization of prosperity and poverty, Maasai often regard agricultural and town people as poor precisely because they do not possess livestock wealth.) Another word for poor people in Maasai is *iltorrobo*, referring to scattered and small groups of people (Okiek, Ndorobo) who live on the forest edges of Maasai territory, surviving on hunting and gathering, in particular the gathering of honey (Spear, 1993a). (Pauperization is increasingly a reality for more and more pastoralists; however, the perception and experience of being 'poor', although not dissociated from these material processes, set in at an earlier stage.)

Namanga town: a place of 'danger'

Namanga is a Maasai word (*manka*) referring to the red ochre abundant in the area, which traditionally has been used as a dye and, mixed with fat, as a ceremonial anointment. The red-coloured Maasai 'warrior' (*olmurrani*, anglicized form *moran*) is still one of the most powerful and famous tourist images of East Africa. For a long time, ochre was an important item of merchandise in the local barter trade. When the border between Kenya and Tanzania reopened in 1983, after having been closed for several years, Namanga began to expand markedly. The population on the Tanzanian side, where this study was conducted, is roughly 3000 and consists of many different ethnic groups from Tanzania and beyond (population census, 1988; the population in the Kenyan part of the town may be even larger, considering its longer history). The illegal trade of consumer goods, in particular beer, across the border is lucrative. The goods are bought at wholesalers on the Kenyan side, carried across the border and ferried to the larger towns in northern Tanzania and to destinations even further away. Goods also go in the other direction. The fluctuating value difference between the Kenyan and Tanzanian currency has created ample opportunities for economic enterprise.

Those involved in the border trade usually come without their families and stay in Namanga temporarily. Some visit the place only for the day. The number of guest houses, restaurants, bars, groceries, retail shops and other businesses is increasing at a high rate. Being a border town, Namanga also has a substantial number of civil servants, mainly men, within the customs and police forces, which effectively mark the presence of state control in the local setting. Long-distance trucks and tourist buses cross the border daily, thereby linking Namanga to larger international networks. The livestock trade of Maasai cattle across the border, mainly from Kenya to Tanzania during colonial times, in the opposite direction in the 1970s and 1980s and lately from Kenya to Tanzania again, has effectively exploited market opportunities on either side of the border. Situated on the border, Namanga is, in fact, a major venue for this informal trade and as such attracts cattle dealers from all over the Maasai area.

In brief, Namanga town is a place characterized by quick profit, rapid cash circulation, high mobility and temporary encounters between people. The image of the frontier town comes to mind. When walking the streets of Namanga, you meet an impressive mixture of people from far and near and from different walks of life, all seemingly looking for an opportune moment to make money. Well-travelled observers claim that they have seldom seen a place with higher beer consumption or greater promiscuity, both of which they attribute to a quick and high cash flow, cheap beer and fluidity in social relations. Namanga is indeed a place of divergences and boundaries, epitomized in the national border (*mpaka*) running through the middle of the town, dividing it into two distinct and separate entities. Within each one of these, there are marginal and central, private and public, ethnically neutral and ethnically marked, dangerous and safe places. People hurry past the customs area, lest they be detected with illegal goods; waitresses and customers sit on display in front of street bars, consuming their beer; sophisticated Kenyan women parade the main streets; Arab and Somali women are seldom seen outside the family compound. And so on. Spaces are marked and inscribed by activities and persons; simultaneously, spatial boundaries are incessantly crossed, generating and reflecting a dynamic configuration of 'places'. Namanga town is one and several places at the same time. As a locality, i.e. as a place situated in space and time and as a dimension of social life, Namanga synthesizes the parochial and the global.

The pastoral Maasai visit Namanga regularly for many different purposes. Women come for their own or children's medical treatment or to buy consumer goods, sell milk or trade Maasai bead jewellery with the tourists stopping on their way from Nairobi to the game reserves in

Tanzania. Women also come to Namanga sometimes to fetch water. Men visit the place for similar as well as for additional purposes. Namanga, furthermore, is a transit *en route* to other places; buses and *matatus* (large taxis) trafficking between Nairobi and Arusha, the largest urban centre in northern Tanzania, make a stop-off in Namanga.

Except for the few Maasai who hold government positions or own shops, most of them do not remain in Namanga for long. As a general rule, once their errand is completed, they return home. In particular, the women make a point of the fact that they 'just' go there, do their 'business' and return home immediately, consciously communicating that Namanga is not their place. The FAO survey referred to above confirms that the majority of the Maasai use the rural homestead as the base for their social and economic activities, even though these often take them to distant places. As far as town life is concerned, the pastoralists are ambivalent; economically the town represents opportunities, a place for sales, purchases and the acquisition of services; socially and morally, however, it is basically a place of disorder and danger. At first glance, Maasai appear to be everywhere in Namanga; their relatively high number, their divergent appearance and the fact that the town is located right inside their territory give an impression of Maasai omnipresence. Upon a second look, however, they stand forth as spatially concentrated. Whenever Maasai men, for instance, visit the main street bars where bottled beer is served, they seldom stay for a long time, but drink their beer and hurriedly disappear. Some just enter, cast a quick glance around the room and leave, having spotted no familiar sights. For the unaccustomed, such places are 'frightening', instilling in the bad performer a feeling of disorientation. When in Namanga, the Maasai typically occupy 'marginal' urban spaces, which underscores their peripheral position in a modern setting. For example, Maasai male customers are found more frequently in the 'local' bars (*-a kienyeji*) on the backstreets than in the main-street establishments; Maasai patients more often visit private dispensaries located on the outskirts of the town along roads leading to the rural hinterland than the centrally sited government dispensaries; the female hawkers on the edges of the market place are notoriously Maasai women. Those of them who engage in 'prostitution' are said to be found in the partly hidden local bars trading in home-brewed beer (or spirits), which is cheaper than bottled beer. Livestock transactions are settled in locales beyond the border of the town. Examples can be multiplied. Although geographically close and a place they frequent, to most Maasai, Namanga, largely inhabited and occupied by foreigners, is an alien place in which they themselves are mere ephemeral visitors. Namanga residents do not normally speak the Maasai vernacular, and they dress differently, have other food preferences and adhere to another moral order.

The Maasai experience the town as a place of the 'Swahili', a paraphrase of the traditional *ilmeek* (i.e. non-Maasai), chiefly agricultural people of Bantu origin, translated into English as 'savage' (Hollis, 1905; Mol, 1978). The Swahilis represent everything opposite to the Maasai: they do not herd cattle but till the soil, wear trousers, roam around, live in crowded places, lack respect for elders. Most significantly, Swahili men are not circumcised in the same way as the Maasai, a cultural marker that makes them incommensurable in status terms to adult Maasai men.[3] Because the non-Maasai lack the bravery and moral integrity brought about by circumcision and age-group initiation, Maasai males simply cannot relate to such people, whom they basically regard as 'children' (*olayioni*, a young uncircumcised boy not yet permitted to have sex with women); there is no appropriate term of address, no way of sharing meat, no mutual sentiments through common upbringing. Although a notion with multiple and variable meanings, Swahili is on the whole negatively charged and, to most Maasai, signifies distance and exclusion. Educated Maasai who wear trousers, are conversant with urban life and speak the Swahili language are, however, often referred to as 'Swahili'. The term may also be used jokingly sometimes, particularly with respect to children's behaviour. Wealthy and generous family members, even though they have settled in towns, are always respected and welcomed among the Maasai. In contrast, the poor ones, those working as watchmen, for instance, are constantly admonished to return home. The latter, as far as the Maasai see it, are 'lost' people, as they are of benefit neither to their families nor to the community.

In towns, the pastoralists are 'displaced' spatially and morally. By the haphazard mixing of people without due respect to gender, age or kinship, towns become insecure and polluting places. Not only do Maasai find themselves crowded together with an indiscriminate variety of people strikingly different from themselves – a situation they basically do not like – but the town is also the site where authorities of control most habitually demonstrate their power. The police, who take the Maasai to be ignorant city-dwellers, cynically exploit the latter's vulnerable position and demand bribes from them whenever the opportunity arises. To avoid 'problems' or prolonged arguments with the police, they normally pay without much resistance. Historically, the Maasai are renowned for their avoidance of officialdom by secluding themselves within their own territories and strategically withdrawing from communication with the state authorities.

Town visits, a necessity but also undoubtedly journeys of joy and leisure, are recurrent states of liminality, making the pastoralists vulnerable by exposing them to a 'dangerous' world. To the Maasai, however, Namanga, despite being a modern place in terms of spatial arrangements, mechanisms of control and social relations, is more familiar than most other towns. A stone's throw from their homesteads, the place after all has a strong Maasai 'component', not only by its location within Maasai territory, but also by the pastoral 'presence' in the production of 'local subjects' (Appadurai, 1995:205). References and experiences of Maasai cultural preferences and practices are immanent in Namanga residents' construction of reality, particularly in their images of poverty, prosperity, development and sexuality.

Poverty smells

A physician making home visits in a working class apartment building in Oslo, the capital of Norway, in the 1950s, claimed that, as soon as he entered the premises, he could 'smell the poverty' (*lukte fattigdommen*). The poverty was not visible from the outside, as this particular building happened to be located in a middle-class residential area. The distinctive odour of poverty, however, was unmistakable once he opened the door. In a similar fashion, some years back, residents in Moshi town in northern Tanzania would refuse to enter a bus carrying Maasai passengers because of their 'smell' (*arufu*). For the sake of personal care, Maasai customarily smear their bodies with sheep fat, giving them a different and character-istic odour, to which the other passengers reacted. This resulted in the more ambitious and expensive bus companies operating in Moshi refusing to take on Maasai passengers for a long time.

Smell carries messages and images of poverty, wealth, primitivity and can be cheap, expensive, foul or sweet or take on any other quality, depending upon a person's olfactory knowledge and experience. For Moshi residents, as for the Oslo physician, the perception of poverty was associated with a certain olfactory quality, with rancid fat and the stuffy smell of cooking, respectively. These particular odours were encoded with meanings of deprivation and lack of sophistication. In comparison, modern Tanzanians experience foreign and expensive fragrances, whether emanating from a person or sprinkled on wedding guests, as sure signs of progress and prosperity. Although a sensory ability, the meaning and interpretation of odours vary considerably. Our thinking about odours is morally charged: 'what smells good *is* good', and vice versa (Synott, 1993: 190). In contrast to other senses, odour has the potential of radiating from the subject, contaminating or shrouding those in the vicinity (Howes, 1990). A bad smell may linger for a longer time than a good smell on your body and in your hair and clothes and thus, in a very tangible way, invade your personal integrity. Olfactory codes carry a physical, experiential dimension, which makes the 'other' repulsive and potentially dangerous and contagious, but also attractive. An American journalist, sympathetic to the Maasai, ended her description of her first meeting with a Maasai *moran* in a crowded lift in Nairobi with an olfactory note: 'At the fourth floor, he stepped off the elevator and turned right. We all looked to see where he was going, but the door slid shut. Nobody said anything, but a *faint odor lingered, like the smoke of a cooking fire deep in forest'* (Bentsen, 1991:14, my italics). While the journalist interpreted the odour of the young Maasai man as related to something authentically natural, which she as a Western, modern person searched for and found intriguing, the Moshi residents were reminded of 'past times' (*zamani*) when they themselves were still 'poor' and 'did not know how to wash'. For those constantly struggling to improve their lives, memories of the past may be painful.

In Namanga, as elsewhere in Tanzania, poverty is associated with foul odours, dirtiness (*uchafu*) and ignorance. Beggars are the embodied poor. Although a relatively infrequent sight in Namanga, except for a few destitute elderly people, who are often also slightly mentally retarded, they are nevertheless held to be 'dirty', to smell and to be hapless creatures unfavoured by God. They do not wash, are clothed in rags and wander aimlessly around; beggars move in a bodily and spatial borderland. Their presence is somewhat disturbing and people avoid intimate contact with them.

The likening of Maasai to beggars surfaces in the development discourse. The Maasai are not considered destitute, like the beggars, but their appearance and way of life nevertheless conjure images and fantasies of the 'poor'. *Wana pesa, lakini* ... ('they have money, but ...'), an expression frequently heard, points to the fact that, irrespective of Maasai money possessions, by Namanga standards, their nomadic lifestyle does not bespeak prosperity and progress. As they do 'nothing' with their riches by converting them into material comfort, i.e. permanent houses, good hygiene, a composite diet or 'proper' clothes, their property 'serves no purpose' (*haina faida*). What is the use of owning several hundred livestock when you continue to live in a house like a *kombi*, non-Maasai argue? The analogy between the igloo-shaped Maasai house and the white Volkswagen Combi carrying tourists seems to chime with the pastoralists' lack of enlightenment and conservatism. 'Development' commentaries routinely blame and ridicule the Maasai priority of livestock at the expense of the welfare of the humans. 'Maasai poverty', as worked on in the development discourse, is both imbued with a multitude of sensory images and would appear to be less an issue of destitution than of loose morals.

The female bar attendants, who in general were meticulous about their hygienic standard by always keeping their bodies washed, shaved and oiled, elaborated on the 'dirt' (*uchafu*) of the Maasai. This was, according to the women themselves, a major reason why they were reluctant to entertain them sexually. Their 'dirtiness' did not only make them unattractive to the 'eye', but also made them dangerous as far as disease transmission was concerned. People are afraid of diseases 'these days', the women claimed, alluding to the unspoken, but nevertheless acknowledged reality of the spread of AIDS. Health workers hold that venereal diseases are rampant in the Maasai communities causing, among other things, a high rate of infertility among the women. They attribute the prevalence of such diseases to the pastoralists' lack of personal hygiene, to 'promiscuous' sexual practices by age-mates having access to each other's wives and to poor health facilities in the Maasai localities. For fear of being contaminated, men say they shy away from bar women known to associate with the Maasai. In a place such as Namanga, where relations are fluid and norms and standards of behaviour to a large extent creations of the moment, bodily cleanliness appears to be an imperative to secure moral respectability.

Maasai 'dirtiness' is primarily associated with the wearing of the *shuka* or *rubega* (cotton togas) and the smearing of the body with animal fat (*mafuta*). The habits of blowing their noses and spitting 'everywhere' are particular revolting bodily practices to outsiders. The term *shuka* embodies a number of Maasai characteristics: pierced ear lobes, shaved head, removal of lower incisors, lumps of chewing tobacco stuck behind ears, wearing sandals without socks and a number of other 'abnormalities' caught by the observant eye of the bar women. Even if he washed (as admitted by some women that they do), a person clad in a toga would still be 'dirty'. As a garment, the toga simply 'has no respect' (*haina heshima*). Being wrapped loosely around the body, the risk is always there, whether moving, sitting or standing, of exposing nakedness. Showing one's genitals in public, which some Maasai elders occasionally do, as they wear no shorts underneath, duly confirms Maasai 'backwardness' to others.

An ethnic Maasai in shirt and trousers is, on the other hand, considered 'civilized' (*staarabu*). He not only is properly dressed, but also most probably has attended school and, furthermore, has good manners in terms of speech and body language. These are all visible signs of progress, transforming him into a *safi* ('clean') person. *Wale wa shuka* ('those in togas') is an expression frequently used by the bar women to distinguish the traditional from the modern Maasai, but the phrase is not only used descriptively. It is also an idiom in the development discourse. For example, the Maasai dress became a large issue in Tanzania in the late 1960s and early 1970s. The Tanzanian government simply forbade the Maasai to wear their traditional clothes, on the pretext that they were 'indecent' and 'primitive'. The order was that Maasai men and women should change their togas for trousers and dresses, respectively. The government took a strong stand and declared that, if the Maasai refused to obey, they would be denied essential services, such as medical care, public transport and entrance to bars and restaurants. As a compromise, the Maasai men began to wear trousers whenever they moved in public places outside their own area. At home, however, they continued to dress as usual. The dress issue was recently on the political agenda in Tanzania again, but the response from the Maasai was all too familiar. In particular, the elders voice an intense dislike of modern clothes, such as shorts and trousers. They find them impractical, uncomfortable and unaesthetic; the 'tying' of the body with clothes like trousers not only constrains its movability, but also hampers easy and quick removal of body effluvia.

Among Namanga bar women as among Moshi residents and other urban dwellers, Maasai appearance symbolizes underdevelopment and ignorance, having reference to *zamani*, a time they are proud to have left behind. Irrespective of many Maasai having substantial amounts of cash tucked into their togas, their very look embodies primitiveness-cum-poverty and, in the urban context, typifies ambiguity and lack of order. Persons with shaved scalps and untailored clothing are, to the common Namanga dweller, simply an anachronism in a modern society. This irregularity is a matter-out-of-place phenomenon ('dirt'), to paraphrase Mary Douglas. Within the discursive field of development, 'Maasai traditions are in themselves dirty' (*asili ya Maasai ni chafu*).

Dirtiness has been a prevailing theme in representations by others of the Maasai. To mention but one example, Joseph Thomson, traversing Maasailand in the 1880s and, for his time, surprisingly accepting towards the Maasai, thought 'the ladies' would have been 'without fault [he admitted their beauty], if they had only discarded clay and grease and used Pears' soap' (1968 [1885]:195). He goes on, reasoning that the introduction of Pears' soap into the Maasai country would be a 'philanthropic effort' (ibid.). Thomson's view is echoed in the bar workers' elaboration on Maasai dirtiness and in many other voices outside confined Maasai circles. The definition of Maasai dirtiness and bad smell, as it were, is closely linked to cultural particularities. The fact that the pastoral Maasai continue to wear their traditional dress, however, even in settings requiring otherwise, is construed as a refusal to take on ideas of progress and change. The ideology embedded in the citation from the *Daily News* opening this chapter is that 'development' is an act of will. The lack of willingness to change is, in fact, taken by the authorities as a major factor contributing to the poverty of the Maasai.

The prejudices against the Maasai in terms of dirtiness appear to carry little weight for Maasai self-images; in fact, they seem to be more preoccupied with their own dislike of others. As early as 1905, Hollis reported that the Maasai thought that people from the coast stank like 'fowls' and they would never go near them or touch them if they could avoid it. There are also stories of Maasai who openly hold their noses, even vomit, when they get close to people who wash with soap. They find the smell of perfumed soap, in particular the brand Rexona, detestable. Perfumed soap is not associated with poverty, but with foreignness and non-Maasai values.

Intimacy as a discursive field

A Maasai woman married to a man who had three wives plus a mistress in town declared that her husband was particularly attracted by her 'soft skin'. In contrast to his rural wives, she explained, his mistress – a 'Swahili' of Maasai descent – could offer him warm baths, regular meals and soft mattresses. Her husband had no formal education, but was wealthy and attracted by the comfort and leisure that urban living offered. Many claim that his age-set, the *ilkingonde*, heralds preferences and behavioural practices that are 'ruining the Maasai'. Education is widespread among this age-set and many of them are involved in livestock trade, as well as other businesses, activities taking them well beyond Maasai fields of interaction and experience.

Hitherto, it has not been a widespread practice for non-educated Maasai to seek sexual solace from town women. Such relations happen occasionally, however, and, as far as the bar women in Namanga are concerned, they happen precisely because of money. In the words of one: 'If he has money, he is welcomed.' This statement implies that she would not mind his appearance or 'bad' odour as long as he pays well: after all, she has come to town in search of money. The Maasai, in order to compensate the women for their attributed dirtiness, will normally have to pay more dearly than other customers. The women rationalize their higher prices by bringing up their clean and shiny bodies on which they have invested considerable amounts of money, buying and using soap and body lotion. This is an argument that is accepted as the order of things by the Maasai customers and for which they agree to reciprocate with money.

Maasai men, particularly the livestock dealers, often carry large amounts of cash on them, and, as cash by itself is not a form of wealth they have learnt to appreciate in terms of savings, coupled with cash expenses still being relatively limited in the Maasai households, many, but definitely not all, squander substantial amounts of money at a time. The female bar workers appreciate this kind of behaviour and tend to see Maasai customers as an untapped resource. Their acknowledgement of Maasai money possessions does not change their basic opinion of the Maasai as 'poor', in the sense of being ignorant and primitive. In fact, their carelessness with cash is yet another sign of their 'poverty'.

Maasai male sexuality is a topic of much concern in Namanga. First, their special form of circumcision appears to give rise to lively speculation and fantasies. Some educated Namanga men thought of the remaining piece of foreskin after circumcision as an additional satisfaction to women during intercourse. That small piece of flesh, in their opinion, was a major reason why some women, against all odds, liked the Maasai. The women, less convinced about the satisfaction argument, would jokingly say that, when meeting with Maasai men, they were having sex with two penises simultaneously, euphemistically expressed as 'the driver and the co-driver'. No doubt, the image of two penises alludes to sexual potency and virility. Secondly, Maasai also have a reputation of having large penises and are held to possess considerable sexual stamina, of which some women claimed to be apprehensive. Describing the poor, the blacks, the working class and so on as sexually insatiable and unbridled is a well-known and common instrument of power, 'othering' and depreciation. Attributes of untamedness and physical defects depict the Maasai male as an animal-like creature, as 'wild' and 'uncivilized' (Knowles & Collett, 1989).

Their presumed physical abilities notwithstanding, Maasai men in general were held by Namanga women to be sexually 'ignorant', not knowing how to court a woman (*kufanya romans*; 'do romance'). The bar women are 'people of the town', who appreciate, covet and seek a modern living by pursuing individual experiences. Romantic love, as far as they see it, is part of this modern paradigm; a 'woman' wants to be entertained with bottled beer and roasted meat, hear sweet words spoken, be caressed and desired. They 'need' to be satisfied in all respects, economically and sexually, some of the Maasai complain, but nevertheless they succumb to the women's wishes. Young Maasai men with modern ambitions and attracted by the Swahili women are eager to learn how to 'satisfy' them. The novices consult those with more experience. If he does not perform well during the courting, the women may see him as a *maasai mshamba* ('Maasai from the bush'), a country bumpkin. The outgoing and independent bar woman acts her role well, by displaying, whenever the occasion arises, her professionalism in the field of love-making and eroticism, an attribute of a modern identity. In that respect, the Maasai male, in particular, the non-educated, constitutes a striking contrast, a situational 'other'.

Episodes of Maasai meeting with Swahili women (i.e. 'prostitutes') have informed local discursive expressions of 'otherness' and modernity, development and poverty. On the whole, Maasai men are not used to the idea of prostitutes and find it both ridiculous and slightly embarrassing to spend money on sex. Why should they pay for giving away their 'blood' (i.e. semen) which basically is to a woman's benefit? None the less, some of them, and, in particular, the younger ones, get involved in such relation-ships, either out of curiosity and a feeling of attraction to the Swahili women, appreciating variety, or because they are lured into them under the influence of alcohol and ready cash. One Maasai man who had sex with a bar woman got frustrated when she, according to her understanding of their relationship, began to twist and turn her body (-*kata kiuno*, 'break the waist') and make sounds during intercourse. 'Lie still,' he told her, 'so I may finish my work.' Another man asked the woman when she began to move, whether it was he 'doing it' on her or she on him. In the latter case, he wanted the money back! During sexual intercourse, Maasai men expect the woman to play a passive role or she risks being marked as immoral.

One Maasai even stole the women's money and disappeared while she went to the bathroom. Stories about encounters between Maasai men and Swahili women are told and retold, by both Maasai and non-Maasai, as proof of Maasai 'difference'. By narrating such stories, non-Maasai nourish their prejudices of the Maasai as ignorant and backward people; conversely, when Maasai elders reproduce the stories, they underscore the stupidity and weirdness of the Swahili. To the non-educated Maasai, these episodes are yet another example of the lack of aesthetics of the Swahili mode of behaviour and why it does not befit respectable Maasai to mix with such people. Educated Maasai narrate these and other stories with overt admiration and fascination for the Maasai demonstration of autonomy, cultural integrity and lack of respect for 'imposed' authorities.

The stories are always about relations between Maasai men and Swahili women and not vice versa. Sexual relations between Maasai women and Swahili men is a far more serious transgression of Maasai mores and dignity. Pastoral women, therefore, whenever they are involved in such activities, exercise the utmost care. If detected, they risk social isolation; they will be prohibited from participating in important age-grade promotion ceremonies and their fellow women will recount their stories in songs performed at ceremonies. 'Why do you bring back all this "dirt" to us?' the women are blamed. Swahili men, by not being circumcised the Maasai way, are, by definition, children, and within the Maasai moral order they are thus inappropriate and 'unclean' (*enturoto*) partners for adult, circumcised women.

Maasai women are not widely represented among the female bar attendants in Namanga. Recently, however, evidence of Maasai women getting involved in commercial sexual activities has come from several places, in both Kenya and Tanzania. Some ten to 15 years back, such occurrences were almost unheard of or not spoken of among the Maasai in Kenya, where I was conducting research (Talle, 1988). Prostitution as a means of survival, however, is not a totally new phenomenon to the Maasai. Luise White's historical account of prostitution in colonial Nairobi notes Maasai women frequently working as prostitutes at the beginning of the century. During that particular time, Maasai communities had gone through a veritable breakdown following a number of disasters, which were related to livestock epizootics and successive droughts. White's analysis of prostitution rests on an economic argument: first, income from daughters working as prostitutes was sent home for the benefit of the whole family and, second, female sexual and domestic services, by offering food and comfort, contributed to the production of the urban male labour force (White, 1990).

The pastoral women who are involved in commercial sex while in Namanga do not normally act within a modern paradigm, like the town women. Notably, also, the Maasai women are paid less than other women or are even paid in kind. They are said to be 'poor' and too ignorant to appreciate their body in terms of cash value. They 'meet with' their customers, are given their sugar or tea and return home to cook for their families. A general comment was that the Maasai women did it 'because of poverty' (*shauri ya umaskini*) and, unlike the Swahili women, were not in search of another kind of life. One educated Maasai, who runs a shop in Namanga, claimed that Maasai women are popular because they are 'cheap'. Consequently, they attract men with less purchasing power, which reinforces the others' conceptualization of the Maasai as 'poor' and marginal people.

Maasai often express disgust at the way the Swahili make love; they lick each other 'just like cats', touch 'here and there and cannot do one thing at a time, but fool around'. Also, within the intimate sphere of erotics, the Swahili and the Maasai are mutually 'dirty' to each other. While the Swahili associate Maasai 'dirt' with poverty and backwardness, Swahili 'dirtiness' is a matter of lack of aesthetics and incongruent morality for the Maasai.

A poverty icon

Within contemporary cultural and political debates, the educated Maasai élite continue to emphasize Maasai difference and 'otherness'. Two cultural conferences in Arusha town (1991 and 1994), organized and led by educated Maasai men, and the recent parliamentary election campaign (1995) in one of the Maasai districts, for example, underscored the historical and cultural uniqueness of the Maasai. Among all Tanzanian ethnic groups, the Maasai are the most authentic culturally and, as such, represent the cultural heritage of the country. By implication, it was argued, the position of the Maasai people within the national state merits special consideration. This line of argument is generally not approved by Tanzanian politicians and officials (often even including Maasai), who tend to see all ethnic mobilization as a form of 'tribalism'.

Educated Maasai are voicing concern that, as a group, they are 'losing their grip on their culture', at the same time urging Maasai elders to send their children to school, so as not to be left out of the development process. By reconciling the traditional with the modern, these relatively young men are trying to carve out a position for the modern, pastoral Maasai within the development discourse. Over the years, Maasai elders have repeatedly demonstrated, by practical examples, their will to combine technical innovation with a Maasai identity. Being politically marginalized and without power, however, they have not been able to raise a voice in the evolving debate on Maasai identity.

The conferences and the election campaign could be seen as a revival of an often vaguely defined concept of 'Maasainess', but now targeting an international or global audience. In order to underscore the disadvantaged position of their people within the nation-state, educated Maasai, as a plea for survival, increasingly refer to themselves as an 'indigenous group'. In recasting Maasai cultural uniqueness in such terms, they are, with considerable success, appealing to agents of development operating beyond the national scene. Within the contemporary global development discourse, emphasizing identity and authenticity, Maasai 'difference' has become a 'sign of distinction'. Representatives of the élite sometimes appear in togas (above their trousers or suits) at meetings and conferences, and traditional food and lodgings are offered to foreign guests. By bringing ethnic Maasai attire into wider, national and international contexts, they exalt their traditions – to the delight of foreigners, but sometimes to the embarrassment of other Tanzanians. The *shuka* has been 'cleansed' (even in a literal sense), also become harmless, as it were, by a situational redefinition.

As to the controversial issue of the Maasai *shuka*, curiously, bar women in Hedaru, a town south-west of Namanga, have begun to accept the Maasai in their togas. There, the Maasai, even those in the traditional garment, are said to wash and, besides, due to a long-established relationship between the pastoralists and their agricultural neighbours, Maasai speak their vernacular. These days, I was told, women in Hedaru do not associate the *shuka* with 'dirt' but with 'traditionalism', an attribute they, in contrast to Namanga women, find attractive. Apart from 'traditionalism', Maasai men may be attractive for other reasons as well, such as 'generosity' with money or locally based rumours of pastoralists being less exposed to HIV transmission, as they are considered to be 'fresh from the bush'. The positive evaluation of the 'bush' as free of disease and of the *shuka* as 'traditional', but not dirty, may signal a re-evaluation of Maasai living within the development discourse. The historically grounded representation of the Maasai as antiprogressive and inherently poor, however, continues to be heard in the current development discourse. When some educated Maasai have begun to talk about themselves as *sisi ni watu wa maskini* ('we are poor people'), they continue the story line of the grand narrative of Maasai 'backwardness'. The Swahili word *umaskini* is commonly used as a descriptive term for material destitution, as well as a reference to those deserving pity. The Maasai development spokesmen use *umaskini* as a euphemism of 'not yet being developed'. *Umaskini* implies that they lack 'everything': tractor, shops, schools, proper houses, sufficient food. The élite prefer to use the Swahili *umaskini*, even when they are speaking in their own vernacular, as their own term, *olaisinani*, does not work as a contrastive term to 'development'; it refers to poverty in terms of cattle holdings. In the context of the aid business and the tourist industry the 'modern' representation of the Maasai, alluding to cultural commitment and historical deprivation, has proved to be a particularly fortunate combination for generating funds.

In the development discourse, as noted, Maasai 'poverty' embodies multiple meanings, ranging from paucity of material goods to personal carelessness and low morality. Poverty has become synonymous with life-style: being Maasai simply means being poor in the sense of unenlightened and backward. Non-Maasai parents frequently use Maasai cultural specifics as a model negation for their children. A child in a kindergarten in Arusha scolded another who could not sit still in front of the TV screen while watching a cartoon for behaving 'like a Maasai'. To the young child, the term 'Maasai' served as an image of disorder. For development-orientated politicians, civil servants, bar attendants, parents or playmates, 'Maasai' social and cultural practices work as markers of bygone days and signal stagnation and inherent lack of progress. In the nation's struggle to forge ahead, the Maasai trope may, depending upon the context, work positively as a non-exemplary metaphor, but also negatively as a metonym of an 'uncivilized' state. The pastoral Maasai, the prototypical conserva-tive, is a poverty icon in the modern state.

Maasai themselves see things differently. They associate their pauperiza-tion precisely with 'development', which to them is synonymous with agricultural expansion, the establishment of schools, tourism promotion, market penetration and corrupt politicians. These factors, they claim, have contributed to the rapid loss of pastoral lands and to growing livestock sales in response to steadily increasing consumption needs. One young educated Maasai was illustrating the dire fate of his people by referring to the deteriorating pasture resources in one particular area, familiar to both of us, which had been subject to development initiatives in the form of land demarcation. 'They have all become beggars,' he stated, deploring the fact that the families could not survive any longer as pastoralists but were eking out a living from sporadic sources of income from non-pastoral pursuits. The cognition of the vanishing cattle herds, coupled with the expanded agricultural fields, continue to inform Maasai codification of poverty.

By way of contrast, Maasai cultural particularism seems to provide a rich ground for discursive arguments and elaborations on development and progress. In almost all respects, the Maasai differ from other Tanzanians: by sight and smell, management of space, body language, erotic performance. In local expressions of the development discourse, such as those evolving in the streets and bars of Namanga, Maasai 'poverty' is not primarily linked to materiality or survival, but rather to images of backwardness and disorder. Basically, poverty is communication through goods (Douglas, 1982). By being 'traditional'; the pastoral way of life rightly brings *zamani* into *sasa*, a continuity that cannot be accommodated within the development discourse of progress; the 'traditional', repre-senting authenthic Tanzanian culture, however, may continue into the present. What seems to be particularly disturbing to politicians and the

123

agents of authorities is that the Maasai appear to prefer to remain 'undeveloped' and, to that end, are, not without success, looking for outside resources. The re-representation of 'traditions' as something valuable, and not inherently bad, may very well create a 'crisis of category' within the current development discourse; and transforming 'traditions' into a discursive argument of 'culture' links up with other discourses of urgency in contemporary Tanzania.

Notes

1. This excerpt from an article in the largest daily in Tanzania quotes the Regional Commissioner of the Arusha region, the traditional domicile of the Tanzanian Maasai, as he gives an opening speech at a Maasai conference in Arusha town (June 1994).
2. This chapter is based upon material collected during a three-year engagement (1991–4) with the Norwegian–Tanzanian Acquired Immune Deficiency Syndrome (AIDS) Project. Field research was carried out in several Maasai localities. Sakita Olekaura's assistance during the field research is highly appreciated. Thanks also to colleagues of the Africa Seminar Group at the Department and Museum of Anthropology, University of Oslo, for valuable comments on an earlier version of the chapter.
3. At circumcision Maasai do not sever the foreskin completely, but leave it attached by a narrow string of flesh at the back of the glans penis. Earlier, this way of circumcision was common among other ethnic groups as well, such as the Kikuyu in Kenya.

6 'We are as Sheep & Goats': Iraqw & Datooga Discourses on Fortune, Failure & the Future[1]

OLE BJØRN REKDAL & ASTRID BLYSTAD

Like so many other pastoral and agropastoral peoples in Africa, the Datooga[2] and the Iraqw of northern Tanzania[3] have experienced dramatic changes during the course of this century. In this chapter we should like to discuss the highly divergent manner in which these two neighbouring peoples, who have had close inter-ethnic bonds for centuries, perceive, talk about and act upon the dramatic transformations connected with the distribution of land and livestock in the area where they reside. We shall try to show how the encounter between two sets of beliefs and practices embedded in a particular historical–political context have had, and continue to have, considerable effects on the development and future prospects of Datooga and Iraqw.

Among the Datooga who still remain in northern Tanzania, processes of marginalization, impoverishment and disintegration are today highly visible, and Datooga increasingly perceive their future prospects as bleak. This development has reached levels which Datooga, in particular contexts, read as signs of an unavoidable end to their lineages, and thus to the continuation of Datooga life. In contrast to this, the Iraqw, as a quickly expanding population, both geographically and demographically, commonly talk of themselves as relatively successful and prosperous and as a people who manage to manoeuvre victoriously through the challenges the modern world poses. We shall attempt to make sense of these diverging discourses on success and failure in a rapidly changing environment. The commentaries on such a substantial topic are obviously innumerable, complex and conflicting. We shall try to do justice to some of this complexity while at the same time focusing on certain dominant notions that continuously influence and are influenced by the way people act.

Deviating ideas related to what 'property' is, how wealth is measured and what it is to be wealthy or poor in these two communities seem to be significant in this context. Iraqw notions of wealth in particular reverberate around cultivated fields and livestock. A poor person or a pauper (*narkutmo*) will, in Iraqw thought, have neither cattle nor substantive fields for cultivation. Iraqw have been described as having a 'practical way of regarding stock', and the fact that there is 'little of the mystical about their attitude [to livestock]', was listed by Meek (1953:161) as an important reason for the 'outstanding' or 'spectacular success' of the Mbulu destocking scheme in the 1950s (Iliffe, 1979:473; Winter, 1968:22).

Among Datooga, the cattle herd is talked of as the only measure of true wealth. The Datooga expression *siida bar bar*, 'a person without anything', refers to a man without cattle. A farmer who has no cattle, no matter the size of his fields, is referred to as a 'person without anything'. In Datooga thought a major distinction is made between 'people with cattle' (*fuga dugwa*), and 'people without fat to smear' (*fuga murjeewi*), i.e. people without cattle. Diverging perceptions of land, as 'personal property' and as the 'property of God', respectively, will also be shown to be of significance.

Our material points to the necessity of taking a fresh look at some central religious notions and ritual practices in which discourses on fortune, failure and the future are embedded. A focus on diverging perceptions surrounding sources of fertility and the essence of ritual power appears to be particularly revealing if we are to understand the dynamics of poverty and prosperity in this area.

Situating the discourse

The Datooga and the Iraqw have been classified as Southern Nilotic pastoralists and Southern Cushitic agropastoralists, and their numbers have been roughly estimated to some 50,000–100,000 and 500,000 individuals, respectively.[4] Iraqw subsist primarily on the cultivation of maize, beans, and sorghum. Most families also keep cattle and some sheep, goats and chickens. In the area of study, this is increasingly a fitting description of Datooga subsistence as well.

Datooga, or Tara, as they are called by Iraqw, figure prominently in the latter's songs and tales. Let us start out with the presentation of the story that comes closest to an Iraqw origin myth, since it pinpoints some central Iraqw moral norms and political strategies and their relationship with the neighbouring Datooga. The following is a condensed version of the story:[5]

> Many years ago the Iraqw lived further to the south than they do today, in the fertile land of *Ma/angwatay*. The people prospered and became rich and strong in the favourable environment. Iraqw youth gained courage as their health and wealth improved, and at a confident moment they demanded that their leading ritual expert (*qwaslarmo*) go to the Datooga and arrange a battle between the young men of the two peoples. The *qwaslarmo* refused, but the youth forced him to comply by kidnapping and threatening to kill his child. He went to talk to the Datooga, and large numbers of Datooga youth were eventually sent off to

meet their Iraqw counterparts. The battle that ensued was disastrous for the Iraqw, and the survivors fled *Ma/angwatay*, following the *qwaslarmo*. He led them to an area he, by ritual means, turned into a fertile and habitable land, today called *Irqwa Da/aw*.

A key issue in the story is the emphasis on the power and wisdom of the *qwaslarmo* and the elders in opposition to the rebellious youth. In defiance of the *qwaslarmo*'s words, the youth forced violent conflict upon their community, with catastrophic consequences. By their action, they not only violated norms of legitimate political and religious authority, but they also defied the strong ideological emphasis on non-confrontation and non-violence in Iraqw culture. The Datooga youth enter the stage not primarily as an enemy, but rather as a force that legitimately punishes those who have broken internal Iraqw norms. It is, however, hardly incidental that it is the Datooga who engage in battle with the Iraqw in the myth. We shall see below that the lesson of *Ma/angwatay* is strongly manifested in the way the Iraqw of this century are approaching the Datooga in an entirely different kind of battle and with an entirely different outcome.

Where the story of *Ma/angwatay* ends, in *Irqwa Da/aw*, the documented history of the Iraqw begins. Iraqw were confined to this mountainous area until the beginning of this century, when they started to move into the surrounding highlands. The subsequent population growth and the territorial expansion of Iraqw have been a most spectacular feature of the general development of this region (see, for example, Mitchell, 1932:7; Southall, 1961:161; Winter, 1963; Schultz, 1971; Snyder, 1996:318). A great majority of Iraqw today live in areas that were dominated by Datooga and, to some degree, by the Maasai at the end of the nineteenth century, and Iraqw expansion has been the single most important factor in the dramatic shrinkage of Datooga territory during this century.[6] Perhaps the most striking feature of this expansion is that it has occurred at the expense of neighbouring peoples who were stereotyped as both aggressive and militarily strong, without having prompted any large-scale retaliation or conflict.

Iraqw movements out of *Irqwa Da/aw* coincided with the arrival of European colonialists. Since colonial times, national policies have worked in favour of settled agriculture. Cultivating populations were perceived as easier to govern, to levy and to draft as labourers. Moreover, nomadic pastoralism has been discerned as incompatible with mandatory primary education, advances of national health programmes and development of the national economy. The creation of arbitrary borders, settlement schemes, cattle confiscation and state subsidies to farmers are policies that have worked against pastoral adaptation. Agriculturalists have taken advantage of the favourable policies, and Datooga land has shrunk due not only to Iraqw migration from the north but also to Nyaturu movements from the south, Iramba from the west and a number of ethnic groups coming in from Babati in the east (Wada, 1975:67).

The rapid expansion of state-subsidized cash-crop cultivation in the region after the Second World War continued unabated after independence. These policies were particularly successful among Iraqw (Raikes, 1975:96; Coulson, 1982: 58, 164) and implied an increasing rate of cultivator encroachment on Datooga land. Datooga land was again dramatically reduced when the Tanzania Canada Wheat Project (TCWP) took some 100,000 acres for large-scale mechanized wheat farming on the Bassotu plains in the 1970s and 1980s. The area seized by the wheat project amounts 'to as much as 50% of the area that was once available to Barabaig herds for grazing' (Lane, 1991:278).

In their encounters with the colonial power, crucial differences arose between Iraqw and Datooga modes of interaction with 'the outside' world. While Iraqw leaders engaged in dialogue with the colonialists, the Datooga sought to keep the new rulers at a distance. Although there had been a certain degree of fascination for both peoples on the part of the European administrators,[7] their characterizations of Iraqw and Datooga were soon fixed in images of docile and peaceful agropastoralists and hostile and aggressive pastoralists. These stereotypes became increasingly powerful and consequential in the following century. Agriculture officer J. Hartley wrote in the Mbulu District book in 1942 (cited by Snyder, 1993:24) that the Iraqw 'seem a tractable people', whereas the Datooga were described as 'practically unadministered' (Perham, 1976: 103). The policies against them reflected this stand. Public executions, recurring incidences of arbitrary imprisonment, forced enrolment in the army, collective cattle fines and discrimination in resource allocation have characterized Datooga modern history and, indeed, make up central parts of the Datooga calendar of this century.

The representations of the two peoples' responses to the Maasai offensive at the end of the nineteenth century exemplify the stereotypes of the Iraqw as peaceful and defensive[8] and the Datooga as offensive and violent. While Iraqw in the core area of *Irqwa Da/aw* built defensive subterranean caves in order to hide people and cattle from the Maasai scouts (Fosbrooke, 1954), the Datooga developed an institution which ensured rewards for the men who proved the most daring and effective in killing the enemy and capturing or recapturing cattle. This so-called custom of 'ritual killing' (*lilicht*) has, up to this day, been closely associated with the Datooga (Klima, 1970).

Aggression, warfare, raiding and killing have been recurring themes in the pastoral literature (Bollig, 1990; Galaty, 1991, 1993a; Sutton, 1993). Among the pastoral Datooga it is the Barbayiig sub-section in particular that has gained the dubious image as raiders and killers. Margery Perham, an influential lecturer in government and administration who travelled in the area in the 1920s, wrote that the Barbayiig:

cannot graduate as men and claim a wife until they have performed some valiant deed. The result is that no traveller in their country is safe, and the Barabaig are famous for the numbers of senseless and cruel murders they commit. (Perham 1976:103)

The quote is representative of writings on the Barbayiig, and reveals lack of knowledge (killing is not related to marriage among the Datooga) and lack of analytical distinction between ideology and practice. There is no question about the fact that throughout the years a number of killings have been carried out by Datooga against individuals of neighbouring ethnic groups: but highly erroneous accounts about what has taken place, as well as a lack of analysis about the particularities and socio-political contexts of each violent event have characterized both the older and many of the newer writings on the subject (e.g. Wilson, 1952: 44; Fouquer, 1955; Faust, 1969; Umesao, 1969: 87; Loiske, 1990: 97). Moreover, the scale of the killings has been blown quite out of proportion.[9]

Waller & Sobania (1994:47) write:

it is often asserted that pastoralism is by its nature aggressively warlike and expansionist, as communities seek more lands to accommodate their herds, which increase through breeding and raiding (Galaty, 1991) ... Though warfare and expansion are certainly an integral part of pastoral history, they are by no means the whole story ... peaceful interaction with the neighbours has generally been the norm except during short periods of extreme stress.

The account below will provide substance to this statement. Datooga modern history has indeed been a history of recurring incidents of violence, but the violence is characterized not by *lilicht* killings but by confrontations with armed government forces, with confiscation and killing of cattle by the latter and collective and random punishment and imprisonment of thousands of Datooga men (see, for example, Ndagala, 1991:82). During the course of the following analysis, the images of the 'peaceful' Iraqw and the 'aggressive' Datooga will become more nuanced and ambiguous and, we believe, more true to real life.

Iraqw have developed close ties with Datooga.[10] The Iraqw notion *hoomo* is indicative in this context. *Hoomo* refers to a member of another ethnic group and has clearly negative connotations. Datooga are frequently said to be outside this category (Rekdal, 1994:73–5). For their part, Datooga never regarded Iraqw as targets and legitimate prey for their ritual killings. The relationship between the two, as we shall see below, is hardly unambiguous, but the two peoples do regard each other as associates and allies. Neither their mutual interest in the exchange of crops for cattle nor the raids by the common enemy (the Maasai) during the second half of the nineteenth century can sufficiently account for the intimacy of the Iraqw–Datooga relationship. More significant, but not unrelated to the above factors, is the fact that the two groups have intermarried extensively for as long as genealogies can take us back in time.[11] The complexity of the interaction is reflected by the numerous individuals who claim Datooga descent, but who live in Iraqw-dominated areas and who are, in many cases, virtually indistinguishable from the Iraqw themselves. Simultaneously, one will find large numbers of individuals of Iraqw clan affiliation who use the Datooga language, dress and decoration, living in the Datooga dominated areas. These processes of incorporation of people from the one ethnic group into the other have been accompanied by a considerable diffusion of core cultural traits in both directions.

The intermingling of the two peoples has taken place to such a degree that the ethnic categories of Iraqw and Datooga are becoming increasingly blurred. A consequence of these processes is that one single individual can legitimately introduce himself or herself as belonging to more than one ethnic group or category. We recorded numerous examples of people who, in various contexts, made use of a range of seemingly mutually exclusive 'ethnic' labels. They appeared as Iraqw and Datooga, Mang'ati and Mbulu, as Barbayiig, Gisamjanga and Bajuuta, or as Swahili, all according to the context. The picture is further complicated by the fact that certain clans have both Iraqw and Datooga branches, implying the ethnic ambiguity of whole clans. These ethnic labels thus increasingly appear as flexible categories, internally ambiguous and contradictory and open to strategic manipulation.[12]

This complex scenario has important consequences for our discussion of Iraqw and Datooga idioms and practices, and it highlights the fact that the distinctions we attempt to explore are hardly as clear-cut and unproblematic as they may at first appear. It should be emphasized that it is the commentaries made by the people themselves about what is Iraqw and Datooga that we wish to discuss.

'We are as sheep and goats': Discourses on how to manoeuvre in a challenging world

The Datooga was noticeably affected when he responded to an enquiry about the consequences of graves being destroyed by the wheat project in Hanang. 'How can our parents, whose houses have been levelled with the ground, ensure the growth of our lineages? The trees that were there sprouting with life are gone, and so are we.'

A young Iraqw who was present commented on the incident at a later point by saying: 'Talking about such matters is what makes the Datooga vulnerable. We, the Iraqw, know what to keep quiet about, and therefore we win. Our two tribes are as sheep and goats: the one quietly watches the world before slowly moving; the other passionately acts upon it for everyone to see and hear.'

Statements like these were not out of the ordinary. The sheep/goat metaphor was frequently used by both Iraqw and Datooga to characterize

130

modes of discourse. The sheep is in both Iraqw and Datooga thought a most noble animal, which, due to its inherent grace and tranquillity, is the animal sought for ritual sacrifice.[13] The docility of the sheep and the fieriness of the goat are quite revealing metaphors for certain aspects of the two peoples' discourse and action. Interestingly, the sheep/goat metaphor also has other denotations. Goats are known to be quicker and more intelligent than sheep. Sheep are rarely herded alone, as they will roam aimlessly around if not led by goats. The metaphor is thus an ambiguous one and is used by Datooga to indicate their own wits and quick remarks, which contrast with the reserved demeanour and controlled commentary of Iraqw.

It was our almost daily experience that Datooga would share large and small events with us, talking openly about their thoughts and frequently their longings, worries, fears and pain.[14] In contrast to this, even after years of acquaintance, many Iraqw would talk to us only after thoroughly questioning us about our motives and only after being reassured that no one, neither Iraqw nor Datooga, was listening. Moreover, Iraqw would frequently present their stories in such a manner that the information could not be taken at face value, i.e. it would often not reflect how the matters were actually experienced by the speaker. The secrecy, scepticism and reserved demeanour of Iraqw have been found quite noteworthy, and the phenomenon has repeatedly been referred to in introductions to ethnographic contributions from the area. These generalizations are based on more than the stereotypes made by outsiders, whether they were neighbouring ethnic groups or foreign researchers. Iraqw themselves comment on this cultural feature, and its value is expressed in numerous Iraqw sayings and proverbs, as well as in folk-tales (see, for example, Kamera, 1978; Hauge, 1981). The youth's alleged loss of the ability to keep secrets is indeed referred to by present-day Iraqw elders as a sign of the degeneration of Iraqw culture.[15]

The emphasis among Iraqw on the virtue of secrecy does not, however, imply that they are generally without interest in telling stories or in getting their opinions across. Pride about their achievements and successes was a common topic of discussion. Stories about how Iraqw outwitted Datooga, Iraqw imaginative strategies and their ability to maintain a mute and unpretentious image and, last but not least, stories about their wisdom in keeping outsiders outside when deemed appropriate were brought up on innumerable occasions. Extensive knowledge of medicines, spells and rituals to be utilized when facing problems or new challenges was said to be crucial. According to Iraqw informants, this knowledge was continuously manipulated in their quest for land and for women who would enlarge Iraqw families and clans. As proof of their success, Iraqw would often refer to the land they had recently seized, and to the growth of their clans.

131

'We are as hyenas and the lion': the story of acquiring land

A typical account of how Iraqw manage to enter and take over Datooga land was presented by a central informant who told us about how he managed to get his family settled in a Datooga-dominated area:

> We had for several years been ready to move from Endagulda. My father had left my mother with 13 children and many sons, and the land in Endagulda was becoming scarce and overcrowded. We had a relative in the south in Endaba-langda, so we decided to pay him a visit and ask about the conditions in the area. Rumours told that the land was fertile and plenty there, but we were reluctant to enter the area since it was Datooga land. But we went and talked to our cousin, and he confirmed what we had heard: 'There is land here, good soil and water is not far away. From here it all depends upon our wits.'
>
> We decided to give it a try, and started the procedure which eventually facilitated the movement of our whole family. Our cousin went to visit the Datooga neighbour he was on best terms with, a man who had married his mother's sister. He told him he had some brothers who were in great trouble because of the drought, and who had nowhere to herd their cattle. He asked him to accept us on the land one dry season. Nothing troubles the Datooga more than to hear that cattle suffer, so he accepted the request, but stressed that we would be expected to move when the rains started.
>
> A few of us moved on to the new land, and later more came, all of us living crowded in a tiny grass hut. We tried to hide the fact that we were so many, since our only task was supposedly to herd a few cows. During the nights we put up a thorn fence enclosing about an acre where we planned to cultivate the following season. We hooked our enclosure on to the fenced-in area where our cousin kept his cattle grazing at the end of the dry season, so the Datooga would not notice what was going on.
>
> It all went well at first, but one day our neighbouring Datooga discovered that something beyond the agreement was taking place. There were meetings, frightening meetings, where it seemed as if we would have to get out of the area immediately. But we spoke about the hardships at home, and that it was indeed a temporary solution in order to save the lives of cattle, women and children. Our cousin and his Datooga in-law supported our pleas and confirmed our good intentions. We managed to stay on, but at this point we contacted a ritual expert who supplied us with medicines that diminish Datooga vigilance, which we applied to the surrounding land.
>
> Keeping a low profile, we continued to struggle, constructing the fence and applying medicine. The complaints ceased for a time, only to return later with greater force. At this point we realized that we needed more help. Several of the village leaders were Iraqw and could read and write, and it was not the first time they had assisted immigrants in matters like these. We gave them some shillings, and the complaints soon ceased. We don't know exactly what happened, but the main Datooga complainants have moved to Manyoni, so we are fine now. These days our children can even play freely outside.

Similar stories were numerous, and many of them implied that this type of movement was not a new trend. Iraqw informants readily recognized that Iraqw needed Datooga to prosper, but emphasized that secrecy, inventiveness and manipulation in their relations with Datooga ensured their continued growth and well-being. The conquest of Datooga land is a common theme in Iraqw ritual prayers:

> Those people from the south,
> from another tribe.
> Those who are Barabaig.
> Their island there,
> let us take it from them.
> The bracelet which their elders wear,
> let it be lost and let our elder pick it up.
> (Snyder, 1993:299)

Datooga hold that they are well aware of the manner in which Iraqw enter their land. Informants would tell us that they know about the first careful Iraqw 'intruders', who are later accompanied by their numerous relatives, about the efficacy of the medicines they apply to their fields and about the 'clever words' and contacts of Iraqw. However, although Datooga may talk with aversion about the strategies of their Iraqw neighbours, Datooga frequently choose not to confront directly what they regard as 'invading' people. Instead, they will often move away and commonly leave nothing behind that can help them to reclaim the land they lived on at a later date. The following verse from a Datooga cattle song talks about Iraqw farmers, their witchcraft and the Datooga reaction to it:

> I start out the song of the bull Gillagen
> who has white fore feet
> The fore feet are not like those of the Iraqw[16]
> who only cultivate
> If he [the bull] says let us move in the middle of the night,
> I start to sharpen the axe if it is dull
> I call on the women to milk the cows
> so that we can get off to Gideweer
> If the cows bellow
> the Iraqw will hear it,
> and they will use their witchcraft if you are near them
> I do not want to be bothered by their witches
> so I got away early,
> and moved to the place where Gillagen said:
> 'here we are agreed upon' [by the spirits]

Datooga informants told us that they looked upon Iraqw as annoying weeds. The expression *neyekcheanda siginiida* refers to Iraqw (*neyekcheanda*) being like the *siginiida*, a type of weed it is almost impossible to get rid of. The *siginiida*'s roots grow laterally underground, suddenly penetrating the surface of the earth, sprouting and exhibiting excessive growth within a short period of time. Informants would tell us that, when Iraqw first moved on to their land, they knew they had come to stay and would ultimately force people to move, just like the *siginiida* does.

Ideologically, Datooga disdain living for long periods of time in one spot, and moving is praised in song and myth, despite the fact that Datooga themselves are increasingly adopting fairly permanent settlement patterns. Ensuring the livelihood of the herds through the search for satisfactory grazing and watering conditions is the primary incentive for Datooga to move away from the land on which they reside. Moreover, such moves are linked with the concept that land is 'growing old' *(wosinda ng'yeanyiida*, lit. 'old land') and needs renewal. The complex traditional Datooga rotational grazing system, which implies moving between a number of different forage regimes, is based upon a comprehensive knowledge of local species of grasses, herbs, shrubs and trees, on seasonal changes and geographical variability and on disease threats to human beings, livestock and vegetation.[17] Iraqw also recognize that land needs rest and renewal, but to a large extent solve the problem by extensive use of cow dung as fertilizer, intercropping and fallowing.

The diverging manner in which Iraqw and Datooga perceive their supreme deities to acknowledge possession of land is most noteworthy in this context. For Datooga, land is the property of *Aseeta*, and can only be used temporarily by human beings and livestock. Datooga do, however, have complex norms of rights to 'protect land' (*weta ng'yeanyiida*) and 'usufruct rights to land' (*ghang'wanyi ng'yeanyiida*). These imply rights either for the entire ethnic category, for clans or for individuals, and involve rights over homesteads, certain trees, water sources, sacred locations, enclosures of grass reserves for grazing and farming land (Lane, 1991:233–5). But the rights do not involve individual ownership, and there are powerful notions of what is morally acceptable and what is not. Claims to large areas of land reserves *(radaneda)* or permanent possession of land are perceived as 'a sin against God' *(ring'eed Aseeta)*. Such impetuous acts are said to awaken the wrath of the spirits and the deity and to cause misfortune and death.[18] Political leaders' continuous attempts to encourage Datooga to legalize land titles have fallen on deaf ears.

Iraqw acknowledge rights to possession of land which go beyond those of Datooga: farming land is regarded as a particular individual's property as long as he cultivates it. Datooga informants told us that Iraqw acted as if they 'owned' the land they lived on, and made claims on land which for a Datooga were immoral in both scope and content.[19] The inclination of Datooga to move is also connected with their conceptualizations of land and spirits. Hardships of people or cattle are read as signs or warnings from the spirits that the time has come to change habitat. Disease, drought or deaths perceived as exceeding the normal are in this way partially linked up with the relationship between human beings and the moral authority of the spirits. We shall return to this below.

Datooga informants held that living in overcrowded conditions also cause the spread of pollution and illness among human as well as livestock populations. Witchcraft, rare among Datooga, was said to proliferate with the arrival of Iraqw. The few Datooga witches who were pointed out to us were all said to have 'Iraqw blood'. As was expressed in the song presented above, living close to Iraqw is therefore also associated with dangers of becoming a target of these evil forces.[20] With this understanding, it is not difficult to grasp that it makes many Datooga uneasy to stay on in one location for a long period of time, particularly when they are surrounded by Iraqw farmers. None the less, today many choose to remain in one location due to lack of livestock or, in a few instances, as part of a strategy of dividing up wealthy polygamous households into several units.

The 'Iraqw problem', however, is a continuous one since, as Datooga see it, Iraqw are bound to follow in the footsteps of the Datooga. Datooga will frequently substitute the sheep/goat metaphor with another dichotomous animal metaphor when they describe the manner in which new land is secured. They refer to themselves as the lion who daringly goes in front, being the 'killer' and the true conqueror. Iraqw are the hyenas who follow behind and who consume the rewards earned by Datooga courage, strength and hardships.[21] An Iraqw informant referred to the same phenomenon by citing an Iraqw proverb, 'The first harvest is eaten by birds,' and explained that the Iraqw will always be able to follow the Datooga 'because they marry our daughters'.

The story of acquiring wives

A brief look at the dynamics at work in connection with the exchange of women, and indirectly of children, is of significance in this context, since the logic involved in the acquisition of wives seems to be similar to the one we have encountered when talking about Iraqw acquisition of land.

Let us grow fat
Let us press to the north
And also press to the south
And let us increase our power
Let us tread the mountains under our feet
Let us take the young women of other tribes as brides
Young women, come from afar, and give birth in our land
Women, come from afar, and increase the offspring in our land
Cows, come from afar, and increase the offspring in our land
Sheep, come from afar, and increase the offspring in our land
(Wada, 1978:48)

There is a place in the south
Where is that place?
There among the Barabaig.
The cattle thoroughfares remaining between the fields
Now even these are finished (by us)
Like this we shall finish it all
The Barabaig women

Oh yes
Shall stoop
To take our hoes in their hands
(Thornton 1980:122)[22]

As we see in these Iraqw prayers, the theme of acquisition, as well as that of incorporation and conquest, appears in discourses both on seizing new land and on acquiring wives.

Datooga intermarriage with Iraqw women often seems to be perceived and talked about in a different manner from that when Iraqw men marry Datooga women. Intermarriage with Iraqw women has been, and to some degree still is, thought of as a Datooga strategy for getting out of a cycle of poverty (see, for example, Talle & Holmquist, 1979). Today, however, it is not only poor Datooga who marry Iraqw women. It is quite common for educated Datooga men to marry Iraqw women with school education. The typical way of talking about intermarriage between Datooga men and Iraqw women none the less appears to be Datooga men who are unpopular on the marriage market going to the Iraqw to search for a wife, e.g. men with handicaps, men who have got into mischief or men who are struck by misfortune or poverty. The last category is a not insignificant group. One poor Datooga man whom we first encountered while he was cutting grass on the hospital grounds in order to pay off the bills for his Datooga wife, who had just died, later married an Iraqw woman. The woman, according to the man, had 'exceptional farming skills' and would most certainly get their life back on track.

Iraqw women who were initially given in marriage to Datooga were also said to have had certain hardships which affected their marriageability status in their own society. They were often women who had become pregnant before marriage or who had lost an illegitimate child while still nursing it. These incidents are perceived as threatening to the surroundings, causing pollution (*doroway* or *xawi*) and requiring extensive quarantining (*meeta*). The Datooga man, in the example above, married an Iraqw woman who had had several pregnancies out of wedlock. As a factor promoting interethnic marriage between Datooga men and Iraqw women, however, these pollution beliefs are becoming less significant. This is so because these unfortunate girls are becoming less feared among educated and Christianized Iraqw, but also because Datooga are incorporating the fear of these types of ritual pollution.

The vantage point for marriage between Iraqw men and Datooga women is, to a certain degree a consequence of the factors we have mentioned above; Iraqw women marrying Datooga men implies the creation of an affinal relation which can later be exploited by male Iraqw relatives in search of land (e.g. Rekdal, 1994:95–6). The sparsely populated Datooga areas have been particularly attractive for Iraqw men who were rich in cattle and who would, for this reason, be popular on any marriage market in the region. When Datooga give their daughters in marriage to economically powerful Iraqw individuals, they seek to ensure the well-being of their daughters and simultanously create affinal alliances of substantial political and economic potential. Moreover, these immigrating, largely pastoral, Iraqw often secure their position on the land by marrying additional Datooga wives, thus establishing further and stronger ties with various sections of the dominant population in the area[23]. The individual who was undoubtedly the richest in cattle in the area where we conducted our second period of fieldwork appears to have followed precisely such a strategy. As a wealthy Iraqw cattle owner with affinal ties to Datooga, he moved into a Datooga-dominated area and, in the coming years, married three Datooga women. Several of the man's sons are today engaged in mechanized agriculture and cultivate vast areas of land which only a generation ago was Datooga pasture. Evidence from Hanang and Mangola indicates that similar processes have taken place throughout the region. Tomikawa (1970) and Fukui (1970) mention largely pastoral Iraqw who live among Datooga and marry their women. Tomikawa describes the phenomenon as 'assimilation', and Fukui claims that 'their lives are not different from those of the Datoga'. To what extent these processes may be talked of as 'assimilation' or 'incorporation' can possibly be questioned, but the fact that Iraqw male immigrants retain their clan affiliation implies that ties and obligations are maintained which may be activated by other Iraqw on the search not only for pasture, but as is increasingly the case, for areas to cultivate.

We can broadly sum up this scenario in the following manner. Both Iraqw and Datooga men marry women from the other ethnic category for strategic reasons, but the primary motivating factors behind these inter-ethnic marriages seem to differ between the two. While Datooga men who, for some reason, are undesirable as marriage partners among their own seek Iraqw wives in order to reproduce their lineages and to gain the cultivating skills that can ensure the well-being of their families, Iraqw men who marry Datooga women are often successful individuals who seek Datooga wives in order to get access to new land for grazing. Both cases, we argue, establish kinship relations which may later be mobilized by Iraqw who need access to new land, for both grazing and cultivation.

Tension that arises in households with both Iraqw and Datooga wives is a common theme in Datooga song and tale:

My husband married an Iraqw woman
She is like an Iramba
who cannot wear the leather skirt of the Datooga
I will not talk to her and I will not compete with her
We are not equal
I don't want to be compared with a woman
who is more burden than help

This woman can't cross a river
she doesn't know how to walk
She is like the watchmen of Mbulu
who deprive people of their rights.

…

When I was still in confinement
I went to milk the cows in the evening
The Iraqw woman came up behind me
She made noise like a vulture
because of her greed for milk
When my children cried
I told them to keep quiet
A woman has entered this home
who has no shame
She acts like a poisonous scorpion
and prevents Datooga children from getting their milk

Both Iraqw and Datooga continuously denounce various aspects of one another's culture. The quiet comments about the other's dubious or evil traits and mischief in one context, however, are substituted by open demonstrations of friendship and brotherhood in other contexts. While conflict and controversy continue to go hand in hand with comradeship and cooperation, the crux of the problem is visibly apparent to everyone: Iraqw are taking over Datooga land.

The 'docile sheep' appears throughout the last several pages to have gained qualities beyond those of quietude, gentleness and nobility. The docility seems rather to have been substituted by assertiveness, initiative and conquest, while the fieriness and passion of the goat have been replaced by avoidance and withdrawal. The following verses from Iraqw and Datooga ritual prayers highlight this point:

We [the Iraqw] will be alive forever
Oh! our mother land!
They were born on this land
from where we have come
We have accepted alien tribes.
The authority falls on us.
They have accepted the rule and the order of our community.
(Wada, 1969:120)

And when their spears have been stuck into the ground,
Let them use the hoes which have been used by us …
And the Barabaig who decides to live amongst us,
let him merge with our tribe and become Iraqw
(Snyder, 1993:303)

Spirits, whose hands are of mastery
the Datooga are calling you
We, the daughters of the houses
who are neither going west nor east
If we go east to the Mbugwe we are speared

If we go to the Iraqw we are called names
The Iraqw have never made us fertile
they did not cause our lineages to thrive
And to heaven we cannot go
There is no path

On space and spirits

In the next section, we should like to move from the discourses on land
and livestock, fortune and failure, to an encounter between differing
religious concepts and ritual practices. We should like to focus on certain
central concepts of faith among these two peoples, as we believe this is
essential for reaching a better understanding of the diverging discourses
we have outlined above. Important aspects of the relationship between the
Iraqw and the Datooga are pinpointed by the activities of their ritual
experts and by certain characteristics of the respective clusters of beliefs
they derive their legitimacy and power from. We shall argue that these
beliefs and practices influence the two peoples' potential access to
resources.

Both Iraqw and Datooga traditional religions have high gods, called
Looaa and *Aseeta*, respectively. These supreme beings appear to be
relatively distanced from the everyday life of people, but are regarded as
the ultimate sources of fertility and blessings for people, cattle and land.

The land is, in both Datooga and Iraqw thought, inhabited by the
spirits of the dead. The contrasting significance placed on these spirits,
however, is most noteworthy. The transformation of a human being into a
spirit at death by means of the *bung'eed* ceremony is a prominent feature in
Datooga ritual life. Certain distinguished men and women are buried
'officially', i.e. a decision is reached to honour a particular person with an
elaborate funeral ceremony in which large numbers of people, men and
women, young and old, are involved. The corpse is placed in a foetus-like
position in a burial mound which is enlarged in height and width for nine
months, after which time the deceased is said to be reborn into the spirit
world. This takes place in front of the 'entire' Datooga community in
grandiose displays of fertility and growth.[24] The large burial mound will
gradually deteriorate and through the years be transformed into a sacred
grove of trees which is sought for blessings and redemption, both by
individuals and by groups of people, for many generations after 'the spirit
was born'. The reborn spirits (*meanga* or *fuguuta ng'yeanyiida*, literally,
'ancestors of the land') become the guardians of Datooga fecundity and
well-being, but may also act punitively towards individuals or towards the
community as a whole, as a response to immoral behaviour. The spirits
appear visibly in the form of certain small black snakes, which often enter
Datooga homesteads. Their voices are heard through female mediums,

they frequently express both anger and advice via the dreams of the diviners and they are continually called upon in prayer. In Datooga thought the spirits, both male and female, are the mediators between *Aseeta* and the people, and thus facilitate communication between them.

The significance of the spirits 'of the dead' is rather restricted among Iraqw. The funerals are far more limited in scale and scope, and are commonly only attended by the immediate family and neighbours. The dead are transformed into spirits (*gi'i*), but *gi'i* are rarely referred to or called upon in prayer, and graves are not returned to for sacrifice or prayer by anyone but the immediate relatives (Winter, 1964; 1968:7). Unlike Datooga *meanga*, the influence of Iraqw *gi'i* is said to have mainly negative impact upon the living. Any sacrifice made to them is explicitly motivated by a wish to keep them content and at a distance. While the *meanga* are invariably spirits of elders with numerous descendants and may adequately be translated as 'ancestor spirits', the *gi'i* may well be the spirits of young members of society who did not have offspring at the time of their death.

The *daremgajeega*, certain members of six clans who have both healing and prophetic powers, are perceived as the mundane extension of the Datooga *meanga*. They may even be referred to by the same term, and are regarded as earthly guardians of Datooga moral order. Their faithful and authentic replication of ritual activity is perceived as being a vital part of ensuring that their community is blessed with fertile women and herds by satisfied spirit protectors. The distress which follows incidents of immoral behaviour or a deviation in the notions and practices which constitute the 'Datooga', particularly on the part of the *daremgajeega*, is substantial. The disputes and anxiety which arose in response to the death of Gidashiid are indicative of this phenomenon:

> Gidashiid, a prominent member of one of the most prestigious *daremgajeega* clans, died in the autumn of 1994. He was not very old, and had appeared healthy until just days before he died. He died at Haydom Lutheran Hospital, his body covered in blisters, and the doctors concluded that the cause of death was a rare infection. The Datooga community immediately initiated a search for the ultimate reason behind this peculiar and morbid death. It was of great importance to reveal what had taken the life of Gidashiid. In their opinion, it was not only the life of one man which was at stake, but the fertility and health of an entire community. Despite the disturbing circumstances of his death, he was now being honoured with an elaborate funeral ceremony, which was to bring blessings and fecundity upon the Datooga community.
>
> A number of explanations were brought forward during the nine months of preparation for the final phase of his funeral. Some centred around the ritual powers of other *daremgajeega*, who were accused of fighting with Gidashiid to the point that he died. Others argued that some Iraqw were envious of this man's ritual competence and killed him with their remedies or sorcery. That some Iraqw were envious of Gidashiid's son's agricultural success was well known, and this was also brought up to account for his death.

It then became apparent that Gidashiid's inclination to incorporate foreign elements into Datooga rituals was of great concern to many Datooga. Gidashiid had always been fond of inviting strangers to his home. This was thought of as a curious but permissible and amicable aspect of Gidashiid's personality. What was less tolerable, however, was that he had accepted missionary activity in his homestead, had welcomed spectators during important ritual sessions and had allowed picture taking and sound recording on such occasions. He had lately involved the male author of this chapter in the ritual *ginealda ghamunga*, in which he initiated two of his sons and the anthropologist into the elders' world of handling and consuming honey mead, the most significant medium used in communication between human beings and spirits. Through this act, it was said, Gidashiid might have brought the wrath of the spirits upon himself to the point that he was removed from earthly life.

The controversy over the cause of Gidashiid's death once again exemplifies the hidden struggle between Iraqw and Datooga. More importantly in this context, however, is that the discourse highlights the ideal role of the *daremgajeega* as guardians of an eternal Datooga moral order. Irregularity in a *daremnyand*'s (singular) thought and practice is perceived as a serious threat to Datooga life and prosperity.

The Iraqw *qwaslarmo* may act as ritual expert, healer, diviner or prophet, not unlike the Datooga *daremgajeega*. Their roles and the manner in which power is attributed to them, however, are rather different. The ultimate role of the *qwaslare* (plural) is not to guard an eternal moral ordinance, and their authority is not derived from unique links with the spirits. Rather, the *qwaslarmo*'s ritual power is, to a large extent, drawn from sources entirely external to Iraqw culture and the spirits. Their legitimacy as healers, diviners and ritual experts seems, in fact, to partially derive from the foreign ethnic origin of the *qwaslarmo* clans (Rekdal, n.d.).

Another category of central ritual importance in the Iraqw community is the *kahamuse*. One of their roles is to obtain from the *qwaslare* the 'medicine' (*maso aya*) required for the communal rituals of purification and protection of the land, rituals which they lead and supervise. The *kahamuse* earlier also had the responsibility of distributing land to Iraqw immigrants and others who wished to establish a household in their locality. The *kahamusmo* (singular) and the *qwaslarmo* represent the two most central positions of ritual and political authority within traditional Iraqw society. A focus on their roles may further our understanding of the connection between Iraqw religion and Iraqw expansion into areas dominated by other ethnic groups.

The now deceased *kahamusmo* Tua Masay told us that he had originally lived in *Irqwa Da/aw*. At the beginning of the 1950s, he was sent into the Iraqw expansion areas by Nade Bea, the most powerful *qwaslarmo* this century. Tua Masay was given medicines in order to protect himself and the Iraqw emigrants who followed him. The land he moved into had, up to that point, been infested with the tsetse-fly and was only sparsely

populated by Datooga. He settled in Maghang, approximately 12 kilometres from the Harar mountain. This mountain, whose characteristic
conical shape may be seen in the distance from the outskirts of *Irqwa
Da/aw*, is central in Iraqw cosmology. It was feared as a place of the
cursed, and the expanding Iraqw now found themselves living in close
proximity to it. In a ritual held at the foot of Harar, Tua Masay 'undid the
curse' of the mountain, opening the surrounding area for Iraqw
expansion. The great significance of this event is reflected in the way it is
spoken about in ritual prayers today, 40 years after it took place. The
following text was recorded at a harvest celebration held in an Iraqw-
dominated village close to Harar in 1994:

> Let us continue to live in peace
> Let us live here
> There is a place
> That place is Harar
> That place used to be cursed
> We have removed the evil
> That curse, let it be transformed
> Like a gourd adorned
> Our brothers have moved there
> Let the calves be branded
> Let that curse be transformed
> Like a gourd adorned

The pragmatism and inventiveness that characterize the lifting of the
curse of Harar can also be discerned in a number of other events referred
to in the Iraqw ethnography. Thornton (1980:124, 147, 244), who was
struck by the *ad hoc* nature of Iraqw rituals, provides examples of how
Iraqw leaders used similarly innovative means in order to achieve their
goals, such as the opening of the northern expansion areas and the
establishing of peaceful relations with the Maasai. The stories of the
victories of Iraqw political or religious leaders in fact often focus as much
on the wits and clever strategies of particular men as on the strength of
their ritual powers.[25]

The contrasting properties of the ritual experts of Iraqw and Datooga
may be illustrated by the kind of relationship they established with the
colonial administration. Gidamowsa, who was the most influential among
Datooga ritual experts at the beginning of this century, was captured and
hanged by the Germans in 1908 (Jellicoe, 1969:5). In contrast, the most
powerful among the Iraqw ritual experts during the colonial period, Nade
Bea, 'came down four-square on the side of government' (Meek,
1953:161) and became 'a great ally to have going for one', according to
the District Commissioner (Allen and Fry, 1979:85). According to
Ramadhani (1955:12), Nade Bea was even awarded the King George
Certificate and Badge of Honour by the British.

We shall argue that we are witnessing the encounter between two contrasting sets of religious concepts and practices. Datooga religion is centred around the *meanga*, who either reside on the earth, as *daremgajeega*, or under the earth, as spirits, and who guide and protect Datooga fertility with reference to eternal moral norms. Iraqw, on the other hand, are guided by ritual leaders, whose lack of strong ties to the ancestral spirit world give them a different base of power and what appears to be an altogether freer hand in their dealings with religious notions and ritual practices. However, the characteristically manipulative and innovative activity of Iraqw ritual leaders should not lead us to think that they are not acting as guardians of Iraqw culture. On the contrary, what is important to note is the manner in which they contribute to the incorporation of new elements (such as modern health services, the market economy or the Harar mountain) in ways which simultaneously preserve fundamental Iraqw beliefs and practices (Rekdal, 1994, 1996). The ritual redefinition of Harar may be regarded as an event that illustrates the manner in which the flexibility of Iraqw ritual promotes social change while simultaneously ensuring cultural continuity.

We have tried to show that the encounter between the dynamic Iraqw religious concepts and practice and the powerful but less adaptable Datooga religion thus creates grounds for advantageous Iraqw moves into Datooga land. Ideas of 'space' and ideas of 'spirits' must thus be analysed hand in hand if we are to reach a further understanding of the manner in which wealth is shifting hands in Hanang and Mbulu. Most significant in this context is the fact that the 'aggression' expressed in Iraqw daily discourse and ritual prayers under particular historical and political conditions is realized in actual practice. The Datooga 'island in the south' is indeed being 'finished' by Iraqw, and the remaining Datooga in the former Barabaig Chiefdom find themselves complying with 'the rule and the order of [Iraqw] community', as was expressed in the Iraqw texts presented above. Perhaps the most powerful illustration of what is taking place is the sight of Datooga labourers on Iraqw fields. These pastoralists, who so strongly dislike 'scratching the earth' under which their powerful spirits reside, may today be seen tilling the land with Iraqw as their patrons. The new order, which is ever more often transforming Datooga pastoralists into docile labourers on Iraqw farms, is, to Iraqw, a visible manifestation of their successful strategies of peaceful conquest. Datooga are literally 'putting their spears in the ground' and 'taking our hoes in their hands'. To Datooga, the sight is a reversal of the traditional interethnic ranking and one of the many disturbing signs of what lies ahead.

Again, it should be emphasized that the scenario we have outlined cannot be understood outside a larger political context. During the 1970s and 1980s, the TCWP ploughed down more than 50 burial mounds in order to clear 100,000 acres of Datooga land for mechanized, large-scale, wheat farming (Lane 1991:292). For Datooga, the destruction of these graves meant the demolition of the homes of their guardian spirits, the extermination of sanctuaries for prayer, shrines for offerings and sacred refuges where calm and solace had been sought for generations.

Statements by Datooga, such as 'the houses of our spirits are destroyed', 'our women are ceasing to wear the leather skirt', 'brothers are fighting', 'there is no more respect in the world', 'the Datooga marry like dogs nowadays', 'our children are eating maize now', all point to the manner in which the Datooga world is changing in ways perceived as threatening. Such statements are frequently presented together with more direct references to the poor physical condition of the landscape, the herds and the human population: 'the grass is dying', 'these days calves don't thrive', 'our herds are wasting away' and 'our children are dying'. The ultimate consequence of this scenario is the frequently expressed notion of 'Datooga lineages coming to an end' and of 'the death of the land' (*miyeeda ng'yeanyiida*).

Concluding remarks

We have argued that differing motions and notions among Iraqw and Datooga need to be recognized as a significant part of the dynamics of poverty and prosperity in the area in question. We should like to emphasize that our aim has not been to turn from stereotypes of 'aggressive' pastoralists to another set of simplified and outdated models presenting pastoralists as passive spectators of a dying way of life. In this chapter, we have rather tried to emphasize the importance of incorporating detailed analyses of the dynamics of local encounters in our accounts if we are to gain further insights into the flux of agricultural and pastoral adaptations.

Notes

1. We should like to thank Yusufu Q. Lawi, Festo Basso Samuhenda, Ørnulf Gulbrandsen, Georg Henriksen and the participants at the Workshop on Poverty and Prosperity of Pastoral Peoples (Uppsala, Sweden, September 1995) for useful comments on earlier drafts of this chapter. We should also like to thank Annemarie Heggenhougen for help with language editing. The Norwegian Research Council and the Scandinavian Institute of African Studies provided the funding of the fieldwork on which the present study is based. We are also grateful to the Tanzania Commission for Science and Technology for the necessary research permits and to the Centre for Development Studies and Centre for International Health, University of Bergen, for invaluable help and support.
Most personal names and some place names have been changed for confidentiality.
2. We use the spelling 'Datooga', as suggested by representatives from the Summer School of Linguistics, now working on a translation of the Bible into the Datooga language. Other variations include 'Dadog', 'Datoga', 'Tatog' and 'Tatoga'. The Datooga category

consists of some 13 sub-sections, which today are highly intermingled and of which the Barbayiig is numerically the largest.

We follow the convention of not conjugating ethnic terms according to sex and numbers.

3. The majority of the two populations live in the Mbulu, Karatu, Hanang and Babati districts of northern Tanzania, although large numbers of Datooga have, in recent years, moved out of these districts. As a result of these migrations, the Datooga may today be encountered in numerous other regions of the Tanzanian territory.

We carried out fieldwork in four separate locations in the western part of Hanang and the southern part of Mbulu Districts of Arusha Region between 1989 and 1995. We should like to emphasize that, in this chapter, we are writing primarily about the Iraqw and Datooga in the area where we have carried out fieldwork. There is good reason to expect that some of the ethnography we are presenting here may not be pertinent to Iraqw populations further north in Mbulu District, and even less so to the Datooga, who have dispersed over vast areas of Tanzania.

4. The Iraqw figure is based on Mous (1992:1). The Datooga estimate is derived from Lane (1990:6), who indicates that there are between 30,000 and 50,000 Barbayiig in Hanang District alone. Even a rough estimate of numbers is difficult to obtain, due to a lack of data on ethnic affiliation in Tanzanian censuses.

5. The story about the land of *Ma/angwatay* has been recorded in slightly different versions by a number of researchers (Fouquer, 1955:55; Ramadhani, 1955:1–4; Kamera, 1978:1–3; Nordbustad and Naman, 1978; Thornton, 1980: 205–6; Harri, 1989:2–4; Snyder, 1993:319; Berger and Kiessling, n.d.:110–13).

6. The extent to which this has occurred is exemplified by the fact that even what was originally Barabaig Chiefdom, becoming Hanang District in 1985, is now dominated numerically by the Iraqw. See also Schultz (1971) for a graphical illustration of the Iraqw expansion into areas previously dominated by the Datooga.

7. See Rekdal (1998) for a review of how the 'Hamitic hypothesis' shaped the Europeans' attitude towards the Iraqw and other 'Hamites', and in fact became a determining factor for the rise of a new Iraqw origin myth.

8. Bagshawe (1926:64), one of the District Officers in Mbulu, describes the Iraqw as 'experts in semi-passive resistance'.

9. See Blystad (1992, n.d.) for reviews of the *lilicht* tradition.

10. These representations seem to be somewhat at odds with the more general thesis that conflict between pastoralists and agropastoralists has been more common than between pastoralists and agriculturalists, who often have established relationships of mutual interdependence.

11. At least 25 of the approximately 150 Iraqw clans trace their origin to a male Datooga.

12. A Datooga we interviewed right after he was released after 18 years of imprisonment said that the most astonishing thing about his meeting with his homeland was that 'the land is not ours any more', and that 'the Datooga and the Iraqw are almost indistinguishable now'.

13. The use of the docile sheep as a metaphor for the Iraqw is also reported from the *Irqwa Da/aw* area (Snyder, 1993:264–5).

14. E.K. Lumley, a District Commissioner in the 1930s, makes the following comment about the Barbayiig: 'In manner they were frank and extrovert, and gave their views to me and others without hesitation' (1976:79).

15. See Salzman (1983) and Edgerton (1971) for discussions on the contrasting patterns of behaviour of pastoralists and cultivators. Their conclusions are very much in line with the data we are presenting here.

16. 'White forefeet' refers to the reluctance of many Datooga to engage their oxen in the work in front of the ploughs. They dislike the hardships the bulls suffer when they are used to farm the land and prefer to keep their 'forefeet white'. Despite the fact that they have suitable oxen to pull a plough, many Datooga use hand hoes or donkeys to cultivate.

17. See Lane (1991) for a detailed description of the traditional grazing rotation among the Datooga of Lagaujeanda in southern Hanang District.

18. See Lane (1991) for a discussion on Barbayiig concepts of property.

19. As Yusufu Q. Lawi (personal communication) has pointed out to us, the contrast between

the two ways of conceptualizing rights to land may be a recent development, related to a more general 'shift towards a market-oriented economy' among the Iraqw and 'a rather quick transformation of the values, attitudes and beliefs which in the past has held human society in organic unity with nature' (Lawi, 1992:51).

20. This observation is in accord with Baxter's assertion that witchcraft accusations are relatively rare among pastoral peoples in East Africa and that, when they occur, they are frequently directed at strangers or outsiders (Baxter, 1972).

21. The metaphor is highly ambiguous as both 'the spirits of the dead' (*gi'i*) and witches (*da/aluuse*) are associated with hyenas. When the hyenas cry at night, a common comment among the Datooga is that 'the Iraqw have come with their hyenas'.

22. It is revealing that these texts are recorded in areas with populations far more homogeneously Iraqw than is the case in the border areas where we conducted our research. We have made recordings from numerous Iraqw ritual occasions in the southern Mbulu and Hanang Districts, comprising several thousand pages of transcripts, but did not encounter statements about the Iraqw incorporating, taking over or alienating Datooga land or women which were as explicit as those presented in the texts above (and those below from Wada 1969; Snyder, 1993). The reason for this should be connected to the fact that both Datooga and Iraqw are commonly present at the larger ritual occasions in the area of our study, and it would obviously not be appropriate to voice such sentiments in the presence of the people who are to be 'conquered'.

23. Yusufu Lawi suggests (personal communication, June 1998) that an additional motive among these Iraqw for marrying Datooga women would be that the latter are generally regarded as having greater skills related to the tending and caring for cattle than do their Iraqw female counterparts.

24. In connection with large funerals (*bung'eed*), several thousand Datooga from all over Tanzania and quite a few Iraqw may be present on the last day of the ceremony.

25. See, for example, Berger and Kiessling (n.d.:97–101) for a story about a man without 'magical powers' who manages to outwit a powerful ritual expert.

III Coins & Calories

7 Health Consequences of Pastoral Sedentarization among Rendille of Northern Kenya

ELLIOT FRATKIN
MARTHA A. NATHAN
& ERIC ABELLA ROTH

The settling of formerly pastoralist populations is occurring at a rapid rate throughout northern and eastern Africa. While human and livestock populations grew in Africa throughout the 1950s and 1960s in response to both good rainfall and improved health services, pastoralists in Africa have suffered greatly since the late 1960s due to increasing ecological, social and political crises. Sahelian countries (e.g. Mali, Niger, northern Nigeria) experienced drought-induced famine in 1968–73, resulting in 100,000 deaths, while civil war and famine in the Horn led to over 1,000,000 deaths and the displacement of 8,000,000 people, particularly in 1982–4 in Ethiopia, 1988–91 in Sudan and 1991–2 in Somalia (Clay & Holcomb, 1986; Clay 1988; Cultural Survival, 1993; US Committee on Refugees 1993).

Though not facing the tribulations of civil war, many Kenyan pastoralists have abandoned their nomadic livestock economies to settle in or near towns, both in Kenya's arid northern districts (Turkana, Marsabit, Wajir, Garissa, Mandera) and in the Maasai areas of the south (Narok and Kajiado Districts). Pressures to settle include: (i) the loss of livestock to drought, particularly in 1984, 1992 and 1996; (ii) the loss of common-property rangelands to private ranchers and farmers, and the expansion of national game parks; (iii) the increased commoditization of livestock and the movement of pastoralists to market centres; and (iv) the massive distribution of famine-relief foods, especially in the north, leading to permanently settled populations as among the Turkana, Boran, Gabbra and Rendille (Campbell, 1984; Hogg, 1986, 1992; Fratkin, 1992, 1994, 1997; Galaty, 1992). The processes of social dislocation due to famine and war are not new to East African pastoralists (Johnson & Anderson, 1988; Spear & Waller, 1993), but movements towards sedentarization are occurring at accelerated rates as former nomads settle in response to political insecurity, loss of lands and the attractions of town life.

149

Throughout Africa's pastoralist regions, international development agencies and non-government organizations (NGOs) have encouraged the settling of nomadic pastoralists, often with the active cooperation of national African governments, which are usually made up of people from agricultural rather than pastoral backgrounds. In the development literature, the nomadic pastoral lifestyle has been variously characterized as 'primitive, irrational and wasteful', both environmentally harmful and detrimental to the national economy (Hardin, 1968; Horowitz, 1979; Lamprey, 1983). International aid donors, including the US Agency for International Development (USAID) and the World Bank, emphasize the benefits of commercial and private ranching over subsistence livestock herding on communal grazing resources. Large NGOs, including World Vision and Catholic Relief Services, actively encourage nomads to settle in towns or periurban locations to take advantage of increased educational, health-care, market and religious institutions (Fratkin, 1992).

Despite these claims of a better life, it is not clear that sedentarization benefits former pastoralists. Settled pastoralists do have better access to health-care, education, employment, the market economy and grains obtained in trade or relief (Fratkin, 1991; Ensminger, 1992); however, pastoralists are often separated from their animals – their main source of food, income and social identity. This identity is strongly tied to the daily and seasonal rhythms of livestock production, wherein men, women, adolescents and children have clearly demarcated roles, responsibilities and rewards in raising and exchanging domestic animals. Although many settled pastoralists may continue to own livestock, they are usually herded in distant areas, diminishing the role of their herds in the diet and daily life of settled communities.

Despite the centrality of livestock to pastoral populations, development agencies and national governments often discourage pastoral production, while promoting in its place alternative food strategies, such as farming, fishing or commercial ranching. These pronouncements continue today, despite repeated evidence from anthropologists and ecologists to demonstrate that mobile livestock pastoralism is the best adapted and, in many cases, the only food production system possible throughout much of the semi-arid and arid lands of eastern Africa (Coughernour *et al.*, 1985; Horowitz and Little, 1987; McCabe, 1990; Baxter, 1991; Homewood & Rodgers, 1991; Schwartz & Dioli, 1992).

What are the consequences of pastoral sedentarization, and how do we measure the costs and the benefits of this large social transformation? We believe that there are some basic measurements that allow us to judge the success of a human community, and that is the survival and development of its children. Specifically, higher rates of malnutrition, disease and infant and child mortality indicate a less successful strategy than those strategies with lower rates. Therefore we chose to compare the predictors of child survival – nutritional status and infectious disease prevalence – as indicators of successful social adaptation strategies by the communities we studied. Beginning in 1990, we (a social anthropologist, medical doctor and anthropological demographer) began a longitudinal study of women and children in three (later five) Rendille communities – one fully nomadic, a second settled with animals and small gardens and a third settled and dependent on famine relief. In our initial study in 1990 and 1992, we compared morbidity patterns, diet, income and anthropometric measurements (height, weight, arm circumference) of settled and nomadic children and their mothers; we also interviewed women about their children's diet, clinic visits, vaccinations and economic status. Our objective was to determine whether settled or nomadic life was more beneficial in terms of child nutrition and health.

Diet, nutrition and health among pastoralists

African pastoralism represents a particular food-getting strategy especially adapted to semi-arid regions, where herding domestic animals (particularly cattle, camels, goats and sheep) enables humans to convert scarce and patchy grazing resources into a steady supply of food calories and nutrients for the human population in the form of milk, meat, blood and trade of animals and their products for grain (Galaty & Bonte, 1991; Fratkin *et al.*, 1994).

There exists wide variation in diets, social organization, economic production and mobility among pastoral groups. Agropastoralists, such as the Gourma Fulani of Mali, obtain only 25 per cent of their diet from milk (Loutan, 1985), gaining the rest of their nutrients from millet and garden vegetables. East African herders including Maasai, Turkana and Rendille, obtain over 75 per cent of their caloric intake from milk, meat and blood, supplementing their diet with grains during extensive dry periods. Some sectors of these societies, particularly warriors herding animals in distant camps, receive their total diet from animal products (Nestel, 1985a; Galvin, 1988; Fratkin, 1991). Pastoral diets are highly nutritious in protein and fat. Milk, meat and blood provide more than 200 per cent of recommended daily protein among Maasai and 400 per cent among Turkana (Nestel, 1985a; Galvin, 1988). However, energy or caloric intake is typically low from milk products, where one litre of milk contains only one-fifth of the calories of an equivalent market value of maize – one litre of milk yields 700 kcal and 38 grams of animal protein, versus 3560 kcal/kg and 95 grams of amino-acid-deficient protein for one kilogram of maize (Grandin, 1988). Pastoralists must consume over three litres of milk daily to maintain RDIs of more than 2000 kcal per adult. Although pastoral diets are low in fruits and green vegetables, vitamin and mineral deficiencies are rare and seasonal. Hilderbrand (1985) found night-blindness, probably due to vitamin A deficiency, among the Fulani of Mali at the end of the dry season, when milk yields are lowest. Iron deficiencies are widespread, however, particularly among women and children who may consume large quantities of milk but have less access to meat and blood than men, as among Turkana and Somalis (Murray *et al.*, 1978, 1980). 25 per cent of the Maasai women and children studied by Nestel & Geissler (1986) were anaemic, suggesting iron deficiency.

Seasonality exerts a considerable influence on the nutritional status of most pastoral populations. Following short rainy seasons, milk production decreases sharply as grazing resources dry up. An East African zebu cow, which produces one to two litres of milk daily in the wet season, yields less than 250 cc of milk in the dry season (Dahl & Hjort, 1976). In addition to seasonal stresses, there also exists considerable variation in nutritional status based on sex and age differences. Tuareg women consume 1.5 times as much milk as men, owing in part to their primary role in milking tasks (Wagenaar-Brouwer, 1985). However, men and boys consume more meat and blood than women and girls, as reported in Turkana and Maasai (Galvin 1985; Nestel, 1985a). Grains are purchased mainly by the sale of livestock, an endeavour typically carried out by men, who give their wives allowances to purchase foods. However, when pastoralist women participate in the market, such as selling milk, more income goes directly into buying food for the household's children (Fratkin & Smith, 1995).

Nutrition plays a strong role in the incidence of disease and mortality, especially among small children. A malnourished child is 200 times as likely to die from measles as a well-nourished child (Morley, 1973). Pastoral populations face many of the same health problems as agriculturalists in Africa, including high infant and child mortality from infectious diseases, particularly malaria, measles, diarrhoea and respiratory illness. Pastoralists are less prone to water-borne diseases (cholera, hepatitis), and studies among Turkana in Kenya and Tuareg in Mali show low internal parasite loads compared with agriculturalists (Hill, 1985; Little *et al.*, 1988).

Little is known about the health effects of sedentarization on pastoralists. Chabasse *et al.* (1985) compared health and nutritional statuses of pastoral and sedentary populations in Hill's Mali study (1985), obtaining medical examinations and serological tests of 1995 nomadic Tamasheq (Tuareg), Fulani agropastoralists and Sonrai agriculturalists. This study showed that the nomadic groups had higher rates of tuberculosis, brucellosis, syphilis and trachoma, and higher child mortality (children five and under) than the agricultural groups, which the authors attributed to a greater isolation from health-care services. The settled agricultural populations, however, had higher rates of bilharzia, intestinal helminths and other parasites, and higher malaria and anaemia rates, which the authors attributed to their proximity to riverine locations.

The comprehensive study of morbidity and mortality among pastoralists

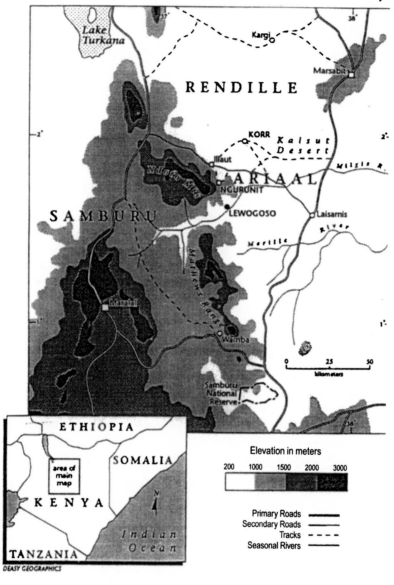

Figure 7.1 Map of Rendille study sites, northern Kenya

153

carried out by A.G. Hill (1985) and his associates in Mali found malaria in up to 35 per cent of all groups surveyed, with rates twice as high in Gourma Tamasheq as in Gourma Fulani (Chabasse *et al.*, 1985). Among Fulani infants and children, diarrhoea and conjunctivitis were the most frequent disorders, in addition to malaria, where 20 per cent of children showed symptoms of diarrhoea and twice that number had conjunctivitis (Hilderbrand, 1985). Hill found 25 per cent infant mortality in all groups surveyed in Mali, with 51 per cent mortality in Fulani children born alive of mothers aged 45–49. Although there have been no direct studies of acquired immune deficiency syndrome (AIDS) among pastoral populations, they are at risk in many African countries, where the incidence of AIDS is high (Caldwell *et al.*, 1989; Nathan *et al.*, 1996).

Our study of health and nutrition among settled and nomadic Rendille emulated Hill's, in that we are concerned with a holistic approach that incorporates socio-economic, health and demographic data in order to understand the consequences of sedentarization; we differ in that we focus on one ethnic group engaged in several economic pursuits (herding, gardening, wage labour, living on relief), rather than comparing different ethnic groups.

The Rendille health and nutrition study

Until quite recently, the Rendille subsisted exclusively on camel, cattle and small stock pastoralism in the Kaisut Desert of Marsabit District, northern Kenya. Marsabit is Kenya's largest but least populated district, receiving an average of 500 mm of annual rainfall (and less than 250 mm in the Chalbi and Kaisut Deserts). The majority of the district's 110,000 people are livestock pastoralists, comprising Rendille (25,000), Gabbra (30,000), Boran (30,000) and Ariaal (7000) herders; an estimated 15,000 people live in or near the district's towns, this population living principally by agriculture or engaging in trade, manufacture, or wage labour (Republic of Kenya, 1988).

In 1990, we began a longitudinal study of nomadic and sedentary Rendille communities, comparing women and their under-six-year-old children for diet, economic status and nutritional indices through anthropometric measurements, morbidity and anaemia. Unlike Hill's study, which compares different cultural groups as well as different economic strategies, we look at different economic strategies within the same ethnic group, which enables us to hold certain cultural practices constant, including marriage patterns, inheritance rights, residence, language and religious beliefs. This research is described in greater detail in Nathan *et al.* (1996).

Three Rendille communities were selected for their distinct ecological settings and economic specializations. The first, Lewogoso, is a nomadic camel-keeping community of Ariaal (Samburu-speaking) Rendille, consisting of approximately 250 people. This clan-based community has been studied extensively by the social anthropologist Fratkin (e.g. Fratkin, 1989, 1991) and forms a control community to compare with the sedentary villages. The Lewogoso community lives along the base of the Ndoto Mountains in western Marsabit District, subsisting on milk camels and the trade of goats and sheep; they also keep large cattle herds in distant highland camps, the cattle being used for bride-wealth, for age-set rituals and in trade. The second community, Ngurunit, is a sedentary agro-pastoral community of approximately 800 people, located in a forested valley in the Ndoto Mountains in western Marsabit District. The community is made up of poor Dorobo (foraging) populations, as well as sedentary and generally poor Rendille and Ariaal (Samburu-speaking Rendille), who keep small numbers of camels, cattle and small stock, as well as having small gardens, irrigated from the mountain run-off. There are two Christian missions here, with the Catholic Church running a primary school and the African Inland Church (AIC) operating a small dispensary; there are also half a dozen shops, largely owned by Somali tradesmen, who buy livestock and sell food commodities, including maize meal, sugar and tea. Ngurunit town is quite isolated from the district's main road and commerce, but represents an important sedentarization option, because town residents are able to keep large numbers of animals, both camels and cattle, in the immediate area. The third community is at Korr, a wind-blown town in the Kaisut Desert, located 40 km east of Ngurunit and 120 km west of the district capital on Marsabit Mountain. Korr town did not exist, except as a dry-season watering-hole, before the droughts of the 1970s when the Catholic Diocese of Marsabit established a church and famine-relief centre. Today Korr has about 800 town residents and a large periurban population of several thousand Rendille living within a 15-km radius. Many of Korr's residents depend on famine-relief foods, while others earn a living from running shops or buying and selling livestock. There is not enough vegetation to keep animals in Korr, and it represents a settled community dependent to a large degree on famine-relief foods. Korr has been extensively surveyed by Roth (1991, 1993).

The three Rendille communities, nomadic Lewogoso and Korr and Ngurunit towns, were visited in July 1990 and again in late June 1992. While rainfall was above average throughout Marsabit District in 1990, 1992 was a drought year, characterized by well-below-average-levels for both the long spring rains and the shorter winter rains (Fig. 7.2). Although our sampling during both years occurred in the same period (June–July), negating seasonality analysis, we compare a wet year (1990) with a very dry year (1992), particularly at the height of the summer dry season, a difficult phase of the East African pastoral annual cycle.

Child health was assessed in the three different communities by measuring morbidity, dietary and growth patterns for a study population

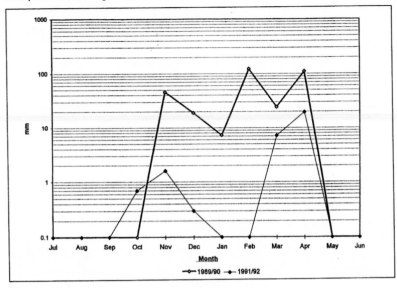

Figure 7.2 Rainfall, 1990 & 1992, Korr Town

of children under six years of age. Thirty-five women of childbearing age (approximately 16 to 45 years) were interviewed from each of the three communities; their children under six formed the original study population (60 children from Lewogoso, 60 children from Ngurunit and 54 children from Korr). A second survey was conducted among the same women and their children (adding new births) in 1992, where in all, 93 women from the original study were located (29 from Lewogoso with 59 children, 31 from Ngurunit with 59 children and 33 from Korr with 66 children). Children's ages were determined by referral to their immunization records, when possible, or, if unavailable, by reference to a historic events calendar developed and used in previous Rendille studies (e.g. Spencer, 1973; Sobania, 1980).

Breast-feeding patterns were similar for all three groups, as was the age of weaning, with no children over 24 months still breast-fed and only one child under 18 months of age fully weaned. Women were asked about their pregnancy and childbearing history and previous child and infant mortality, and mothers were questioned as to how many days in the previous month they and each of their study children suffered respiratory, febrile and diarrhoeal diseases. Women were also asked to recall what foods they and their children had eaten in the past 24 hours, which were recorded separately for morning, afternoon and evening meals. These foods included servings of milk, meat, cooked maize meal (*posho*), fat, tea, sugar, fruit (e.g. mango, papaya, bananas) or green vegetables, including local kale (in Kiswahili, *sukumu wiki*). Frequency of servings was reported

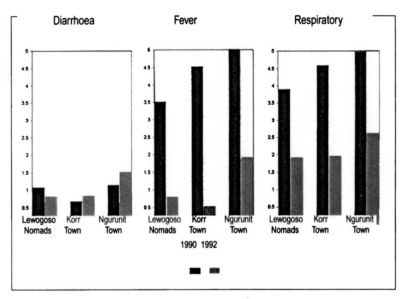

Figure 7.3 Morbidity by location, 1990 & 1992

rather than actual amounts consumed (e.g. calories or volume), which were not possible to observe or otherwise measure. An important exception to this was the estimation of milk consumed based on the standard metal cups widely used in the area, so that 'one small cup' was listed as one cup, 'one large cup' as 1.5 cups and milk served with tea or porridge estimated at 0.25 cups.

Families were identified as 'poor' or 'sufficient', according to the number and type of animals available to each woman and/or the amount of money spent on food per week. Using a method we employed in previous studies to determine wealth differences (Fratkin & Roth, 1990), households were classified as 'sufficient' if they owned more than 4.5 tropical livestock units (TLUs) per capita or if they earned incomes above $50 per month, and 'poor' if they owned fewer livestock units or had a lower income. The highest proportion of children from poor households were from Ngurunit town (53 per cent), followed by Korr town (28 per cent) and the nomadic Lewogoso settlement (20 per cent). The differences reflect the large number of impoverished people without any livestock living near Ngurunit town. Famine relief was available to all three communities to varying degrees. Maize and beans constituted the bulk of this food aid, distributed by local missions. As this food was available to all study communities – less to the nomadic community because of distance to distribution points – 'poor' households did not necessarily reflect lack of access to food.

Finally, we obtained measurements of weights, heights, mid-arm circum-

Table 7.1 Immunization data, children > 12 months of age, sedentary (Korr and Lewogoso) vs. nomadic (Lewogoso) communities, by year

Immunization	1990 Sedentary	Nomadic	X^2
BCG			
Covered	98	16	
Not covered	0	43	98.4*
DPT			
Covered	85	5	
Not covered	13	54	92.2*
OPV			
Covered	82	5	
Not covered	16	54	84.3*
Measles			
Covered	82	4	
Not covered	16	55	87.9*
	1992		
BCG			
Covered	109	3	
Not covered	2	46	137.2*
DPT			
Covered	80	0	
Not covered	31	49	70.6*
OPV			
Covered	80	1	
Not covered	31	48	66.7*
Measles			
Covered	105	35	
Not covered	6	14	16.7*

* = $p < 0.001$

ference and triceps skin folds for mothers and their children under six years old. We also obtained haemoglobin values in the 1990 survey by analysing blood from finger pricks in a portable Haemacue optical scanner.

Morbidity data were gathered by asking mothers the number of days each child in the household was ill in the past month with diarrhoea, fever and respiratory infections ('colds' or 'cough'). The town samples had more reported cases of diarrhoea, colds and fevers, although these differences were not significant (based on pairwise Student's t-test); all three communities showed decline in illnesses during 1992, the dry year (Fig. 7.3).

There are significant differences in immunization rates, however; in 1992 children over 12 months of age in Korr and Ngurunit towns had 100

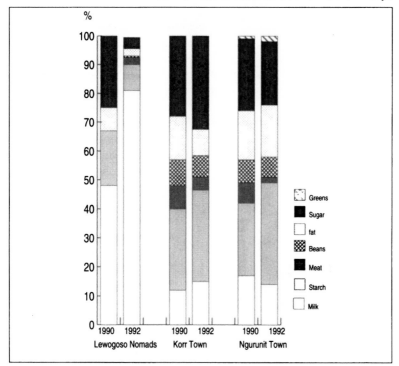

Figure 7.4 Diet by location, 1990 and 1992

per cent Bacillus Calmette-Guerin (BCG), DPT and OPV immunization protection, compared with 6, 0 and 2 per cent, respectively, for nomadic Lewogoso. Measles immunization rates were more nearly equal, because an epidemic which struck in 1990 prompted a campaign to immunize all the children in the district before our return in 1992 (Table 7.1).

Haemoglobin levels obtained in each location in 1990 show relative anaemia in all three communities, below −2 standard deviation (SD) from the World Health Organization (WHO) median of 12.5 mg/dl (Anon., 1993). However, there was significantly higher mean anaemia at Korr town (9.47 mg/dl) than in Ngurunit town (10.83 mg/dl) or Lewogoso nomadic children (11.03 mg/dl). We are not certain why there is more anaemia in Korr. Ferritin levels were not obtained, so distinctions between iron-deficiency and parasite-induced haemolysis cannot be made, although we suspect that there is more malaria at Korr. It is also likely that nutritional differences are at play, as a livestock-based diet of meat, blood and milk produces more iron than a grain-based urban diet.

As one would suspect, the 24-hour dietary recall data revealed strikingly different daily regimes between nomadic Lewogoso, and Korr and Ngurunit towns (Fig. 7.4). Lewogoso children drank two to three times as much milk as their sedentary counterparts, even during the dry year of 1992. In

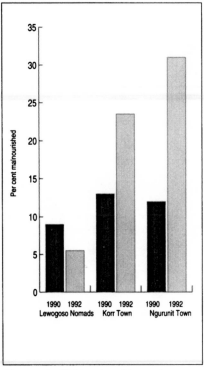

Figure 7.5 Child malnourishment by location, 1990 and 1992

fact, the average amount of milk intake actually increased for Lewogoso in the dry year, from 2.32 cups in 1990 to 3.17 cups in 1992. As expected, servings of starch are much higher among the sedentary communities for both wet and dry years. Tea and sugar are also more frequently consumed in the sedentary towns, particularly in Korr. Residents of Ngurunit, the only community capable of supporting gardens, ate the most greens, while high bean consumption in Korr represents distribution of this food as famine relief. Residents in towns ate more meat and fat than the Lewogoso nomads, however, reflecting nomadic pastoralists' reluctance to kill their subsistence animals for meat and the sedentary communities' tendency to purchase processed fat (ghee) through the market economy (Table 7.1).

As an important measure of child health, we compared nutritional status by community and year, based on weight-for-height measurements, which indicate immediate malnutrition (wasting) and which are age-independent. We compared Rendille child growth patterns with the WHO reference standard (World Health Organization, 1983). The great majority of Rendille children were 1–3 SD below the median of the WHO standard, as shown in Fig. 7.5, where 2 SD below the mean is considered severe and immediate malnutrition, or wasting. However, there were large differences in weight for height, both between nomadic and settled communities and between the wet (1990) and dry years (1992) in our study. Where the 1990 wet-year sample showed comparatively low levels of childhood malnutrition relative to the dry-year 1992 sample in all three communities, Lewogoso had significantly lower malnutrition rates than the towns during the drought year of 1992.

These findings are particularly surprising, in light of the previously cited studies from nomadic pastoral communities, such as Turkana, which show severe nutritional stress during the dry season (Galvin, 1988; Little *et al.*, 1988). Among Rendille pastoralists in Lewogoso, children's milk consumption remained high during the dry year, more than compensating for their lower intake of starch, sugar, fat and greens compared with settled children. Consequently, nomadic Lewogoso children in the 1992 dry year exhibited a far lower incidence of malnutrition than did children in the sedentary communities of Korr and Ngurunit towns. These results confirmed our view that a nomadic diet based on consumption of livestock production, particularly camel's milk, offers better nutrition to children than diets found in towns.

Conclusions

Our study of health and nutritional consequences of pastoral sedentarization is based on measurements of diet, morbidity and anthropometrics drawn from women and children under six in three Rendille communities, one nomadic and two sedentary, in both a wet year (1990) and a dry year (1992). Morbidity patterns of diarrhoea, respiratory disease and fevers were similar for all communities in both years, although children in all three communities suffered fewer episodes of respiratory illness and fever in the 1992 sample, probably due to more arid conditions that year. Both towns showed a higher number of respiratory-disease and fever days than the nomads, and Korr town had a higher anaemia rate, due either to a higher incidence of malaria or iron deficiency. If the anaemia at Korr is nutritional in nature, it would give added support for these initial findings on the enhanced nutritional potency of the nomadic diet. Dietary recall data showed wide differences in types of foods consumed in the three communities, with the nomadic Lewogoso consuming three times the amount of milk compared with residents in Korr or Ngurunit towns. These sedentary communities relied much more on fats, starch and meat relative to Lewogoso. We believe that these dietary differences are the reasons for greater child malnutrition in the towns than among the nomads.

Comparing the study groups via anthropometrics of weight for height, childhood malnutrition levels were comparable for all three communities in the wet year, 1990. However, a major finding in our study was that, while there was much more wasting among the town children in the dry year, malnutrition did not increase in the nomadic Lewogoso sample and was significantly less than that found in the towns in 1992. This finding was surprising, since Lewogoso is the most dependent of all communities upon livestock products and hence we assumed it to be the most susceptible to dry season fluctuations, which reduce livestock milk production. The nomadic pastoral production system appears to be far more effective in dry season times than the sedentary systems sampled here, even though the latter were regularly receiving famine food relief to augment their diet. This finding is at variance with the Turkana studies, which show seasonal malnutrition (Little, 1989). We attribute these differences to the large number of animals Rendille keep in the nomadic settlement, particularly camels with their copious milk supplies, as well as the larger communities within which Rendille live, contributing to a greater sharing of food resources (Fratkin & Roth, 1990; Fratkin, 1991).

Economic differences do not seem to affect child health or nutritional status in any of the communities. Children from poor households are found in all three communities, with more poor households in Korr and Ngurunit towns. Impoverishment and sedentarization are co-related, with many families moving to towns because they are poor. However, settlement also has a positive side, featuring improved access to jobs, education and primary health-care and access to famine-relief foods. Yet the 1992 findings reveal that nomadic children in Lewogoso, despite the absence of famine relief foods, enjoyed far better nutritional status, while even children from poor families received non-significantly different amounts of milk relative to food-sufficient children from Lewogoso. In terms of nutrition, the sharing of milk animals and milk itself between wealthy and poorer kin in the nomadic communities tends to negate livestock ownership differences. This suggests that the effects of poverty are considerably levelled in a kinship-based pastoral society, while they may threaten to decline in town-based settings. For these reasons, as well as promoting child health in general, we encourage development agencies to allocate resources that improve pastoral livestock economies, and not to settle nomads if this means alienating households from their animals. The trend to sedentarization of pastoral nomads appears to have strong health consequences, especially for children, leading to increased malnutrition and susceptibility to disease. Our study demonstrates that alienating pastoralists from their livestock leads to impoverishment, not only of the spirit but of the body as well.

8

Of Markets, Meat, Maize & Milk: Pastoral Commoditization in Kenya

FRED ZAAL & TON DIETZ[1]

The fate of African pastoralist communities in the twentieth century has been to suffer a loss in power and a loss of control over resources. This image of decline and marginalization is almost universally acknowledged: but is it true in all cases and, if not, can lessons be learned from the exceptions? This question will be addressed here in relation to two case studies from Kenya. In the first, that of the Pokot of Kenya's West Pokot District, there is little doubt that increasing social, economic and political insecurity have combined with ever more apparent poverty in the wake of the series of environmental disasters that began in 1979. However, in the second case, that of the Maasai of Kajiado District, the typical image of decline fits less well, mediated by other changes in the local political economy and ecology. In particular, this chapter will examine the extent to which involvement in the market has allowed pastoralists – or, to be more precise, some pastoralists – to improve their economic position. For those who have done so, we shall explore further what this has meant in terms of risk for their security of production.

Any discussion of poverty and prosperity among East African pastoralists must include a thorough analysis of trends in pastoral commoditization and its impact on wealth and accumulation. The study of commoditization can offer insights into the changing position of pastoralists in the wider economy, reveal many of the risks involved in adapting to market changes, allow the differential impact of these risks (combined with environmental risks) to be evaluated across segments of the pastoral population and give a measure of longer-term trends of income and wealth differentiation within pastoralist communities.

To give a general definition of the term, commoditization is a process whereby assets, goods and services gradually shift from having a use value purely in terms of subsistence to having an exchange value as well, meaning that they will be increasingly sold and acquired on the market. In

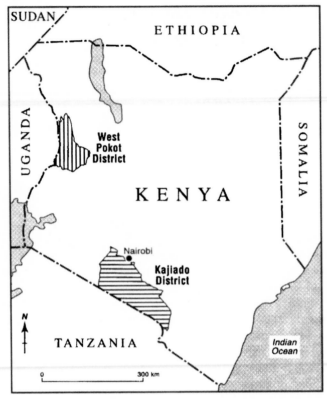

Figure 8.1 Pokot and Kajiado Districts in Kenya   (*Source:* Republic of Kenya, 1985.)

the early stage, this exchange may take place without money, as barter trade, but increasingly it will become monetized. In the debate about commoditization within pastoralism several specific elements of the process need to be highlighted. First, the commercialization of livestock production (through the sale of milk, meat, wool, hides and skins, manure, draught-animals) takes place when the balance between own use and sale changes in favour of the latter. Typically, local livestock trading will become part of the national trend in supply and demand, with an impact on price formation. Second, the acquisition of food through the market becomes more important with commoditization. This change is often accompanied by a move in diet from one based on livestock products to one based more upon grains. Third, the acquisition of non-food consumption items through the market – both material goods (often starting with ornaments and clothing; items for the house; medicinal drugs and stimulants) and services (education, health-care) – is given overriding priority. Fourth, inputs to be used in the production process may be purchased increasingly (buying of water or land-use rights, for example, or, more commonly, the

164

purchase of veterinary medicine, salt, additional feed, fencing materials, breeding animals or semen). Fifth, moves towards the privatization of land and/or water ownership become evident. And, finally, the commoditization of labour relations within the pastoral production system may occur, waged workers being employed by herd-owners.[2]

The debate about pastoral commoditization in eastern Africa has long been dominated by the issue of 'livestock commercialization' and 'off-take rates', often prompted by the growing demand for meat in the ever more dominant non-pastoral sector of the economy of the three East African countries (Aldington & Wilson, 1968). Commoditization has less commonly been viewed as a possible answer to growing tensions in the pastoral economy itself. From time to time, the Kenya government has sought to take measures to capitalize upon the wealth held in livestock by pastoralists. The earliest efforts at compulsory marketing came in the second half of the 1930s, provoking the famous Kamba political protest against forced destocking in 1938 (Forbes Munro, 1975) and failed attempts to develop stock auctions. A second wave of policies in the second half of the 1950s, again using ecological arguments to justify forcing a higher off-take rate (e.g for Karamoja: Evans-Jones, 1960; Baker, 1967; Quam, 1978; for Kenya: Raikes, 1981), and a third came with the launching of the World Bank-financed livestock development programmes in the late 1960s and early 1970s (in Kenya this took the form of the Livestock Development Programme).

Scholars looking at these government-led drives to increase offtake rates from the perspectives of the pastoralists have often drawn attention to the apparently unfair terms of trade offered to herders. These criticisms were particularly evident in works published during the early 1980s. Raikes (1981: 97) blamed the East African governments for the failure to increase offtake, because the pastoralists' 'reluctance (to sell livestock) is at least in part due to low prices'. Evangelou wanted 'more favourable national pricing policies' for livestock (1984a:140), arguing that the transition to market-orientated production had been hindered because the Kenyan government had succumbed to 'short-term political advantages gained by "cheap meat" and other urban-biased policies' (1984b:50). In 1980, Campbell & Axinn (1980:7–8) complained that beef prices had 'remained controlled and low during the past 15 years in Kenya', while Aronson (1980:181) deplored the 'sharp decline in the terms of trade, so that more and more livestock product is necessary for a given amount of grain or industrial goods'. Giving a more specific case, Hjort (1981) cited Swift (1979) and Kjaerby (1976) to suggest a decrease in exchange ratios for cattle and camels against maize, while Little (1983) was convinced that 'in recent years ... the rate of inflation for consumption items (particularly maize and finger millet) has increased faster than livestock prices, eroding the purchasing power of the herdowners'.

These arguments tend to suggest that the impact of commoditization among pastoral communities has been negative, contributing towards a decline in their economic position. Taking up questions already touched upon in the earlier work of Dietz (1987, 1993), the effects and extent of commoditization will be re-evaluated here in relation to three main issues: (i) How successfully can (partial) commoditization ease the tension between the capacity of pastoral production and the needs of household consumption? (ii) What would be the pastoralists' requirements for commoditization at the market level? (iii) To what extent is commoditization actually taking place and how does it affect patterns of accumulation among pastoralists? The effects of commoditization will be modelled first under differing conditions, followed by a presentation of empirical findings from among the Pokot in north-western Kenya and the Kajiado Maasai of southern Kenya.[3]

Commoditization: caloric terms of trade and market risks analysis

To elucidate the main elements affecting the process of commoditization among pastoralists, we will offer four models of production, each operating under differing market conditions, beginning with a model in which market forces are absent and ending with one in which commoditization is prompting marked diversification in the local economy.

Model 1: subsistence production

Our first model, subsistence production, assumes that pastoralists who produce milk, meat and blood for their own consumption, with the aim of being self-sufficient in food, need enough animals to do so. The absolute amount of food that provides energy as well as proteins, minerals and vitamins is generally dependent on household composition (children–adults; men–women, breast-feeding women), on the average weight and the body efficiency in handling food, on the climate and on work-related energy requirements. People can do with temporary lower energy inputs, but these cannot be sustained over the longer term without damage to health. The food people produce from their herds and flock has a certain caloric (and protein, etc.) value, which can fluctuate depending on the fat contents of milk and meat.

Given these basic conditions, we can make a number of general assumptions regarding the minimum requirements. On average, an adult living in a pastoralist environment in East Africa can be assumed to require 800,000 Calories (Cal) per annum. If each household unit is taken to consist of seven people, the household will require 5.6 million Cal in all. One litre of milk contains 700 Cal and an average (zebu) cow gives 400 litres of milk per annum for human consumption. (There is competition with milk for the calves, and milk production for human consumption will generally be between two and three litres per day in the short rainy season and between one and two litres per day in the long dry season.) Cows form, on average, 60 per cent of the herd. Turning to the meat supply, one kilogram of cattle meat contains 2,300 Cal (for goat meat the figure is lower, for sheep meat it is much higher) and each zebu has a consumable meat weight of 100 kg. The natural life of zebu cows is 13 years and the culling of most male animals is at three years, which results in an average lifespan for all newborn calves of eight years. This implies an average 'normal' offtake rate of 12.5 per cent per year. Looking at labour requirements, our pastoral household unit can manage a herd of 30 to 40 animals without labour problems. Teaming up with other herders and herds for seasonal mobility is often useful for security and labour-efficiency reasons, but beyond 40 animals additional labour is often required.

These assumptions give rise to a number of outcomes. If the average pastoralist drinks only milk, then 1140 litres of milk will be needed by each adult in a year, that is, 8000 litres per assumed household unit. To achieve this the household will need to have 20 cows within a total cattle herd of 33 animals. Similarly, if the average pastoralist eats only meat, then 350 kg of meat will be required per person in a year, giving a total annual requirement of 2450 kg for the household unit. Thus, 25 cattle will have to be slaughtered for food. In 'normal' circumstances, with an offtake rate of 12.5 per cent, this would require a herd of at least 200 animals. Combining the milk and meat production, to give a more realistic picture, full dependence for all food requirements on animals would mean that a pastoral household needed a cattle herd of at least 28 animals (producing 6720 litres of milk and 350 kg of meat). This is within the labour potential of the average household, and implies an ownership ratio of only four head of cattle per capita.

Such averages are, of course, only analytical tools and can be very far from individual households' and herds' real situations. This model discounts a number of important social uses of livestock – for example, in bridewealth transactions, in loans and gifts and in ritual slaughter (Dahl & Hjort, 1976). But, even without these elements of livestock use, the narrow focus on calorific requirements shows significant complicating variables. A large seasonality in milk production would require dependence on other food sources during part of the year. In pastoral societies, the 'hunger period' is generally during the dry season when milk yields are lowest and labour energy requirements highest. The assumed 'normal' offtake rate for cattle is based on the assumption that all animals end up as meat for the household. However, not all meat will be consumed, either because of losses due to predators or disease or, less commonly, because cultural practices inhibit the consumption of certain animals. Likewise, the assumed 'normal' off-take rate for cattle is based on a 'natural' life for cows and on the culling of (most) male animals as soon as they are adults. In fact, social factors and cultural considerations may inhibit the slaughter of young males – for example, because of shared ownership with far-away stock friends or cultural taboos against early slaughter (or sale). And, of course, with regular droughts, animals die of starvation and/or lack of water and, if these animals are eaten at all, they will inevitably have a much lower food value. Within the household itself, norms prescribing diet behaviour might complicate the food (milk and/or meat) entitlements of particular members of the household. Even if certain households have herds big enough to provide them with milk and meat during dry seasons and droughts, other households might be faced with structural or temporary food problems, and customary sharing of meat and milk among a larger group than the own household may still jeopardize the availability of food to the household.

Model 2: production with minor commoditization

Our second model adds to the pattern of subsistence production the modification of limited involvement with the market. This, in fact, has been the reality for many pastoralists in eastern Africa over the past three decades or so. Over that time population densities in many pastoral areas have increased, because of natural growth, immigration of pastoralists from elsewhere (for example, Boran from Ethiopia to Marsabit; Upe Pokot from Uganda to Kenya; Somalis from Somalia to Kenyan Somali areas); and the incursions of non-pastoralists pushed out of the high-potential agricultural zones (Dietz, 1986). It is generally assumed that long-term pastoral population growth since 1960 has been much higher than livestock growth, partly because of the devastating consequences of the droughts (which affected most Kenyan pastoral areas in 1960–61, 1965, 1968–9, 1974–6, 1979–81, 1984–5, 1987, 1989, 1991–3), preventing the rebuilding of herds and flocks. At the same time, it is probable that the total absolute number of animals in the pastoral areas is higher now than it was in the 1950s. But, on the whole, the overall trend of livestock per capita has been downward and, for many pastoralists, this has meant a loss of wealth to a level below the requirements for subsistence production, as described above in model 1.[1]

Pastoralists have adopted a number of strategies to avoid a food crisis in these circumstances. The pressures have undoubtedly been greatest during periods of drought (Dietz, 1991). Pastoralists have always participated in marketing during these periods, selling or bartering milk, hides and skins or hunting trophies and getting non-livestock food in exchange (Schneider, 1981; Kerven, 1992). They may also seek additional food by hunting and gathering (or by stealing food from neighbouring cultivators), even if this is regarded as culturally taboo. Some may even try to grow their own food, many taking up what is sometimes called 'hit and run' cultivation of millet or sorghum, others adopting more labour-intensive forms of rain-fed or water-harvesting agriculture. The problem is that it is during years in which droughts cause most stress in the livestock economy that the chances of a harvest are most meagre. But, in years with adequate rainfall, the cultivation of cereals by pastoral households can enable livestock to recover more quickly. In recent years, however, there has been a growing problem of access for pastoralists to the few environmental niches where cultivation has in the past been possible, as these have been gradually permanently occupied by non-pastoral immigrants or former pastoralists. Formal relationships with groups in these niches or living in higher-potential areas adjacent to pastoral lands are commonly formed through marriages, especially where this can be accomplished within the same ethnic community. Bride-wealth arrangements in such circumstances often include livestock, which can be retained as part of the son-in-law's herd in the lowlands but owned by the highland-based father-in-law. These relationships often form the basis for the temporary migration of women and children to the higher-potential areas. Migration is an important way of reducing the energy requirement of households during droughts.

Model 3: market production, positive terms of trade between livestock and grains

Growing tension between the capacity of pastoral production and house-hold consumption needs can also force a more active involvement in the market economy. Selling a steer or milk on the market and buying cereals instead can offer considerable advantages to the herder, as long as the 'caloric terms of trade' (CToT) are in favour of the livestock owner. The CToT relates pastoral production, expressed in energy values, with pastoral consumption of cereals, also expressed in energy values, through the price of the respective products and their energy value on the market. We can assume that 1 kg of maize or sorghum provides between 3000 and 3600 Cal (let us say 3,500), depending on milling and storage losses. For an exchange of this kind to be positive in caloric terms, the pastoralist must get more than 65 kg of cereals for selling a steer, and more than 200 grams of cereals for a litre of milk.[5]

There is, of course, a danger that pastoralists engaging in such exchanges will become ever more dependent on the market. Ideally, there should be traders willing to buy the animal or the milk at a time when the pastoralist is in need of cash to buy food and at a market-place that can be reached without too many problems (distance, security, etc.), and also traders willing to sell food at a time when the pastoralists want to buy it and at places that are accessible. But it is not always obvious that urgent or foreseen food needs in the household will be covered by the sale of animals or milk for cash to buy cereals. Decision-making is often gender-specific: it is mainly the women who are confronted with lack of food to feed the household, and often they cannot make the decisions concerning the sale of animals; the decision is made by the male head of the household, and even he may have to consult others in the family hierarchy or 'stock friends' who have a partial claim of ownership. Even if an animal can be sold, the money goes to the man and it may be diverted to purposes other than buying cereals for the consumption of household members. In some households, male heads simply regard it as their wives' responsibility to provide for food and they will not contribute. It then depends on her ownership of animals (usually small stock) and the possibilities she may have to participate in the livestock and milk markets. Where there is a market for milk nearby, women will generally take the opportunity to sell independently.

The availability of food aid, provided by government or non-governmental organizations (NGOs), can complicate the situation further still. Occasional food hand-outs or food-for-work arrangements often undercut the position of local food and livestock traders, undermining the trading infrastructure in the months after food aid comes to an end. At worst, the collapse of trading infrastructure could well mean that 'positive CToT' are no longer achievable and people become ever more dependent on food hand-outs.

However, even under this model, it must be remembered that not all commercialization of livestock results from a gradual or dramatic process of diminishing livestock per capita or of short-term disaster sales. Commercialization can also be a deliberate strategy for rich pastoralists (and absentee herd-owners-cum-politicians in particular) *en route* to becoming ranchers. They may focus on purely commercial production as an accumulation strategy. The emphasis then shifts to meat production, off-take maximization, market-derived inputs (medicine, top-quality breeds, special feed, etc.) and secure control of fixed assets (water facilities, dips and sprays, fences). When livestock become a commodity as well, this can lead to pressures for reform in land tenure. Behnke (1984:265) argues that, under such conditions, pastoral nomadic systems of land use give way spontaneously to an 'open range ranching system'.

Model 4: commoditization, with intensification and diversification of the pastoral economy

With a further diminishing of livestock-per-capita ratios, growth of additional non-food consumption needs or a change to a 'ranchers' mentality', pastoralists might be forced to intensify or diversify their economy in more dramatic ways. When access to adequate land and water is restricted, investments in private water facilities and commercially available feed will be required (starting, perhaps, with payment for access to cultivators' stubble fields after harvests). In some cases, individual herders may succeed in acquiring pasture as property, so that the land itself becomes a commodity. Some herders will then start to invest in fencing to keep others out or, at least to control access by demanding payment for the use of pasture and water.

According to Behnke (1984), this phase is often characterized by a shift from what he terms the 'open-range ranching system' to a 'fenced ranching system'. This notion of a fenced ranching system had its origins in the USA, where ranchers wanted to better control their land, not their cattle. Land had become a commodity and had to be protected from occupation by others. At this stage, cattle had already been a commodity for a long time. After fencing, the ranchers were trapped in their ranches and had to adapt their practices to reduce grazing pressure. This shift can thus be seen to have been initiated by the commoditization of land. Subsequently, many commentators have viewed this as a necessary step towards commercial production, and it was introduced in parts of East Africa under colonial rangeland policies in the 1950s. For the most part, these projects failed. The change demanded a shift from a labour-intensive subsistence production system to a labour-extensive commercial production system. This resulted in higher incomes being achieved by a few people, while others were expelled from the production system due to lower labour demands. Consequently, migration increased, while the pressure on those areas that remained unfenced increased sharply. In contrast to Behnke, Rutten (1992) explains this change in terms of mounting pressure for land tenure change *per se*, and not through demands for improvements in productivity, arguing that fenced ranching as practised in the USA actually resulted in lower productivity (in terms of protein production per hectare) (see also Grandin, 1987). Improved natural resource management, especially soil conservation aimed at the maintenance of carrying capacities, is often cited as a further reason for reform of this kind, but degradation can be found in both systems.

Productivity per animal can also be raised by improved veterinary care, improved breeds, better feeds and improved access to water. To achieve this kind of intensification of pastoral production, cash may be acquired through informal or even formal forms of credit. This can mean that interest payments become an additional force pushing the herder toward increased levels of commoditization, although this is not a necessary effect.

More commonly, a higher level of commoditization in land, production and consumption is accompanied by a higher level in commoditization of labour. Pastoralists who accumulate animals beyond levels which they can manage with family labour will start to employ fellow pastoralists as labourers, a process that is often disguised by a variety of patron–client arrangements of labour, in which non-cash payments may feature strongly. At the bottom of the economic scale, those losing control of adequate pastoral resources will seek wage-paying employment, and some may become paid herders. Rebuilding their own herds or flocks becomes a possibility through this mechanism, especially if payment is partly in the form of animals and if the pastoral employer allows the dependent herders to share the management of the small number of their animals with the employers' herd or flock. In some cases, the pastoral sector has been invaded by absentee herd-owners, who invest in animals but put the care of their herds in the hands of paid managers and labourers.

Two Kenyan examples: West Pokot and Kajiado Districts

In this section, the processes of change and increasing social differentiation implied in these models of commoditization, and especially the role of the terms of trade, will be illustrated with two examples in Kenya. But before looking in detail at the examples, some general points must be made regarding recent economic and political trends in Kenya.

The changes in Kenya's political economy in recent years have been of a scale and intensity that are difficult to overestimate and that make themselves felt at every level of society. Most obviously, the moves toward multiparty democracy in the period leading up to the elections in 1992 contributed to an inflationary spiral. The exchange rate of the Kenya shilling against other currencies collapsed at this time.[6] But the drought of 1991–2 contributed further to the country's economic difficulties in the early 1990s, while Kenya's export commodity prices went down or stagnated. Due partly to the apparent resistance in government to multi-party democracy, partly to the slow implementation of the structural adjustment programme (SAP) and partly to discontent with widespread corruption, major donors decided to withhold development aid. While the cost of living climbed higher, the costs of imported inputs went up even more rapidly. With donors no longer willing to make up fiscal deficits, these were taken care of by increases in money supply until 1992 and, after the new government was installed in 1993, by the issuing of short-term high-interest treasury bonds. The exchange rate was left free to float, as one of the SAP measures, and fell further to almost Ksh.70 to the dollar. By the end of 1993, when donors resumed development aid, there was an expectation that this situation would hold and help the Kenya economy to recover through increased exports.

However, due to a combination of the declining value of the dollar itself, the repatriation of money from outside the country attracted by the high-interest treasury bonds, improved agricultural production and good export earnings, the value of the Kenya shilling went up and inflation went down. Fig. 8.2, which presents the cost of living index for low-income families in Kenya, shows how the index went up as a result of these developments. It also shows how prices for cattle and maize meal

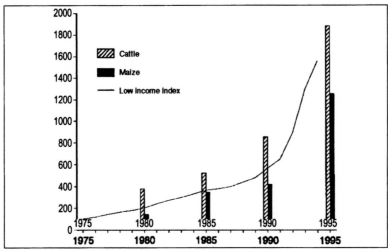

Figure 8.2 Indices, 1975–95

have developed relative to the national index, as, traditionally, these are the most relevant products for pastoralists. The ratio referred to above with a more solid footing of parity, the CToT, was around 6 in 1995. In 1975 the CToT ratio was 4, in 1980 just below 11, in 1985 around 6 and in 1990 slightly above 8.[7]

From the early 1990s, market liberalization went ahead with a gradual reduction of barriers to trade. Increasing amounts of maize were allowed to be transported,[8] although this process was a long-drawn-out one, in which measures were reversed at regular intervals (*Nation*, 21.8.94 and 27.11.94). In the recent past, maize shortages have been covered by imports from Uganda and Tanzania (Argwings-Kodhek, 1992:53). This situation continued well into 1994 and producers in Loitokitok (Kajiado District), for example, complained about the low price levels in the border area, especially in the irrigated areas around Loitokitok itself, because of competition from Tanzania.

The livestock and meat trade was also liberalized in the early 1990s. The slaughterhouse of the Kenya Meat Commission (KMC, the parastatal organizaton for the meat trade) at Athi River, near Nairobi, had been out of operation periodically since the mid-1980s. It finally collapsed in 1993 because of overwhelming liquidity and management problems, political inter-ference and corruption. Plans were under way at the beginning of 1995 to reopen KMC in partnership with Mitsubishi Corporation, with a capacity roughly that of the other, private slaughterhouses combined (600 head per day). Export from the plant was to be through the Mitsubishi Corporation to the European Union, assuming an export licence could be obtained.

With the effects of these broader economic trends in mind, we can now look more closely at our two case-studies.

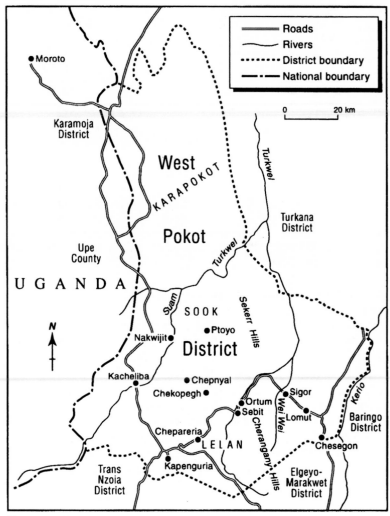

Figure 8.3 Household wealth in TLU.

West Pokot District, north-west Kenya

The Pokot people are recognized to be divided between those who make their living by agriculture (they are often, in fact, agropastoralists) and those who depend solely upon pastoralism. The agricultural sections lived in the northern foothills and nearby plains of the Cheranganis and in the Sekerr hills. In common with their Marakwet neighbours to the south-east, they have developed an ingenious system of gravity irrigation for their sorghum crops, but they also keep goats and sheep, along with a small number of cattle. In recent years, many have moved into the upland areas of the Cheranganis, where they combine maize and potato cultivation

174

with commercial sheep farming, while others have moved into the area around the district headquarters at Kapenguria-Makutano, where there are opportunities for commercial farming (maize, dairy cattle) and where employment in non-agricultural occupations is more easily available.

The pastoral Pokot live in the lowlands north and north-west of the Cherangani mountains and east and west of the Sekerr hills in West Pokot District (which includes Karapokot), their territory extending westwards into Uganda (the Upe county of Karamoja) and eastwards into the northern parts of Kenya's Baringo District. Pastoral and agricultural Pokot have always been connected by extensive social and economic contacts, through bride-wealth arrangements, stock friendships (*tilianan*) and barter trade (mainly goats against millet, sorghum and, after the 1950s, maize). In a geographical sense, Pokot present a classic example of a 'vertical society', where different agroecological zones, from dry lowlands to moist mountain areas, all contribute to the livelihood and organization of society as a whole (Porter, 1965).

Population and livestock figures collected by colonial officials during 1926 showed that there were approximately 210,000 head of cattle in West Pokot (including the 'Karapokot' area, that was to be administered by Uganda from 1926 to 1970) and 220,000 sheep and goats, together with a human population of 'between 24,000 and 45,000'. This amounts to 169,000 tropical livestock units (TLU), or between 4 and 7 TLU per capita.[9] Looked at purely in terms of food availability, this can be regarded as more than sufficient, even without wider trade links beyond the district and with a relatively low grain element in the pastoral diet. However, in the years just before the 1926 survey, the pastoral Pokot were recovering from a disastrous period of drought and disease, which had lasted from 1918 to 1923. During these difficult years we know definitely they had relied upon trade links with their (irrigating) agricultural counterparts in the nearby mountains (Dietz, 1987).

From the 1920s to the 1950s, the pastoral economy of West Pokot gradually strengthened, with numbers of cattle increasing to about 300,000 and goats and sheep to beyond 250,000. But the human population also enlarged, to at least 66,000 (including Upe and the whole of West Pokot), meaning that the average TLU per capita figure fell to between 3 and 4. Over the same period, improved grain consumption in the diet was made possible by increased cereal production by the agricultural Pokot, more barter trade and the emergence of weekly markets at places such as Chesegon and Sigor. In these markets, food trade was in the hands of Pokot and Marakwet women and trade in goats mostly in the hands of Somali men. In some of the lowland areas, colonial officers reported the start of forms of 'hit-and-run' sorghum and millet cultivation by the 1950s.

In the meantime, the colonial administration tried to force the Pokot to sell some of their cattle. During the Second World War and again between 1954 and 1960, compulsory quotas for cattle sales were imposed across the district. As a result, official registered trade in cattle went up from a level of 1000–2000 to 8000–10,000 per year in West Pokot (excluding Karapokot and Upe), representing a rise in off-take from 1 per cent only to between 6 and 9 per cent. Officially registered sales of small stock in this period stood at between 7000 and 14,000 in drought years and 4000 and 6000 in other years. In the Pokot areas administered by Uganda (Karapokot and Upe), officially registered cattle sales fluctuated between 1300 to 2500 in years of good rainfall and between 3000 and 4000 in years with droughts, which was still below an estimated off-take rate of 4 per cent per annum for those areas. Figures for the sale of small stock in Karapokot and Upe are unknown. With the drought of 1961, soon followed by the ending of colonial rule (and effective taxation), the official registration of trade collapsed.

During the mid-1970s, cattle numbers were still around 300,000, but sheep and goats had increased to 400,000 and the Pokot population to 150,000. The marked growth in population reflected major investments in health care by government and missions, coupled with considerable immigration of non-Pokot to the highland areas of West Pokot District. By the 1970s, the average TLU per capita figure had fallen to between 1.5 and 2. As a consequence, fewer Pokot were dependent solely upon pastoralism, the majority having increased their sorghum cultivation. None the less, Pokot in the north-west and north-east parts of the district continued to regard themselves as pastoralists, even if milk was often supplemented with 'grains and greens' in their diet. These supplements were acquired through purchase, not barter. The trade in cattle and goats which allowed the accumulation of cash necessary to facilitate this went largely unrecorded, with the exception of drought years, when the need for distress sales forced herders to come to the official markets. For example, distress sales in West Pokot in 1973 were as high as 9000 cattle and 6000 small stock.

If we look at the total commoditization picture for the pastoral Pokot during the mid-1970s, it becomes evident that some commercial sale of livestock existed for most pastoral households. Ceremonial slaughter of cattle was probably more important than sale of cattle and slaughter of goats and sheep for home consumption more important than sale of small stock. Milk was not sold at all, with the exception of some exchange on weekly market-days. The need to buy other consumer goods remained minimal, and what little schooling was available to Pokot children was wholly paid for through the local missions. Livestock inputs were then only beginning to be acquired through the veterinary services.

The years 1979 to 1981 saw the beginnings of a dramatic and disastrous downturn for the pastoral Pokot. It started with a major disease outbreak, which wiped out most of the goat flocks across the district. This was followed by an exceptionally long drought, lasting three years and accompanied by cattle epidemics. Lastly, and most devastatingly of all, Idi Amin's flight through Karamoja resulted in the opening of the armoury at Moroto barracks and the distribution of weapons among Karamojong and others. As a consequence, heavily armed cattle raiders, known locally as *ngorokos*, became the scourge of West Pokot. It took the Pokot only a few years to get access to heavy weapons themselves to protect their animals, but the Kenya government moved to disarm them in 1984 and again in 1986. In the process, the Kenyan authorities seized Pokot cattle as hostages for the surrender of weapons, but so mismanaged the animals during drought that thousands died. By 1983, it was estimated that the total number of cattle in West Pokot (again including Karapokot) had decreased to less than 100,000, with only around 200,000 sheep and goats. By this time most of the Upe Pokot had fled from Uganda into West Pokot with their few remaining animals. The Pokot population had consequently risen to 180,000, with a TLU per capita figure of around 0.5. To survive these dramas, pastoral Pokot were propelled into agriculture, many even becoming dependent upon food aid, some trading in gold and *miraa*[10] and others taking casual labouring jobs in the highlands and in nearby Trans Nzoia District (Dietz, 1987: 118–27; 1991).

By 1987, district livestock officers estimated that local cattle herds had recovered to 170,000 and sheep and goats to 230,000, with a further 10,000 grade and cross cattle and 70,000 wool sheep on the farms in the highlands (Republic of Kenya, 1989–93: 64). This implied an improvement in the TLU per capita figure to between 0.6 and 0.7. In the lowlands, Pokot pastoralists-cum-cultivators-cum-gold-diggers now tried to re-establish their pastoral economy, assisted by government and NGOs through water development, disease control, and goat breeding and pasture improvement schemes. They also tried to make good use of the positive CToT between livestock products and grains, although money was by then ever more needed for other goods and services as well. During the 1980s, the government forced most of the pastoral Pokot to wear 'decent' clothing, and these had to be purchased. Many pastoral Pokot children had joined primary and even secondary education, partly because of the attractions of school food and missionary food assistance through schools. These were signs of growing commoditization, but neither grazing land nor pastoral labour had yet been drawn into full commoditization. Although group ranches had been created in theory, they had never functioned properly and individual claims to land were limited to new areas of cultivation, such as along the Suam River.

In these circumstances, it is not surprising that West Pokot's pastoral resource base should have failed to recover after the 1979–81 disasters.[11] An example of one community's experience can illustrate the impact of the disaster. In an area called Nakwijit, west of the Sekerr massif, below *Maral* (the 'mountain of thirst'), a small community of isolated pastoral

Pokot existed mainly on their herds and flocks, with some sorghum cultivation. They herded their animals across the Suam River into the Karapokot area. In 1979, before the onslaught, they had 37 TLU per household of nine people on average (38 head of cattle, 86 goats and 16 sheep). This gave a reliable pastoral food base, although some additional sorghum was produced as a reserve. Not much food was bought during years without droughts, and barter exchanges at the Nakwijit market nearby mainly functioned to cement ties and maintain personal networks. In bad years, however, these trade contacts became crucial. Between 1979 and 1982, Nakwijit households lost on average six cattle and more than ten sheep and goats to *ngorokos* and each exchanged on average two cattle for guns and ammunition. In addition, many animals died of diseases, while others were sold for cash. A survey completed in 1982 showed that an average Nakwijit household had by then only 16 TLU (13 cattle, 36 goats and 36 sheep, meaning cattle were only 56 per cent of the total TLU value). Half of the remaining cattle had been farmed out to stock friends in areas that were regarded as safer than Nakwijit (Dietz *et al.*, 1983).

The Nakwijit area was revisited in 1995 to reconstruct what had happened to people and livestock between early 1984 (before the drought had started and after the good years of 1982 and 1983) and early 1995 (after the droughts of 1984–5, 1986–7, and 1991–3).[12] Compared with late 1982, the livestock situation had considerably improved in early 1984: an average household owned about 30 TLU (73 per cent cattle; 21 per cent goats and 6 per cent sheep) and the 1982 anomaly of 'too many sheep' in the eyes of the Pokot had been corrected.[13] By 1995, though, the situation was back to what was regarded as the disaster level of late 1982, with the average Nakwijit household reduced to 15 TLU (an average of 15 cattle, 32 goats and ten sheep). With one household owning four camels, cattle thus formed 72 per cent, goats 21 per cent and sheep 7 per cent of the total TLU value. Compared with the situation of late 1982, livestock numbers had not increased overall, but the composition had changed considerably, with a stabilized number of goats, a rather improved number of cattle and a strongly decreased number of sheep. In 1995, livestock wealth per capita was about 1.6 TLU, potentially providing less than half the food needs of the average person.

There is also evidence that the livestock distribution had become more skewed over this period than it had been before. In early 1984, there was one extreme case of destitution – a household without cattle and only ten goats – and at the other end of the economic spectrum there was a household with 80 cattle, 300 goats and 60 sheep. At this time, 21 per cent of all households surveyed owned 43 per cent of all animals and only 11 per cent of the households had less than 10 TLU. In 1995, there was again one destitute household without any cattle and, at the other extreme, a household with 60 cattle, 80 goats and 35 sheep. However, in 1995, 19 per cent of the households owned 50 per cent of the total livestock wealth (all above 25 TLU) and 57 per cent of all survey households had below 10 TLU (of whom 24 per cent below 5 TLU). It is indicative of the increasingly marked economic differentiation of the Nakwijit community that the five most wealthy households had 82 per cent cattle, 13 per cent goats and 4 per cent sheep in TLU terms (with 179 TLU in total among them), while the five poorest households had 52 per cent cattle, 34 per cent goats and 14 per cent sheep (with only 16 TLU among them). Young households had a very low TLU per capita ratio (households with children below five years old only 0.4, households with children between five and 15 years 0.7), while well-established, older households (with at least one child above 15 years old) had an average TLU per capita value of 2.0). With one exception, all older households experienced a rather drastic decrease in TLU value between 1984 and 1995, from 35 per household to 18.[14]

The large majority of pastoral households in West Pokot now have to combine three major sources of food. They produce some sorghum themselves, but there is a high chance of harvest failure. Their own herds and flocks produce some milk, but this covers less than half the food needs. And some food is acquired through the market, either by selling animals (making use of good CToT) or by selling gold that they dig up in one of the various gold sites in the district. Seasonal migration with animals has been restricted, due to the dangers involved, but seasonal migration to gold places has become an important activity. As these 'hunger trips' take place mostly in the rainy season, they have a negative impact on labour availability for cultivation and herding at home.

This brings us back to a fuller analysis of changes in the CToT. During the first decades of this century, sorghum and goats were exchanged on the basis of a CToT of between 4 and 6, so that pastoralists selling a goat could get four to six times the caloric value in return in the form of sorghum grains. Gradually the pastoralists' position improved further, until the CToT had reached a level of between 8 and 10 in the mid-1970s. After the mid-1970s, the situation changed to the detriment of the pastoralists, although even in very bad years (such as 1979) the CToT remained positive for the pastoralists. However, the relevance of the goats-for-sorghum trade was soon to become negligible, because the pastoralists started to prefer to buy and eat maize. The supply of maize grains from the Pokot highlands increased considerably during the 1970s. The maize-for-goats trade was less dominated by traditional obligations than was the equivalent trade in sorghum for goats, where even during drought years traders exchanged according to the established custom of 'a goat for a bag'. New, non-Pokot maize traders entered the scene, replacing the long-standing networks of Pokot and Somali traders. The trade in goats also changed, as young Pokot traders took over from Somalis, who mainly concentrated on the gold trade after 1979. All this meant that prices became more responsive to fluctuating supply and demand, and this in turn strengthened the economic position of livestock producers, because the CToT for maize grains against goats was between 8 and 17 throughout the period after 1980, well above the level reached by the CToT between sorghum and goats. In addition, pastoralist women close to trading centres improved their position by selling milk, which also had good CToT. The people around *Maral*, for example, have become much more dependent on maize, sorghum, millet and also beans from the market-places (Nakwijit in the lowlands, Ptoyo and Chepnyal in the Sook highlands). Although prices have become increasingly unstable (with strong seasonal variations), 'normal' CToT in 1995 were between 12:1 and 16:1 for maize grains against goats or cattle, but only between 4:1 and 6:1 for millets or sorghums against goats or cattle. In some dry years, however, extreme situations were experienced, with CToT ratios of below 1:2 for maize grains against goats and probably below parity for millet against goats. In addition, at such times people must spend a lot of time and effort in finding traders.[15]

During the 1980s, regular lowland markets in particular expanded rapidly. Most of them functioned weekly (the larger market-places of Chepareria, Chepkobegh, Ortum and Lomut) or twice weekly (Sebit and Chesegon). In addition, there were smaller markets, either held once a week or irregularly. According to an inventory made by the Arid and Semi-Arid Lands (ASAL) Programme, at least 8000 head of cattle were on offer at these markets during an average year, along with at least 40,000 goats and at least 25,000 sheep (Republic of Kenya, 1990: 36–7). These markets also provided chickens and eggs, hides and skins, grains, fruits and some clothing and utensils as well. In most of the market-places, shops were started, and increasingly pastoralists could buy maize meal there. If the 8000 cattle, 40,000 goats and 25,000 sheep offered for sale in a year had been consumed locally, then 5000 pastoral people would have been provided for. With a CToT of 10:1, 50,000 people would be able to survive on grains alone. With 75,000 people living in the lowlands, most of whom are at least partially pastoralists, the estimated exchange situation therefore appears to be adequate, at least in theory.

But the most important threat to this market system-based form of food security is the availability of grains in the market-places. Most grains in the 1980s came from the Pokot highlands, in the south-western part of the district (the Kapenguria area and Lelan). Already during the 1980s, large-scale traders linked with government-owned enterprises or private companies started to buy highland maize for transportation to the urban centres in Kenya, far beyond West Pokot District. Trade was thus redirected from a northern, lowland direction to a southern, highland/ urban direction. Some of it came back as maize meal, at double the price of maize grains. Of course, a growing dependence of pastoralists on meal instead of grains would lower the CToT considerably (although they would still remain positive). But, more seriously, during times of national food scarcity, traders in the lowlands of West Pokot cannot get adequate supplies. With the liberalization of the livestock and grain prices after 1990, as part of the structural adjustment package, the market system has become very unreliable and dangerously insecure for potential buyers at the tail-end of these exchanges. The more distant from urban centres, the more volatile and vulnerable the market system.

Olkarkar group ranch, Kajiado District

Kajiado District is mostly semi-arid (agroclimatic zone V, about 50 per cent of the area) or arid (zone VI, about 30 per cent), with rainfall figures between 400 and 800 mm a year (White & Meadows, 1981; Republic of Kenya, various years). Although rainfall in the highland areas of the Ngong hills and around Loitokitok near Kilimanjaro, is adequate for cultivation, and there is some agriculture along seasonal rivers, as well as cultivation using techniques such as *Fanja Juu* terraces, this is as yet on a very limited scale and the district is dominated by grazing lands. The carrying capacity, based on average rangeland qualities in the zones, was estimated by Bekure *et al.* (1991) to be 465,700 TLU in the dry season and 1,304,000 TLU in the rainy season.[16] However, the Ministry of Livestock Development appears to use a much more conservative estimate of about 285,000 TLU for the district, as computed from figures in Rutten (1992:123, 346).

The earliest livestock data for Kajiado date from 1912, when the Maasai had been moved from a reserve in Laikipia District to the more southern area of present-day Narok and Kajiado Districts. From the early 1890s to 1910, they had suffered heavy losses in stock and human population from consecutive outbreaks of rinderpest, smallpox, contagious bovine pleuropneumonia and East Coast fever (ECF). Further huge losses were caused by the moves of 1904 and 1911, in the wake of which it was estimated that a population of some 10,000 Maasai held 200,000 cattle. Despite recurrent losses over the previous years, this still gave a figure of 20 head of cattle per capita, which, if correct, would have sustained pastoral subsistence. Further periods of drought and outbreaks of diseases in 1915–16, 1918, the mid-1920s and the mid-1940s brought fluctuating fortunes for Kajiado District's herders. By 1943, the district cattle herd was estimated at 360,000, while the Maasai population was stated to be 16,215 (Republic of Kenya, various years) that is, 15 TLU per (Maasai) capita. The number of non-Maasai in the district was by then already starting to increase. The years 1943 to 1947 saw further stock losses to drought and disease, but by 1954 a recovery to around 600,000 head of cattle had been achieved. A peak of 750,000 head of cattle was reached in 1960, before the disastrous drought of 1961–2 killed massive numbers of animals. Even

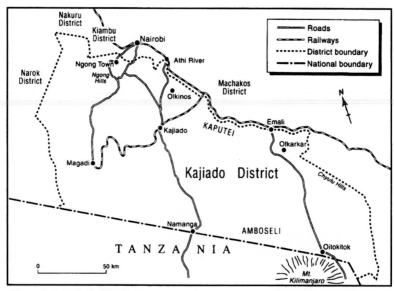

Figure 8.4 Kajiado District (*Source:* Republic of Kenya, 1990a.)

as the herd size peaked, increases in the human population had already seen a lowering of average holdings to 10 TLU per Maasai. In 1962, however, this had dropped to 3 TLU on average. Most Maasai – some 40,000 out of 53,200 in the district – received food aid during this time.[17]

Rainfall in the years after 1962 was relatively good until the early 1970s, when another drought caused heavy stock losses. By the end of 1975, after several years of low rainfall, an estimated 566,000 cattle survived in Kajiado. With around 90,000 Maasai then resident in the district, this represented just over 4 TLU per Maasai.[18] By 1979, when 93,560 Maasai were counted (apart from 55,445 non-Maasai), an estimated 602,000 cattle were kept in the district. Assuming that these cattle belonged to the Maasai, this represented 4.5 TLU per Maasai. By 1983, the estimated cattle numbers had risen to 675,000, but this dropped sharply to a low of 350,000 the following year when a combination of drought and ECF culled nearly 50 per cent of the district herd. Only five years later, in 1989, cattle numbers had recovered from the losses to 670,000, but the human population was then estimated at 146,268 Maasai and 112,391 non-Maasai. Again, leaving aside the impact of the non-Maasai population, this dramatic growth implied a reduction to just over 3 TLU per Maasai.

The most recently available livestock estimates, for 1992, give surprisingly high figures of 886,000 cattle, 969,000 sheep and 896,000 goats, amounting to a total of 992,000 TLU. Though very high compared with earlier data, these estimates reflect the clear impression of those living in the area that herds were then very large, a consequence of no disaster having struck since the mid-1980s.[19] This is all the more interesting since livestock marketing continues to be very important throughout the district. With livestock/population ratios as high as these figures imply, a large part of the population would apparently be able to subsist on milk and meat alone without recourse to the sale of livestock. Of course, such aggregate figures give no indication of the impact upon poorer households who may still be compelled to sell stock to survive and who could not continue to do so over the longer term.

Cultivation and the expansion of the urban environment are slowly but steadily spreading their influence into the district. The Ngong area carries the burden in this respect, where overflow from Nairobi is causing a rapid increase of cultivation and urban land use. But even in the group ranch areas along the road to Tanzania, cultivation is becoming more apparent. Here we find group ranches that were among the earliest lands in Kajiado to be subdivided among individual owners. Immediately after subdivision, land in these areas was quickly further subdivided to be sold off, allowing the sellers to accumulate capital for reinvestment in the ranching, to repay debts, to diversify into businesses or simply for consumption. Buyers were motivated variously by speculation, a desire to acquire cultivable land and demands among non-Maasai to gain a stake in commercial ranching. In this process, land has become a highly valuable commodity, fetching tens of thousands of shillings per hectare. This important development has triggered a number of other changes, which were at first slow to spread, but have now gained considerable momentum.

In the Maasai area, conditions for livestock marketing are incomparably more favourable than in many other dry regions of Kenya. Kajiado District, in particular, has a good connection with Nairobi through the tarmac road to Tanzania that runs through it, while the northern part of the district borders the railway line, the main road to Mombasa and the densely populated Machakos District. Of course, in the interior of the district the roads are sandy, and the south-eastern part of the district is more easily reached from Tanzania, but on the whole the majority of the district's herd-owners have relatively easy access to the livestock trade.

Usually, herders either sell or give animals to brokers who collect the livestock at the producers' homes until they have a sizeable herd ready for market. Alternatively, the herder may take the animal to a nearby market himself. Small markets serve as collection points, from which the bigger markets are supplied. In Kajiado Diistrict, Emali market has always been one of the most important for livestock sales (Bekure *et al*, 1991) and, even though other markets recently have grown in size, it has retained its primary position. A study of the Emali cattle market in Kajiado District in 1990–1 revealed that supply varied considerably, from 1500 head per week in November 1990 to January 1991, to a peak of 5000 per week in June–July 1991. Between 30 per cent and 90 per cent of the numbers offered for sale were actually sold at Emali. Despite fluctuations in supply and in percentage of sales, average prices remained relatively high throughout the year, varying between KSh. 2200 and KSh. 3200 (weighted average) (Zaal, 1993).

There are a number of explanations for these high average prices. The most obvious relates to changes in the marketing infrastructure, with the problems and ultimate collapse of the operations of the KMC at the Athi River abattoir and the liberalization of the meat trade. Private slaughter-houses had already taken over the bulk of the trade from Kajiado, long before liberalization in the early 1990s. Meat from private slaughterhouses in Kajiado was transported directly to Nairobi markets, via wholesalers and butchers, bringing customers closer to producers, with the effect of improving meat prices realized in the district. All along Kajiado District's main roads, slaughterhouses have been erected in response to this oppor-tunity, each privately owned. Livestock is also imported from Tanzania to be processed through these slaughterhouses in quite considerable numbers, contributing greatly to their economic viability (although with the low value of the Kenya shilling this trade temporarily reversed in December 1993). The most important slaughterhouses are in the Ngong area, near Nairobi, where more than half the animals are taken,[20] but now increasingly slaughterhouses further away are becoming significant. After slaughtering, the carcasses are transported to Nairobi by car, so-called 'meat *matatus*', high-speed unchilled pick-up trucks with special boxes in the back, that take about an hour to reach Nairobi. Since the early 1990s, politically inspired conflicts between various groups in Rift Valley Province have disrupted flows of animals to Nairobi from these areas, opening up a larger slice of the market to traders from Kajiado. Similarly, the conflict in Somalia has caused a slump in supply to Nairobi from the northern districts through Isiolo.

How have the CToT in Kajiado been affected by these most recent developments? Under these circumstances, pastoralists do gain on average when they sell their animals for maize. To sell a goat of average weight for Ksh.1000 in 1995 is giving up about 11 kg of meat and 2 kg of *matumbo* (liver, heart, stomach, etc.), equivalent to 29,250 Cal. Buying maize meal at the price of KSh.15 per kg gives 67 kg, or 230,000 Cal, a ratio of 8 to 1. To feed a family of seven, one would need to sell almost 25 goats from a flock of 80 at average off-take rates, or 120 at a very low off-take rate of 20 per cent. A similar ratio (7:1) is obtained when cattle are sold to buy maize meal. The ratio for milk is 5 to 1, but better for pastoralists in the dry season; there is a clear profit to be made in food energy terms from the sale of milk.[21]

Over earlier years the situation has fluctuated greatly. In 1990, one head of cattle was sold for an average KSh.3000, for which 600 kg of maize meal could be bought. This represents a ratio of 8:1 in caloric terms. In 1985, an estimated KSh.1830 for an animal would buy 445 kg of maize, a CToT ratio of only 6:1. In 1980, one head of cattle sold bought 800 kg of maize meal, for a CToT of 11:1. In 1975, one head of cattle (of admittedly lower quality) was equivalent to 300 kg of maize meal, giving a CToT of only 4:1 – probably the lowest ratio at any time over the past three decades. Comparing the 1995 situation with earlier periods thus demonstrates considerable fluctuations in the relative position of pastoralists, although even the worst years still provide positive terms of trade in respect of food energy.

However, it is not enough to look only at gross price trends in maize meal and livestock. With the increased use of commercial in-puts in animal husbandry, especially on the part of wealthier herd-owners, the price trends of these in-puts need to be taken into account. Prices of livestock in-puts recently increased at a greater rate than the price of maize. As a consequence, few pastoralists using sprays will now apply these to their entire herd, instead restricting spraying to the better, more highly valued stock (generally including improved breeds, cows in calf and sick animals). For these herders, the terms of trade have deteriorated recently, but they can still afford to continue buying at least some quantity of the necessary supplies. They find themselves in a position similar to the farmers in western Kenya who produce maize for the market; improved seeds, fertilizer and pesticides have become expensive, while the price received for their maize has risen less.

We can explore and disaggregate the impact of such shifts to better effect by considering the example of the Olkarkar group ranch. The division of larger group ranches, such as Olkarkar, into smaller, individually owned ranches is progressing at a great pace throughout Kajiado. This change is but the latest in a long list of changes in land tenure over the past half-century (Rutten, 1992).

The first controlled grazing scheme in Kajiado was introduced in the Konza area in 1949, with group ranches being launched among the Kaputei Maasai in 1964 as part of the World Bank-funded Kenya Livestock Development Programme. Despite these innovations, herders were very slow to alter their production parameters to accommodate land-tenure reforms. Sub-division of the group ranches was first proposed in 1982, with the Olkinos group ranch leading the way with sub-division in 1986. Since then, sub-division has accelerated, the Olkarkar ranch being sub-divided in 1994–5, local pastoralists quickly adopting the sub-division even before title-deeds had been issued. With this smaller, more focused example of Olkarkar, we can evaluate issues of income and expenditure more precisely, to reveal some quite sharp distinctions between wealthier and poorer pastoralists.

To assess wealth distribution among the herders of Olkarkar, we have calculated TLU by quantifying cattle numbers along with sheep and goats to give a single measure. In addition, a high percentage of improved breeds and crosses in the herds was considered a sign of wealth, as was the ownership of a hand-spray to control ticks. Though not a direct indication of wealth, the hypothesis was that, through their labour needs for intensive production, wealthy pastoralists would be less likely to migrate to townships and Nairobi and would have fewer non-agricultural jobs, in view of the higher labour needs of improved breeds. In discussions with respondents, we asked them to identify the people they considered very poor and very rich, and interviews with these people were then conducted so as to assess these perceptions.

In their 1980–81 survey of this area, White & Meadows (1981:16–17) found relatively high levels of stock ownership. They divided the population into three broad bands: below-average households, with 3.7 head of cattle and 6.1 head of small stock per capita; average households, with 8.1 head of cattle and 8 head of small stock per capita; and above-average households, with 20.5 head of cattle and 10 head of small stock per capita. From these figures, even those households reckoned to be below average had sufficient livestock to survive in the subsistence pastoral economy described in model 1. Calculating from the household sizes estimated by White & Meadows, average herd sizes in 1980–81 were 215 head of cattle and 156 small stock per household, with an average of 14.3 head of cattle and 10.4 small stock per capita. Expressed in TLU, this represents 166.1 TLU per household and 11 TLU per person. Obviously, some very rich Maasai lived in Olkarkar at this time, but wealth was not evenly distributed. In 1980–81, one-third of the households owned 69 per cent of the cattle. Since rich households were larger in size, per capita differences were smaller, and the upper third of the survey owned five times the number of cattle owned by the lower third.

By 1994–5 the situation remained rather similar in per capita terms, even if households appear somewhat less wealthy on average. The TLU was calculated at an average of 59 per household, still a considerable figure when set against the average household size of 7.5, giving a TLU of 7.9 per capita. Allowing for possible underenumeration of younger children and young adults and making a rough estimate of average household size in the population as a whole, a higher estimated figure of 8.7 members per household still gives an average of 7 TLU per capita. As in 1980–81, the pattern of distribution of this livestock in 1994–5 reveals substantial differentials between rich and poor households. Of the households surveyed, 21 per cent had herds below the threshold of 4 TLU per capita, and, unchanged from 1980–81, the upper third of the households surveyed had five times the number of livestock (in TLU) possessed by the lower third.

The average 1994–5 figure of 7.9 TLU per capita among the Olkarkar community compares favourably with our estimate of the minimum

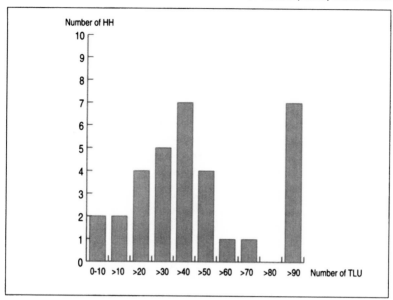

Figure 8.5 Household wealth in TLU

requirements of 4 TLU per capita, but it is apparent from Rutten's surveys (1992:346) in another part of Kajiado District that these figures are not exceptional: in another group ranch survey, Rutten has found an average of 9.1 head of cattle and 12.9 head of small stock per capita, giving a total of 7.6 TLU per capita.[22] He has argued that these figures suggest there has been a break in the trend of declining per capita stock ownership levels, and the Olkarkar data appear to support this assertion. Thus, even though district livestock figures have fluctuated hugely in the past, the average pastoralist in the Olkarkar area has been able to hold on to a number of animals that is more than adequate to feed the household.

The distribution of livestock within the population is highly skewed, as indicated in Fig. 8.5. The poorest household surveyed held only 6.1 TLU (six cattle and five small stock), while the richest owned 327.9 TLU (comprising a herd of 422 cattle and a flock of 305 small stock). This range is considerable by any standard, but it is even more interesting to note that there seems to be a 'wealth gap' between those with average-sized herds and the very rich. As we shall see, it is the wealthier owners of these huge herds who have led the shift to commercial production. At the same time, there is marked differentiation among poorer households also, both in ownership of livestock and in access to alternative sources of income.

There proved to be a negative correlation between livestock ownership (in TLU) and involvement in non-agricultural jobs and between wealth and migration as a whole (although the correlations were low). Income

other than from cattle sales was relatively small, even for wealthy
pastoralists. White & Meadows (1981: v) found a positive correlation in
these indicators in 1980–81, and further enquiries will be needed to establish what has caused the shift. No correlation between wealth and ownership of hand-sprays could be identified, since practically everybody
possessed one, regardless of wealth in livestock. It may well be that
possession of hand-sprays is more closely correlated with availability of
water; the only nearby permanent source of water is just outside the group
ranch area. In other areas of the district dipping is still common, but for
dipping a reliable source of water is required.

*Table 8.1 Average numbers of introduced/cross-breeds of cattle & small stock per
wealth class (< 90 TLU, > 90 TLU), Olkarkar 1994–95, in TLU per household
and percentage*

Type	< 90 TLU		> 90 TLU	
	heads	%	heads	%
Local breed, cattle	16	28	24	19
Introduced/crossed, cattle	42	72	102	81
Total cattle	58	100	126	100
Local breed, small stock	6	10	10	6
Introduced/crossed small stock	56	90	171	94
Total small stock	62	100	181	100

Source: own survey.

Relating wealth and household size reveals that average household size
is much smaller in 1994–5 than in 1980–81, but that bigger herds are
more often owned by bigger households. There was a positive correlation
between average number of animals and size of households. Still, all but
one of those producers owning big herds (between 90 and 327 TLU per
household) also have the highest number of animals per capita (between
9.5 and 22 TLU). There has been only a slight shift in sex distribution of
animals in the herds. While in 1980–81 percentages of between 72 (the
above-average group) and 64 female stock were found, with an average of
69, we found an average of 64 per cent cows in 1994–5. This is still at a
level characteristic of subsistence milk-orientated pastoralists. It is also
clear, from Table 8.1, that the wealthy pastoralists have relatively high
numbers of cattle and fewer small stock. This is a phenomenon described
elsewhere, but it appears here very prominently. Poorer livestock
producers rely more on small stock; rich pastoralists have more small stock
than poorer pastoralists, but the percentage of small stock declines.

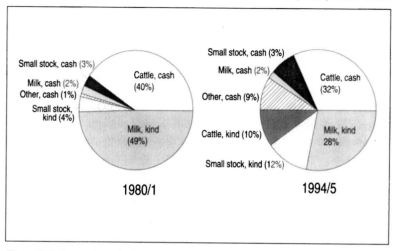

Figure 8.6 Income in cash & kind, 1980–81 & 1994–5

Table 8.1 further indicates, perhaps not surprisingly, that wealthier households owned more improved breeds and crosses as a percentage of total cattle holdings than did poorer households, although the figures for both groups are relatively high by most standards. Not only are improved breeds more expensive to acquire, but they also need more care and more regular watering. The capital and recurrent costs this implies can be met only when productivity and marketed offtake are higher. Water is one of the major problems in the Olkarkar area, and those who live furthest away from the permanent source of water often have their breeding bulls in another group-ranch area. This involves additional costs for grazing as well. How do pastoralists gain the income to meet these costs?

In 1980–81, when White & Meadows studied the production systems of a number of group ranches,[23] Olkarkar was the only one where average cash income was lower than average income in kind (Fig. 8.6). Other group ranches studied at that time had income in cash percentages of 58 (Longosua), 59 (Poka), 60 (Elang'ata Wuas) and 62 (Kiboko). To evaluate the changes by 1994–5, we employed similar categories to those used in the White & Meadows study, from which cash income from the sale of cattle, small stock and milk can be computed and combined with income in kind. The latter is mostly the consumption of meat and milk produced from the herds. In addition, we studied income and expenditure patterns for a full year within the Olkarkar group-ranch area.

From Fig. 8.6, it appears that diversification in income generation by pastoralists at Olkarkar was quite marked between 1980–81 and 1994–5. A large part of their cash income comes from small-stock sales and from other sources, such as jobs and self-employment (running a shop, a bar, etc.). The dominance of milk consumption in income in kind is disappearing, and instead consumption of cattle and small stock (22 per cent of total income) is becoming more important. Slaughter for food accounts for only part of total meat consumption. For small stock, for example, only half of the animals eaten were slaughtered, consumption of animals that died adding another 40 per cent (animals killed by wild animals or that died of diseases or accidents). Total off-take of cattle is not lower. Combining cattle sales and income in kind (slaughter, consumption of animals that have died and gifts being the most important) we arrive at 42 per cent, which is roughly the same percentage as for cattle sales in 1980–81. Slaughter of cattle was extremely rare in 1980–81. Income from milk is low in relative terms, and sales and consumption combined now contribute 30 per cent of total income, whereas White & Meadows found it to be almost 50 per cent.

Table 8.2 Average annual household income in cash in Olkarkar, per household wealth class, in current Kenya Shs. and percentages, 1994–5

Category	all households		< 90 TLU		> 90 TLU	
	Shs.	%	Shs.	%	Shs.	%
Cattle	88,920	64	52,836	57	223,380	73
Small stock	19,200	14	17,352	19	26,206	9
Milk	6,468	5	6,588	7	5,964	2
Other	23,844	17	16,524	18	50,040	16
Total	138,432		93,300		305,590	

Source: own survey.

Large herd-owners are not necessarily more involved in the cash economy than poorer households. Pastoralists with smaller herds may have to sell part of their production (both milk and young animals) to buy food, thereby obtaining a gain in caloric value. But, in the case of Olkarkar, the large herd-owners have incomes three times those of the average poorer herd-owner, and their dependence on income from cattle sales is higher as well. Table 8.2 shows that there is indeed a gap between these groups in both the level and the source of their incomes. While rich herd-owners have more small stock (though representing a smaller percentage of their herd in TLU), they rely strongly in relative terms on cattle for their income. Milk sales by rich pastoralists are lower even in absolute terms. But, in the category 'other sources of income', there is hardly any difference in relative terms. As the wealthier households rely on cattle sales, they can retain the milk for home consumption and for the calves. This affects the position of women in wealthier households, in that their access to an independent income diminishes as milk sales decline.

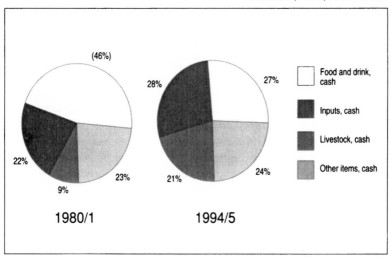

Figure 8.7 Expenditure in cash, 1980–81 & 1994–5

Turning from income to expenditure, there are further interesting comparisons between the findings of White & Meadows from 1980–81 and those of 1994–5. Here again, the earlier 'traditional' dominance of food and drinks has disappeared, and expenditure on livestock inputs is high, in particular veterinary medicine (Fig. 8.7). The figures for 1980–81 were restricted to cash expenditure only, and so animals given away were not included, although the practice is universal in pastoral production systems and probably formed a relevant part of expenditures in 1980–81. In 1994–5, animal gifts formed about 5 per cent of total expenditures. This is remarkably low, even allowing for a degree of underenumeration, and it indicates the extent to which commoditization has taken place in this area. Also, in 1980–81, Olkarkar was rather particular in that much more money was spent on food and drinks than in the other group ranches. On average, expenditure on food and drinks for all group ranches together was 33 per cent in 1980–81, 37 per cent being spent on costs related to livestock production (of which livestock represented 18 per cent, and inputs another 19 per cent), leaving 29 per cent spent on other items (including health services, etc.). The equivalent percentages for Olkarkar in 1994–5 are given in Fig. 8.7. By 1994–5, the amount spent on food and drinks at Olkarkar had declined to about a quarter of total expenditure in cash. Expenditure on inputs (salt, veterinary medicine, labour, money for grazing and water, hand sprays, etc.) had climbed to 28 per cent. Expenditure on livestock is now quite high, indicating its increasing commoditization: instead of exchanging animals, they are now sold and bought. This is partly for trading purposes, but mostly for breeding.[24]

The wealthiest people in Olkarkar have taken the greatest steps towards commercial production, based largely on commoditized inputs and trade in animals. It is also clear that even poorer households must invest in livestock production. At Olkarkar, the former group-ranch lands have been divided in a process of privatization, but fencing is not yet considered necessary. Most of the barbed wire one sees in the district is owned by non-Maasai who have acquired plots for cultivation or by Maasai who depend on other sources of income (Rutten, 1992:362). Typically, fenced private ranches of this sort are kept at low levels of productivity. In contrast, many Maasai in Olkarkar spend money on grazing, water, veterinary medicine and improved breeds. This is reflected in the differences in spending between the two groups of pastoralists (Table 8.3). This pattern of emerging commercial production corresponds to the conditions described in our model 4. Traditional grazing flexibility is maintained, while resources and services formerly freely given to clansmen and age-mates increasingly become commodities.

Table 8.3 Average annual household cash expenditure in Olkarkar, per household wealth class, in current Kenya Shs. and percentages, 1994–5

Category	All households		< 90 TLU		> 90 TLU	
	Shs.	%	Shs.	X	Shs.	Z
Food/drink	34,452	27	31,908	31	44,628	21
Inputs	35,328	28	24,120	23	80,700	37
Cattle	21,780	17	18,144	17	35,628	16
Small stock	4,368	3	5,280	5	948	0
Other	30,516	24	23,940	23	55,640	26
Total	126,444	99	103,392	99	217,548	100

Source: own survey (errors due to rounding).

Two Maasai we talked to are particularly interesting as examples of how some of the richest Maasai at Olkarkar have changed their production system in recent years. Both live on their own ranch, although neither has an individual title-deed yet. They have together bought a Sahiwal steer for breeding purposes, and one of them has another besides to service his own herd. As he bought his own animal in the dry season, he had to sell ten head of cattle to pay for the cost of water and feed. The two Sahiwal steers are kept in neighbouring individual ranches, where the chances of catching diseases are lower. The two herders use money for veterinary medicine, salt and spraying, and have fenced part of their land with *Osilalei* (a small tree particularly suitable for this purpose). They still call these fenced areas by the traditional term *Olopololi* – to denote land set aside for young animals and sick and lactating cows – although the area is larger than would be usual for such a purpose. The zebu cows they have are used for breeding, being crossed with the Sahiwal bulls. Neither will sell cross-breeds, but they allow others to keep one or two heifers in the herd for breeding with the bull. They want their herds to consist of improved breeds or crosses only. They have invested in grazing and water, although water-supply remains one of the biggest problems they face. They have access to a small dam, but the water does not last beyond August. One of the men has a square house with iron-sheet roofing, and both have bicycles. Neither man will allow the women in their households to sell any milk, because it would result in competition between calves and children over the remaining milk. They prefer dams and rain-pans to boreholes, as these are cheaper to maintain and there is always lack of maintenance with communal boreholes. When the local grazing is finished, usually sometime in August or September, they move to the neighbouring Kiboko group-ranch area and sometimes on to Makueni and into the Machakos District further north. They will sell animals to pay for inputs during that shift, in particular for veterinary medicine and grazing, because the animals get exhausted. For most herders at Olkarkar, spraying is usual once a week, but these men spray twice weekly.

Contrast the experience of the two wealthy pastoralists with another Olkarkar producer with very few animals, who made the best of the fact that his neighbours migrated during part of the year. He chooses to stay and take on small jobs, such as the fencing of other people's *Olopololi*. Migration is a strain on the animal, which needs additional veterinary medicine, grazing and water, costs which he avoids by staying put. During that time his animals graze on the small patches of grass and herbs left by the bigger herds, in particular in those areas where the soils are slightly waterlogged for part of the year. The owners let him graze there and he does not have to pay for grazing. On the other hand, he sometimes allows the neighbours to graze their animals on his land, for which he receives a small amount of money. His house is small, of the traditional kind and in a poor state of repair. The compound likewise is small and, because he lives in an area with few trees the fence is incomplete. The lack of trees is an extra burden on his wife, who fetches wood and water from considerable distances (up to 15 km), especially in the dry season. She has to get water at Masimba in the dry season, at the other end of the group ranch, since he does not have his own dam. Most of the money he earns he spends on maize, other food and livestock inputs.

As these examples of rich and poor households both indicate, the roles of men and women in the production and consumption of goods is changing in Olkarkar. Women in Maasai areas are usually dependent for their cash income on the sale of milk and hides and skins. In relative terms, the role of milk as a source of cash declines when wealth increases and production becomes more commercial. Increasingly, women complain about the fact that men prevent them from milking enough for household consumption. The relative importance of income from milk, be it in kind or cash, has declined. The sale of hides and skins has gone up, but this hardly makes up for the loss. On the other hand, women in poorer households still have control over a large part of the family income. Also, there are now women who decide on expenditure themselves and go shopping, instead of asking their husbands to pay for the goods the women subsequently carry home on their backs. Usually, these women are married either to men who have a job somewhere else or to men who have more than one wife. The second wife, often living in close proximity to the market centre, caters for the needs of children in school, and has some of her own animals with her. The men provide them with food aid, a regular supply of small animals or money whenever they visit the market-place. In Olkarkar, we also found some women who formed a group to save Ksh.5 on each milk sale and who bought 20 young steers for fattening from the proceeds. While there are initiatives of this kind, they receive little subsequent support. This particular initiative was threatened by a loss of control over the young steers to the male herders and by dominance of the men in relationships with outside actors (such as researchers and government and NGO or development project personnel) over what kind of help should be provided.

In relation to the shift of income away from milk, from the discussions with women it seemed that they felt they had lost control over their lives in a more general sense. The shift from subsistence production to increasingly commercial production, accompanied by individualization of land, to which women have less access than before, makes them dependent on the man's decision-making. Following subdivision, the *engkangs* (the traditional residential units) split up, as has clearly happened in Olkarkar, and the separate households – almost becoming nuclear families – go and live on the new ranch. All women we talked to complained about the isolation that was the result of this move. While men went off to the market-places, their women stayed behind.

But not everyone within the former group ranch has managed the shift toward individual commercial ranching successfully. The most successful are often those who were influential in earlier phases of land-tenure and production reforms. According to Hedlund (1971:4), in earlier times 'registration itself was considered more important than other kinds of development' by these pioneers of change, while Galaty (1980:165) has observed that 'the major significance of the group ranch structure lies not in the field of economic innovation, which was occurring previously through individual and neighbourhood channels, but in the essential area of political security'. The group of very wealthy people we described above, owning more than 100 head of cattle, are increasingly dependent on their cattle for their cash income and will no doubt continue to invest in their animals. In the process of land privatization, the more influential and richer pastoralists have been quickest to register title, thus getting first choice of land and location and often obtaining the best ranches. Wealth may be enough to buy the advantage, and it certainly gives richer pastoralists the economic and political power to secure their own interests. The security that subsistence production and the social structure in general no longer provide will be sought increasingly through contacts with politicians and civil servants.

Conclusions

Over the twentieth century, pastoralists have found it increasingly difficult to secure the resources they depend upon to maintain their production system. They seem more vulnerable than ever to the impact of climatic variability and disease episodes and, in some areas, such as West Pokot, they are beset by violent attacks and a lack of personal security. More recently, other uncertainties have become more pronounced: loss of control over and even ownership of land through privatization and sale. As a consequence, pastoralists are now more dependent on the increased marketing of produce or on other sources of income. Economic forces, in the shape of traders in livestock and grains, and the vagaries of government policies have become very important determinants of pastoralist success or failure in places as diverse as Kajiado and West Pokot.

In these circumstances, commoditization is a strategy that can ease the tensions between pastoral production capacity, household food requirements and the need for production inputs. Positive terms of trade, especially CToT, are the key requirement, enabling the pastoralist to employ the commoditization strategy effectively, even in times of crisis. Several other market-level conditions are also important if commoditization is to be applied successfully. Liberalization of the livestock, meat and grains markets have helped in food provision in the districts examined here and in generally improving the marketing of livestock. The commercial system that developed over the 1990s has had particularly favourable effects in Kajiado, but less so in West Pokot. A small group of influential businessmen and ex-politicians has seen the opportunity to start in this business, which has helped in developing a slaughterhouse and butchery sector in both districts, but at the cost of increasing inequality. In general, as the economy in Kenya is influenced heavily by political decision-making, involvement in the market has its risks as well. Conditions may change suddenly, as is the case with the planned redevelopment of the KMC as a private enterprise, at the expense of the smaller-scale slaughterhouses. Conflicts between ethnic groups have disrupted markets in Kenya before, and may do so again. Greater engagement with the market offers alternatives, but it does not necessarily lessen risks.

Commoditization is evident in both Kajiado and West Pokot, but each is taking a different road. In West Pokot, commoditization is the road to survival, in Kajiado, it is the road to the ranch. The road to survival is mapped out by a gradual decrease in the TLU per capita figures, especially among the pastoralists at the lower end of the wealth spectrum. In the wake of the disasters of 1979–82, these now form the large majority of the remaining pastoralists in West Pokot. In contrast, the road to the ranch in Kajiado is being laid down by pastoralists following an accumulation strategy at the upper end of the wealth spectrum, who feel an increasing need to improve livestock productivity through purchased inputs. This strategy of accumulation is being pursued by a large group among current Maasai herders and only a very small group among the Pokot. But in both districts the accumulation strategy tries to diminish risks related to the market by connections with politics and politicians. In both societies a clear process of wealth differentiation is visible. Among the poor, we see a strategy of diversification of sources of income, in which livestock-related activities are only part of a broader survival package. Among the rich, both specialization and diversification are found. Where marketing options for livestock are good and stable, specialization is a safe option.

To understand what is happening in current pastoral development in Kenya, the concept of CToT between livestock and grains (or maize meal) offers many significant clues, but it is clearly not enough on its own to explain all the changes taking place, especially with regard to the wealthier pastoralists. The whole bundle of purchases and sales needs to be included as part of an overall analysis of all the trends in commoditization, including inputs, land and labour.

Notes

1. The research among the Pokot was partly funded by the Dutch Ministry of Development Cooperation (as research for the Arid and Semi-Arid Lands Programme); the research among the Maasai was partly funded by the Netherlands Israel Development Research Programme and in collaboration with the ASAL Programme in Kajiado. In both cases, the recent work was part of the collaboration between the University of Amsterdam and the Moi University in Eldoret, Kenya.
2. Of course, there is a complex debate going on about the type of wage, because in so many cases the 'wage labourers' get their rewards in non-monetary forms (e.g. food or livestock wealth) and also many of them have family ties (or age-mate or clan ties) with the 'employer' in various forms of patron–client relationships.
3. The evidence offered comes from a project on the 'caloric terms of trade', as part of the collaboration between the University of Amsterdam and Moi University, Eldoret. Other more recent projects in Kenya along the same lines have started in Garissa, among the Kenyan Somali and in Marsabit, where the Gabbra, Boran and Rendille in this northern part of the country are compared as to their marketing behaviour. In addition, trends in East Africa and West Africa are compared.

4. The unit most widely used in Kenya (Peden, 1984; Bekure *et al.*, 1991; Kilewe & Thomas, 1992:77): 1 TLU = 1.42 head of cattle, ten hair sheep or goats, one camel.
5. A steer = 100 kg of meat x 2300 Cal = 23,0000 Cal. This is equivalent to 65 kg of maize or sorghum. A litre of milk = 700 Cal. This is equivalent to 200 g of cereals in energy terms.
6. The depreciation against the Tanzania shilling and the dollar was considerable.
7. Any trend in index figures depends, of course, on the basis from which the index is computed. Started five years later, the figures for 1995 would be quite different: 909 for maize, 499 for cattle. When we compare national-level animal and maize prices for the years mentioned in Fig. 8.2, expressed in caloric terms (the CToT discussed above), the discussion is put on a more solid footing. A CToT of 4 would mean that, with the sale of an animal, about four times its food-energy value in the form of grains can be bought.
8. From only one bag of maize in the mid-1980s, first to ten bags in 1988, then to 44 bags and later to 88 bags in the early 1990s, and now transportation of maize between districts in the country as well as imports is supposed to be free.
9. The total population included agropastoral Pokot, probably one-third at the time. Since they had animals, as well as intensive links with pastoral Pokot, they are included in the estimate.
10. Related to the kat family of stimulants.
11. These days, it is very difficult to say who is a pastoralist and who is one no longer. The population census of 1989 (Republic of Kenya, 1994) showed that the district of West Pokot had 225,000 inhabitants, 190,000 of them Kalenjin (and Pokot the overwhelming majority of those Kalenjin). The areas generally considered 'pastoral' are Alale Division in the north-west, Kacheliba Division in the south-west and most of Kipkomo, Batei, Lomut, Masol, Weiwei and Cheptulel locations (half the population there estimated to be pastoral). These 'pastoral areas' had about 75,000 inhabitants, owning probably two-thirds of the animals in the district. This would give a TLU per capita figure of 1.3 for these lowlands. It is interesting to note that, in the census reports of both 1979 and 1989, all Kalenjin were grouped together, unlike earlier census reports, where Pokot and all the other Kalenjin subgroups are mentioned separately.
12. By human-geography students Nanda Haverkort and Els Veldhuizen, assisted by local research assistant Simon Lopeyok, who had also done the survey in 1983.
13. The improvement may be attributed partly to the shift in power between the Pokot and the Karamojong in favour of the former, resulting in considerable counter-raiding of cattle. Also, the Pokot successfully increased their number of goats through purchase and gifts from their relatives in the highlands.
14. The exceptional household improved its livestock wealth from 19 to 54 TLU.
15. For a fuller discussion of the figures cited in this paragraph, see Dietz (1993: 93). In 1993, maize grains had gone up to Ksh.40 per tin, while goat prices were below Ksh.300 per animal. During the first part of 1995, maize grains sold at Ksh.8-10 per 2-kg tin; finger-millet at Ksh.20-30 per tin and beans at Ksh.25-50 per tin. Goat prices were above Ksh.500 per animal and cattle prices above Ksh.4000 (Haverkort, Veldhuizen and Lopeyok, personal communication).
16. With all its limitations, see De Leeuw & Tothill, 1993:77-88 for a recent comprehensive view. Stocking rates of between 1.5 ha/TLU and 4.2 ha/TLU were the basis of this estimate. Olkarkar group-ranch area was rated as a 1.8 ha/TLU area.
17. Both figures of 750,000 head of cattle and 53,200 people, derived from the *Annual Reports*, seem too high.
18. There were probably around 50,000 non-Maasai in the district by that time.
19. We have no indication that the drought in 1993 caused the stock loss in Kajiado District it was said to have caused by the authorities.
20. Of an official (under-recorded) slaughter figure of 26,298 head of cattle and 21,965 small stock in 1994 in Kajiado District, 55 per cent and 52 per cent, respectively, were slaughtered in Ngong division, serving both Nairobi and local residents (Republic of Kenya, 1995).
21. Compare this with the farmer who sells maize to buy meat at the butchery! He or she pays KSh.120 per kg of meat, and has to sell 13 kg of maize, which in terms of food energy values is a negative ratio of 1 to 18 at present prices.

22. Olkinos, Embolioi, Kiboko, Elang'ata Wuas, Lorngosua and Meto.
23. Apart from Olkarkar, Poka, Kiboko, Elang'ata Wuas and Lorngosua were studied, together with individual ranchers in the vicinity of these group ranches.
24. Of course, more generally there were under-recording errors similar to those reported by White & Meadows in their study, but, comparing the cash income and expenditure levels, it appears that this under-recording is probably not very great. We found that total recorded expenditure amounted to 91 per cent of total recorded income. Part of the difference was spent on drinks in bars (there was a difference, for example, between what was stated as expenditure on drinks and what was recorded in the bars). However, there were additional livestock-related expenditures during migration as well. Data are being gathered now to fill in the remaining gap.

9 Mutual Assistance among the Ngorongoro Maasai

TOMASZ POTKANSKI

This chapter, based on field research conducted between 1991 and 1993 among the Maasai of Tanzania, mainly in the Ngorongoro Conservation Area within the Ngorongoro District, offers an analysis of forms of traditional mutual assistance practised by Maasai herders. The pastoral economy of the approximately 40,000 Maasai living in this area has recently been subject to severe strains, primarily caused by epidemics of tick-borne livestock diseases, the effects of which have been accentuated due to the lack of adequate veterinary services within the Conservation Area. The limited subsistence cultivation practised by over half of the Maasai households in Ngorongoro as an anti-poverty measure is opposed by the government, who view it as being incompatible with conservation objectives of the area.

The clan-based system of cattle redistribution to impoverished families will be central to this discussion of mutual assistance, although its importance has not been recognized widely in the existing literature on Maasai pastoralism. Perhaps more than any other pastoral group in eastern Africa, Maasai society has commonly been characterized in idealized and even stereotypical terms. The emphasis this tended to place upon the strength of cultural 'norms', and especially upon self-reliance and independence, has contributed to a neglect of the internal societal dynamics of mutual assistance (Spear & Waller, 1993). Also, the experience of poverty has increased markedly among some Maasai sections in recent years and this has brought mechanisms of mutual assistance into sharper profile. For the Maasai of Ngorongoro, poverty is now a reality and its solution is a concern that affects the whole community.

In describing traditional Maasai systems of mutual assistance, one has to distinguish between two distinct categories. The first is individual assistance, in which individual gifts and/or loans of food and livestock may be made from one person to another. This category constitutes the majority of transactions that take place between herders. The basis for such assistance can be close family ties (patrilineal and affinal), personal friendship between recipient and donor or their relationship as age-mates. These individual gifts or loans are based on the expectation of future reciprocity. Viewed from a comparative perspective, individual assistance of this kind does not differ significantly from what we know of many other pastoral societies. In contrast, our second category is collective, clan-based mutual assistance. This constitutes the core of the mutual assistance system as practised by Maasai in the Ngorongoro area, and through its operation poverty-stricken families are enabled to move back toward self-sustaining pastoralism once again. The existence of similarly sophisticated and complex systems has been documented for several other pastoral societies, including Borana and Somali. The collective clan-based system should not be considered as just an aggregate result of individually made gifts, but rather as a separate, distinct and consciously maintained system of mutual assistance within clans. It is known as *ewoloto* or, more properly, *engelata ewoloto*. This is actually only one of four types of *engelata*, and a detailed description of this institution will follow in the next section.

The objective of the system is to assist families that 'cannot help themselves' to break out of the vicious circle of poverty to become self-sustaining pastoralists. Although the system appears to be male-centred, with men mostly dominating the negotiations, in fact it is the family unit, and not the male herder alone, which is targeted for assistance. The system is primarily operated among clan members in each locality, although an individual family in need can approach fellow clan members in other localities as well and has a right to expect assistance. The widespread functioning of this system at the level of the local community (*enkutoto*) is possible, since members of all seven clans found in Ngorongoro (Laiser, Lukumai, Laitayok, Molellian, Makasen, Tarosero, Mamasita) are dispersed throughout 'Maasailand' and it is therefore usual to find representatives of all seven clans in each locality.

The underlying ideology of the Maasai clan is that 'we are brothers and the children of each of us are our common children'. The social obligation within the clan is exemplified by the common belief that 'cattle belonging to each of us at the same time belong to all of us'. Sharing cattle in the event of a fellow clansman's misfortune gives substantive social meaning to this loose ideology of diffused property rights. The ideas of 'brotherhood', 'common responsibility for children' and 'common cattle' are thus the basis for the traditional redistribution of cattle to destitute clan members (for a fuller discussion see Potkanski, 1994a and 1994c). However, within this generalized notion of a 'common good', Maasai culture also accommodates the idea of the 'deserving poor' – that is, those whose poverty is to be distinguished from persons whose behaviour brings ill-fortune upon themselves. Before describing the operation of the *engelata ewoloto* mutual assistance system in greater detail, we first need to discuss the accepted criteria by which those in poverty can be judged to be elligible to receive the assistance of clansmen.

Measuring wealth and poverty in Maasai pastoral society

The major tool employed in external assessments of levels of wealth and poverty among pastoralists is the concept of 'cattle per capita', or more precisely, 'livestock units per capita' (expressed as LU, SSU, tropical livestock units (TLU), etc.). Where sociological data are detailed enough, such calculations may even be expressed in 'livestock units per adult equivalent', but at that level of sophistication the numbers generated can become less meaningful to the local authorities and development planners who seek to interpret them in terms of policy. This method of assessment originally derived from attempts to measure the minimum nutritional requirements of pastoralists, based upon crude assumptions about pastoralists' diet in relation to pastoral production. While such calculations provided the bases for comparisons across groups and territories, the practical weakness of the method lay in the demonstrable fact that most pastoralists either employ cultivation themselves or barter their products with agriculturalists for cereals to be used for domestic consumption. Rarely is it that any pastoralist community in East Africa lives off livestock products alone. Aware of this shortcoming, Kjærby (1979) attempted to estimate the minimum herd per capita in an exchange-orientated pastoral economy, making the more sophisticated assumption that caloric requirements would be met by purchasing grain with income generated from commercial off-take, while protein requirements would be met by the consumption of milk and meat from the family herd. Accordingly, he estimated that the average pastoral family needed to have a minimum herd equivalent to around 5 LU per capita in order to meet their subsistence requirements. This formula is, of course, vulnerable to fluctuating terms of trade and to changes in the practicability of effecting barter exchanges, but it remains the most appropriate academic method of measuring the basic level of livestock requirements among pastoralists.

When these externally derived estimations are set alongside Maasai internal expressions of relative wealth or poverty in livestock, it quickly becomes apparent that the minimum nutritional requirements for pastoralists as calculated 'scientifically' in terms of TLU seem high when compared with the pastoralists' own perceptions, based on their daily experience. However, although Maasai concepts of poverty and wealth are described easily, they cannot be defined so easily in empirical terms, since they combine sociological and subsistence aspects.[1] Maasai traditions assert that wealth is measured in children and cattle. But to lose one's cattle does not necessarily mean becoming socially disadvantaged. In order to rank people's wealth or poverty, the Maasai utilize the concept of the number of livestock per *engaji*. This term refers to the usual unit of one wife and her children in a polygamous family living in one house (the *engaji*) within a larger homestead. The *engaji* (pl. *inkajijik*) is, in effect, a basic consumption unit within the larger Maasai family. When deciding whether a family has entered one of the socially accepted categories of poverty which make it eligible to receive assistance from clan members, Maasai will therefore investigate the number of livestock in relation to the number of *inkajijik*. Although the Maasai themselves do not verbalize this in numerical terms, for convenience we can express it as 'LU per *engaji*', or more simply as 'livestock per *engaji*'. Once livestock holdings have been calculated in this way, it is subsequently possible to make an arithmetic conversion to livestock per capita if this is needed for comparative purposes.

Table 9.1 Maasai wealth/poverty categories as interpreted by the author

Category	Livestock per *engaji*	Equivalent in livestock per capita
Destitute	0.00–2.00	0.0–0.50
Very poor	2.01–5.00	0.50–1.25
Poor	5.01–10.00	1.25–2.50
Medium	10.01–20.00	2.5–5.0
Rich	Over 20.01	Over 5.0

Source: Potkanski, 1994c.

To employ the internally derived method of estimation, it was first necessary to determine more precisely how differing categories of poverty were defined. This was done through the analysis of a number of cases of *ewoloto* in the area of Ngorongoro, Monduli, Simanjiro and Kiteto Districts, which occurred over a five- to seven-year period. Within Ngorongoro District, most cases studied were actually in the Conservation Area and on the Salei Plain. In each case, a profile of the socio-economic position of the family was established – the property status of the family assisted, its size, any significant occupations besides pastoralism, the number of marriageable girls in the household, any appearance of alcoholism among the adult males (especially the head of family), and so on. In addition to examining real cases, fictitious cases were discussed with informants in order to set the benchmarks affecting their categorizations of eligibility for mutual assistance. Through a combination of real cases and fictitious examples, I was able to determine more closely the actual thresholds of poverty that, if crossed, changed the property status of the family. The broader aim was to assess how the poverty categories translated into practice, triggering rights of mutual assistance.

In order to describe the scale of poverty, five conventional categories were used: destitute, very poor, poor, medium and rich. The locally based logic of defining these categories was based upon a set of observations, which will be described now for each of the five groups.

Beginning at the top of the scale, Maasai informants had problems in defining a 'rich' category of households from a purely subsistence point of view in relation to longer-term security, since for them the term 'rich' only has a cultural meaning in the context of the concepts of *olkarsis* or *olparakuoni*, denoting 'a man with many wives, children and cattle'. Given this conceptual difficulty, for the sake of the model an arbitrary figure of over 20 LU per *engaji* was taken as the parameter in defining a 'rich' household. With this many livestock, there is little doubt that the herder should be able to sustain subsistence requirements from the herd over the longer term. Pastoralists in the next category ('medium') were those found to hold 10 to 20 LU per *engaji*. These households can be considered secure from the subsistence point of view over the short term, but in the longer run their herds are still vulnerable to adverse climatic conditions and epidemic diseases and may easily decline.

Those in the third category, 'poor' households, were defined as holding between 5 and 10 LU per *engaji*. From a purely subsistence point of view, Maasai recognize a herd of about ten cattle (or their equivalent in small stock) per wife in a polygamous family to be at the borderline of poverty. According to my estimates, this is equivalent to about 2.5 livestock per capita, given that the average *engaji* consists of four people. The Maasai argue that any family below this level 'does not have enough food and hunger is a constant feature of its life', especially in the dry season. This means, in observable practice, that the family herd is likely to decrease year by year because off-take, mortality and home consumption or outgoing gifts will be greater than the combination of natural increase and gifts received. A family in such a position will try desperately to limit offtake, and this results in limiting human food consumption to the bare minimum. Throughout the dry season, a poor family may consume only a light porridge and black tea, while during the wet season only milk mixed with water to add volume (*olomelok*) is likely to be available.

Given that ten livestock per *engaji* can be defined as marking the threshold of poverty, it is significant that the ideal herd offered by a husband to his new wife should not be lower than nine animals (eight heifers and one steer).[2] Maasai consider this to be the minimum herd per *engaji* which ensures natural growth, allowing for necessary off-take and mortality. In reality, the ideal herd, which is not always provided by poor husbands, is worth more than ten livestock per *engaji*, since it is composed of high-value reproductive heifers, compared with the average *inkishu engaji*, or family herd, where the number of reproductive animals may not be as great. But 10 cattle per *engaji* should be understood only as an approximate borderline of poverty in the subsistence, exchange-orientated pastoral economy. These households were not considered to be living necessarily below the 'poverty line', when alternative survival strategies for securing family livelihood, such as agriculture, cattle trading, herd reconstruction and food and livestock sharing were taken into account. Discounting the possible effects of prolonged drought or epidemic disease, it was assumed that a good herd manager might increase his herd above the level of ten livestock per *engaji*, by carefully manipulating his animals and exchanging adult animals for more productive younger ones, by receiving more gift stock and giving fewer away or by minimizing commercial off-take and home consumption. 'Poor' households were accordingly not recognized as being in need of mutual assistance, although it was understood that such households would be likely to seek individual assistance from their *osotua* (relatives), who include members of the immediate family, the extended family, affines, age-mates of the household head and other friends. These 'relatives' may be requested to provide a few animals (cattle or small stock) or alternatively food, money, clothes or medicine, depending on specific needs. A wide network of relatives and 'cattle friends' builds security for a household, allowing the head of a poverty-stricken family to ensure survival while the herd is rebuilt.

Moving down to the lower parts of the scale, households with between two and five LU per *engaji* were considered to be 'very poor'. These households were generally not thought capable of rebuilding their herds on their own, and so were considered eligible for mutual assistance from the clan. In recent times, however, the general process of impoverishment of Maasai in some parts of Maasailand, notably within the Ngorongoro Conservation Area, has created a growing number of herders who can be said to be 'destitute', owning less than two LU per *engaji*. Consequently, in the Ngorongoro Conservation Area, it was in practice herders in this category who emerged as being most frequently the recipients of organized mutual assistance by fellow clan members. Like those in the category of the 'poor', those defined as 'very poor' in Ngorongoro were therefore increasingly expected to seek individual assistance from kinsfolk, friends and age-mates, rather than through the organized, clan-based assistance they were in theory entitled to expect. As the ranks of the 'destitute' have swollen here, they have become the principal recipients of mutual assistance. In other, relatively richer areas, such as the Salei Plain or Simanjiro, where there are fewer destitute herders, those households with between two and five LU per *engaji* can still expect to receive the assistance of the clan.

It is difficult to compare these internally derived Maasai categories with others used in the literature on East African pastoralists with any

Table 9.2 Wealth distribution of the pastoral households in the NCA

Wealth category	% of all NCA households	Number of households in each category
Destitute	21	1039
Very poor	16	755
Poor	21	1029
Medium	20	977
Rich	22	1024
Total	100	4824

Source: NCAA General Census, 1994.

precision. Using the general census of the Ngorongoro Conservation Area taken in 1994, which gives an average of four persons per *engaji*, and applying this to the figures given for household status in Table 9.2, we can see that some 58 per cent of households are unable to subsist from livestock production alone. Only those herders in the 'Rich' category (22 per cent of Ngorongoro Conservation Area households) would meet Kjaerby's minimum requirement for a subsistence herd of 5 LU per capita. Over the longer term, average livestock per capita ratios in the Ngorongoro Conservation Area have dropped sharply from 14.2 in 1966 to only 3.4 in 1994. These figures emphasize the extent of poverty now being experienced by the pastoralists in this once favoured area.

Fratkin & Roth (1990:394), who analysed nutritional requirements of Ariaal pastoralists in northern Kenya, have calculated the minimal viable herd at the level of 4.5 LU per capita, which again came out at around 20 LU per subhousehold (equivalent to Maasai *engaji*). Approximately the same figure was calculated for Rendille by Field & Sampkin (1985:171), and for Barabaig by Kjaerby (1979). The interpretation of the Waso Borana figures provided by Swift & Umar (1991:48) is more problematic, since they only use the concept of a household, although in most of the cases this was a one-wife household. They have calculated the minimum viable herd at 5 TLU per household, comprising seven cattle or 50 goats, which is equivalent to 7 LU per *engaji* in the Maasai case. The Oxfam restocking projects in northern Kenya reported by Kelly (1993) have also used the same estimation of 50 goats as a minimum viable herd. These cases reported by Swift & Umar and Kelly fit the Maasai customary conceptualization of poverty pretty well, and indeed the categorizations employed in each study were derived from local concepts. In contrast, the other cases mentioned above were based upon external, 'scientific' estimations of minimum nutritional requirements in a pastoral economy, and gave results which are much higher than the internally derived, Maasai estimations of poverty. On the other hand, the definition of a 'rich'

Maasai household – one that is self-sustainable in the longer term – seems to fit the external scientific estimations more closely when converted into subsistence terms. This implies, by Maasai definitions, that only the 'rich' are able to cover basic subsistence needs from pastoral resources.

Maasai clan-based mutual assistance

The existence of a clan-based institution for the redistribution of livestock has been relatively well documented in the case of Borana pastoralists (Dahl, 1979b:173; Bassi, 1990:32; Swift & Umar, 1991:36), but nowhere in the published accounts of Maasai ethnography is a similar system elaborated. Some writers, however, have provided important clues as to the role played by clans in providing mutual assistance. Århem (1981:7), for example, makes a vague passing reference to clan-based livestock-sharing among Maasai, writing that:

> Patrilineal clanship ... also forms a basis for allocation of diffuse rights in livestock owned by fellow clansmen; clansmen are expected to help each other build up herds for future marriages and in situations of individual misfortune.

Jacobs (1965:201–2) offers a fuller account of the importance of the clan:

> in matters of cattle exchange, whether to replace stock lost in a cattle epidemic or to build up a residual herd for purposes of securing a wife, a man turns first to his brothers of the same gate-post group for assistance and then to local members of his sub-clan and clan, later calling them by the cattle-names appropriate to the beast given. The degree of their relationship or their ability to trace genealogical links is unimportant, it is being assumed that since they share the same cattle ear-mark, they are like 'brothers' of the same gate-post.

Ndagala (1990:175) confirms the principle of clan-based property in livestock, but without adding any substantive detail:

> Livestock belonging to a clan member do, through him and like him, belong to his clan. In principle those animals are available to the clan whenever the need arises. Given the fact that clan members are scattered, their livestock are identified by ear-marks.

Despite these unpromisingly generalized earlier references, a field survey conducted during 1993 in Monduli, Simanjiro and Kiteto Districts, in the central and southern parts of Tanzanian Maasailand, revealed that clan-based mutual assistance was in fact an elaborate, widespread and socially more significant practice than earlier writers have allowed. There were found to be four different kinds of redistribution of livestock, known generally as *engelata*, each of which is operated at a community level through the social mechanism of the clan. The first three will be described briefly here, before the fourth, *engalata elowoto*, is examined in detail.

The first, *engelata enkaputee*, is the collecting of cattle from among clan members for a man to pay bride-wealth, where the payments are to be made in a single transaction and where the livestock demanded exceed his resources. These 'one-off' marriage transactions involve higher bride-wealth payments than is usual, but, unlike other types of marriage arrangement, no further claims can be made subsequently upon the husband. Currently, the 'selling of a girl' (*emirata entito*), whereby payments are extended over a longer period, is becoming increasingly prevalent in this part of Maasailand as a consequence of poverty. Failure to maintain payments leads to many formally arranged marriages being broken off. However, locally it is said that this difficulty is restricted to poor families only. The second redistributive mechanism, *engelata embolwa*, is relevant here, for it denotes the collecting of cattle from among clan members for a man to pay back bride-wealth and other marriage payments received earlier for a daughter, in case of divorce or a broken engagement. The third type of redistribution, *engelata oloikop*, occurs when clan members collect cattle to pay 'blood-wealth', a traditional payment made when one Maasai has killed another.

The last and most important category of clan-based assistance is termed *ewoloto*, denoting the collection of cattle from among clan members to assist a destitute family. Within the *ewoloto* system, the assistance of the clan is ostensibly offered to the male head of the household, but, in fact, he is viewed as a representative of the family, and it is understood that the assistance given is for the benefit of all family members. This fact is graphically expressed in sayings which make it clear that cattle are offered to 'feed hungry children' so that they 'do not go to other clans': 'We collect these cattle not for the man, for he can go and stay in the homestead of his age-mate, but for his children who are dying, and who are our children.' In a sense, this is another way of stressing the importance of maintaining marriages, for, in a situation of hunger, poverty and desperation, it is more likely that the distraught wife will return to her father's clan, taking the children with her. Children, like cattle, mark the wealth of the clan. But, although it is accepted in principle that livestock donated under *ewoloto* will benefit the family as a whole, clansmen who make donations to the poor do not seek to involve themselves in the 'intra-household' distribution of the allocated stock between wives.

The head of a household has a right to approach his fellow clan members in the locality, as well as from further afield, to collect cattle for his family when the number of livestock in his herd has fallen below five cattle per *engaji*. Usually, this is done through a formal request, but in some cases action is taken by the clan even before a formal request is made. It is obligatory for clan members living in the same locality to attend the meeting (*enkigwana*) which is called on such occasions. At the *enkigwana*, the prospective recipient of *engalata* will be expected to provide locally produced beer for consumption, which in itself may be costly. Failure to attend this meeting by any local clansman would be considered a serious abrogation of social responsibility. Each case is examined to establish the level of need. There are two typical outcomes, depending on the level of poverty of the applicant. If the herder is found to have between two and five cattle per *engaji*, his ability to deal with the problem himself will be closely evaluated. Consideration is given to factors such as his capacity to engage in cattle trading, or to take up some cultivation, or whether he has any daughters who can be 'sold off' in marriage. The availability of marriageable daughters was a matter very frequently discussed in such cases among the Maasai of the Ngorongoro Conservation Area. If it is found that he cannot help himself through these means, then he will be offered assistance by his clan members. In contrast to these detailed investigations of means, if a man is found to have two or less cattle per *engaji*, he will be offered help immediately without further discussion. Only if he were known to have misused his herd, for example through excessive drunkenness, might such assistance be withheld. Even within a strong culture of mutuality, there are those who exclude themselves by their own anti-social behaviour. But, once it is agreed to lend assistance to a clansman, every effort is made to provide sufficient livestock to raise the holdings of the household above five cattle per *engaji*. However, because of the general state of impoverishment in some parts of Maasailand at present, notably the Ngorongoro Conservation Area, it is not always possible for clansmen to raise the resources of a 'very poor' or 'destitute' family above five livestock per *engaji*. This aspect appears to be a new feature of the system and obviously has extremely important consequences.

Once it has been decided that *ewoloto* should be given, which clan members will provide such assistance is then a matter for further deliberation. There is a strong cultural obligation for clan members to give in accordance with their own wealth status. Less wealthy clan members will contribute goats and sheep, while the richest may contribute a heifer, a lactating cow or even a steer. If the richer members are reluctant to give in accordance with their wealth, and this is often the case, they may be encouraged or persuaded by other clansmen. Offers of assistance may be promised for some time in the future, as a way of acknowledging the obligation but trying to postpone it. These negotiations can be protracted and must always be conducted in keeping with Maasai ideals of social etiquette, but in the end clansmen have no way of refusing to contribute to the *ewoloto* payment.

Specific examples can help to illustrate the way in which mutual assistance operates in practice. The following case of *ewoloto* was recorded in Oloirobi-Ilmesigio during November 1990, involving a young man of the Simaga subclan of the Laitayok clan, whom we shall call X.[3] The father of X had died several years previously, leaving two widows. The first wife, the mother of X, had run away from her husband some time earlier and X had been brought up by the second wife. After the death of the father, the sister of X, who was married to a man from a different clan, took care of him until his circumcision. Members of the Laitayok clan were then informed about his case, and subsequently organized an *engelata ewoloto* to collect cattle for X. Two sub-clans each donated two cattle, and a third sub-clan donated three cattle. A fourth sub-clan donated three further cattle, and offered a girl to be married to X, while X's own Simaga sub-clan donated five cattle and offered another girl in marriage. As a result of these interventions, X was offered a total of 15 cattle and two marriageable girls were provided for him without the need to pay bride-wealth.

This case demonstrates the system at its best, but not all the needy are provided for so well. The dynamics of the process can be better understood when it is realized that certain limits may be imposed affecting those seeking assistance. When people were asked why there are still families in the destitute category that were not helped through *ewoloto*, they pointed to the widespread extent of poverty in Maasai society, implying that all those in need could not be helped, and also to the fact that some of those not given assistance had disqualified themselves from community sympathies through their behaviour, for example by being known to be heavy drinkers. The problem of alcoholism among the Ngorongoro and Salei Maasai has been increasing rapidly over recent years. Informants pointed out that herders selling livestock for cash in order to buy alcohol had become a major problem and was partly responsible for the apparently high commercial offtake rates in some families. Despite the increasing scale of the problem and the fact that drunkards are generally excluded from the category of those eligible for clan assistance, the clan members can find ways to help the family of the drunkard, if not the drunkard himself. On the initiative of an influential clansman or as a result of a request from one of the wives of a drunkard, cattle can be collected for such a family and control over the donated animals allocated to the wives' eldest sons, if they have been circumcised. If the sons are as yet uncircumcised, livestock may be put in the care of a 'guardian', who would usually be a brother of the drunkard. Together with the wives, the sons or guardian will take decisions regarding the management of animals given in this manner. The drunkard is thereby excluded from decision-making over the donated herd, although he may still be permitted to supervise herding. If he impinges upon the authority of the sons or the guardian in this situation, he risks the social sanction of being beaten by other men. In short, the drunkard is undeserving of assistance.

In extreme cases, where the negligence of the household head is seen to be a cause of the family's problems, the clan members can order the wives and children to move to the homestead of a fellow clan member (usually the guardian). Known drunkards are accordingly often reluctant to ask for *ewoloto* for fear of the public humiliation the request may bring upon them. More often, such individuals prefer to do nothing while their wives beg for food. When the situation becomes desperate, it is the wives who will seek help or fellow clansmen who, observing the plight of the family, will take it upon themselves to organize assistance. The rationale for their intervention will invariably be to prevent the children of that family from dispersing, which is what would surely happen if the wives returned to their own fathers' clans with their children. Should this be allowed to happen, then it effectively means losing the 'children of the clan'.

Another case can be cited, this one from the village of Oloirobi in the Ngorongoro Conservation Area, to illustrate in concrete terms how this kind of community intervention can operate to effect *ewoloto*. This case was reported to have taken place in 1976 and involved a man belonging to the Molelian clan. Informants who gave this information did not want the man's identity to be revealed in public, so we will again refer to him as X.

As a young man, X took a wife, who bore him four children. X then started to drink heavily and sold all his cattle to pay for alcohol. The Molelian clan members now became concerned lest the wife should run away to her father, taking her children, who would, over time, be absorbed into the father's clan. At first, the Molellian clansmen considered appointing the younger brother of X as guardian, but they feared that X would have influence over this younger brother. In the end, they took the ususual step of asking the father of the wife to look after her and her children, in return for five cattle being allocated to this family through *ewoloto* and it being accepted by all parties that the children would remain members of the Molelian clan. At the same time, they decided to 'sell off' X's two adolescent daughters in marriage, and also give the resultant livestock to X's wife's father to keep in trust for the growing sons of X. All this was accomplished, and by around 1990 the wife and sons of X had accumulated around 40 head of cattle. However, in 1991–2, a year before the case was recorded, 32 of these cattle died as a result of the tick-borne disease bovine cerebral theileriasis (*olomilo*).

The above case illustrates an extreme situation in which the clan has become intimately involved in a family's affairs. Maasai informants were at pains to stress that drunkards assisted by the clan were often thereby placed under considerable social pressure to reform their behaviour and stop drinking. Subsequently, such reformed characters were reputedly the first to assist others in cases of misfortune, either through individual gifts or through participation in *ewoloto*.

Recent changes in mutual assistance

Although the participation of clan members in all four forms of *engelata* is generally said to be obligatory, observation reveals that the obligation to participate is stronger in cases of *engelata oloikop* and *engelata embolwa* than in cases of *engalata enkaputee* and *engalata ewoloto*. Besides the general threat of being ostracized from the 'community of sharers' by refusal to participate in clan assistance, it is notable that both *engelata oloikop* and *engelata embolwa* bring the honour of the clan into play, since the clan is obliged to repay the already existing debts of one if its fellow members towards another clan. Thus, *engelata oloikop* and *engelata embolwa* demand assistance beyond the more widely recognized realms of individual subsistence or costs of marriage for which a person may be thought to be personally responsible for organizing. Where the public honour of the clan is less under threat, particularly in cases of *engalata ewoloto*, the wider impoverishment of the community may inhibit the proper functioning of the system of mutual assistance and members of the clan may seek to avoid their social obligations. These problems will now be further elaborated.

Table 9.3 presents a breakdown of recorded *engalata* cases for named communities within the Ngorongoro Conservation Area over the period 1985 to 1993. The statistics indicate some important shifts in the practice of *engalata*, but they do not fully reveal the extent of the social evolution in the functioning of the system. The increased intensity of *engelata*, and especially *ewoloto* cases, is clearly apparent from the recent aggregated annual figures. However, there has also been a qualitative change. Recorded case-studies reveal that the average scale of *ewoloto* collection is rapidly decreasing. The majority of donors seem no longer to mind whether the collected herd is sufficient to allow the recipient destitute family to escape from their poverty. Rather, it appears to have become more important merely to be seen to take part in the collection in order to fulfil only the minimum expected social requirements of the clan. Consequently, individuals give as small a contribution as possible or delay handing over the declared contribution until long after the *ewoloto* meeting has taken place. As a result, *ewoloto* contributions do not effectively solve the problems of the destitute households. Therefore, as in a quantitative sense *ewoloto* cases have become more numerous, their qualitative value and effect has diminished. It is also significant that emerging patterns of insufficient *ewoloto* collection were especially marked in the poorest Ngorongoro Conservation Area villages of Endulen and Nayobi. No such strategies of avoidance are apparent anywhere in cases of *embolwa* or *oloikop*, where delay in providing animals would endanger the clan's reputation with other clans.

One of the worst and potentially most destructive consequences of this change in practice is the impact it would seem to be having in the minds of the poorest herders who have most to gain from the system of mutual assistance. These herders appear to have gradually ceased to have faith in the capacity of their clansmen to offer effective assistance. All are aware of examples where destitute families were promised livestock, but these were not ultimately delivered. Although exposing one's poverty by requesting assistance from clansmen is not perceived by Maasai to be humiliating, the failure to receive assistance having made a request is viewed as a deep

Table 9.3 Incidence of engalata cases in the NCA, 1985–93

Village, year	*Ewoloto*	*Enkaputee*	*Embolwa*	*Oloikop*
Endulen				
1993	4	–	1	1
1992	3	2	–	–
1991	–	1	–	–
1985–90	10	6	5	?
Kakesio*				
1992	5	–	3	–
1985–91	20†	–	10	?
Oloirobi				
1993	2	3	4	–
1992	–	1	–	–
1991	2	–	1	–
1985–90	9	?	2	–
Olbalbal				
1993	2	n/a	n/a	n/a
1992	3	–	–	–
1991	3	3	2	–
1985–90	10	10	5	–
Irkepusi*				
1992	3	3	3	–
1991	3	5	–	–
1985–90	7	7	–	–
Sendui				
1993	–	–	–	–
1992	6	3	3	–
1991	1	5	–	1
1985–90	6	7	4	5
Nayobi				
1993	1	–	1	–
1992	3	1	6	1
1991	4	2	2	–
1990	3	1	6	1
Total				
1993	9	3	6	1
1992	17	10	15	1
1991	13	16	5	1
1985–90	65	31	32	6

* no data available for 1993 for Kakesio or Irkepusi.
† The high number of *ewoloto* cases here arises from cattle losses caused by Tatoga and Sukuma raiding.
n/a = not available.
Source: Potkanski, unpublished survey of 1993.

humiliation. As a result, destitute families now increasingly prefer to rely upon their relatives for assistance instead. Once again, this development is most starkly evident in the poorest Ngorongoro Conservation Area localities of Endulen and Nayobi, but it is recognizable to a lesser extent elsewhere. Informants in Endulen and Nayobi explained that poverty is so widespread within their immediate communities, that they are ashamed to ask others, knowing that the majority of potential donors may be equally poor or only marginally better off than themselves.

Even the observable rapid increase in *ewoloto* cases in 1991–2 is disproportionally low when compared with the dramatic enlargement in the number of households classified as 'destitute' and 'very poor' over the same period. The overwhelming majority of families deciding to ask for *ewoloto* in both Endulen and Nayobi in recent years were either people returning to the area from outside, having lost their animals, or those who had come to the area because of poverty and were seeking relatives with whom they might stay. Long-term local residents in these villages would have to be in the most extreme circumstances before seeking assistance. For example, one such case at Endulen in 1993 concerned a family whose cattle had been stolen in a Sukuma raid. In an example from Nayobi, the supplicant was blind and therefore unable to cultivate, and in a further case from the same community a man planning to circumcise a daughter found that he had insufficient livestock to invest in the necessary ceremony. These examples, seen in conjunction with the aggregate figures, indicate that the system of generalized reciprocity implicit in the *ewoloto* institution is in danger of breaking down.

According to my own research findings, which were confirmed by the general census conducted in 1994 by the Ngorongoro Conservation Area authorities, the average livestock : human ratio in both Endulen and Nayobi was around 2 to 2.5 livestock per capita. Herders in these locations were signifcantly poorer on average than those throughout the area, reflected by an overall figure of 3.4 livestock per capita. In contrast, in the wealthier Salei Plain localities, which still enjoy human : livestock ratios of five livestock per capita, recourse to *ewoloto* and other types of *engelata* has not been nearly as frequent. The same is true of Terat and Kitwai localities in the Simanjiro District, as can be seen in Table 9.4, where the number of *engalata* cases has remained stable and was anyway not very high. The marked increase in the incidence of *ewoloto* and other *engelata* cases in certain localities in 1991–2 was due to the high rates of livestock losses experienced there as a consequence of the outbreak of bovine cerebral theileriasis. In the whole of the Ngorongoro Conservation Area by 1994, between 30 and 40 per cent of all households were in the 'destitute' or 'very poor' categories, and yet few were able to benefit from relief through *ewoloto* because of the generalized poverty currently characterizing the whole area. This analysis suggests that the institution of

Table 9.4 Incidence of engalata cases in localities in Monduli and Simanjiro Districts, 1991–3

Village	Ewoloto	Enkaputee	Embolwa	Oloikop
Engaruka				
1993	–	1	3	–
1992	3?	2	1	1
1991	1	2	4	2
Arketani				
1993	1	1	5	–
1992	3	1	3	–
1991	2	n/a	3	1
Monduli Juu				
1993	–	–	–	1 (expected)
1992	–	1	1	2
1991	–	1	2	3
1989–90	2	2	2	–
Simanjiro Terrat				
1993	2	–	–	–
1992	1	–	–	1
1991	1	1	–	–
Kitwai				
1993	2	2	1	–
1992	1	3	–	1
1991	2	2	3	1

n/a = not available.
Source: Potkanski, unpublished survey of 1993.

ewoloto has begun to malfunction in the poorest localities, where the larger number of households live in poverty, while still operating effectively in other, wealthier localities.

Another factor undermining the effectiveness *ewoloto* is the increasing extent of permanent reliance on agriculture among Maasai households. The impact of this is already recognizable in Endulen and Nayobi within the Ngorongoro Conservation Area, and clear evidence of a shift toward agriculture is also to be seen in the Monduli Juu village in Monduli District. To show the difference in patterns of clan-based livestock redistribution between communities that rely heavily on agriculture and those that are mostly pastoral, we can examine data on the incidence of *engelata*, and especially *ewoloto* cases, from several surveyed localities from the Simanjiro and Moduli Districts (see Table 9.4).

In Monduli Juu village the last case of *ewoloto* occurred more than four years ago, and the people do not expect any more cases in the near future. Since most of the people successfully cultivate, relative poverty in cattle, due to recent bovine cerebral theileriasis and East Coast fever epidemics in the 1990s, is less important. In these localities, nobody is suffering hunger, even though many have little or no stock. Rather than seeking *ewoloto*, poorer families here, the majority of whom are from Arusha, concentrate their energies on crop production.

In these increasingly difficult circumstances, the practice of *ewoloto* has thus silently died. Other types of *engelata* are still practised, however, as these concern debts or payments that can only be made in livestock. Should these other types of *engalata* also fall into disuse, then forms of individual assistance will be the only alternative remaining to poorer families confronted by larger debt demands and payments, and this will make already disadvantaged families even more economically vulnerable. It seems likely that this is also the potential scenario for the Nayobi and Endulen communities in the Ngorongoro Conservation Area, if their reliance on agriculture continues to grow in the face of declining livestock holdings.

A key conclusion to be drawn from these findings is that the more firmly rooted a local community is in the pastoral economy, the more reliable and effective the system of clan-based livestock redistribution is likely to be. Conversely, the greater the dependence on seasonal local agriculture, the weaker will be the system of clan-based mutual assistance. In the Ngorongoro Conservation Area, it is clear that already severely disadvantaged families are becoming poorer in livestock and that this will inevitably drive them towards cultivation. In a year of relatively favourable rainfall, they have sufficient food for adequate subsistence, but, in a year of drought and crop failure, their vulnerability is exposed and they are thrown back upon the assistance of relatives, who may themselves be only marginally better off. In the next year, learning from their experience, they will cultivate an even larger area than before. This conclusion has very considerable relevance for development planning in the Ngorongoro Conservation Area, where cultivation is considered undesirable. The only practical way to avoid this cycle of decline would appear to be to introduce an effective method of restocking – in other words, to re-create an effective system of *ewoloto*, allowing poorer pastoralists to re-establish themselves.

Restocking – a development intervention

To seek to reverse current trends in the Ngorongoro Conservation Area, a self-sustaining economic recovery programme has been proposed that will rebuild the pastoral economy. It is hoped that the programme can eventually be extended to all of Ngorongoro District, where the situation seems to be only marginally better than in the Conservation Area. The proposed economic recovery programme consists of three interrelated technical interventions: the reduction of livestock losses from disease through an effective tick-control programme, as well as the provision of preventive and curative veterinary services; the improvement and increase of range utilization, to be effected mainly through the development of better watering facilities for livestock and through controlled burning of pastures; and the eventual institution of a restocking project to bring 'destitute', 'very poor' and 'poor' households to the level of pastoral self-suffiency.

It is anticipated that improved veterinary health services and better water provision will reverse negative mortality trends in calves and adult cattle. As a limited amount of small-scale subsistence agriculture will be allowed to continue over a period of three to five years, this will help to reduce the need for commercial offtake from the Maasai herds. As a result, it is hoped that the overall Ngorongoro Conservation Area livestock herd, which according to the 1994 census amounted to only 143,000 livestock units, will begin to increase. It is assumed that over five years the average LU per capita ratio can be restored to the minimum subsistence level of 4 to 5. It is further assumed that, after the end of the project, this ratio will not decrease and human population growth will be balanced by the natural increase of the herds. For this to happen, range utilization must be improved. The recurrent costs of improved veterinary services and water provision will be covered from income accruing to the Ngorongoro Conservation Area authorities from tourism, augmented by a stratified set of fees for the use of veterinary services.

Restocking holds the key to the effective recovery of pastoralism in the area. Livestock will be purchased by the project personnel, assisted by the local Maasai, both locally at three buying centres within the Conservation Area (where it is estimated that 11,000 LU can be bought within two years) and at markets in Arusha and Shinianga regions (where a further 16,000 livestock units will be acquired). Distribution of the livestock will follow the culturally accepted rules of assessing household poverty and need associated with the Maasai customary institution of *engalata ewoloto*. However, clan linkages will not be the operative arena for this process. Instead, the selection of beneficiary families and formal allocation of stock to these families is to be carried out by ward or village development committees, consisting of traditional and modern Maasai leaders and other persons of authority. This is broadly the same group of people who participate in similar traditional clan-based allocations, although the system of relationships with which they will deal will be different. Recognized Maasai standards of poverty and necessary social assistance will be employed in making these assessments, as traditionally applied in cases of *engalata ewoloto*, and it is hoped that this will lessen the likelihood of misallocation or corruption. It is proposed that the livestock distributed through the restocking scheme will be given as outright gifts to particular needy families, rather than as loans or group allocations. Those families identified in the 1994 census as 'destitute', 'very poor' and 'poor' were considered to be below or at the edge of sustainable pastoralism and will be the targeted recipients of the restocking programme.

The proposed programme will last not longer than two consecutive years, in order to prevent the creation of a dependency syndrome among local herders. 'Destitute' families will receive more livestock, while the wealthier will receive fewer, with 10 LU per *engaji* taken as the upper limit. Woman-headed households, of which there appears to be a growing number in Ngorongoro, will be treated as separate units, fully eligible for assistance. The problem of formal ownership of cattle allocated to women has yet to be worked out, but the practice of formally allocating such animals to the sons of women, as would happen in traditional *ewoloto* arrangements, may be adopted.

If the programme is successful, it is anticipated that, after two years, all the 'destitute' and 'poor' families will have herds restored to subsistence levels. Thereafter, it should be possible for traditional *engelata ewoloto* to be re-established. The sustainability and success of this project should be measured not only in terms of restoration of the self-sufficient pastoral economy of the Ngorongoro Maasai, but also in terms of revitalizing concepts of social responsibility and restoring the practice of local mutual assistance.

Notes

1. The term *olkarsis* or *olparakuoni* denotes a man with many wives, children and cattle. Its opposite, *olaisenani* or *olokirikoi*, denotes 'a man lacking relatives and cattle'. Although terms such as *olaiterani* and *olokishi* refer to 'a man lacking cattle', they do not have a quantitative meaning.
2. I am indebted to Dr Daniel Ndagala for drawing my attention to this point, which was subsequently confirmed by Maasai informants.
3. I was asked by my informant, Ole Wanga, from Endulen-Olmekeke, not to release the name of the person.

IV DEVELOPMENT DIALOGUES

10 Images & Interventions: The Problems of Pastoralist Development

DOROTHY L. HODGSON

Although the problems of pastoralists and development have been the subject of numerous international conferences and scholarly publications,[1] the problems seem to continue unabated; they include lack of participation by pastoralists in projects, declining livestock production, failure to repair and maintain water-project and other infrastructures, limited off-take for beef sales and lack of interest in income-earning opportunities. Meanwhile, there has been a recent resurgence in the conferences, publications and organizations devoted to detailing and resolving the unique problems of pastoralists, including the conference where the papers on which the chapters of this book are based were first presented. My purpose in this chapter is not to deny the importance of addressing these concerns, but to argue that part of the problem is the formulation of the problem itself, especially the images of pastoralists that shape how scholars, policy-makers and development practitioners understand the problems of pastoralists, and then design and implement development interventions to solve them.

For example, Maasai in Tanzania and Kenya – those ultimate icons of pastoralists for many Westerners[3] – have been the target of numerous interventions designed to change or sustain their economy, society or culture. From early water conservation and veterinary control measures to contemporary projects designed to improve Maasai animal husbandry, most of these projects have failed, however, with the blame cast on Maasai culture. In fact, despite over 80 years of development, the Maasai are still viewed as culturally conservative, stubbornly persistent in their pursuit of pastoralism and rejection of farming, sedentarization, education and other more modern ways of being (see especially Chapter VI in Hodgson, 1995).

Using the Maasai case as an example for the dilemma of many pastoralist groups throughout East Africa, this chapter challenges such perspectives by arguing that it is not Maasai (and other pastoralists) who have persevered unchanged by history, but the cultural images which shape how state administrators, non-governmental organizations (NGOs), and other development agents perceive pastoralists, particularly the Maasai. In other words, it is the ways of seeing Maasai, not being Maasai, which have persisted. That development projects have consistently failed to meet their own objectives, yet are repeatedly implemented in almost identical versions has less to do with any inherent Maasai conservatism, and more to do with these fixed images which produce invariable definitions of the problem, and therefore similar measures to solve it.[4]

Within the scope of this chapter, I analyse two interrelated aspects of this image which has defined how Maasai have been perceived for decades: first, that real Maasai are pastoralists and only pastoralists; and second, that these real Maasai pastoralists are male. To substantiate my argument about the influence of these paradigms in shaping development interventions, I examine briefly the United States Agency for International Development (USAID) Masai Livestock and Range Management Project (MLRMP) of 1969–79. In contrast to the numerous evaluations of the project which detail its resounding failure to meet most of its own objectives,[5] I argue that the objectives themselves were misguided from the beginning; shaped by a narrow, ahistorical, gendered image of pastoralists, the project produced interventions, considered appropriate for the Maasai, which were designed to improve livestock production, but never agricultural production, and to direct all project components, resources and training to Maasai men, not women. The consequences of such misdirected interventions included not only the project's failure in its own terms, but the intensified economic insecurity of Maasai households, the increased disenfranchisement of Maasai women from their rights in livestock and the further consolidation of state power over Maasai. In the remainder of the chapter, I first present a brief history of changing Maasai relations of production. After an overview of the USAID project, I turn to a more detailed discursive analysis of the images which shaped its policies and practices. In the conclusion, I explore the significance of my argument for contemporary development interventions designed to solve the problems of pastoralists.

Being Maasai

Despite extensive scholarly debate about the origins of the term Maasai, and the establishment of its referent ('Maa-speaking pastoralists') (Berntsen, 1980), most scholars do agree that while the majority of Maa-speakers were originally agropastoralists, cultivating sorghum and millet and raising cattle and small stock, in time a group emerged with an increasing specialization in pastoralism and an intensifying linkage between their sense of a distinct identity as a group and their mode of production.

By the early nineteenth century, communities of Maa-speakers existed with different economic specialities: as pastoralists, agropastoralists, farmers and hunter-gatherers. The issue of whether they were all considered Maasai or some were considered more Maasai than others is obscured by the perceptions of early traders, travellers, missionaries and scholars, as well as the fragmentary evidence. By the late 1880s, however, the term Maasai had become standard usage among Europeans as an ethnic descriptor for Maa-speakers who were primarily pastoralists, as opposed to the Wakwafi (later Arusha), the name used for Maa-speakers who were primarily cultivators (Berntsen, 1979, Sutton, 1990, 1993; Galaty, 1993a; Sommer & Vossen, 1993; Hodgson, 1995).

The particular type of pastoralist system followed by these Maasai was as follows. Cattle were primarily raised for milk production, although beef was occasionally eaten when cattle were slaughtered for certain ceremonial occasions or special events. Cattle were also important symbols of prestige and wealth, and contributions and/or exchanges of cattle marked important social transactions, such as marriage, stock partnership and death payments. Although of lesser symbolic importance, small stock were crucial to the maintenance of daily life. They were the primary source of meat, a key currency of trade by both men and women for agricultural foodstuffs and commodities and a common gift between family members and friends, as well as for smaller ceremonial occasions.

Early European reports, including a detailed ethnography by a German colonial officer (Merker, 1904), portray the relations of production in the late nineteenth century among the Maasai – that is, Maa-speaking pastoralists – as organized by age and gender.[6] As they grew older, the responsibilities and obligations of Maasai males shifted from herding small stock and later calves and then cattle as young boys (*olayioni/ilayiok*), to protecting settlements and livestock as young circumcised men (*olmorani/ilmurran*), to marrying, beginning a family, and managing the affairs of livestock and people in their homestead (*enkang'*) as junior elders. Their political power in terms of clan and community affairs peaked when they became senior elders, and then waned once they became venerable elders, although they still attracted great respect.

Maasai women followed a similar trajectory of increasing power and respect through their lives. As young, uncircumcised girls (*endito/intoyie*), they worked hard helping their mothers in child care, collecting wood and water and other household chores. Once circumcised and married, they built their houses, cooked for their household, collected wood and water, cared for calves and small stock, milked cows and cared for their young children. As they and their children grew older, Maasai women gained respect, especially once they had sons who became *ilmurran*. Once their sons began to marry and they became mothers-in-law, their authority increased and their workloads decreased as they managed their daughters-in-law. These same sons and daughters-in-law would in turn care for these women when they became elderly and feeble grandmothers (*koko*).

For the purposes of this chapter, what I want to emphasize is that, although married Maasai men and women operated in separate and yet overlapping spheres in the tasks of daily life, they shared both roles and rights in the care and management of livestock. Women cared for calves, small stock and sick animals. They milked cattle (and sometimes small stock) in the morning and evening and controlled the distribution of milk to household members and visitors, as well as trading the surplus. Women also processed animal skins, either trading the skins or producing clothing and sleeping skins. Men made the broad management decisions about the timing and location of grazing and watering the herd. Besides the rights of women to livestock products, both men and women shared rights in cattle themselves and conferred and agreed on decisions to slaughter, trade or give an animal away. Rights to small stock seemed to vary, with husband and wife sharing joint rights in some animals and separate rights in others. When a woman married, her husband transferred a certain amount of cattle to her as house property, to be managed by her for her household's immediate benefit in terms of milk and hides, but also to be kept in custody for her sons' inheritance.

The advent of first German colonialism in the late 1880s and then British colonialism after the First World War, had significant consequences for Maasai pastoralism. As I document these in great detail elsewhere (Hodgson 1995), here I shall summarize what is important for this chapter.[7] First, pastoralism became less viable as a productive system, because of increased land alienation, decreased mobility of both people and their herds, repeated devastation of the herds from disease and drought and on-going interventions in the form of veterinary controls, taxation and pressure to increase off-take. As early as the 1930s, some Maasai began to cultivate in order to either supplement their dietary intake or use their profits from their harvest to rebuild or expand their herds. Wealthy Maasai would hire non-Maasai to cultivate their land, while in poorer families the women began to farm small subsistence plots, with occasional help from their sons and husbands. By the 1950s, as more and more Arusha families moved into Maasai District, cultivation increased further, as Maasai not only learned from Arusha men and women how to farm, but Maasai men began increasingly to marry at least one Arusha woman as their farming wife. By 1956, some Maasai were not just farming old homestead sites, but quite large *shambas* [farms]'.[8]

Second, Maasai were subjected to repeated development interventions, usually designed to improve the productivity of their livestock or improve the quality or carrying capacity of their rangeland. Specific project objectives included the provision of permanent water sources (since most of their former dry-season grazing and watering lands were rapidly alienated in the form of settler farms, forest reserves and game parks), improving Maasai animal husbandry practices and integrating them into the colonial economy through commoditization and monetization by encouraging them to sell their cattle and purchase various sundries and commodities. Although many of these interventions were more significant for their rhetoric than their reality and many Maasai men and women resisted their implementation, they did have cumulative effects over the years, especially in terms of gender relations. Most importantly, although Maasai men and women retained the same responsibilities for pastoralist production, there was a gradual shift in rights. These development interventions targeted Maasai men as the individual owners of cattle and the primary handlers of money, a discursive practice that Maasai men used to usurp women's former shared rights and to claim sole rights to cattle as their property (Llewelyn-Davies, 1978, 1981; Talle, 1988; Kipuri, 1989).

A final result of colonial policies was to marginalize Maasai as a stigmatized ethnic group *vis-à-vis* other non-Maasai Africans. Paradoxically, despite the primarily economic interventions directed at livestock development, paternalistic sentiments about preserving Maasai culture were used to justify only minimal social interventions, such as education or health services, thereby undermining Maasai political power and presence in relation to other ethnic groups. The numerous failures of colonial development projects, together with the resistance of many Maasai to these intrusions, were blamed on Maasai's cultural conservatism, contributing to the perceptions of non-Maasai that the Maasai were uninterested in development and resistant to change. For their part, many Maasai were tired of contributing cattle and money to endless failed projects, while others felt betrayed by the on-going land alienation and suspicious of government promises. The consequences of these processes and practices were starkly evident at independence, when development became the legitimating project of the postcolonial nation-state in Tanganyika. The African élite who took power embraced the modernist narrative with its agenda of progress. For them, the Maasai represented all they had tried to leave behind, and persisted as icons of the primitive, the savage, the past. Thus, although Maasai people had undergone significant changes in their pastoralist production system during the colonial period, their image as pastoralists and its associations with traditionalism and 'primitivism' obscured their changing realities.

From backward pastoralists to modern ranchers

The MLRMP began during this period, when the drive by the newly independent Tanganyikan government to increase productivity renewed and intensified attempts to develop the beef industry as a potentially lucrative source of state revenue. Not only did urban areas of Tanganyika[9] have a large unmet demand for beef, but beef was a profitable export commodity. In 1959–60 an economic mission from the International Bank for Reconstruction and Development (IBRD, the World Bank) visited Tanganyika to formulate a programme for the economic development of the country.[10] Among other conclusions in their dense report (IBRD, 1961), the mission claimed that 'the pastoral areas are contributing far less than their potential to the income of Tanganyika' (IBRD, 1961:81). This problem of pastoralist production was conceived as one beyond history: 'As with crops, so with livestock, existing African methods differ little in essentials from those practiced from time immemorial, and lead to a combination of low yields and deterioration of the land' (IBRD, 1961:79). A key cause of this land degradation, according to the IBRD, was the conjuncture of communal land ownership and individual rights in livestock, which produced a version of the 'tragedy of the commons' (Hardin, 1968), so that 'each *man* is anxious to increase his herds and to possess as many beasts as possible') (IBRD, 1961:79, my emphasis).[11] To address these concerns, the IBRD proposed, among other ideas, group ('partnership') cattle ranching. These 'organized, large-scale ranches', established in selected localities on land cleared from tsetse and provided with water-supplies would be run under the expert management of the Tanganyika Agricultural Corporation, supervising the 'tenant cattle keepers' (IBRD, 1961:160).

Although the idea of government-managed ranches with African cattle-keeping tenants was never realized, the idea of group ranches as the solution to the problems of pastoralist development persisted. Based in part on this IBRD report, in 1962 the Tanganyikan government requested that the USAID finance a study to prepare a 'livestock and range management program' for Masai District, which could be used as 'a model for extending improved practices and production' throughout the district (Deans *et al.*, 1968:2). The study's recommendations formed the basis for the Range Management and Development Act of 1964, which provided 'the legal basis' for 'increased livestock production and improving land use on 155,000 square miles of grazing land in Tanzania'. Under the Act, local herders could form 'ranching associations' with 99-year leasehold rights, and district 'ranching commissions' would be formed to supervise, set policies and manage the activities of such associations within their area (Deans, *et al.*, 1968:2).

In 1964, the government started Komolonik, a pilot demonstration ranching association covering 220,000 acres of Maasai land near the town of Monduli, the district headquarters of Maasai District (Fig. 10.1). To prove that the Government 'was really serious this time', the Masai Range Commission[12] financed over US$210,000 worth of improvements on the land, including a 16-mile gravity pipeline system with six tanks in Mfereji (a dispersed settlement of Maasai on the floor of the Rift Valley on the far

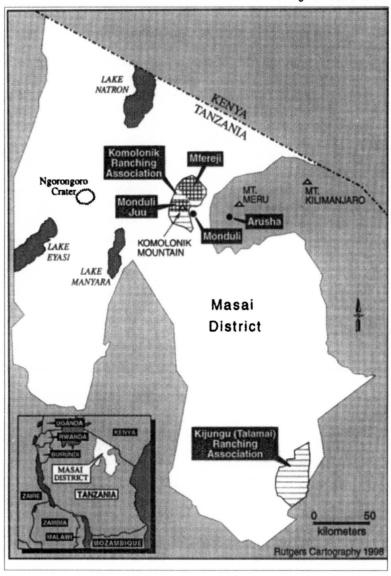

Figure 10.1 Masai District c. 1970, showing approximate location of major Masai Range Project Ranching Associations.

(*Source*: Adapted from USDA map, Deans *et al.*, 1968: Figure A)

227

side of Komolonik Mountain (Fig. 10.1), a two-mile pipeline supplying one watering point and a dip, other dams and water points, road construction and cattle dips.[13] A 30-member steering committee (of Maasai men) selected by Maasai (men) was formed to mediate between the Masai Commission and the Komolonik association members, but by 1969 the Association was still not registered. Maasai refused to accept the budget for the improvements or the stock quotas presented by the commission and saw little reason to form such an association.

Besides the reluctance of Maasai men to institute formally the required ranching associations, the Komolonik Pilot Project was facing other major problems as well. First, the concentration of water and dips in Mfereji was causing 'acute overgrazing', as herds from neighbouring areas converged on the area during the dry season to drink the water (ole Parkipuny, 1979:141). Second, Maasai felt no responsibility for maintaining, repairing or expanding the project infrastructure. In fact, a five-month study of the association in 1968–9 by a team of USAID 'experts'[14] concluded that:

> The move by the Range Commission to get the backing of the Masai through capital improvements has not succeeded. The Masai feel little responsibility for the improvements made, possibly because they were not involved enough in the planning and construction of improvements. They definitely do not feel it was a partnership arrangement. Their attitude is that the government has done this much, let them finish the job. (Deans et al., 1968:56)

Finally, these USAID 'experts' found that Maasai were intensely suspicious of the project's objectives, in part because of a significant disparity between the felt needs of Maasai and the government plans, and the patronizing, top-down approach of the government officials:

> The majority of the Masai have not perceived the need for an association nor how an association would work. They have difficulty in seeing how their needs will be solved by the scheme presented by the Range Commission. The Masai feel strongly that the government officials do not fully explain their proposals so that they can understand them. What they do not understand, they distrust and hesitate to commit themselves to support. The Masai have been suspicious of the Government and the Range Commission, primarily because they have not understood what the Commission and its officials are trying to do and why. (Deans et al., 1968:56)

Despite these indications of Maasai reluctance (if not resistance), the recognized problems of accountability, participation and communication and the rapid, acute overgrazing in Mfereji, the ranching association concept became the cornerstone of the largest development project among Maasai in Tanzania to date.

Based on the above 1962 and 1968 studies, USAID designed and implemented a series of projects over a ten-year period (1969–79) in Tanzania, known collectively as the MLRMP, contributing over US$10 million to a total project cost of US$23 million.[15] The project's goal, explicitly set by the nation-state and not the Maasai, was: 'to assist the Government of

Tanzania to achieve its objective of self-sufficiency and an exportable surplus to earn foreign exchange in the livestock sector')(Utah, 1976:5).[16] To reach its implicit economic goal of converting the Maasai into commercial beef producers, MLRMP's purpose was phrased in economistic terms: 'to achieve a high level of livestock offtake in the Maasai District consistent with proper resource management and Tanzanian development goals' (Utah, 1976:6). Seven specific changes in herd management (e.g. a decrease in calf mortality) were designated to measure the successful realization of this purpose by 1980.[17]

(To meet their goals, project administrators produced an ambitious array of project components, designed to improve range management and livestock production; control diseases; improve land-tenure security; train Tanzanian specialists; develop training for Maasai and Tanzanian livestock and range officers; and assemble baseline data on all facets of Maasai population, economic life, and range conditions, climate and other topics. A key objective of the MLRMP was to increase the productivity of Maasai livestock.) Such efforts included attempts to teach Maasai men 'improved' methods of animal husbandry; veterinary interventions, such as inoculations, quarantines, dipping and permits to control and prevent diseases; and livestock programmes such as the introduction of improved bulls and the formation of the ranching associations. In fact, the formation of ranching associations similar to those formulated in the 1960s was central to the project's objectives.(Comprised of groups of Maasai men, who would register with the government in return for legal rights of occupancy and certain water rights, these ranching associations had three purposes: first, 'to develop an improved herd and raise improved bulls for distribution to upgrade member herds'; second, 'to serve as an educational instrument to introduce modern range and livestock management practices'; and, third, 'to make the ranch economically profitable and pay for its development as well as improvements in the Association'.)[18] In order for an association to be officially registered, at least 60 per cent of the prospective members had to consent, a range officer was posted to the area, a census was taken of members and their stock and a 'ten-man' steering committee was elected by members (ole Parkipuny, 1979:141). Promised project inputs for each ranch included the construction of a manager's house, a dip, a permanent water supply, stock *bomas* (corrals) and paid herders, as well as pledges for continued financial assistance until the associations became 'profitable'.

(Maasai men responded positively to some of the project components, especially the construction of new facilities for stock watering and the provision of veterinary services, including dips, for improving animal health. Although initially they were reluctant to form ranching associations, reports of the success of dips and the provision of water points in Talamai and Komolonik spread, and soon Maasai demands for forming associations surpassed the capacities of project personnel. Maasai men sometimes travelled long distances to use dips, contributed cash to the construction of dips and paid dipping fees during the first two years of the project. About 60 new dips were constructed (bringing the total number of dips in Maasailand to 94), and over 28 million cattle, 6 million sheep and 7 million goats were dipped during the project period (project documents cited in DEVRES, 1979:144–6). The problem was no longer how to entice Maasai to form associations, but how to meet the overwhelming demand for new associations, with dips and water. In 1973, one project report lamented that 'Masai willingness to cooperate has exceeded ability of technical staff to implement'.[19] But delays and even failure to build the promised dips and water points soon stifled Maasai interest. Problems also developed with embezzlement of membership dues and other funds by some ranching association officials (ole Parkipuny, 1979:147).

Furthermore, as in the case of the Komolonik Pilot Project at Mfereji described above, the concentration of water sources and dips in the two associations attracted large numbers of people with their livestock from other areas. Most of these people became association members, but even non-members were allowed to graze within the bounds of the associations, resulting in significant overgrazing:

> For example, a new dam was constructed at Monduli Juu during the past year. The area was previously grazed properly because of a lack of water. When the dam was constructed, many people moved into the area. The people that were there began to keep cattle for other people. The results were overgrazing around the dam and the use of all the water in the dam. The water was completely used and most of the people had to leave the area.[20]

'The results of this development', according to the range management specialist, 'are that the most developed associations are the worst over-grazed.'[21] As early as 1976, experts were forecasting disaster if the project continued to supply water and dips without a concurrent programme to limit livestock numbers: 'I feel that the continued existence of the Range project in its present form significantly increases the probability that Masailand will become a desert due to overgrazing.'[22]

In time, the hugely ambitious, bureaucratically top-heavy project sunk under its own administrative weight. The reams of finely-tuned detailed plans could not overcome the logistical problems of transport delays, inadequate equipment, staff shortages and erratic funding that are part of any project's implementation. The size of the project only magnified the effects of these problems.[23] For example, the maintenance and recurrent costs of boreholes and dips were an ongoing problem:

> One problem area has been lack of recurrent expenses for transportation and for maintenance of dips and boreholes. Many dips and some boreholes were not functioning for various lengths of time due [sic] pump failures, engine breakdown, lack of diesel, lack of acaracide, transport, and in some cases, almost no testing and cleaning of dips.[24]

Furthermore, several unexpected problems, such as drought, disputes over land tenure with the Tanzanian government and the hostility of many non-Maasai Tanzanian project personnel towards Maasai, contributed to the project's failure. And, finally, as with prior development projects, no provisions were made as to how the project should be run and maintained once USAID ended its involvement. Administrators merely hoped that Maasai would see the benefits, and that the ranching associations would eventually become profitable and self-supporting.

Ultimately, the project failed even to meet its own goals of increasing the sale of Maasai livestock on the Tanzanian market. The numerous terminal evaluations of the project were overwhelmingly negative in their assessments (see, for example, DEVRES, 1979). While better access to water and dips created an increase in stocking levels, Maasai did not increase their commercial off-take. Thus the primary goal of the project – increased beef for domestic and international markets – was not even partially fulfilled. Development experts attributed the limited off-take to a lack of market incentives in Tanzania, but evidence indicated that Maasai were in fact selling large numbers of cattle illegally in Kenya.[25] Furthermore, some project areas, such as Talamai, which attracted large numbers of people and stock, soon experienced high stocking levels, land deterioration, bush encroachment and inadequate water supplies to meet the inflated demands (Århem, 1987:38).

As in the case of previous development projects (Hodgson, 1995), Maasai were once again blamed for the failure of a project not of their own design or choosing. Several of the evaluation reports repeatedly cited the unwillingness of the Maasai to participate in either the implementation or the maintenance of most project components, noting that, once the government subsidized such services, the Maasai attitude was characterized as 'they have done this much, let them finish it' (DEVRES, 1979:90). Many of the 38 'important assumptions' on which the project objectives were based assumed a willingness on the part of the Maasai to change voluntarily fundamental aspects of their lives (including their seminomadic movements, their livestock management techniques, and their attitudes toward cattle and land) when shown the advantages of alternative modes. Furthermore, given these obvious advantages, the project assumed that the Maasai would be willing to contribute labour and share the costs of the projects. But, as the following excerpt illustrates, many Maasai saw the government-designed, government-financed, government-controlled projects as the government's property and responsibility:

> The ... dip was not operating because the iron water pipe had rusted through in one 10 foot section. When asked why there were so few cattle and so much grazing, the herders, standing at the water trough, reported that there was much ECF [East Coast fever] and that the dip had not been operating for 18 months. When asked why they didn't fix the pipe, an easy task ... they

expressed surprise that we thought they should do this and explained that they were waiting for the Mifugo [Livestock] Office to do it.[26]

In fact, according to Jacobs, Maasai were explicitly prohibited by the government from financing the construction of water supplies 'because the government argued that such installations should be provided free by the government, even though the government did not have the resources to do so themselves' (Jacobs, 1980a:12).

While the project evaluators severely criticized the project's design and implementation, Maasai were not as critical. The DEVRES evaluation team were told by some Maasai that the new wells, dams, reservoirs and tank trucks for emergency distribution were the 'Project's greatest contribution to them and it was the project activity they would most like continued' (DEVRES 1979:46). Although the evaluation team found faults in the water project component of the project, including continual delays in project implementation and rapid silting of some boreholes, these problems (based on project, not Maasai, criteria) did not sour the Maasai's evaluation – they were satisfied with their net gain in access to water.

Images and interventions

Although, as discussed above, the MLRMP failed to meet its own objectives, my concern here is to distil the assumptions about Maasai as pastoralists which guided planners in the design and implementation of project interventions.[27] My point is to argue that the MLRMP's objectives and interventions, like those of most Maasai development projects before and since, were misguided from the beginning, since they were informed by a static, gendered image of pastoralists that had little relationship to Maasai realities. The problem, in other words, of pastoralist development, was partly due to the formulation of the problem itself.

The first assumption that is clear from project documents is the belief that Maasai were pastoralists and only pastoralists. Despite evidence since the 1950s of increasing diversification of subsistence strategies among Maasai, especially through cultivation, the purpose of the MLRMP (as its very title suggests) was to support and reinforce Maasai livestock production. Project planners ignored not only the visible evidence of small-scale cultivation in their field visits, but their own survey findings: in his 1971 *Report on Cultivation Activities*, the range ecologist reported scattered small-scale cultivation and occasional large-scale cultivation throughout Masai District (Van Voorthuizen, 1971), and almost half of the homesteads surveyed as part of the 1974 USAID census of the Komolonik ranching association were both herding and farming (Hatfield, 1975:20). By the early 1980s, soon after the end of the MLRMP, Ndagala (1982) found that almost all households in Monduli Juu (part of Komolonik) were farming.[28]

The point here is that, although being a pastoralist might still be a (male) cultural ideal (but see Hodgson, 1994, 1995; cf. Galaty, 1982a), the cultural reality is that even at the time of the MLRMP, increasing numbers of Maasai were agropastoralists.[29] Mistaking ideals for reality, however, the MLRMP administrators and planners made no systematic efforts to reinforce and strengthen Maasai cultivation by the provision of supplies or training, for example. But even those project personnel who recognized the extent of cultivation among Maasai argued against bolstering Maasai cultivation. Their arguments (which occurred during the colonial period and persist today) generally took one of two forms: increased cultivation would destroy the fragile rangelands (Van Voorthuizen, 1971); or cultivation would destroy Maasai culture (since, echoing arguments in functionalism and cultural ecology, Maasai culture was presumed to be intricately related to and a product of their pastoralist mode of production). Such arguments were directly contradicted by the increasing embrace of cultivation by many Maasai and their success at small-scale (and occasionally large-scale) subsistence cultivation in many highland areas.

Of course, project planners believed that Maasai were not just pastoralists, but a particular kind of pastoralist. A second, related assumption was that the primary productive strategy of Maasai pastoralists was to raise cattle for beef. As evidenced in the focus of project components on increasing the sale of Maasai cattle for beef, planners took little cognizance of at least two Maasai actualities: first, that Maasai livestock production strategies were shaped by their objective of raising cattle for milk, not beef; and, second, that Maasai small stock (goats and sheep) were absolutely central to the daily currency of Maasai life (especially meat consumption and marketing). Both biases, as discussed below, have had consequences in terms of Maasai gender relations.

Finally, the androcentric assumptions that pastoralists must be men blinded project planners – whether technical experts or USAID administrators – to women's roles in pastoral production, as well as their overlapping rights in most livestock. The gendered assumptions of the project are clear from the language used in almost any project documents: the cattlemen, stock-owners, herdsmen, and decision-makers are all male. 'Since the Masai cattleman is proud, independent, and conservative he must be convinced not coerced', writes Hess (1976:15), for example, in a report on the ranching associations. They directed all of their training, access to veterinary medicines and membership in ranching associations only to Maasai men as the presumed owners of livestock, contributing to the failure of their projects. As Bennett remarked in his evaluation of the MRLMP, 'No role for women was envisaged by the project from the beginning. The team considered this to have mitigated against improvements in calf mortality and weaning, since Maasai women are mainly responsible for raising calves' (Bennett, 1984:108). Similarly, the final project evaluation by DEVRES, of which the anthropologist Alan Jacobs was a participant, ends the evaluation of almost every project component with the remark that participation of Maasai women was never considered (DEVRES, 1979).

The gendered assumptions and effects of the MLRMP were also clearly evident in the training and extension components. From the beginning, a key objective was to train 30 Tanzanians (all men, most Maasai) in US universities in the various technical specialities necessary for livestock development (such as range management, animal production, livestock production). No Maasai women were sent or even considered for training.[30] Similarly, when a shift in USAID development policy to more social concerns[31] prompted an increased emphasis on training by extension workers in the field, funds were allocated for the construction of a rural training centre (RTC) in Monduli to provide instruction for men in animal husbandry and for women in nutrition and maternal child care.[32] But, when finally the RTC was opened in 1978, its first two seminars were for 48 Maasai (male) leaders and 15 (male) elders from Komolonik, including lessons on animal parasites, some disease conditions, care of improved bulls, dairy cattle, artificial insemination, castration and cleaning and using a syringe. Only when such 'female' concerns as health and nutrition were proposed for study through the RTC in 1977, did Maasai women become the target of possible interventions. As the project sociologist commented, 'the fact that it focuses on women means that a major segment of Maasai, who have virtually been ignored, would be given special attention'.[33]

The almost complete absence of women from consideration contributed in no small way to the failure of various project components. For example, as discussed above, the USAID experts assumed that Maasai raised cattle for beef rather than milk. This was partly due, as Kettel (1992) has noted for pastoralist development projects generally, to Western assumptions that men were always the primary economic providers. According to this ethnocentric gendered logic, since women were involved in milking, milking could not be that important economically to the maintenance of the household. Despite the retinue of livestock experts, the fact that Maasai breeding and production strategies were designed to increase milk rather than beef production was noticed seriously only in the final year of the project. As the USAID animal production specialist meekly noted in his 1979 end-of-tour report:

> It has not been earlier recognized that the Masai are also very much involved in milk production. Besides for reasons of security and wealth, large numbers of cattle are needed to provide for a preferred milk diet. When visiting a boma one is not offered roast meat but a cup of milk. When one asks about the condition of the boma the reply most often comes in terms of how much milk is available. People who become sick are often considered sick because they are

drinking only a little milk. When one discusses improved bulls, female offspring are judged not only on their size but how much milk they produce.[34]

Of course, once the economic potential of dairy farming was finally acknowledged, project personnel ignored the roles and rights of women in managing and controlling milk and directed their efforts towards men. The Monduli Juu dairy project registered households according to the (male) head of household, facilitating the appropriation by men of the milk and income earned (Ndagala, 1992:140–42). And, when 50 dairy cattle were introduced to local farmers, these farmers were all men.[35]

The cumulative impact of development interventions such as those described in this chapter on Maasai gender relations was significant. The experts' discursive practice of treating Maasai men as the individual owners of cattle and therefore directing all animal husbandry training, advice and inputs to them, made men the *de facto* livestock 'experts,' undermining women's roles in pastoral production and their rights in livestock. For example, in age-stratified interviews held in 1992 of Maasai men and women in three communities encompassed by the former Komolonik ranching association, the eldest men and women spoke of shared rights in livestock, while younger men and women agreed that men were the sole owners of cattle (Hodgson, 1995). Furthermore, since rights in land (however tenuous) were vested in the association members, men became the controllers, if not the owners of the land as well. A lasting consequence of this policy component was that once Maasai were resettled in villages, farm plots were naturally allocated to men as the heads of households.

Thus, images that Maasai were pastoralists and that pastoralists were men shaped the design and implementation of the components of the MLRMP. Administrators implemented interventions designed to sustain Maasai as pastoralists, not cultivators; and Maasai men, not women were the targets of these interventions as they were assumed to control not only cattle and small stock, but the resources, such as water and pasture, on which they subsisted to make their allotted land habitable.

Conclusion

Although I have used the MLRMP as the focus for analysis, since it was one of the largest development projects to be undertaken among Maasai in Tanzania, it was hardly unique in terms of its project objectives or interventions. Elsewhere I have documented how similar images have produced similar interventions, from the early British development initiatives among Maasai during the colonial period to contemporary development interventions by the Tanzanian government and NGOs in the 1990s. What is remarkable is the power of this particular image of pastoralists to persist, despite repeated project failures and changing

Maasai realities (Hodgson, 1995). In fact, these images have done more to undermine and prevent development than to enable it. That is, rather than producing increased food security, collective empowerment *vis-à-vis* the nation-state and adequate health and education opportunities, they have contributed to increased stratification, limited food production and income strategies and the increased economic and political disfranchisement of women.

Despite their repeated failures, however, development interventions in both the colonial and postcolonial eras have been a useful means of consolidating state control, as well as obscuring the political conflicts producing certain development problems by depoliticizing them through redefining them as mere technical matters (Ferguson, 1990). In the case of the USAID project, ranching associations and the provision of dips and water points became the first step towards resettling Maasai in villages. The data collected by the project, such as the censuses of Maasai and their livestock and detailed land-use surveys, further facilitated the government's villagization plans. The project's goals were set by the state, not the Maasai, and the primary project beneficiaries would be the state's urban populations and foreign exchange accounts, not the Maasai. Maasai reluctance to participate in aspects of the project could be read as efforts to evade and resist such control.[36] They voted with their feet by participating in those project components that they perceived as beneficial (the dips, veterinary services and water facilities) and ignoring components (increased offtake) they found unhelpful. Thus this project, like many before and after, was explicitly about developing livestock, not people, for the benefit of the state rather than the people themselves. The disparity between the state's agenda and that of the Maasai was revealed by the failure of the Maasai to translate their increased herd size into increased offtake, an outcome that the state and project designers had assumed as given.

In conclusion, the recent resurgence of interest in the issue of pastoralist development suggests that my findings for the MLRMP have contemporary relevance. Despite the numerous international conferences and scholarly publications addressing the problems of pastoralists and development, the problems seem to continue unabated. But the paradigms persist also; rarely do such conferences consider the alternative economic strategies, such as cultivation, that many pastoralists are pursuing, nor do they consider the roles and rights of pastoralist women in livestock production and management (but see, for example, Broch-Due *et al.*, 1981; Wienpahl, 1984; Dahl, 1987; Talle, 1987, 1988). As the analysis and conclusions of this chapter suggest, I believe it is time to make a change.

[handwritten marginal note:] cultivation not in USAID project !!

Acknowledgments

Sections of this chapter appear in Chapter VII of my dissertation, 'The politics of gender, ethnicity and "development": images, interventions and the reconfiguration of Maasai identities, 1916–1993'. Research for the dissertation, carried out from 1991 to 1993, was supported by a Fulbright–Hays Doctoral Dissertation Abroad Award; an International Doctoral Research Fellowship funded by the Joint Committee on African Studies of the Social Science Research Council and the American Council of Learned Societies with funds provided by the Rockefeller Foundation; a National Science Foundation Doctoral Dissertation Improvement Grant (BNS No. 9114350); and an Andrew W. Mellon Candidacy Fellowship from the University of Michigan (summer and autumn, 1991). Dissertation write-up was supported by an Andrew W. Mellon Dissertation Fellowship (1993–4) and a Rackham Fellowship (1994–5), both from the University of Michigan. I am indebted to the Tanzanian Commission for Science and Technology for permission to carry out the research, and to Professor C.K. Omari and the Department of Sociology at the University of Dar es Salaam for research affiliation. Special thanks are also due to Neil Smith and George Levine of the Center for the Critical Analysis of Contemporary Culture for providing me with an Associate Fellowship (1994–5), and a vibrant intellectual space in which to think and write. Finally, I am grateful to Rick Schroeder, Vigdis Broch-Due, David Anderson, Elliot Fratkin, Sara Dickey and Pete Vayda for helpful comments on earlier drafts of this chapter.

Notes

1. See, for example, Galaty & Salzman (1981); Galaty *et al.* (1981); Raikes (1981); Evangelou (1984b); Fratkin (1991).
2. In Tanzania alone, several organizations devoted to solving the problems of pastoralist development have been formed recently, including the Pastoralist Network in Tanzania (PANET), the Maa Development Organization (*Inyuat e Maa*), the Korongoro Integrated People Oriented to Conservation (KIPOC) and the Olkonerei Integral Pastoralist Survival Programme.
3. See, for example, Knowles & Collett, 1989; Bruner & Kirshenblatt-Gimblett, 1994; Hodgson, 1995.
4. For similar studies that distil the images and social representations used by development planners and others to design and implement particular interventions, see, for example, Roe (1989); Ferguson (1990); Pigg (1992); Dove (1994).
5. For other analyses of the MLRMP, see Jacobs (1980a, b); Bennett (1984); Århem (1985) and Holland (1987). Official evaluations include Hoben (1976); Utah (1976); and DEVRES (1979). Primary materials from the MLRMP files, which were found in the Regional Water Department (Arusha), are cited as MLRMP/file number or file name. Reuben ole Kunei, the Tanzanian counterpart sociologist trained by the project, kindly provided me with access to other project documents.
6. These accounts include Krapf (1968 [1860]); Farler (1882); Wakefield (1882, 1883); Last (1883); Thomson (1968 [1885]); and Johnston (1886).
7. For historical studies of the encounter between the British and Maasai in Kenya, see the important work by Waller (1976, 1984, 1985b, 1988, 1993a). Other studies of Maasai in Tanzania include Ndagala (1982, 1992); and ole Parkipuny (1975, 1979). Works on Maasai in general include Jacobs (1965, 1968, 1975); Llewelyn-Davies (1978, 1981); Galaty (1982a, b, 1993a, b); Talle (1987, 1988); Spencer (1988); Kipuri (1989); Kituyi (1990); Homewood & Rodgers (1991); and Spear & Waller (1993).
8. Provincial Commissioner, 1956, *Northern Province, Annual Report*, p. 99.
9. Tanganyika was the name given to the mainland until it united with the island of Zanzibar in 1964 to form the United Republic of Tanzania.
10. See also Barclay's Bank (1958). Chapter 2 in Escobar (1995) provides an intriguing analysis of the first such World Bank mission to Colombia in 1949.
11. Peters (1994) and McCay & Acheson (1987), among others, have noted the problems with Hardin's early formulation, especially its assumption that communal lands lacked any regulations for use and access. Hardin himself revised his paradigm (Hardin, 1991),

and yet its power in shaping development interventions among pastoralists and other groups still persists. For a historical perspective on struggles over the meanings and uses of land among Maasai in Tanzania, see Hodgson (1995).

12. The Masai Range Commission was formed under the auspices of the Ministry of Agriculture to supervise the formation and management of ranching associations for the entire Maasai District. One representative from each of the five divisions in the district was appointed, as well as six government officials as ex officio members (Deans *et al.*, 1968:20).

13. Deans *et al.*, (1968:55); Moris (water development engineer), 'Maasai Range Management Project Water Development: past – present – future,' 27 Jan. 1976, MLRMP.

14. The Livestock and Range Improvement in Masailand, Tanzania survey illustrates well the rise of technocratic experts in designing, implementing and evaluating development projects during this period. The survey was conducted by a livestock economist, a range management specialist, an agricultural engineer, a sociologist and an agronomist, seconded from the US Department of Agriculture by USAID (Deans *et al.*, 1968).

15. Although the USA made a significant financial contribution to the project, the Tanzanian government paid dearly for the project, including substantial payments to the USA in the form of local contributions, the required purchase of US-manufactured equipment and supplies and long-term debt obligations to the USA to be repaid in US dollars ('Project Agreement between the Department of State, AID an Agency of the United States of America and the Treasury and United Republic of Tanzania', 11 Sept. 1975, MLRMP/Jim L. Fisher). See also ole Parkipuny (1979:142–3) and Hodgson (1995: 285–6).

16. The project also became integrally related to a major, large-scale beef development scheme, which the Tanzanian government initiated with International Development Association loan financing, based on a comprehensive 1971 IDA sector analysis for livestock. Light *et al.* (evaluation team), 'Evaluation Report, Masai Range and Livestock Development Project,' 4 Feb. 1973, MLRMP.

17. The seven changes in herd management included: '1) Eight Ranching Associations will have increased offtake to 12% or more; 2) Average slaughter steer liveweight increased to 650 lbs; 3) Calf drop increased to 60%; 4) Calf mortality reduced to 20%; 5) Effective calving rate increased to 50%; 6) Average age of slaughter steers at market weight reduced to four years; 7) Average age of females at first calf reduced to four years' ('Logical Framework' for MLRMP, 1970, reproduced in DEVRES, 1979:103).

18. Thomsen (animal production specialist), 'End of tour report, Jan. 24 1977–Jan. 24, 1979,' MLRMP/55.

19. Light *et al.* (evaluation team), 'Evaluation report, Masai Range and Livestock Development Project', 4 Feb. 1973, MLRMP.

20. Engle (range management specialist), 'Evaluation report for range management activities of the Masai Range Project,' 27 Jan. 1976, MLRMP.

21. Ibid.

22. Salk (veterinarian), 'Evaluation report on the activities of the veterinarian – Masai Range Project,' 1976, MLRMP/1975 & 1976 Project Agreements, with revisions.

23. The 'end-of-tour' reports filed by American project team members are full of such complaints. See, for example, Esler (heavy equipment specialist), 'end of tour report, Feb. 1, 1974–Jan. 31, 1976,' 10 Nov. 1975; Vorhis (hydrogeologist), 'Hydrogeologic work on the Maasai project: end of tour report,' 1979; both in MLRMP.

24. Fisher (Chief of Party/MLRMP), 'Progress report for Masai Livestock and Range Development Project:621-0071, Nov. 1976–April 1977,' 30 June 1977, MLRMP/loose.

25. Based on 'discreet inquiries' among Maasai, Jacobs estimated that from 60,000 to 100,000 head of cattle per year were being sold 'illegally' by Maasai in Kenya, and a similar number of sheep and goats (Jacobs, 1978:18; cf. Jacobs, 1980a:12).

26. Thomsen (animal production specialist), 'End of tour report, Jan. 24 1977–Jan. 24 1979,' MLRMP/55.

27. In a similar fashion, Knowles & Collett (1989) examine how images of 'the Maasai' shaped colonial and postcolonial interventions among Maasai in Kenya. They argue that Maasai do want to persist as pastoralists, and that their efforts at cultivation and interest in education are merely 'superficial transformation[s]' (1989:49) produced by difficult

times. Furthermore, although the gendered aspects of images of Maasai are implicit in many of their examples, they never explicitly discuss the issue (see also Collett, 1987).

28. Scholars of Maa-speaking peoples, as well as Maasai themselves, have often tried to argue that any Maasai man or woman who cultivated must really be an Arusha. Although Arusha, a closely related ethnic group to Kisongo Maasai, began moving into the Monduli area in the 1950s, all the researchers discussed (Hatfield, Ndagala, Hodgson) sorted their data by self-identified ethnicity. For more on the debates among scholars as to the historical and contemporary relationships of 'Maasai' and 'Arusha Maasai,' see Spear & Nurse (1992), Spear (1993a and b) and Hodgson (1995).

29. My data from 1992 showed almost 90% of households farming in two communities encompassed by the former ranching association. Even in Mfereji (the site of the Komolonik pilot project), where cultivation is virtually impossible, almost 30% of the women walk miles to farm small plots on nearby Monduli Mountain (Hodgson, 1995).

30. 'Masai Livestock and Range Management Project' [typed list of 'Return participants', 'Participants in training', 'Participants scheduled to go'], MLRMP/58C.

31. Initially, the project was seen primarily as a technical intervention, applying the modern, scientific expertise of American scientists to the technical problems of Maasai animal husbandry. But, in the mid-1970s, as part of a broader shift in its development philosophy, USAID started demanding that its projects contain components devoted to the social development of the people involved, ensuring that each project was not only financially sound, but socially and environmentally sound as well (Hoben, 1976; Jacobs, 1980a:9). The project's goals were revised to reflect these new humanitarian concerns; rather than helping the Tanzanian government, the project was now designed 'to assist the Masai People in improving water and range resources, control livestock parasites, and decrease diseases and increase animal production through integrated ranges and livestock management systems' (Fisher (Chief of Party/MLRMP), 'Progress report for Masai Livestock and Range Development Project:621-0071, Nov. 1976–April 1977,' 30 June 1977, MLRMP/loose). See Hodgson (1995) for more discussion.

32. Salk (veterinarian), 'First quarterly report (May through July 1975)', July 1975, MLRMP/73.

33. Hatfield (project sociologist) to Fisher (Chief of Party), 19 Apr. 1977; Fisher (Chief of Party) to Kriegel, 28 Apr. 1977; both in MLRMP/Jim L. Fisher.

34. Thomsen (animal production specialist), 'End of tour report, Jan. 24 1977–Jan. 24 1979,' MLRMP/55.

35. Ibid.

36. Worby (1988) describes a similarly antagonistic development relationship between Setswana pastoralists and the government of Botswana.

11 Rehabilitation, Resettlement & Restocking: Ideology & Practice in Pastoralist Development

DAVID M. ANDERSON

This chapter examines the ideology and practice of development in the pastoral areas of eastern Africa over the past six decades. Over that period, trends in development in the pastoral sector have differed sharply from other sectors of rural development in several respects. The most important divergence concerns the failure of both the development agencies and the governments who engage them to devise and implement programmes aimed at sustaining pastoral production. Where in the area of agrarian production more generally the issue of sustainability has been the most prominent and in policy terms the most significant issue since the late 1970s, in the pastoral sector sustainability has been accepted only rarely as an achievable goal (Baxter & Hogg, 1990). The majority of interventions have begun from the position that eastern African pastoralism is intrinsically self-destructive and that a more progressive approach to development should steer pastoralists into other, allegedly more secure means of assuring their livelihood. Some degree of diversification away from pastoral production has been implicit, therefore, in much of the development offered to pastoralists in the region (Galaty et al., 1981). The outcome can be stated plainly: it is that development in the context of pastoral peoples in eastern Africa has commonly meant the implementation of programmes that will result in a diminution of the pastoral sector.

This view may be considered unduly polemical. There are agencies involved in pastoralist development, many of them smaller non-governmental organizations (NGOs), who succeed in promoting local sustainability in partnership with pastoral communities (Scott-Villiers & Scott-Villiers, 1995). And it can be demonstrated that larger donor agencies are increasingly following this lead in looking for ways to assist pastoralists without undermining their production systems (Iles, 1994; Johnson & MacAskill, 1995). There is also, of course, a rich literature on eastern African pastoralism which stoutly defends pastoral systems against their critics and advocates the cause of herding peoples (for recent examples, see Homewood & Rodgers, 1991; Spear & Waller, 1993; Fratkin *et al.*, 1994; cf. Anderson, 1993). Even taking account of these factors, however, the dominant image of pastoralism remains one of a system in decline, marked by a shrinking of the rangelands, as alienation of lands causes compression and as cultivation creeps into drier, lower-lying savannah areas, and by the visible destitution of large numbers of pastoral peoples in the wake of drought, famine or disease episodes (Moris, 1988b).

Most pastoralist development schemes in fact start out as relief projects. This characteristic is shared by the earliest colonial interventions aimed at pasture improvement and destocking and by the most recent efforts at restocking. Impoverishment and destitution have long been motivational themes justifying external interventions and promoting particular approaches. Interventions have, accordingly, been either: (i) ameliorative – to solve an identified problem in production; (ii) reformist – to modify production so as to bring greater security or enhanced returns; or (iii) restorative – to re-establish the structures of pastoral production so as to re-accommodate marginalized groups. Despite their stated intentions, such interventions have only rarely worked to strengthen local institutions, as even those with a restorative agenda find it difficult to model and replicate the social mechanisms of pastoralist societies.

Development interventions in pastoralism are typically intended to address failure. The 'failure' of pastoralism is at once a consequence of events over which individuals have no control – drought, epidemic, war – and the simultaneous impact of commoditization brought about by the increasing penetration of wider economic forces. Over the last three decades in particular, the interaction of the two over vast areas of eastern Africa has worked to create more destitute pastoralists and to widen the gap between the wealthy and the poor within pastoral society (Baxter & Hogg, 1990: ii–iii).

This chapter will present an account of three key paradigms of intervention in pastoral systems, arranged chronologically over the past six decades. To facilitate easier comparison, the majority of examples to be cited will be drawn from studies of pastoralists in semi-arid Kenya. The first and second paradigms to be described, 'rehabilitation' and 'resettlement', are already well established with a wide supporting literature. These paradigms, reflecting the emphasis upon ameliorative and reformist policies, will be set out briefly. Greater attention will be paid to the third, and less thoroughly documented paradigm of 'restocking'. Schemes for the restocking of eastern Africa's pastoralists have been framed around a rhetoric of restoration, and it will be shown that these programmes are considerably more sympathetic to the sustainability of pastoral systems than those aimed at rehabilitation or resettlement. However, in practice such programmes are hampered by currents of change within pastoral societies driving towards commoditization. The overall intention is to demonstrate the connectedness of these three paradigms and to show, not that developers have been devising alternative strategies for pastoral areas, but that the sequential effect of policy formulation and implementation has worked in a cumulative way. Restocking programmes can be shown to be aimed toward the sustainability of pastoralism, but they are, none the less, still being implemented in a wider policy environment that is geared towards relief and not development.

Rehabilitation

The rehabilitation paradigm took shape in eastern Africa beginning in the 1930s, as colonial governments mounted the first interventionist programmes in pastoral areas. The principal aim of the earliest schemes, the most notable being those mounted in Baringo and Machakos Districts of Kenya, was to ameliorate the environmental decay attributed to pastoralist land use practices)(Anderson, 1984, forthcoming; Tiffen et al., 1994). As Ian Scoones has noted, cases such as these contributed to the emergence of a development narrative of range (mis)management, based upon assumptions about the causes of ecological calamity which stress 'the damaging potentials of livestock grazing, the threats of degradation and desertification, and the need for control of livestock numbers and grazing movement'. Such ideas have a long history, and in Scoones's view they are still dominant in development perceptions of traditional pastoral land use systems (Scoones, 1996: 34).

Built upon a well-rehearsed narrative of overstocking, and reinforced by 'tragedy of commons' views on the limitations of communal landholding systems (Homewood & Rodgers, 1987), the legitimation of policy interventions to constrain pastoral land use under the banner of rehabilitation have been buttressed latterly by broader debates over property rights and investment in resources (Baxter & Hogg, 1990; Roe, 1994). Rehabilitation is presented as a neutral and supportive package of policies aimed at improving the security of pastoralists, but it is in practice always highly intrusive, involving wholesale changes to management of pastoral lands (Sandford, 1983). It alters the economics of the range. It is closely linked to commoditization of land. Nothing has been more destructive of eastern African pastoralism than this. Drawing upon the general experience from Kenya and Tanzania, we can model the evolution of rehabilitation interventions through a number of sequential stages. (Migot-Adholla & Little, 1981; Raikes, 1981; Evangelou, 1984b; Dietz, 1987; Ngadala, 1992; Rutten, 1992; Anderson, forthcoming).

Within the paradigm of rehabilitation, policy thus moves logically along a continuum from amelioration to reform, which begins with pasture reconditioning and anti-erosion works. These measures are designed to prevent further degradation, but the techniques employed have sometimes been questionable and have invariably proved expensive. From the 1930s to the 1950s, herders in many parts of semi-arid Kenya and Tanganyika were temporarily removed from lands undergoing reconditioning and communal labour was often called out to facilitate anti-erosion work. Among the earliest rehabilitation programmes were those mounted in the Baringo and Machakos Districts of Kenya during the 1920s (Forbes Munro, 1975; Tiffen et al., 1994; Anderson, forthcoming). In both districts these policies were unpopular, being resisted by local herders, who refused to cooperate in the exclusion of animals. Where formerly communal lands were fenced for reconditioning, stock-owners frequently ignored restrictions upon access and trespass was widespread. As a consequence, the need to enforce compliance added significant policing costs to the budget of these rehabilitation programmes, to the extent that attendant high costs of implementation and control could not justify the meagre economic results of marginally improved pasturelands – an improvement that could be sustained only through continued policing and regulation. Without the cooperation of local communities, sustainability came to depend upon restricting access to the reconditioned lands.

These initial schemes therefore gave rise to a second phase of rehabilitation, in which controlled grazing systems were introduced on reconditioned lands. These schemes were designed to maintain grazing quality by restricting access to residential or locality groups. This was the first step towards enclosure of the range. A limited number of pastoralists could enjoy any improvements on such lands, including wells or boreholes, while the majority were displaced to the remaining unreconditioned lands, increasing burdens there (Government of Kenya Colony, 1962). Without adequate controls, and without formal registration of herders, these schemes were chaotic, with endemic trespass and many herders straddling between the closed and the open range (e.g. Dietz, 1987; Anderson, forthcoming).

Registration of herders, often supported by the branding of stock, accompanied the introduction of paddocking systems on higher-potential lands and early forms of group ranches on areas deemed less viable for intensive systems of production. At this stage commercial principles become more overtly part of the rehabilitation package, with members typically paying grazing fees as a contribution towards the infrastructure of dipping, other veterinary services and the provision and maintenance of stock routes that will be required to sustain a marketable offtake of livestock. By the early 1960s, Migot-Adholla & Little (1981:147) report that Kenya's African Land Development Board (ALDEV) was administering no fewer than 40 schemes of this kind in pastoral areas throughout the Rift Valley and Eastern and Northern Provinces (Government of Kenya Colony, 1962).

In practice, many such schemes have failed to realize a commercial return, because stocking levels cannot be controlled effectively and restrictions upon mobility prove to be far too severe a constraint in times of drought. However, success or failure in commercial terms seems unrelated to pressures which mount for further land consolidation and security of tenure for herders engaged in such schemes. Individual title within schemes was often introduced experimentally in the first instance, to test and effectively demonstrate the viability of full enclosure and individualization of property. Once such a process is begun, however, it cannot easily be reversed, and there is a tendancy for other herders to quickly seek similar security in title, if only as a hedge against the fear of subsequent exclusion. In many parts of Kenya, the move toward individual title in the 1950s and early 1960s led to a dramatic rush of spontaneous enclosure of lower-potential lands outside the designated scheme areas. In common with more recent trends in Maasailand, detailed by Rutten (1992) and Campbell (1993), these developments were in part provoked by wealthier speculators, sometimes from outside the local community, and in part by the anxieties of poorer herders, who feared further restrictions on access to pasture and water. While some developers were no doubt satisfied to see herders on high-potential lands with security of title, which provided new opportunities to raise investment against the collateral of their land, this was countered by the simultaneous creation of 'inappropriate' landholdings in neighbouring areas that were not likely to prove commercially viable. By 1960, officials in Baringo District, for example, openly admitted that the spontaneous registration of uneconomic holdings had already moved beyond effective government control (Anderson, forthcoming:ch. 7).

In the final stage along this continuum, the commoditization and individualization of the range is completed with sub-division and the sale of title. Sub-division of title further undermines any initial calculations of the viability of holdings that were made at the planning stage. Owners will subsequently need to further intensify production in order to maintain levels of return and to reinvest in their holdings directly. This is a process which was evident over many parts of Kenya's Maasailand by the 1980s, and has been especially well documented for Kajiado by Marcel Rutten (1992; see also Zaal and Dietz, this volume).

The motor force which propels this model of rehabilitation from ameliorative measures to more dramatic reform of pastoral systems is economic: extensive systems of pastoral production cannot sustain the costs of amelioration of pasture, let alone the investment costs of bringing about range improvements – water, dipping, marketing infrastructure and other services. Rehabilitation begins as a technical intervention to improve carrying capacity, but its end-point is a fundamental shift in land tenure. Pastoral production can be maintained only with a shift from extensive to intensive systems of range management. In addition, the difficulties of regulation and control of access to herders continue to be seen as threatening the sustainability of resources. At the core of these interventions is the ideological belief that pastoralist land use needs to be regulated in order to prevent degradation. One of the most important outcomes of this path from amelioration to reform must inevitably be to reduce the number of herders who have access to the enclosed pasture and, in so doing, to accentuate socio-economic differentiation between wealthier and poorer herders – those who can make claims on resources and those who cannot.

Resettlement

Whereas the rehabilitation paradigm was rooted initially in an apparently benign approach to pastoral systems, suggesting their potential recoverability, the idea that pastoralists could be made more secure by resettlement has never had any pretence of neutrality. Development interventions aimed at the resettlement of destitute herders implicitly presents pastoralism as having reached an end-point.

Resettlement has been advocated and implemented most vigorously in the wake of major regional disasters in eastern Africa since the 1960s. From the mid-1960s onwards, a trend towards the permanent settlement of growing numbers of destitute pastoralists in small trading centres throughout the semi-arid and arid districts of the region was apparent. Some of these refugees had been excluded from resources and pauperized by the uncontrolled collapse of communal grazing rights as the effects of the privatization of landholdings widened. Others came as a consequence of stock losses from drought and yet others because of the effects of raiding, as worsening insecurity affected many parts of north and northeastern Kenya, southern Ethiopia and eastern Uganda. Congregating in these unplanned settlements, close to a source of water and often assisted by famine relief distributed through NGOs, churches or government, the pastoral poor became visible *en masse* as never before (Hogg, 1987).

Governments in the region saw an explanation for this plight in the backwardness of pastoralists. As Jon Moris observed as recently as 1986: 'Most African governments persist in hoping that pastoralists can be sedentarized as quickly as possible, making them amenable to the types of service delivery system used for dealing with settled agriculturalists' (Moris, 1986:18). The increasing intensity of national incorporation marginalized many already remote herding communities in new ways. Pastoralists who had failed to reform their system of production, for whatever reason, were viewed in the 1960s and 1970s as increasingly dysfunctional in the economies of modern states. According to the received wisdom of government, pastoralists tied up precious resources in land and livestock unproductively, leaving themselves vulnerable to a capricious environment, whose effects they apparently did little to ameliorate (Raikes, 1981). When smitten by drought, famine or disease, they became a drain on the state, which was drawn into providing for their temporary welfare through recurrent relief measures.

Here, once again, the narrative of bad pastoralist range management reinforced the view that destitution was the product of overstocking and desertification, both of which were presented as self-inflicted ills (Scoones, 1996; Swift, 1996). The solution was to be found in destocking, so as to restore carrying capacities that would be sustainable. Prevailing orthodoxies in the 1960s held that the communal rangelands of eastern Africa were grossly overstocked and that a 'crash' was imminent (Heady, 1960; Brown, 1963; Migot-Adholla & Little, 1981). This would inevitably reduce the numbers of pastoralists who could be maintained on the land. These individuals would need to be resettled and given alternative means of securing a livelihood. The rationale for providing resources with which to resettle displaced pastoralists was therefore already taking shape before the droughts of the early 1970s took their miserable toll (Hogg, 1987).

In this respect, drought and war pulled off the neo-Malthusian trick of bringing about destocking 'by natural forces' and pushing destitute herders to seek refuge at a growing number of permanent settlements. Between 1966 and 1978, a series of small-scale irrigation projects were started in northern Kenya with financial support from the German Catholic Church and technical assistance from the Food and Agricultural Organization (FAO), as a means of reducing the dependence of these displaced people on food hand-outs. The first pilot project was set up at Kekarongole, in Turkana District, during 1966. With United Nations Development Programme (UNDP) support, further schemes were then established at Katilu (1970), Mandera and Merti (1972), Amolem (1975), Mbalambala and Malka Dakaa (1976) and Gafarsa (1979).

These small-scale schemes were mostly located in unpromising sites for development. Populated predominantly by women and their children, with men absent seeking work or herding for relatives, they had little local labour. Agricultural production was necessarily geared to subsistence needs, with little scope for generating a surplus and no ready market to supply, even if a surplus could be harvested. The gathering of even small populations around the schemes quickly exhausted local resources of fuelwood, and pasture close to the schemes became grazed out as flocks of small stock, mainly goats, were accumulated by the settlers in their efforts to restock themselves. Resettled pastoralists on these schemes made a decent living in good years, but those who really were destitute found themselves in the worst position of all, in some seasons having to seek income outside the scheme to survive (Broch-Due & Storas, 1983; Hogg, 1986, 1987; cf. Sorbo, 1977).

That these schemes appeared so unattractive and yet continued to draw in the destitute revealed the depth of the crisis confronting some pastoral societies. Most of the irrigation schemes in Turkan quickly grew into small towns – Kituli had grown to a po 10,000 by 1980. Richard Hogg has estimated that by 1982 s cent of the Turkana population was living within 5 km of a settlement and that in Isiolo District 'large areas to the north of the Ewaso river were empty of both people and stock, and upwards of 40 percent of Boran were living in small towns and irrigation settlements' (Hogg, 1985:4). Pastoralism was contracting. The logic of assisting the destitute to cultivate seemed to many undeniable, even if the reality of doing this was barely functional.

But establishing irrigation schemes with earth moving machinery and tractor cultivation in such remote areas and giving resettled pastoralists the necessary tools and skills with which to become farmers was an expensive enterprise. In Turkana, for example, Richard Hogg states that irrigation resettlement for pastoralists proved to be 'a costly mistake' (Hogg, 1985:4). The average development costs at the three government-sponsored schemes of Kekarongole, Katilu and Amolem had mounted to US$61,240 per hectare by 1984, that is US$21,800 per tenant household (Hogg, 1987:297). The operating costs of the projects alone amounted to more than three times the gross margin that farmers could expect to realize from their plots and, despite the very high costs, farmers' returns remained inadequate even for reliable subsistence. A similar picture comes from Isiolo, where Kuester & Wiggins (1982) calculated the development costs of the small-scale irrigation schemes at Malka Dakaa, Gafarsa and Merti at nearly US$17,000 per hectare. These schemes had virtually collapsed by the end of 1981, after the withdrawal of UNDP and FAO support, with most tenants again depending upon famine relief and unable to harvest anything from their plots (Hogg, 1985, 1987).

Where the agencies who established the resettlement schemes hoped to encourage destitute pastoralists to become agriculturalists and invest in the technologies, skills and tools required for cultivation, those herders who settled on the schemes had other ideas. Most sought to reinvest anything they could back into pastoralism. They saw the irrigation scheme as a means of re-establishing the capital necessary for herding, and not as a viable alternative to herding (Sorbo, 1977). In doing so, they were reviving a historical pattern in eastern Africa, whereby herding communities had enjoyed a symbiotic relationship with small, settled groups of irrigation cultivators at many points along the edge of the Rift Valley and along the major rivers. During times of drought and stock losses, pastoralists had taken refuge with irrigation farmers; and, in good conditions, when those in the farming communities had accumulated sufficient livestock, they might re-enter pastoral production (Waller, 1985b; Anderson, 1988). Irrigation had in the past represented an important element in the coping strategies of many eastern African pastoralists: from the 1960s, development agencies unwittingly replicated a similar, although less successful, mechanism. The crucial difference was that irrigation had been utilized historically as a means of sustaining pastoralism, whereas its modern reincarnation was presented as an alternative to pastoralism.

Restocking

The schemes established for the resettlement and sedentarization of pastoralists in eastern Africa since the 1960s have reflected the prevailing view of donor agencies (and governments) that the poorest households should diversify out of herding in order to improve their food security. But in the 1980s a number of agencies, many of them small religious organizations and church-based NGOs, began operating schemes to restock pauperized pastoralists. In the Samburu District of northern Kenya, following the 1984 drought, schemes of this type were operated by World Vision and the local Catholic and Lutheran churches, but the scale of such operations was relatively small and they were often linked to church membership or proselytizing activities. Moris reports that the Catholic church assisted up to 150 families, usually giving each less than ten goats as an outright gift. World Vision distributed 3500 goats to some 600 families, at an average of less than six animals per family. The Lutheran mission at Baragoi restocked only 16 families, with no more than 18 animals each (Moris, 1989:17). The numbers of livestock handed over through these interventions were insufficient alone to rebuild herds but did help to meet the immediate subsistence needs of the family. Giving animals to pastoralists was seen as an effective and highly popular way of targeting the poorest and helping them to avoid famine through increasing their access to food (Moris, 1989).

The Soroti Livestock Restocking Programme, supported by Christian Aid, is another scheme typical of many that are now pursued by donor agencies in the region. This scheme was targeted at Iteso and Kumam communities in Iteso District, Uganda, who suffered very heavy livestock losses in Karamojong cattle raids between 1986 and 1989. Estimates that the raiders took up to 1.6 million head of stock over this period may be excessively high, but an acceptance of massive stock losses provided the background to Christian Aid's support for a programme of restocking, which was seen by the agency to get to the heart of the problem of local food security. Characterizing the local population as 'traditionally agriculturalists who depend on oxen as a basic tool for crop production', the restocking programme sought to revive ox cultivation as a means of increasing farming acreage, while reducing farm work drudgery (Christian Aid, 'Soroti Livestock Restocking Programme', March 1996). Although the project was described as restoring 'the cultural values of the people', these values were posited solely in terms of agricultural rehabilitation, making no mention of the cultural and economic importance of cattle in exchange, subsistence and social contracts, such as marriage (Karp, 1978). Restocking with oxen in the Soroti programme is thus a means toward securing the sustainability of agriculture, not livestock production.

The Soroti programme indicates that we should not assume that restocking projects are necessarily to do with restoring the viability of pastoralism. Agencies may have other socio-economic and ideological agendas which restocking can help to facilitate, and in general such interventions are geared more narrowly toward household subsistence and survival rather than to building up the reproductive capital in livestock which sustainable pastoralism requires. Restocking is therefore most commonly seen as part of a bundle of short-term, palliative measures, and not as promoting a longer-term route back to pastoralism.

The existence of indigenous mechanisms for restocking, in the wake of an episode of disease or drought among herding communities throughout eastern Africa, can also be seen as a disincentive to external agencies who would want to avoid replicating or distorting existing coping strategies (Toulmin, 1986; Burke, 1987; Baxter & Hogg, 1990; Iles, 1994). However, although there are accepted means by which impoverished families can make claims upon the assistance of the wider community, for the most part the ability to restock effectively reflects the social standing and economic status of the family concerned (Potkanski, 1994a). Typically, these methods involve the loaning of stock within the community to assist those who have lost animals, the temporary 'ratcheting-down' from cattle to sheep or goat pastoralism in order to build up capital in stock again or the bartering of breeding stock on credit arrangements (Spencer, 1974, 1988; Oba, 1994; Schneider, 1979). In practice, a pastoral family will find it easier to restock if they have a good network of friends, associates and relatives who are wealthy in livestock, or if they have daughters of marriageable age and have sufficient social standing to ensure that brideprice will be paid (Moris, 1988a; cf. Potkanski, this volume). While it is common for herders to loan out stock to be herded elsewhere, poorer families are not necessarily a good choice as partners in such an arrangement. The poorest households, often by definition those with the least reliable networks of reciprocity, are unlikely to be in a position to operate such mechanisms, and anyway their poverty may force them to consume any animals they receive or to sell them in order to purchase grain.

It is therefore apparent that not all needy pastoral families have realistic claims to assistance through indigenous restocking arrangements. Even assuming that they did, there can be many circumstances in which indigenous welfare or redistributive mechanisms might fail to meet the demand (Potkanski, this volume). In a widespread and severe drought, livestock losses may be so acute that the cycle of reciprocity for the wider community will be inadequate to recapitalize those who have lost; there simply may not be sufficient stock to go around, least of all breeding stock. Where pauperization becomes widespread throughout a community, as has happened in parts of Maasailand and in Turkana in the recent past, and it is recognized that it is no longer possible for customary commitments to be honoured, then community pressure to do so will inevitably wane (Burke, 1987; Potkanski, 1994a). It must also be remembered that such customs are negotiable even at the best of times, and how well they can function to assist poorer households depends upon the degree of wider community support. There can be reluctance on the part of richer herders to transfer stock to poorer neighbours, even where custom and circumstance would indicate that they should (Hogg, 1985; Burke, 1987; Potkanski, this volume). Also, in those areas where the impact of commercialization of livestock production has altered relations between herders, the reciprocities that underwrite customary restocking systems will inevitably be eroded, the very process of commercialization having the effect of increasing socio-economic differentiation between rich and poor families (Rutten, 1992; Zaal and Dietz, this volume).

The recognition that pastoralists' indigenous entitlement systems were failing to assist the poorest and most destitute provided 'an important justification' for an exceptional series of restocking schemes launched by Oxfam in northern Kenya (Moris, 1988a). These programmes, mounted during the 1980s in the four semi-arid districts of Isiolo, Wajir, Samburu and Turkana, were aimed explicitly at returning destitute herders to pastoralism, allowing each selected family to become mobile again (Hogg, 1985; Burke, 1987, 1990; Moris, 1988a; Mace, 1989; Kelly, 1993).

The concept of restocking was promoted in the early 1980s in response to the effects of drought in both the West African Sahel and the semi-arid areas of eastern Africa (White, 1984; Hogg, 1985). Oxfam had first begun work in Kenya's semi-arid areas in the drought of 1979–80, becoming involved in food distribution, including food-for-work schemes linked to the Turkana Rehabilitation Project (Burke, 1990:129; Ekwee, 1995:2). In this region, restocking appeared an attractive policy in view of the very large numbers of herders who had been reduced to dependency upon food aid through utter destitution (Hogg, 1986; Moris 1988b), and was presented as being more cost effective than the alternative of resettlement on irrigation projects (Kuester & Wiggins, 1982; Hogg, 1983; Moris, 1988a:11–12). The agency also had earlier experience with the idea of restocking in Ethiopia from the mid-1970s upon which to draw (Moris, 1988a:1).

When Oxfam embarked upon its first restocking project in Isiolo District in 1983, the agency saw its involvement as a pilot venture, 'designed to develop an operational approach which might then be replicated much more widely in response to future droughts'. This project restocked 70 families from the Malka Dakaa Resettlement Scheme with 50 small stock each, comprising eight goats and 42 sheep. The animals were given to the families as a gift, with no expectation of repayment. In addition, each family received one or two transport animals (donkeys) and jerrycans for water-carrying and retained an entitlement to a limited amount of food relief while they were re-establishing themselves in pastoralism. This bundle of resources was designed to allow the family to become fully mobile as quickly as possible, so that they would move away from Malka Dakaa and avoid any danger of overstocking close to the resettlement scheme or of continued dependence (Hogg, 1985; Moris, 1988a; Kelly, 1993).

Such was the pressure at this time for programmes to deal with pastoralist destitution that replication of the Isiolo 'pilot' in fact happened well before any conclusions could reasonably be drawn from the experiment. A second 'pilot scheme' was started from Kalabata, 120 km to the south-east of Lodwar in Turkana District, between May and September 1984. This pilot restocked ten families, whereupon Oxfam approved funding for a fuller programme of restocking targeted at 500 families from various distribution centres in that district over 1985 and 1986. Families here received between 50 and 70 small stock, mostly goats, but in practice a series of conditions were tied to the distribution of the animals, approximating to a 'loan'. It was believed this would help families resist claims against them from friends, and especially relatives, for past obligations, and so prevent any 'redistribution' of the restocked flock – although, as we shall see, this move in fact raised its own problems. In the light of the Isiolo experience, larger quantities of grain were distributed to families in Turkana (Hogg, 1985).

More modest restocking projects were undertaken by Oxfam in Wajir from 1984 and in Samburu from 1985. In Wajir, 30 families were restocked with 30 goats each around Wajir township, while a larger project near Baragoi in Samburu distributed flocks of between 50 and 70 goats to destitute herders in several communities, identified through the recommendation of local chiefs and committees of elders (Moris, 1988a:4–6).

It is notable that in each of the locations selected by Oxfam the restocked herders enjoyed free access to common property in pasture, browse and water across an open range. Although it might have been possible to restock pastoralists involved in commercial production in a similar way, there would undoubtedly have been complications and anyway this would have run contrary to the ideological underpinnings of the Oxfam projects. In many respects, the Oxfam projects can be seen to have mimicked the devices and mechanisms of indigenous restocking strategies. Although customary practices were modified in some important ways, there was a strongly 'restorative' ethos to these schemes, which included the stated aim of redistributing livestock between households so as to bring about 'a more equitable distribution of wealth' (Hogg, 1985:6). At an ideological level, it would not be going too far to suggest that some developers involved in the implementation of these schemes saw them as an antidote to those elements of rehabilitation and resettlement programmes that had contributed to the destruction of pastoral systems in many parts of eastern Africa.

To what extent can Oxfam's adventure with restocking be seen to have been successful in restoring households to pastoralism? It is difficult to answer this question unequivocally. The success of the Oxfam programmes was seen to depend largely upon the continued availability of food aid as part of the restocking process. Families needed to be maintained for many months after the stock had been handed over, or else they would have been compelled to sell or slaughter the animals they had been given. The delivery of food assistance as part of the restocking package was expensive and logistically difficult, and Oxfam was fortunate in Isiolo and Turkana to be able to rely upon other agents – the World Food Programme and the Turkana Rehabilitation Project – to deal with significant aspects of this. Restocking does not offer a short cut to prosperity for destitute herders.

The timing and cost of livestock purchases for the projects was a crucial and vexed matter. It is tempting to buy animals to restock when prices are low, usually before the dry season sets in or when a drought is anticipated. This saves the project money, but herders must then face the difficulty of nursing the newly acquired stock through the dry months to come. The reproductive capacity of a herd restocked in a bad season will inevitably be impaired. A more secure option was to restock when environmental conditions had improved, but this necessarily implied paying more for the stock in the first place. The alternative scenario, of buying when prices were cheap and then holding animals for redistribution at a suitable time, burdens the project with the care and pasturing of large numbers of livestock, with all the risks of loss and mismanagement that implies. There was no easy way around this problem, and the larger the number of animals to be given to an individual family the more acute the difficulty became for project staff wavering between budgetary constraints and project goals. Securing an adequate supply of animals was only the first step; securing them at the right time and at a satisfactory price required detailed local knowledge and an ability to respond quickly to changing circumstances.

Restocking schemes are not cheap. The costs of restocking on the Isiolo project have been estimated at US$1230 per family, but even though this figure discounts a number of centralized costs connected with the running of the project, restocking can still be shown to be considerably cheaper than resettling ex-pastoralists on irrigation schemes (Hogg, 1985:7; Moris, 1988a: 12). In addition, the effects upon the local economy generated by restocking were beneficial, reinforcing the terms of trade for all livestock owners and giving them a better return. However, local traders complained that the schemes inflated the prices for small stock in local markets because of increased demand as the project bought up animals. Such traders are, of course, used to obtaining animals at very cheap prices. Faced with a choice between resettlement and restocking, the latter is thus both socially more acceptable to the pastoralists concerned and more cost effective for the donor agency, while it also has a positive impact on the local economy.

The targeting of destitute households was a principal aim of the Oxfam restocking projects. This was easy enough in Isiolo, where those to be restocked were taken from a failing resettlement scheme, but the sheer scale of Oxfam's operations in Turkana led to poor screening arrangements and strained the ability of the project to purchase sufficient stock at appropriate prices. Accusations were made that some of those receiving livestock through the project were not in fact destitute at all. Contested claims over access to the resources being redeployed through the Turkana project are not surprising, given the immense value these transfers represent in the local economy, but the fact that the project purchased its stock locally tended to feed conflicts. The purchasing of local animals for redistribution was desirable to achieve the goal of recirculating animals within the wider pastoral community, and thereby fuelling the local economy, and as a protection against losses from disease, which would have been more likely with imported stock. But the reality was that local stock could be recognized: 'each animal bought came with a social history, a genealogy and a pedigree'. In Turkana, this resulted in claims and counter-claims against restocked animals (Burke, 1990:131).

This was to some extent accentuated in Turkana by the restorative ethos of the project. Oxfam bought its stock commercially within the district, but distributed them within the more traditional framework of *kojakokonit*. As Kelly Burke explains:

> *Kojakokonit* refers to a practice of loaning an animal to poorer friends or relatives in time of need, as after raids or disease or when the owner does not have sufficient labour to herd all his own stock. The person who is loaned the beast has use of the milk, blood and meat (should it die) and, after an agreed period of one or more years, has to return the original stock plus some or all of the progeny. (Burke, 1990:131)

But how, then, should Turkana conceptualize the stock received from Oxfam? Was each animal to be seen in the terms implied by *Kojakokonit*, carrying with it a set of obligations to the previous owner – obligations that might then typically be used as bargaining counters against claims to other resources? Or were these animals to be seen purely in commercial terms, with no social ties attached? If, as Oxfam said, these animals were a 'loan' and could be returned to the agency, why could they not be returned to the original owner also? In practice, by invoking the custom of *Kojakokonit* in a transformed and deeply ambiguous context, Oxfam placed the animals in both realms, opening up endless possibilities for debate and disputation (Burke, 1987, 1990:131–2). As an external agency, Oxfam found that it could not simply replicate 'traditional practice'; Oxfam's very presence altered the relationships involved in the 'loaning' of stock, while its own ideologically driven bias to 'bet on the weak' placed constraints upon participants' actions that were far from 'traditional'.

Attempts to remove the ambiguous status of the 'loans' of stock made by Oxfam by tightening the conditionalities attached to each restocked animal were only partly successful in clarifying the position. As the project expanded in Turkana, government chiefs, local councillors and even Members of Parliament (MPs) became involved in the selection of families, which added further confusion to the local politics of ownership and control. Because of uncertainties over the status of the animals, restocked families were in fact hampered in their efforts to reconstruct social relationships with wealthier households. It was not clear what social life these animals could have, because it was not clear in what way they or their progeny could be used in social transactions (Burke, 1987, 1990; Kelly, 1993).

The most significant indicator of the success of restocking must surely be the extent to which it can be shown to enhance the sustainability of livestock production for the recipient families: are herders secure in pastoralism once restocked? The answer to this question must be mediated by an assessment of their ability to retain the stock acquired and then rest upon their capacity to nurture the growth of their flock or herd. In the first place, much depends upon how the stock acquired through the restocking scheme are perceived by the wider community. Oxfam learned from experience that animals seen to be 'gifted' to a herder might be less secure as his/her long-term property than animals seen to be 'loaned' on conditional terms which restricted the possibility of further transfers, but the Turkana experience demonstrates that even this apparent 'security' is fraught with difficulty.

Over the longer term, Ruth Mace's follow-up study of two groups of restocked herders shows that, in addition to the bundle of resources delivered by Oxfam, a very high proportion of families continued to depend upon other sources of income, including food assistance from their wider family and friends, over several years following their restocking. Very few households were able to sustain themselves entirely from their livestock, even four to five years after restocking, and even these families were vulnerable to crash again if environmental conditions worsened. Bad luck was more significant than bad management in determining such outcomes (Mace, 1989). This reality tends to dampen the longer-term positive impacts of restocking: households can be propelled back into pastoralism, but the environmental realities of eastern Africa's semi-arid lands are such that no agency can guarantee the sustainability of their production over the next five to ten years. The prospect of having to restock the same household again is all too real.

In these circumstances, it is especially important for the donor agency to demonstrate that its policies really are targeting the most deprived and vulnerable sectors of the community. For Oxfam, gender loomed large in defining their target group. Older women, many of them widowed and others abandoned, and younger women who had been the victims of divorce represented a group who commonly found it impossible to engage in the transactions to allow restocking through traditional networks of mutual assistance. Female-headed households of these types were found to be prominent among destitute pastoralists across all four of the project areas tackled by Oxfam, and they accordingly formed a significant portion of the families targeted for restocking in each location. In the Isiolo project, for example, 15 of the 70 participating families were female-headed, which Hogg reports reflected the large number of such destitute households on the Malka Dakaa irrigation scheme (Hogg, 1985).

Here again, Mace's study offers some intriguing insights. One of her two study groups comprised restocked female-headed families, the other male-headed families. The behaviour of each group differed, the female-headed families being inclined to a more traditional strategy of slow herd growth, unwilling to gamble by slaughtering or selling stock, and prepared to limit other cash expenditure in order to see through this strategy. There was also evidence to suggest that women who had been restocked subsequently remarried more quickly as a consequence. The male-headed group, in contrast, showed a greater propensity to sell stock, often so as to realize the cash needed for school fees and for other activities that diversified the household economy. Overall, female-headed families conformed more closely to a traditional pattern of herding, while male-headed households were more prepared to invest in activities that were not directly related to pastoral production (Mace, 1989).

The apparent success of the restocked female-headed households – they did no worse in Mace's estimation over the first five-year period after restocking than male-headed households, and more consistently fulfilled the conditions of restocking policies – reinforces the current bias in donor agency programmes toward gendered policies that empower women. Of course, evidence deriving only from herd size and household income disguises the wide range of social interactions into which a restocked woman is likely to be drawn by her gaining of property. In the negotiations with relatives and other associates over the management of the property, the woman may encounter difficulties of status and control.

In polygamous societies such as Turkana and Samburu, in common with other Nilotic peoples, the definition of terms such as 'widow' and 'female-headed household', which have been widely used by Oxfam and other agencies in targeting vulnerable groups who should receive assistance, needs to be thought about in context. As Johnson & MacAskill have pointed out with respect to Dinka communities in eastern Bahr el-Ghazal, the exchange of bride-price in cattle-keeping societies creates a bond between the families of the wife and husband which extends beyond the grave. Thus, for a widow, '[i]t is continued membership of her husband's agnatic lineage, and her actual or potential contribution to its size, which guarantees her a right to claim support from a range of her deceased husband's kin'. 'Widowhood', they continue, 'does not automatically create a female head of household along the lines of the Western "single parent family"' (Johnson & MacAskill, 1995). Furthermore, it is precisely in the wake of a significant and widespread disaster, such as prolonged drought, that persons may find it more difficult to honour their obligations to widows within their wider kin group. At a time when there are fewer resources to go around, people will naturally 'attempt to limit or even evade demands placed upon them': the safety net of mutual assistance tends to shrink just at the time when more people are falling into it (Johnson & MacAskill 1995; Potkanski, this volume). This can be seen to justify the targeting of widows and 'female-headed households' at times of stress, as others retreat from obligations toward them. But their marginal status does not mean that their wider kin group has abandoned them for ever. Once such persons are restocked with property, kin will reactivate relations of reciprocity, making claims against past assistance.

The predicament confronting all restocked families is how to maximize the resources they have been given, and the reality is that they may elect to deploy those resources in a way that contradicts the intentions of the donor agencies who provided them with stock. The restocking paradigm has been invoked through a rhetoric of entitlement and sustainability, reaffirming the appropriateness of pastoralism as a lifestyle, but its target group are precisely those who pastoralists themselves have felt compelled to marginalize. It must be realized that the changes which have brought this about are a consequence not of the most recent drought or war, but of the cumulative effects of gradual socio-economic reforms spanning six decades.

Concluding comments

Oxfam's experience of restocking in northern Kenya illustrates the difficulties in devising an intervention that can be articulated successfully with local understandings of need and status. Even those pastoral systems which appear the least affected by commoditization are in fact undergoing important changes in their definitions of property, its value and exchangeability and the social status and potential relationships it imparts. In this sense, restorative projects will tend always to run up against the difficulty of accommodating the dynamic currents of change already flowing through pastoral societies. It is ironic that, in their focus upon restocking, development agencies working among pastoral peoples have acknowledged that the need for relief measures is greater and more widespread than ever before. Restocking is a response to the realization that an increasing number of destitute pastoralists have moved from conjunctural to structural poverty (Iliffe, 1987). It is a shift that the implementation of earlier development paradigms has helped to promote.

References

Agostini, F., Puglielli, A. & Siyaad, C.I. (eds) (1985) *Dizionario Somalo–Italiano* (Rome: Gangemi Editore).

Aldington, T.J. & Wilson, F.C. (1968) *The Marketing of Beef in Kenya* (Nairobi: Occasional Paper No. 3, Institute for Development Studies).

Allen, C. & Fry, H. (1979) *Tales from the Dark Continent* (London: A. Deutsch).

Almagor, U. (1978) 'Gerontocracy, polygyny and scarce resources', in La Fontaine, J.S. (ed.) *Sex and Age as Principles of Social Differentiation* (London and New York: Academic Press).

Almagor, U. (1979) 'Raiders and elders: a confrontation of generations among the Dassenetch', in Fukui, K. & Turton, D. (eds) *Warfare among East African Herders* (Osaka, Japan: Senri Ethnological Series No. 3, National Museum of Ethnology).

Almagor, U. (1987) 'The cycle and stagnation of smells: pastoralist–fishermen relationships in an East African society', *RES*, 14, pp. 106–21.

Anderson, D.M. (1984) 'Depression, dust bowl, demography and drought: the colonial state and soil conservation in East Africa during the 1930s', *African Affairs* 83, pp.321–43.

Anderson, D.M. (1986) 'Stock theft and moral economy in colonial Kenya', *Africa*, 56 (4), pp. 399–416.

Anderson, D.M. (1988) 'Cultivating pastoralists: ecology and economy among the Il Chamus of Baringo, 1840–1980', in Johnson, D.H. & Anderson, D.M. (eds), *Ecology of Survival: Case Studies from Northeast African History* (London: Lester Crook).

Anderson, D.M. (1993) 'Cow power: livestock and the pastoralist in Africa', *African Affairs*, 92, pp. 121–33.

Anderson, D.M. (forthcoming) *Eroding the Commons: Politics and Ecology in Baringo, Kenya 1980–1963.*

Anon. (*c.* 1962) 'A history of the fluctuation of the cattle population in Kajiado Masailand during the last 20 years' unpub. ms.: Nairobi.

Anon. (1983) *The Harriet Lane Handbook: a Manual for Pediatric House Officers* 11th edn (Chicago: Year Book Medical Publishers).

Appadurai, A. (1986) *The Social Life of Things: Commodities in Cultural Perspectives* (Cambridge: Cambridge University Press).

Appadurai, A. (1995) 'The production of locality', in Fardon, R. (ed.) *Counterworks: Managing the Diversity of Knowledge* (London and New York: Routledge).

Argwings-Kodhek, G. (1992) 'Private sector maize marketing in Kenya', in *Policy Analysis Matrix, Proceedings of the Conference on Maize Supply and Marketing under Market Liberalization* (Nairobi: KCB).

Århem, K. (1981) *Maasai Pastoralism in Ngorongoro Conservation Area: Sociological and Ecological Issues,* (BRALUP Research Paper No. 69, University of Dar es Salaam).

Århem, K. (1985) *Pastoral Man in the Garden of Eden: the Maasai of the Ngorongoro Conservation Area, Tanzania* (Uppsala: Scandinavian Institute of African Studies).

Århem, K. (1987) *The Maasai and the State: the Impact of Rural Development Policies on a Pastoral People in Tanzania* (Copenhagen: Documentation Series Paper 52. IWGIA).

Aronson, D.R. (1980) 'Must nomads settle? Some notes towards policy on the future of pastoralism', in Salzman, P.C. (ed.), *When Nomads Settle: Processes of Sedentarization as Adaptation and Response* (New York: Praeger).

Bagshawe, F.J. (1926) 'Peoples of the happy valley. Part IV', *Journal of the Royal African Society*, 25, pp. 59–74.

Baker, P.R. (1967) *Environmental Influences on Cattle Marketing in Karamoja.* (Kampala: Occasional Paper No. 5. Department of Geography, Makerere University College).

Barclay's Bank DCO (1958) *Tanganyika: an Economic Survey* (London: Barclay's Bank).

Bassi, M. (1990) 'The system of cattle redistribution among the Obbu Borana and its implication for development planning', in Baxter, P. & Hogg, R. (eds), *Property, Poverty and People: Changing Rights in Property and Problems of Pastoral Development* (Manchester: Department of Social Anthropology and International Development Centre, University of Manchester).

Baudrillard, J. (1994) *Simulacra and Simulation* (Ann Arbor: University of Michigan Press).

Baumann, O. (1894) *Durch Massailand zur Nilquelle; Reisen und Forschungen der Massai-Expedition des deutschen Antisklaverei-Komite in den Jahren 1891–93* (Berlin: D. Reimer).

Baxter, P.T.W. (1972) 'Absence makes the heart grow fonder: some suggestions why witchcraft accusations are rare among East African Pastoralists', in Gluckman, M. (ed.) *The Allocation of Responsibility* (Manchester: Manchester University Press).

Baxter, P.T.W. (1975) 'Some consequences of sedentarisation for social relationships', in Monod, T. (ed.) *Pastoralism in Tropical Africa* (London: Oxford University Press).

Baxter, P.T.W. (1991) *When the Grass is Gone: Development Intervention in African Arid Lands* (Uppsala: Scandinavian Institute of African Studies).

Baxter, P. & Hogg, R. (eds) (1990) *Property, Poverty and People: Changing Rights in Property and Problems of Pastoral Development* (Manchester: Department of Social Anthropology and International Development Centre, University of Manchester).

Behnke, R. H. (1984) 'Fenced and open range ranching: the commercialization of pastoral land and

References

livestock in Africa', in Simpson, J. R. & Evangelou, P. (eds) *Livestock Development in Sub-saharan Africa: Constraints, Prospects, Policy* (Boulder: Westview Press).

Bekure, S. *et al.* (1991) *Maasai Herding. An Analysis of the Livestock Production System of Maasai Pastoralists in Eastern Kajiado District, Kenya* (Addis Ababa: Systems Studies 4, ILCA).

Bennett, J. (1984) *Political Ecology and Development Projects Affecting Pastoralist Peoples in East Africa* (Madison: Land Tenure Center, University of Wisconsin).

Bentsen, C. (1991) *Maasai Days* (New York: Anchor Books).

Berger, P. & Kiessling, R. (n.d.) *Iraqw Texts* (mimeo).

Berntsen, J. (1979) 'Pastoralism, raiding and prophets: Maasailand in the nineteenth century' (PhD thesis, University of Wisconsin-Madison).

Berntsen, J.L. (1980) 'The enemy is us: eponymy in the historiography of the Maasai', *History in Africa*, 7, pp. 1–21.

Berry, S. (1993) *No Condition is Permanent: Social Dynamics of Agrarian Change in Sub-Saharan Africa* (Madison: University of Wisconsin Press).

Blystad, A. (1992) 'The pastoral Barabaig: fertility, recycling and the social order' (Cand. Polit. thesis in Social Anthropology, University of Bergen).

Blystad, A. (n.d.) 'Lilicht and violence: reconsidering Barbayiig killings' (forthcoming).

Bollig, M. (1990) 'Ethnic conflicts in northwest Kenya: Pokot–Turkana raiding 1969–1984', *Zeitschrift für Ethnologie*, 115, pp. 73–90.

Bonte, P. (1977) 'Non-stratified social formations among pastoral nomads', in Friedman, J. & Rowlands, M. (eds) *The Evolution of Social Systems* (London: Duckworth).

Borgerhoff Mulder, M. & Sellen, D.W. (1994) 'Pastoralist decision making: a behavioural ecological perspective', in Fratkin, E., Galvin, K.A. & Roth, E. (eds) *African Pastoralist Systems: An Integrated Approach* (Boulder: Lynne Rienner).

Brantley, C. (1997) 'Orr and Gilks revisited: Kikuyu–Maasai nutrition: Kenya in the late twenties', *International Journal of African Historical Studies*, 22, pp. 19–86.

Broch-Due, V. (1983) *Women at the Backstage of Development* (Rome: FAO).

Broch-Due, V. (1986) *From Herds to Fish, and From Fish to Food Aid* (Oslo: NORAD).

Broch-Due, V. (1987) 'From sameness to difference in women's lives; some suggestions for improving the relation between women-oriented aid and feminist research', *Nordic Forum*.

Broch-Due, V. (1990a) 'Livestock speak louder than sweet words: changing property and gender relations among the Turkana', in Baxter, P. & Hogg, R. (eds) *Property, Poverty and People: Changing Rights in Property and Problems of Pastoral Development* (Manchester: Department of Social Anthropology and International Development Centre, University of Manchester).

Broch-Due, V. (1990b) 'The bodies within the body: journeys in Turkana thought and practice' (PhD thesis, University of Bergen).

Broch-Due, V. (1991) 'Cattle are companions, goats are gifts: animal and people in Turkana thought', in Paulsen, G. (ed.) *From Water to World Making: Arid lands and African Accounts* (Uppsala: Nordic Institute of African Studies).

Broch-Due, V. (1993) 'Making meaning out of matter: Turkana perceptions about gendered bodies', in Broch-Due, V., Rudie, I. & Bleie, T. (eds), *Carved Flesh/ Cast Selves: Gendered Symbols and Social Practices* (Oxford and Providence: Berg Press).

Broch-Due, V. (1995) *The Poor and the Primitive: Discursive and Social Transformations* (Uppsala: Poverty and Prosperity Occasional Paper Series, No. 3, NAI).

Broch-Due, V. (1996) *Poverty Paradoxes: the Economy of Engendered Needs* (Uppsala: Poverty and Prosperity Occasional Paper Series, No. 4, NAI).

Broch-Due, V. & Rudie, I. (1993) 'Carved flesh – cast selves: an introduction', in Broch-Due, V., Rudie, I. & Bleie T. (eds), *Carved Flesh/ Cast Selves: Gendered Symbols and Social Practices* (Oxford and Providence: Berg Press).

Broch-Due, V. & Storas, F. (1983) *Fields of the Foe: Factors Constraining Agricultural Output and Farmers' Capacity for Participation on Katilu Irrigation Scheme* (Bergen: NORAD).

Broch-Due, V. *et al.* (1981) 'Women and pastoral development: some research priorities for the social sciences', in Galaty, J.G. *et al.* (eds) *The Future of Pastoralist Peoples: Research Priorities for the 1980s* (Ottawa: International Development Research Center).

Brown, D. (1994) 'On pastoralism and poverty', in Brokensha, D. (ed.) *A River of Blessings: Essays in Honor of Paul Baxter* (Syracuse: Maxwell School of Citizenship and Public Affairs, Syracuse University).

Brown, L.H. (1963) *The Development of the Semi-Arid Areas of Kenya* (Nairobi: Government Printer).

Bruner, E. & Kirshenblatt-Gimblett, B. (1994) 'Maasai on the lawn: tourist realism in East Africa', *Cultural Anthropology*, 9 (4), pp. 435–70.

Burke, K. (1987) 'The rehabilitation of pastoralists in Turkana: the ethnography of a restocking project, 1984–87' (MA dissertation in anthropology, University of Manchester).

Burke, K. (1990) 'Property rights in "animals of strangers": notes on a restocking programme in Turkana, N.W. Kenya', in Baxter, P. & Hogg, R. (eds) *Property, Poverty and People: Changing Rights in Property and Problems of Pastoral Development* (Manchester: Department of Social Anthropology and International Development Centre, University of Manchester).

Caldwell, J.C. *et al.* (1989) 'The social context of Aids in sub-Saharan Africa', *Population and Development Review*, 15 (2), pp. 185–234.

Campbell, D.J. (1984) 'Responses to drought among farmers and herders in southern Kajiado District, Kenya', *Human Ecology*, 12 (1), pp. 35–64.

Campbell, D.J. (1993) 'Land as ours, land as mine: economic, political and ecological marginalization in Kajiado District', in Spear, T. & Waller, R.D. (eds), *Being Maasai: Ethnicity and Identity in East Africa* (London: James Currey).

Campbell, D.J. & Axinn, G.H. (1980) *Pastoralism in Kenya. Obsolete Societies en route to Extinction, or Appropriate Technologies for a Fragile Environment?* (Hanover: Field Staff Reports No. 30, American Universities).

Cassanelli, L.V. (1987) 'Social construction on the Somali frontier: Bantu former slave communities in the nineteenth century', in Kopytoff, I. (ed.) *The African Frontier: The Reproduction of Traditional African Societies* (Bloomington: Indiana University Press).

Cerulli, E. (1922) 'The folk-literature of the Galla of southern Abyssinia', *Varia Africana (Harvard African Studies)*, 3, pp. 9–228.

Cerulli, E. (1957, 1959, 1964) *Somalia: Scritti vari editi ed inediti*, 3 vols (Rome: Istituto poligrafico dello stato).

Chabasse, D. *et al.* (1985) 'The health of nomads and semi-nomads of the Malian Gourma: an epidemiological approach', in Hill, A.G. (ed.) *Population, Health and Nutrition in the Sahel* (London: Routledge and Kegan Paul).

Chambers, Robert (1983) *Rural Development: Putting the Last First* (London: Longman).

Chieni, T. & Spencer, P. (1993) 'The world of Telelia: reflections of a Maasai woman in Matapato', in Spear, T. & Waller, R.D. (eds) *Being Maasai: Ethnicity and Identity in East Africa* (London: James Currey).

Classen, C., Howes D. & Synnott, A. (1994) *Aroma: The Cultural History of Smell* (London and New York: Routledge).

Clay, J.W. (1988) 'The case of Hararghe: the testimony of refugees in Somalia', in Clay, J.W., *et al.* (eds) *The Spoils of Famine* (Cambridge, Massachusetts: Cultural Survival).

Clay, J.W. & Holcolmb, B.K. (1986) *Politics and the Ethiopian Famine 1984–1985* (Cambridge, Massachusetts: Cultural Survival).

Clifford, J. (1986) 'On ethnographic allegory', in Clifford, J. & Marcus, G.E. (eds) *Writing Culture: the Poetics and Politics of Ethnography* (Berkeley: University of California Press).

Collett, D. (1987) 'Pastoralists and wildlife: images and reality in Kenya Maasailand', in Anderson, D.M. & Grove, R. (eds), *Conservation in Africa: People, Policies, and Practice* (Cambridge: Cambridge University Press).

Colucci, M. (1924) *Principi di diritto consuetudinario della Somalia italiana meridionale* (Florence: Editrice La Voce).

Comaroff, J & Comaroff, J.L. (1990) 'Goodly beasts and beastly goods: cattle and commodities in a South African context', *American Ethnologist*, 17, pp. 195–216.

Comaroff, J & Comaroff, J.L. (1992) *Ethnography & the Historical Imagination* (Boulder: Westview).

Coughernour, M. *et al.* (1985) 'Energy extraction and use in a nomadic pastoral ecosystem', *Science*, 230, pp. 619–25.

Coulson, A. (1982) *Tanzania: A Political Economy* (Oxford: Clarendon Press).

Cowan, M.P. (1974) 'Patterns of cattle ownership and dairy production in Nyeri, Kenya, 1900–1965' (Cambridge: unpub. ms.).

Cranworth, Lord (1919) *Profit and Sport in British East Africa* (London: Macmillan).

Cultural Survival (1993) *State of the Peoples: A Global Human Rights Report on Societies in Danger* (Boston: Beacon Press).

Dahl, G. (1979a) 'Ecology and equality: the Boran case', in Equipe Ecologie et Anthropologie des Societiés Pastorales, *Pastoral Production and Society* (Cambridge: Cambridge University Press).

Dahl, G. (1979b) *Suffering Grass: Subsistence Society of Waso Borana* (Stockholm: Department of Social Anthropology, University of Stockholm).

Dahl, G. (1987) 'Women in pastoral production: some theoretical notes on roles and resources', *Ethnos* 52 (1–2), pp. 246–79.

Dahl, G. & Hjort, A. (1976) *Having Herds: Pastoral Herd Growth and Household Economy* (Stockholm: Dept of Social Anthropology, University of Stockholm).

Dahl, G. & Hjort, A. (1979) *Pastoral Change and the Role of Drought* (Stockholm: Report No. 2, SAREC).

De Leeuw, P. N. and Tothill, J. C. (1993), 'The concept of rangeland carrying capacity in sub-Saharan Africa', in Behnke, R., Scoones, I. & Kerven, C. (eds) *Range Ecology in Disequilibrium* (London: ODI).

De Waal, A. (1989) *Famine that Kills: Darfur, Sudan, 1984–85* (Oxford: Clarendon Press).

Deans, R. *et al.* (1968) *Livestock and Range Improvement in Masailand: Tanzania Survey Report* (report for USAID and Ministry of Agriculture, Tanzania).

Devereux, S. (1993) *Theories of Famine* (Hemel Hempstead: Harvester Wheatsheaf).

DEVRES (1979) *Terminal Evaluation of the Masai Livestock and Range Management Project* (Dar es Salaam, report for USAID).

Dietz, T. (1986) 'Migration to and from dry areas in Kenya', *Tijdschrift voor Economische en Sociale Geografie*, 77 (1), pp. 18–24.

Dietz, T. (1987) *Pastoralists in Dire Straits. Survival Strategies and External Interventions in a Semi-Arid Region at the Kenya/Uganda Border: Western Pokot, 1900–1986.* (Amsterdam and Utrecht: University of Amsterdam).

Dietz, T. (1991) 'Crisis survival strategies: a summary of concepts and an example from the semi-pastoral Pokot in Kenya/Uganda', in Stone, J.C. (ed.) *Pastoral Economies in Africa and Long Term Responses to Drought* (Aberdeen: African Studies Group).

References

Dietz, T. (1993) 'The state, the market, and the decline of pastoralism: challenging some myths, with evidence from western Pokot in Kenya/Uganda', in Markakis J. (ed.), *Conflict and the Decline of Pastoralism in the Horn of Africa* (London: Macmillan; The Hague: ISS).

Dietz, T. *et al.* (1983) *Locational Development Profile Sook Location* (Kapangaria: report for the Arid and Semi-arid Lands Development Programme, Kenya).

Douglas, M. (1982) *In the Active Voice* (London, Boston and Henley: Routledge and Kegan Paul).

Dove, M. (1994) 'The existential status of the Pakistani farmer: studying official constructions of social reality', *Ethnology*, 33 (4), pp. 331–51.

Dundas, F.G. (1893) 'Exploration of the Rivers Tana and Juba', *Scottish Geographical Magazine*, 9, pp. 113–26.

Dyson-Hudson, R. (1980) 'Towards a general theory of pastoralism and social stratification', *Nomadic Peoples*, 7, pp. 1–7.

Edgerton, R.B. (1971) *The Individual in Cultural Adaptation: a Study of Four East African Peoples* (Berkeley: University of California Press).

Ekwee, E. (1995) 'Poverty and prosperity – the contribution of food aid: Oxfam drought relief programme in northern Kenya, 1992–95' (paper presented to the workshop on 'Poverty and Prosperity among Eastern African pastoralists', Uppsala, Sweden, September 1995).

Ensminger, J. (1992) *Making a Market: The Institutional Transformation of an African Society* (Cambridge: Cambridge University Press).

Escobar, A. (1995) *Encountering Development: The Making & Unmaking of the Third World* (Princeton: Princeton University Press).

Evangelou, P. (1984a) 'Cattle marketing efficiency in Kenya's Maasailand', in Simpson, J.R. & Evangelou, P. (eds) *Livestock Development in Sub-Saharan Africa: Constraints, Prospects, Policy* (Boulder: Westview Press), pp. 123–41.

Evangelou, P. (1984b) *Livestock Development in Kenya's Maasailand* (Boulder: Westview Press).

Evans-Jones, P. (1960) *The Karamoja Development Scheme: a Report on the Work during the Years 1955–59* (Kampala: Special Development Section, Uganda Protectorate).

Fallers, L.A. (1964) 'Social stratification and economic processes', in Herskovits, M.J. & Horwitz, M. (eds) *Economic Transition in Africa* (London: Routledge and Kegan Paul).

Farler, J.P. (1882) 'Native routes in East Africa from Pangani to the Masai country and the Victoria Nyanza', *Proceedings of the Royal Geographical Society*, 4 (12), pp. 730–42, 776 (map).

FAO (1993) *Monduli District: an Agro-economic Survey of the Maasai 1993* (Dar es Salaam: draft report, FAO Marketing Development Bureau).

Faust, H. (1969) 'Courtship via murder', *World Encounter*, 6 (3), pp. 1–7.

Ferguson, J. (1990) *The Anti-Politics Machine: 'Development', Depoliticization, and Bureaucratic Power in Lesotho* (Cambridge: Cambridge University Press).

Ferguson, J. (1992) 'The cultural topography of wealth: commodity paths and the structure of property in rural Lesotho', *American Anthropologist*, 94 (1), pp. 55–73.

Ferrandi, U. (1903) *Lugh. Emporio commerciale sul Giuba* (Rome: Società Geografica Italiana).

Field, C.R. & Sampkin, S.P. (1985) *The Importance of Camels to Subsistence Pastoralists in Kenya* (Nairobi: IPAL Technical Report E-7, UNESCO).

Fischer, G.A. (1885) *Das Massailand* (Hamburg: L. Friedrichson & Co.).

Folbre, N. (1984) 'The feminization of poverty and the pauperization of motherhood', *Review of Radical Political Economics*, 16 (4), pp. 78–88.

Folbre, N (1991) 'The unproductive housewife: her evolution in nineteenth century economic thought', *Signs*, 16 (3), 463–84.

Fosbrooke, H.A. (1955) 'The defensive measures of certain tribes in north-eastern Tanzania', *Tanganyika Notes and Records*, 36, pp. 50–57.

Fouquer, R. (1955) *Irakou: Histoire d'un peuple et d'une mission* (Paris: Editions La Savane).

Fraser, N. (1989) *Unruly Practices: Power, Discourse and Gender in Contemporary Social Theory* (Cambridge: Polity Press).

Fratkin, E. (1989) 'Household variation and gender inequality in Ariaal Rendille pastoral production: results of a stratified time allocation survey', *American Anthropologist*, 91 (2), pp. 430–40.

Fratkin, E. (1991) *Surviving Drought and Development: The Ariaal Rendille of Northern Kenya* (Boulder: Westview).

Fratkin, E. (1992) 'Drought and development in Marsabit District, Kenya', *Disasters*, 16, pp. 119–30.

Fratkin, E. (1994) 'Pastoral land tenure in Kenya: Maasai, Samburu, Boran, and Rendille Experiences, 1950–1990', *Nomadic Peoples*, 34/35, pp. 55–68.

Fratkin, E. (1997) 'Pastoralism: governance and development issues', *Annual Review of Anthropology*, 26, pp. 235–61.

Fratkin, E. & Roth, E.A. (1990) 'Drought and economic differentiation among Ariaal pastoralists', *Human Ecology*, 18 (4), pp. 385–402.

Fratkin, E. & Smith, K. (1994) 'Labor, livestock and land: the organization of pastoral production', in Fratkin, E., Galvin, K.A. & Roth, E.A. (eds) *African Pastoralist Systems: An Integrated Approach* (Boulder: Lynne Rienner).

Fratkin, E. & Smith, K. (1995) 'Women's changing economic roles with pastoral sedentarization: varying strategies in four Rendille communities', *Human Ecology*, 23 (4), pp. 433–54.

Fratkin, E., Galvin, K.A. & Roth, E.A. (eds) (1994) *African Pastoralist Systems: An Integrated Approach* (Boulder: Lynne Rienner).

260

Fukui, K. (1970) 'Migration and settlement of the Iraqw in Hanang area', *Kyoto University African Studies*, 5, pp. 102–24.

Galaty, J.G. (1977) 'In the pastoral image: the dialectic of Maasai identity' (PhD thesis, University of Chicago).

Galaty, J.G. (1979) 'Pollution and pastoral antipraxis: the issue of Maasai inequality', *American Ethnologist*, 6, pp. 803–16.

Galaty, J.G. (1980) 'The Maasai group ranch: politics and development in an African pastoral society', in Saltzman, P. (ed.) *When Nomads Settle: Processes of Sedentarisation as Adaptation and Response* (New York: Praeger).

Galaty, J.G. (1981) 'Land and livestock among the Kenyan Maasai', in Galaty, J.G. & Salzman, P. (eds), *Change and Development in Nomadic and Pastoral Societies* (Leiden: E.J. Brill).

Galaty, J.G. (1982a) 'Being Maasai, being "people of the cattle": ethnic shifters in East Africa', *American Ethnologist*, 9 (1), pp. 1–20.

Galaty, J.G. (1982b) 'Maasai pastoral ideology and change', *Studies in Third World Societies*, 17, pp. 1–22.

Galaty, J.G. (1986) 'East African hunters and pastoralists in a regional perspective: an "ethno-anthropological" approach', *Sprache und Geschichte in Afrika*, 7, pp. 105–31.

Galaty, J.G. (1991) 'Pastoral orbits and deadly jousts: factors in the Maasai expansion', in Galaty, J.G. & Bonte, P. (eds) *Herders, Warriors, and Traders: Pastoralism in Africa* (Boulder: Westview Press), pp. 171–98.

Galaty, J.G. (1992) 'The land is yours: social and economic factors in the privatization, sub-division, and sale of Maasai ranches', *Nomadic Peoples*, 30, pp. 26–40.

Galaty, J.G. (1993a) 'Maasai expansion and the new East African pastoralism', in Spear, T. & Waller, R.D. (eds) *Being Maasai: Ethnicity and Identity in East Africa* (London: James Currey).

Galaty, J.G. (1993b) 'The eye that wants a person, where can it not see?: inclusion, exclusion, and boundary shifters in Maasai identity', in Spear, T. & Waller, R. D. (eds), *Being Maasai: Ethnicity and Identity in East Africa* (London: James Currey).

Galaty, J.G. (1994) 'Rangeland tenure and pastoralism in Africa', in Fratkin, E., Galvin, K.A. & Roth, E.A. (eds), *African Pastoralist Systems: an Integrated Approach* (Boulder: Lynne Rienner).

Galaty, J. & Bonte, P. (eds) (1991a) *Herders, Warriors and Traders: Pastoralism in Africa* (Boulder: Westview Press).

Galaty, J.G. & Salzman, P. (eds) (1981) *Change and Development in Nomadic and Pastoral Societies* (Leiden: E.J. Brill).

Galaty, J.G. *et al.* (eds) (1981) *The Future of Pastoralist Peoples: Research Priorities for the 1980s* (Ottawa: International Development Research Center).

Galvin, K. (1985) 'Food procurement, diet and activities and nutrition of Turkana pastoralists in an ecological and social context' (Ph.D thesis, State University of New York).

Galvin, K. (1988) 'Nutritional status as an indicator of impending food stress', *Disasters*, 12.

Galvin, K.A., Coppock, D.L. & Leslie, P.W. (1994) 'Diet, nutrition and the pastoral strategy', in Fratkin, E., Galvin, K.A. & Roth, E.A. (eds) *African Pastoralist Systems: An Integrated Approach* (Boulder: Lynne Rienner), pp. 113–32.

Geertz, C. (1974) *The Interpretation of Cultures* (New York: Basic Books).

Giblin, J. (1992) *The Politics of Environmental Control in Northeastern Tanzania, 1840–1940* (Philadelphia: University of Pennsylvania Press).

Government of Great Britain (1905) *Report on the East African Protectorate for the Year 1903–4* (London: Cd 2331, HMSO).

Government of Great Britain (1932) *Report by the Financial Commissioner on Certain Questions in Kenya* (London: Cmd 4093, HMSO).

Government of Great Britain (1934a) *Report of the Kenya Land Commission*, (London: Cmd 4556, HMSO).

Government of Great Britain (1934b) *Evidence and Memoranda of the Kenya Land Commission*, 3 vols (Nairobi: Government Printer).

Government of Great Britain (1955) *Report of the East Africa Royal Commission 1953–55*, (London: Cmd 9475, HMSO).

Government of Kenya Colony (1913) *Evidence and Report of the Native Labour Commission* (Nairobi: Government Printer).

Government of Kenya Colony (1962) *African Land Development in Kenya, 1955–1962* (Nairobi: Government Printer).

Grandin, B. (1987) *Pastoral Culture and Range Management: Recent Lessons from Maasailand* (Addis Ababa: ILCA Bulletin 28, ILCA).

Grandin, B. (1988) 'Wealth and pastoral dairy production: a case study from Maasailand', *Human Ecology*, 16, pp. 1–23.

Gregory, C.A. (1982) *Gifts and Commodities* (London: Academic Press).

Gulliver, P.H. (1969) 'The conservative commitment in northern Tanzania: the Arusha and Masai', in Gulliver, P.H. (ed.), *Tradition and Transition in East Africa: Studies of the Tribal Element in the Modern Era* (London: Routledge and Kegan Paul).

Guyer, J. (1981) 'Household and community in African studies', *African Studies Review*, 24, pp. 87–137.

Guyer, J. (1984) 'Naturalism in models of African production', *Man*, 19 (3), 371–88.

Guyer, J. (1993) 'Wealth in people and self-realisation in equatorial Africa', *Man*, 28, pp. 243–65.

Guyer, J. (1995) 'Wealth in people, wealth in things', *Journal of African History*, 36, pp. 83–90.

Haberland, E. (1984) 'Caste and hierarchy among the Dizi (Southwest Ethiopia)', in Rubenson, S. (ed.),

Proceedings of the Seventh International Conference of Ethiopian Studies (Uppsala: Scandinavian Institute of African Studies).

Haberland, E. (1993) *Hierarchie und Kaste. Zur Geschichte und politischen Struktur der Dizi in Südwest-Äthiopien* (Stuttgart: Franz Steiner).

Hakansson, T. (1989) 'Family structure, bridewealth and environment in eastern Africa: a comparative study of house property systems', *Ethnology*, 28 (2), pp. 117-34.

Hallpike, C.R. (1968) 'The status of craftsmen among the Konso of south-west Ethiopia', *Africa*, 38, pp. 258-69.

Hardin, G. (1968) 'The tragedy of the commons', *Science*, 162, pp. 1243-8.

Hardin, G. (1991) 'The tragedy of the unmanaged commons: population and the disguises of providence', in Andelson, R.V. (ed.), *Commons Without Tragedies: Protecting the Environment from Overpopulation − A New Approach* (London: Shepheard-Walwyn).

Harri, H.H. (1989). 'The social significance of "Hante tlesa" among the Iraqw of northern Tanzania' (MA coursework paper, MA [Education] Ed 605 − Social Psychology, University of Dar es Salaam).

Harris, O. (1981) 'Households as natural units', in Young, K. *et al.* (eds) *Of Marraige and the Market* (London: CSE Books).

Hatfield, C. (1975) 'End of tour report of C.R. Hatfield, Jr., sociologist, Masai Range Development Project (1973-75)' (unpublished report for USAID).

Hauge, H.E. (1981) *Iraqw Religion and Folklore* (Fjellhamar: World Folklore Society).

Heady, H.F. (1960) *Range Management in East Africa* (Nairobi: Government Printer).

Hedlund, H. (1971) *The Impact of Group Ranches on a Pastoral Society* (Nairobi: Institute for Development Studies, University of Nairobi).

Hedlund, H. (1979) 'Contradictions in the peripheralisation of a pastoral society: the Maasai', *Review of African Political Economy*, 15/16.

Helander, B. (1988) 'The slaughtered camel: coping with fictitious descent among the Hubeer of southern Somalia' (PhD thesis, Uppsala University).

Helander, B. (1996) 'The Hubeer in the land of plenty: land, labor, and mobility among a southern Somali clan', in C. Besteman & Cassanelli, L. (eds) *The Struggle for Land in Southern Somalia: The War Behind the War* (Boulder and London: Westview and Haan).

Helander, B. (1998) *Bari region*, Studies in Governance No. 4, Nairobi: United Nations Development Office for Somalia.

Hess, O. (1976) *The Establishment of Cattle Ranching Associations among the Maasai in Tanzania*, Rural Development Committee, Cornell University, Occasional Paper 7.

Hilderbrand, K. (1985) 'Assessing the components of seasonal stress among Fulani of the Seno-Mango, central Mali', in Hill, A.G. (ed.) *Population, Health and Nutrition in the Sahel* (London: Routledge and Kegan Paul).

Hill, A.G. (ed.) (1985) *Population, Health and Nutrition in the Sahel: Issues in the Welfare of Selected West African Communities* (London: Routledge and Kegan Paul).

Hillman, E. (1991) 'The pauperization of the Maasai' (unpublished ms).

Hjort, A. (1981) 'Herds, trade and grain: pastoralism in a regional perspective', in Galaty, J.G. *et al.* (eds) *The Future of Pastoral Peoples* (Ottawa: IDRC).

Hoben, A. (1976) 'Social Soundness of the Masai Livestock and Range Management Project' (Washington: report for USAID).

Hobley, C.W. (1929) *Kenya: From Chartered Company to Crown Colony. Thirty Years of Exploration and Administration in British East Africa* (London: Frank Cass).

Hodgson, D.L. (1994) '"Once intrepid warriors": "development", modernity and the modulation of Maasai masculinities' (paper presented to the Department of Anthropology, Rutgers University).

Hodgson, D.L. (1995) 'The politics of gender, ethnicity and "development": images, interventions, and the reconfiguration of Maasai identities, 1916−1993' (PhD thesis, Department of Anthropology, University of Michigan).

Hogg, R. (1983) 'Irrigation, agriculture and pastoral development: a lesson from Kenya', *Development and Change*, 14, pp. 577-91.

Hogg, R. (1985) *Restocking Pastoralists in Kenya: a Strategy for Relief and Rehabilitation* (London: Pastoral Development Network Paper 19C, ODI).

Hogg, R. (1986) 'The new pastoralism: poverty and dependency in northern Kenya', *Africa*, 56 (3), pp. 319-33.

Hogg, R. (1987) 'Settlement, pastoralism and the commons: the ideology and practice of irrigation development in northern Kenya', in Anderson, D.M. & Grove, R. (eds) *Conservation in Africa: People, Policies and Practice* (Cambridge: Cambridge University Press).

Hogg, R. (1992) 'Should pastoralism continue as a way of life?', *Disasters*, 16, pp. 131-7.

Holland, K. (1987) *On the Horns of a Dilemma: the Future of the Maasai* (Discussion Paper Series No. 51, CDAS, McGill University).

Hollis, C. (1905) *The Masai, Their Language and Folklore* (Oxford: Clarendon Press).

Homewood, K.M. (1995) 'Development, demarcation and ecological outcomes in Maasailand', *Africa*, 65 (3), pp. 331-50.

Homewood, K.M. & Rodgers, W.A. (1987) 'Pastoralism, conservation and the overgrazing controversy', in Anderson, D.M. & Grove, R. (eds) *Conservation in Africa, People, Policies and Practice* (Cambridge:

Cambridge University Press).

Homewood, K.M. & Rodgers, W.A. (1991) *Maasailand Ecology: Pastoralist Development and Wildlife Conservation in Ngorongoro, Tanzania* (Cambridge: Cambridge University Press).

Horowitz, M. (1979) *The Sociology of Pastoralism and African Livestock Projects* (Washington: AID Program Evaluation Discussion Paper No. 6, The Studies Division, Office of Evaluation, Bureau for Program and Policy Coordination, USAID).

Horowitz, M. & Little P.D. (1987) 'African pastoralism and poverty: some implications for drought and famine', in Glantz, M. (ed.) *Drought and Hunger in Africa: Denying Famine a Future* (Boulder: Westview).

Howes, D. (1990) 'Olfaction and transition: an essay on the ritual uses of smell', *Canadian Review of Sociology and Anthropology*, 24 (3), pp. 398–416.

Hultin, J. (1987) 'The long journey: essays on history, descent and land among the Macha Oromo' (PhD thesis, Uppsala University).

Humphrey, C. & Hugh-Jones, S. (eds) (1992) *Barter, Exchange and Value: an Anthropological Approach* (Cambridge: Cambridge University Press).

Hutchinson, S.E. (1996) *Nuer Dilemmas: Coping with Money, War, and the State* (Berkeley: University of California Press).

Huxley, Elspeth (1948) *The Sorcerer's Apprentice* (London: Chatto and Windus).

IBRD (World Bank) (1961) *The Economic Development of Tanganyika* (Baltimore: The Johns Hopkins Press).

Iles, K. (1994) *Feasibility Study for Restocking Displaced Dinka and Nuer Peoples in Southern Sudan* (Nairobi: Livestock Sector, UNICEF).

Iliffe, J. (1979) *A Modern History of Tanganyika* (Cambridge: Cambridge University Press).

Iliffe, J. (1987) *The African Poor: a History* (Cambridge: Cambridge University Press).

Iliffe, J. (1990) *Famine in Zimbabwe, 1890–1960* (Gweru: Mambo Press).

Isaac, E. (1985) 'Genesis, Judaism and the sons of Ham', in Willis, J.R. (ed.) *Slaves and Slavery in Muslim Africa.* Vol. One: *Islam and the Ideology of Slavery* (London: Frank Cass).

Jackson, M. (1989) *Paths Towards a Clearing: Radical Empiricism and Ethnographic Inquiry* (Bloomington: Indiana University Press).

Jacobs, A.H. (1963) 'The pastoral Masai of Kenya: a report of anthropological field research' (London: unpublished paper, Ministry of Overseas Development).

Jacobs, A.H. (1965) 'The traditional political organisation of the pastoral Maasai' (DPhil. thesis, University of Oxford).

Jacobs, A.H. (1968) 'A chronology of the pastoral Maasai', in Ogot, B.A. (ed.), *Hadith I* (Nairobi: East African Publishing House).

Jacobs, A.H. (1975) 'Maasai pastoralism in historical perspective', in Monod, T. (ed.), *Pastoralism in Tropical Africa* (London: Oxford University Press).

Jacobs, A.H. (1978) *Development in Tanzania Maasailand: The Perspective Over 20 Years, 1957–1977* (Final report prepared for the USAID Mission in Tanzania).

Jacobs, A.H. (1980a) 'Pastoral development in Tanzanian Maasailand', *Rural Africana*, 7, pp. 1–14.

Jacobs, A.H. (1980b) 'Pastoral Maasai and tropical rural development', in Bates, R. & Lofchie, M. (eds) *Agricultural Development in Africa: Issues of Public Policy* (New York: Praeger).

Jellicoe, M. (1969) 'The Turu resistance movement', *Tanganyika Notes and Records*, 70, pp. 1–12.

Johnson, D.H. & Anderson, D.M. (eds) (1988) *The Ecology of Survival: Case Studies from Northeast African History* (London: Lester Crook).

Johnson, D.H. & MacAskill, J. (1995) *Eastern Bahr el Ghazal Evaluation* (Oxford: report for OXFAM-UK/I).

Johnston, H.H. (1886) *The Kilima-Njaro Expedition: A Record of Scientific Exploration in Eastern Equatorial Africa* (London: Kegan Paul).

Kamera, W.D. (1978) *Hadithi za Wairaqw* (Dar es Salaam: East African Literature Bureau).

Karp, I. (1978) *Fields of Change Among the Iteso of Kenya* (London: University of London Press).

Keenadiid, Y.C. (ed.) (1976) *Qaamuuska Af-Soomaaliga* [Word book of the Somali language]. (Mogadishu: Wasaaradda Hiddaha iyo Tacliinta Sare [Ministry of Culture and Higher Education]).

Kelly, K. (1993) *Taking Stock: Oxfam's Experience of Restocking in Kenya* (Nairobi: Oxfam).

Kerven, C.K. (1992) *Customary Commerce: a Historical Reassessment of Pastoral Livestock Marketing in Africa* (London: ODI).

Kettel, B. (1992) 'Gender distortions and development disasters: women and milk in African herding systems', *National Women's Studies Association Journal*, 4 (1), pp. 23–41.

Kilewe, A.M. & Thomas, D.B. (1992) *Land Degradation in Kenya, a Framework for Policy and Planning* (London: Commonwealth Secretariat).

Kipuri, N. (1989) 'Maasai women in transition: class and gender in the transformation of a pastoral society' (PhD thesis, Temple University).

Kitching, G. (1980) *Class and Economic Change in Kenya: the Making of an African Petite Bourgeoisie, 1905-1970* (New Haven: Yale University Press).

Kituyi, M. (1990) *Becoming Kenyans: Socio-economic Transformation of the Pastoral Maasai* (Nairobi: Acts Press).

Kjaerby, F. (1976) 'Agrarian and economic change in northern Tanzania: a study of the pastoral Barabaig and agro-pastoral Iraqw of Hanang District, Arusha Region' (MA dissertation, Institute of Ethnology and Social Anthropology, University of Copenhagen).

Kjærby, F. (1979) *The Development of Agro-Pastoralism Among the Barabaig in Hanang District* (BRALUP Research Paper No. 56, University of Dar es Salaam).

References

Kjerland, K.A. (1995) 'Cattle breed, shillings don't: the incorporation of the abaKuria into modern Kenya' (PhD thesis, Bergen University).

Klepp, K.-I. *et al.* (1995) 'The local HIV/AIDS epidemic in Arusha and Kilimanjaro', in Klepp, K-I., Biswalo, P.M. & Talle, A. (eds) *Young People at Risk: Fighting AIDS in Northern Tanzania* (Oslo: Scandinavia University Press).

Klima, G. (1970) *The Barabaig, East African Cattle-Herders* (New York: Holt).

Knowles, J.N & Collett, D.P. (1989) 'Nature as myth, symbol and action: notes towards a historical understanding of development and conservation in Kenyan Maasailand', *Africa*, 59 (4), pp. 433–60.

Krapf, J.L. (1854) *Vocabulary of the Engutuk Eloikob* (Tubingen: Ludwig Friedrich Fues).

Krapf, J.L. (1968) [1860] *Travels, Researches, and Missionaries Labours During an Eighteen Years Residence in Eastern Africa*, 2d edn. (London: Frank Cass).

Kuester, P. & Wiggins, S. (1982) 'Proposals for development of the Ewaso Nyiro irrigation scheme cluster' (Nairobi: unpub. paper, Ministry of Economic Planning and Development).

Lamphear, J. (1976) *The Traditional History of the Jie of Uganda* (Oxford: Clarendon Press).

Lamphear, J. (1986) 'The persistence of hunting and gathering in a "pastoral" world', *SUGIA*, 7.

Lamphear, J. (1992) *The Scattering Time: Turkana Responses to Colonial Rule* (Oxford: Clarendon Press).

Lamprey, H.F. (1983) 'Pastoralism yesterday and today: the overgrazing problem', in Bourliere, F. (ed.) *Tropical Savannas* (Amsterdam: Elsevier Scientific Publishing), pp. 643–66.

Lane, C.R. (1990) *Barabaig Natural Resource Management: Sustainable Land Use under Threat of Destruction* (Geneva: UNRISD Discussion Paper 12. United Nations Institute for Social Development).

Lane, C.R. (1991) 'Alienation of Barabaig pasture land: policy implications for pastoral development in Tanzania' (PhD thesis, University of Sussex).

Lane, C.R. (1996) 'Ngorongoro voices: indigenous Maasai residents of the Ngrongoro conservation area in Tanzania give their views on the proposed general management plan' (London: manuscript, International Institute for Environment and Development).

Last, J.T. (1883) 'A visit to the Masai people living beyond the borders of Nguru country', *Proceedings of the Royal Geographical Society* 5 (9), pp. 517–43, 568 (map).

Lawi, Y. Q. (1992) '"Modernization" and the de-harmonization of the man–nature relationship: the case of the agrico-pastoral Iraqw of the old Mbulu District', in Forster, P.G. & Maghimbi, S. (eds), *The Tanzanian Peasantry: Economy in Crisis* (Aldershot: Avebury).

Leach, M. & Mearns, R. (1996) *The Lie of the Land: Challenging Received Wisdom on the African Environment* (Oxford: James Currey, in association with the International Africa Institute).

Levine, D. (1974) *Greater Ethiopia: The Evolution of a Multiethnic Society* (Chicago: University of Chicago Press).

Lewis, H.S. (1970) 'Wealth, influence and prestige among the Shoa Galla', in Tuden, A. & Plotnicov, L. (eds) *Social Stratification in Africa* (New York: Free Press).

Lewis, I.M. (1961) *A Pastoral Democracy: A Study of Pastoralism and Politics among the Northern Somali of the Horn of Africa* (Oxford: Oxford University Press).

Lewis, I.M. (1963) 'Dualism in the Somali notions of power', *Journal of the Royal Anthropological Institute of Great Britain and Ireland*, 93 (1), pp. 109–16.

Little, M.A. (1989) 'Human biology of African pastoralists', *Yearbook of Physical Anthropology*, 32, pp. 215–47.

Little, M.A. *et al.* (1988) 'Human growth, health, and energy requirements in Nomadic Turkana pastoralists', in de Garine, I. & Harrison, G.A. (eds), *Coping With Uncertainty in Food Supply* (Oxford: Oxford University Press).

Little, P.D. (1983) 'The livestock–grain connection in northern Kenya: an analysis of pastoral economics and semi-arid land development', *Rural Africana*, 15–16, pp. 91–108.

Little, P.D. (1985a) 'Absentee herd owners and part-time pastoralists: the political economy of resource use in northern Kenya', *Human Ecology*, 13, pp. 131–51.

Little, P.D. (1985b) 'Social differentiation and pastoralist sedentarization in northern Kenya', *Africa*, 55, pp. 243–61.

Little, P.D. (1992) *The Elusive Granary: Herder, Farmer and State in Northern Kenya* (Cambridge: Cambridge University Press).

Llewelyn-Davies, M. (1978) 'Two contexts of solidarity among pastoral Maasai women', in Caplan, P. & Bujra, J. (eds) *Women United, Women Divided: Cross-Cultural Perspective on Female Solidarity* (London: Tavistock Publications).

Llewelyn-Davies, M. (1981) 'Women, warriors, and patriarchs', in Ortner, S. & Whitehead, H. (eds) *Sexual Meanings: The Cultural Construction of Gender and Sexuality* (Cambridge: Cambridge University Press).

Loiske, V.M. (1990) 'Political adaption: the case of the Wabarabaig in Hanang district, Tanzania', in Bovin, M. & Manger, L. (eds) *Adaptive Strategies in Arid Lands* (Uppsala: Scandinavian Institute of African Studies).

Lonsdale, J. (1992) 'The conquest state of Kenya, 1895–1905', in Berman, B. & Lonsdale, J. (eds) *Unhappy Valley: Conflict in Kenya and Africa* (London: James Currey).

Loutan, L. (1985) 'Nutrition amongst a group of WoDaabe pastoralists in Niger', in Hill, A.G. (ed.) *Population, Health and Nutrition in the Sahel* (London: Routledge and Kegan Paul).

Lovejoy, P. & Baier, S. (1975) 'The desert-side economy of the central Sudan', *International Journal of African Historical Studies*, 8, pp. 551–81.

Luling, V. (1984) 'The other Somali: minority groups in traditional Somali society', in Labahn, T. (ed.) *Proceedings of the Second International Congress of Somali Studies. IV. Studies in Humanities and Natural Sciences*

(Hamburg: Helmut Buske Verlag).

Lumley, E.K. (1976) *Forgotten Mandate: A British District Officer in Tanganyika* (London: C. Hurst).

McCabe, J.T. (1990) 'Turkana pastoralism: a case against the tragedy of the commons', *Human Ecology*, 18, pp. 81–102.

McCay, B. & Acheson, J. (eds) (1987) *The Question of the Commons: The Culture and Ecology of Communal Resources* (Tucson: University of Arizona Press).

McGregor Ross, W. (1927) *Kenya from Within: a Short Political History* (London: Allen & Unwin).

Mace, Ruth (1989) *Gambling with goats: variability in herd growth among restocked pastoralists in Kenya* (London: ODI Pastoral Network Paper 28a, ODI).

Marris, P. & Somerset, A. (1971) *African Businessmen: A Study of Entrepreneurship and Development in Kenya* (Oxford: Oxford University Press).

Massey, G. *et al.* (1984) 'Socioeconomic baseline study of the Bay Region', 2 vols (Mogadishu: unpublished USAID report).

Mauss, M. (1954) *The Gift: Forms and Functions of Exchange in Archaic Societies* (London: Cohen and West).

Mazonde, I. (1990) 'From communal water points to private wells and boreholes in Botswana's communal areas', in Baxter, P. & Hogg, R. (eds) *Property, Poverty and People: Changing Rights in Property and Problems of Pastoral Development* (Manchester: Department of Social Anthropology and International Development Centre, University of Manchester).

Meek, C.L. (1953) 'Stock reduction in the Mbulu Highlands, Tanganyika', *Journal of African Administration*, 5, pp. 158–66.

Merker, M. (1910) [1904] *Die Masai. Ethnographische Monographie eines ostafrikanischen Semitenvolkes* (Berlin: Dietrich Reimer).

Meyer, H. (1900) *Der Kilimanjaro* (Berlin: Dietrich Reimer).

Migot-Adholla, S.M. & Little, P.D. (1981) 'Evolution of policy toward the development of pastoral areas in Kenya', in Galaty, J.G., Aronson, D., Salzman, P.C. & Chouinard, A. (eds), *The Future of Pastoral Peoples* (Ottawa: International Development Research Center).

Mitchell, P. E. (1932). *Census of the Native Population of Tanganyika Territory, 1931* (Dar es Salaam: Government Printer).

Mol, Fr.F. (1978) *Maa: A Dictionary of the Maasai Language and Folklore* (Nairobi: Marketing and Publishing).

Moore, H.L. (1986) *Space, Text and Gender: an Anthropological Study of the Marakwet of Kenya* (Cambridge: Cambridge University Press).

Moore, H.L. (1987) *Feminism and Anthropology* (Cambridge: Polity Press).

Moris, J. (1986) *Directions in Contemporary Pastoral Development* (London: Pastoral Development Network Paper 22a, ODI).

Moris, J. (1988a) *Oxfam's Kenya Restocking Projects* (London: ODI Pastoral Network Paper 26c, ODI).

Moris, J. (1988b) 'Failing to cope with drought: the plight of Africa's ex-pastoralists', *Development Policy Review*, 6, pp. 269–94.

Morley, P. (1973) *Paediatric Priorities in the Developing World* (London: Butterworth).

Mous, M. (1992) *A Grammar of Iraqw* (Leiden: University of Leiden).

Muhammad, A. (1985) 'The image of Africans in Arabic literature: some unpublished manuscripts', in Willis, J.R. (ed.) *Slaves and Slavery in Muslim Africa*. Vol. One: *Islam and the Ideology of Slavery* (London: Frank Cass).

Munn, N.D. (1986) *The Fame of Gwawa: Symbolic Study of Value Transformation in a Massim Society* (Cambridge: Cambridge University Press).

Munro, J. Forbes (1975) *Colonial Rule and the Kamba. Social Change in the Kenya Highlands, 1889–1939* (Oxford: Clarendon Press).

Murray, M.J. *et al.* (1978) 'The adverse effect of iron repletion on the course of certain infections', *British Medical Journal*, 2, pp. 1113–15.

Murray, M.J. *et al.* (1980) 'An ecological interdependence of diet and disease? A study of infection in one tribe consuming two different diets', *American Journal of Clinical Nutrition*, 33, pp. 697–701.

Nathan, M.A *et al.* (1996) 'Sedentarism and child health among Rendille pastoralists of Northern Kenya', *Social Science and Medicine*, 43 (4), pp. 503–16.

Ndagala, D.K. (1982) 'Operation Imparnati: the sedentarization of the pastoral Maasai in Tanzania', *Nomadic Peoples*, 10, pp. 28–39.

Ndagala, D.K. (1990) 'Pastoralists and the State in Tanzania', *Nomadic Peoples*, 25–7, pp. 51–64.

Ndagala, D.K. (1991) 'The unmaking of the Datoga: decreasing resources and increasing conflict in rural Tanzania', *Nomadic Peoples*, 28, pp. 71–82.

Ndagala, D.K. (1992) 'Territory, pastoralists, and livestock: resource control among the Kisongo Maasai' (PhD thesis, Uppsala University).

Nestel, P. (1985a) 'Nutrition of Maasai women and children in relation to subsistence food production' (PhD thesis, University of London).

Nestel, P. (1985b) 'Nutrition of Maasai women and children pastoralists', in Galaty, J.G. & Bonte, P. (eds) *Herders, Warriors and Traders: Pastoralism in Africa* (Boulder: Westview).

Nestel, P. & Geissler, C. (1986) 'Potential deficiencies of a pastoral diet: a case study of the Maasai', *Ecology of Food Nutrition*, 19, pp. 1–10.

Nordbustad, F. & Naman, E.B. (1978) *Iimu/ungw Yaamaa Iraqw. Mwanzo wa Nchi ya Wairaqw* (Mbulu: Christian Literature Centre).

Oba, G. (1994) 'Kenya Boran: sharing and surviving: responses of impoverished pastoralists to food insecurity', *Rural Extension Bulletin*, 4, pp. 17–22.

Oboler, R. (1994) 'The house–property complex and African social organisation', *Africa*, 64 (3), pp. 342–58.

ole Kulet, H.R. (1972) *To Become a Man* (Nairobi: Longman).

ole Parkipuny, L. (1975) 'Maasai predicament beyond pastoralism: a case study in the socio-economic transformation of pastoralism' (MA dissertation, University of Dar es Salaam).

ole Parkipuny, L. (1979) 'Some crucial aspects of the Maasai predicament', in Coulson, A. (ed.) *African Socialism in Practice* (Nottingham: Spokesman).

Orr, J. B. & Gilkes, J. L. (1931) *Studies in Nutrition. The Physique & Health of Two African Tribes* (London: HMSO).

Parry, J & Bloch, M. (1989) *Money and the Morality of Exchange* (Cambridge: Cambridge University Press).

Peden, D.G. (1984) *Livestock and Wildlife Inventories by District in Kenya, 1977–1983* (Nairobi: KREMU).

Perham, M. (1976) *East African Journey. Kenya and Tanganyika, 1929–30* (London: Faber and Faber).

Peters, P. (1994) *Dividing the Commons: Politics, Policy and Culture in Botswana* (Charlottesville: University Press of Virginia).

Pigg, S. (1992) 'Inventing social categories through place: social representations and development in Nepal', *Comparative Studies in Society and History*, 34 (3), pp. 491–513.

Porter, P.W. (1965) 'Environmental potentials and economic opportunities, a background for cultural adaptations', *American Anthropologist*, 67, pp. 409–20.

Potkanski, T. (1994a) 'Pastoral economy, property rights and mutual assistance mechanisms among the Ngorongoro and Salei Maasai of Tanzania' (PhD thesis, University of Warsaw).

Potkanski, T. (1994b) *Property Concepts, Herding Patterns and Management of Natural Resources among the Ngorongoro and Salei Maasai of Tanzania* (London: International Institute for Environment and Development).

Potkanski, T. (1994c) *Pastoral Economy, Property Rights and Mutual Assistance Mechanisms among the Ngorongoro and Salei Maasai of Tanzania* (London: Fieldwork Report, International Institute for Environment and Development).

Quam, M.D. (1978) 'Cattle marketing and pastoral conservatism: Karamoja District, Uganda, 1948–1970', *African Studies Review*, 21 (1), pp. 49–71.

Raikes, P. (1975a) 'Wheat production and the development of capitalism in north Iraqw', in Cliffe, L. *et al.* (eds) *Rural Cooperation in Tanzania* (Dar es Salaam: Tanzania Publishing House).

Raikes, P. (1981) *Livestock Development and Policy in East Africa* (Uppsala: Scandinavian Institute of African Studies).

Ramadhani, M.H. (1955) 'Mapokeo ya historia ya Wa-Iraqw Mbulu' (unpub. ms.).

Rekdal, O.B. (1994) *Kulturell Kontituitet & Sosial Endring. En Studie av Iraqw-folket i det Nordlige Tanzanie* (Bergen: Studies in Social Anthropology No. 48, University of Bergen).

Rekdal, O.B. (1996) 'Money, milk, and sorghum beer: change and continuity among the Iraqw of northern Tanzania', *Africa*, 66 (3), pp. 367–85.

Rekdal, O.B. (1998) 'When hypothesis becomes myth: the Iraqi origin of the Iraqw' *Ethnology*, 37 (1), pp. 17–38.

Rekdal, O.B. (n.d.). 'Cross-cultural healing in East African ethnography' (forthcoming in *Medical Anthropology Quarterly*).

Republic of Kenya (1984) *West Pokot District Atlas* (Kapenguria: ASAL Programme).

Republic of Kenya (1988) *Marsabit District Development Plan 1988–1992* (Nairobi: Ministry of Finance and Planning).

Republic of Kenya (1989–93) *District Development Plan West Pokot District [DDPWPD]* (Nairobi: Ministry of Planning and National Development).

Republic of Kenya (1990) *Kajiado District Atlas* (Kajiado: ASAL Programme).

Republic of Kenya (1994) *Kenya Population Census 1989*, vol. 1 (Nairobi: Government Printer).

Republic of Kenya (various years) *Kajiado District Annual Reports* (Nairobi: Government Printer).

Ricœur, P. (1976) *Interpretation Theory: Discourse and the Surplus of Meaning* (Fort Worth: Texas Christian University Press).

Rigby, P. (1992) *Cattle, Capitalism and Class: Ilparakuyo Maasai Transformations* (Philadelphia: Temple University Press).

Robinson, P.W. (1979) 'The 1890s: a decade of crises, and Gabra responses to them' (Nairobi: unpub. Staff Seminar paper, History Dept, University of Nairobi).

Roe, E. (1989) 'Folktale development', *American Journal of Semiotics*, 6 (2/3), pp. 277–89.

Roe, E. (1991) 'Development narratives, or making the best of blueprint development', *World Development*, 19, pp. 287–300.

Roe, E. (1994) 'New framework for an old tragedy of the commons, and an aging common property resource management', *Agriculture and Human Values*, 11, pp. 29–36.

Roth, E. (1991) 'Education, tradition and household labor among Rendille pastoralists of northern Kenya', *Human Organization*, 50, pp. 136–41.

Roth, E. (1993) 'A reexamination of Rendille population regulation', *American Anthropologist*, 95, pp. 597–612.

Rutten, M.M. (1992) *Selling Wealth to Buy Poverty: the Process of Individualisation of Landownership among the Maasai Pastoralists of Kajiado District, Kenya, 1890–1990* (Saarbruecken: Verlag Breitenbach).

Salzman, P.C. (1983) 'The psychology of nomads', *Nomadic Peoples*, 12, pp. 48–55.

Sanders, E.R. (1969) 'The Hamitic hypothesis: its origins and functions in time perspective', *Journal of African History*, 10, pp. 521–32.

Sandford, G.R. (1919) *An Administrative and Political History of the Masai Reserve* (London: Waterlow).

Sandford, S. (1983) *Management of Pastoral Development in the Third World* (Chichester: Wiley).

Schack, W.A. (1964) 'Notes on occupational castes among the Gurage of south-west Ethiopia', *Man*, 54, pp. 50–52.

Schneider, H.K. (1979) *Livestock and Equality in East Africa: the Economic Basis for Social Structure* (Bloomington: Indiana University Press).

Schneider, H.K. (1981) 'Livestock as food and money', in Galaty, J.G. *et al.* (eds) *The Future of Pastoral Peoples* (Ottawa: IDRC), pp. 210–23.

Schultz, J. (1971) *Agrarlandschaftliche Veränderungen in Tanzania* (Munich: Weltforum Verlag).

Schwartz, H.J. & Dioli, M. (1992) *The One Humped Camel in Eastern Africa* (Weikersheim: Verlag Josef Margraf).

Scoones, I. (1996) 'Range management science and policy: politics, polemics and pasture in southern Africa', in Leach, M. & Mearns, R. (eds) *The Lie of the Land: Challenging Received Wisdom on the African Environment* (Oxford: James Currey, for the International African Institute), pp. 34–53.

Scott-Villiers, P. & Scott-Villiers, A. (1995) 'Poverty as vulnerability in Somali pastoralist society' (paper presented to the workshop on 'Poverty and Prosperity among Eastern African Pastoralists', Uppsala, Sweden, September 1995).

Sen, A. (1981) *Poverty and Famines: an Essay on Entitlement and Deprivation* (Oxford: Clarendon Press).

Shipton, P. (1989) *Bitter Money: Cultural Economy and Some African Meanings of Forbidden Commodities* (Washington: American Ethnological Society).

Shipton, P. (1990) 'African famines and food security: anthropological perspectives', *Annual Review of Anthropology*, 19, pp. 354–94.

Simmel, G. [1900] (1990) *The Philosophy of Money* (New York: Routledge).

Snyder, K.A. (1993) 'Like water and honey: moral ideology and the construction of community among the Iraqw of northern Tanzania' (PhD thesis, Yale University).

Snyder, K.A. (1996) 'Agrarian change and land-use strategies among Iraqw farmers in northern Tanzania' *Human Ecology*, 24 (3), pp. 315–40.

Sobania, N.W. (1980) 'The historical tradition of the peoples of the eastern Lake Turkana basin *c.* 1840–1925' (PhD thesis, University of London).

Sobania, N.W. (1988) 'Fishermen herders: subsistence, survival and cultural change in northern Kenya', *Journal of African History*, 29, pp. 41–56.

Sobania, N.W. (1991) 'Feasts, famines and friends: nineteenth century exchange and ethnicity in the eastern Lake Turkana region', in Galaty, J.G. & Bonte P. (eds) *Herders, Warriors and Traders: Pastoralism in Africa* (Boulder: Westview Press).

Sommer, G. & Vossen, R. (1993) 'Dialects, sectiolects, or simply lects?: the Maa language in time perspective', in Spear, T. & Waller, R.D. (eds) *Being Maasai: Ethnicity and Identity in East Africa* (London: James Currey), pp. 25–37.

Sørbø, G. (1977) 'Nomads on the scheme: a study of irrigation agriculture and pastoralism in eastern Sudan', in O'Keefe, P. & Wisner, B. (eds) *Landuse and Development* (London: IAI).

Sorrenson, M.P.K. (1968) *Origins of European Settlement in Kenya* (Nairobi: Oxford University Press).

Southall, A.W. (1961) 'Population Movements of East Africa', in Barbour, K.M. & Prothero, R.M. (eds) *Essays on African Population* (London: Routledge and Kegan Paul).

Spear, T. (1993a) 'Introduction', in Spear, T. & Waller, R.D. (eds) *Being Maasai: Ethnicity and Identity in East Africa* (London: James Currey).

Spear, T. (1993b) 'Being Maasai, but not people of the cattle: Arusha agricultural Maasai in the nineteenth century', in Spear, T. & Waller, R.D. (eds) *Being Maasai: Ethnicity and Identity in East Africa* (London: James Currey).

Spear, T. & Nurse, D. (1992) 'Maasai farmers: the evolution of Arusha agriculture', *International Journal of African Historical Studies*, 25 (3), pp. 481–503.

Spear, T., & Waller, R.D. (eds) (1993) *Being Maasai: Ethnicity and Identity in East Africa* (London: James Currey).

Spencer, I.R.G. (1983) 'Pastoralism and colonial policy in Kenya, 1895–1929', in Rotberg, R.I. (ed.) *Imperialism, Colonialism and Hunger: East and Central Africa* (Lexington: Lexington Books).

Spencer, P. (1965) *The Samburu: a Study of Gerontocracy in a Nomadic Tribe* (London: Routledge and Kegan Paul).

Spencer, P. (1973) *Nomads in Alliance* (London: Oxford University Press).

Spencer, P. (1974) 'Drought and the commitment to growth', *African Affairs*, 73, pp. 419–27.

Spencer, P. (1988) *The Maasai of Matapato: A Study of Rituals of Rebellion* (Edinburgh: Edinburgh University Press, for the International African Institute).

Sperling, L. (1987) 'Wage employment among Samburu pastoralists of north central Kenya', *Research in Economic Anthropology*, 9, pp. 167–90.

Stiles, D. (1980) 'Historical interrelationships of the Boni with the pastoral peoples of Somalia and Kenya' (paper presented at the First International Congress of Somali Studies, Mogadishu, 6–13 July).

Stiles, D. (1981) 'Hunters of the northern East African coast: origins and historical processes', *Africa*, 51, pp. 848–62.

Strathern, M. (1988) *The Gender of the Gift: Problems with Women and Problems with Society in Melanesia* (Berkeley: University of California Press).

Sutton, J. (1990) *A Thousand Years in East Africa* (Nairobi: British Institute in Eastern Africa).

Sutton, J. (1993) 'Becoming Maasailand', in Spear, T. & Waller, R.D. (eds) *Being Maasai: Ethnicity and Identity in East Africa* (London: James Currey), pp. 38–60.

Swift, J. (1979) 'The development of livestock trading in a nomad pastoral economy: the Somali case', in Lefevre, C. (ed.) *Pastoral Production and Society* (Cambridge: Cambridge University Press).

Swift, J. (1996) 'Desertification: narratives, winners and losers', in Leach, M. & Mearns , R. (eds) *The Lie of the Land: Challenging Received Wisdom on the African Environment* (London: James Currey, for the International African Institute).

Swift, J. & Umar, A. (1991) 'Participatory pastoral development in Isiolo district: socio-economic research in the Isiolo Livestock Development Project' (unpublished manuscript, Isiolo Livestock Development Project).

Synott, A. (1993) *The Body Social: Symbolism, Self and Society* (London and New York: Routledge).

Talle, A. (1987) 'Women as heads of houses: the organization of production and the role of women among the pastoral Maasai in Kenya', *Ethnos*, 52 (1–2), pp. 50–80.

Talle, A. (1988) *Women at a Loss: Changes in Maasai Pastoralism and their Effects on Gender Relations* (Stockholm: Studies in Social Anthropology No. 19, University of Stockholm).

Talle, A. (1990) 'Ways of milk and meat among the Maasai: gender identity and food resources in a pastoral economy', in Palsson, G. (ed.) *From Water to World-Making* (Uppsala: Scandinavian Institute for African Studies), pp. 73–92.

Talle, A. (1995) 'Desiring difference: risk behaviour among young Maasai men', in Klepp, K.-I. *et al.* (eds) *Young People at Risk: Fighting AIDS in Northern Tanzania* (Oslo: Scandinavian University Press).

Talle, A. & Holmqvist, S. (1979) *Barheida og dei tre Konene Hans* (Oslo: Det Norske Samlaget).

Thomas, N. (1991) *Entangled Objects: Exchange, Material Culture and Colonialism in the Pacific* (Cambridge, Massachusetts and London: Harvard University Press).

Thomson, J. (1968) [1885] *Through Maasai Land: A Journey of Exploration among Snowclad Volcanic Mountains and Strange Tribes of Eastern Equatorial Africa*, 3rd edn. (London: Frank Cass).

Thornton, R. (1980) *Space, Time and Culture among the Iraqw of Tanzania* (New York: Academic Press).

Tiffen, M., Mortimore, M. & Gichuki, F. (1994) *More People, Less Erosion: Environmental Recovery in Kenya* (London and Nairobi: ODI).

Tignor, R. (1976) *The Colonial Transformation of Kenya: the Kamba, Kikuyu and Maasai from 1900 to 1939* (Princeton: Princeton University Press).

Todd, D.M. (1977) 'Caste in Africa?', *Africa*, 47, pp. 398–412.

Todd, D.M. (1978) 'The origins of outcasts in Ethiopia: reflections on an evolutionary theory', *Abbay*, 9, pp. 145–58.

Tomikawa, M. (1970) 'The distribution and the migration of Datoga tribe', *Kyoto University African Studies*, 5, pp. 1–46.

Toulmin, C. (1986) 'Pastoral Livestock Losses and Post-drought Rehabilitation in Sub-Saharan Africa: Policy Options and Issues' (ALPAN Network Paper No. 8: ILCA).

Turton, D. (1980) 'The economics of Mursi bridewealth: a comparative perspective', in Comaroff J. (ed.) *The Meaning of Marriage Payments* (London: Academic Press).

Turton, D. (1985) 'Mursi response to drought: some lessons for relief and rehabilitation', *African Affairs*, 84, pp. 331–46.

Umesao, T. (1969) 'Hunting culture of the pastoral Datoga', *Kyoto University African Studies*, 3, pp. 77–92.

US Committee for Refugees (1993) *Beyond the Headlines: Refugees in the Horn of Africa* (Washington, DC: US Committee for Refugees).

Utah State University Team (1976) *Evaluation of the Maasai Livestock and Range Management Project* (Utah: Utah State University).

Van Voorthuizen, E.G. (1971) 'Report on cultivation activities in Masai district' (Nairobi: report prepared for Masai Livestock and Range Management Project, USAID).

Vaughan, M. (1987) *The Story of an African Famine: Gender and Famine in Twentieth-Century Malawi* (Cambridge: Cambridge University Press).

von Hohnel, L. (1968) [1894] *Discovery of Lakes Rudolf and Stephanie; a Narrative of Count Samuel Teleki's Exploring and Hunting Expedition in Eastern Equatorial Africa in 1887 and 1888*, 2 vols (London: Frank Cass).

Wada, S. (1969) 'Local groups of the Iraqw – their structure and functions', *Kyoto University African Studies*, 3, 109–31.

Wada, S. (1975) 'Political history of Mbulu District', *Kyoto University African Studies*, 9, 45–68.

Wada, S. (1978) 'Slufay: Notes on an Iraqw ritual prayer', *Senri Ethnological Studies*, 1, pp. 37–53 (Osaka: National Museum of Ethnology).

Wagenaar-Brouwer, M. (1985) 'Preliminary findings on the diet and nutritional status of some Tamasheq and Fulani groups in the Niger delta of central Mali', in Hill, A.G. (ed.) *Population, Health and Nutrition in the Sahel* (London: Routledge and Kegan Paul).

Wakefield, Rev. T. (1882) 'Native routes through Masai country', *Proceedings of the Royal Geographical Society*, 4 (12), pp. 742–7.

Wakefield, Rev. T. (1883) 'The Wakwafi raid on the district near Mombasa', *Proceedings of the Royal*

Geographical Society, 5 (5), pp. 289–90.

Waller, R.D. (1975) 'Uneconomic growth: the Maasai stock economy, 1919–1929' (unpublished ms.).

Waller, R.D. (1976) 'The Maasai and the British 1895–1905: the origins of an alliance', *Journal of African History*, 17 (4), pp. 529–53.

Waller, R.D. (1979) 'The Lords of East Africa: the Maasai in the mid-nineteenth century, c.1840–1885' (PhD thesis, University of Cambridge).

Waller, R.D. (1984) 'Interaction and identity on the periphery: the Trans-Mara Maasai', *International Journal of African Historical Studies*, 17 (2), pp. 243–84.

Waller, R.D. (1985a) 'Economic and social relations in the central Rift Valley: the Maa-speakers and their neighbours in the nineteenth century', in B.A. Ogot (ed.) *Kenya in the Nineteenth Century* (Nairobi: Bookwise).

Waller, R.D. (1985b) 'Ecology, migration and expansion in East Africa', *African Affairs*, 84 (336), pp. 347–70.

Waller, R.D. (1988) 'Emutai: crisis and response in Maasailand 1883–1902', in Johnson, D.H. & Anderson, D.M. (eds) *The Ecology of Survival: Case Studies from Northeast African History* (London: Lester Crook).

Waller, R.D. (1993a) 'Acceptees and aliens: Kikuyu settlement in Maasailand', in Spear, T. & Waller, R.D. (eds) *Being Maasai: Ethnicity and Identity in East Africa* (London: James Currey).

Waller, R.D. (1993b) 'Conclusions', in Spear, T. & Waller, R.D. (eds) *Being Maasai: Ethnicity and Identity in East Africa* (London: James Currey).

Waller, R.D. (1994) 'What the sheep said: power and wealth in pastoral society' (Toronto: unpub. ASA conference paper).

Waller, R.D. (1999) 'They do the dictating and we must submit: the Africa Inland Mission in Maasailand', in Spear, T. & Kimambo, I. (eds), *African Expressions of Christianity in Eastern Africa* (Oxford: James Currey).

Waller, R.D & Sobania, N.W. (1994) 'Pastoralism in historical perspective', in Fratkin, E. *et al.* (eds) *African Pastoralist Systems: an Integrated Approach* (Boulder: Lynne Rienner).

Watts, M. (1983) *Silent Violence: Food, Famine and Peasantry in Northern Nigeria* (Berkeley: University of California Press).

Watts, M. (1991) 'Entitlements or empowerment? Famine and starvation in Africa', *Review of African Political Economy*, 51, pp. 9–26.

Weiner, A. (1992) *Inalienable Possessions: The Paradox of Keeping-While-Giving* (Berkeley: University of California Press).

White, C. (1984) *Herd Reconstruction: the Role of Credit among Wodaabe Herders in Central Niger* (London: Pastoral Development Network Paper 18c, ODI).

White, J.M. & Meadows, S.J. (1981) *Evaluation of the Contribution of Group and Individual Ranches in Kajiado District, Kenya, to Economic Development and Pastoral Production Strategies* (Nairobi: Ministry of Livestock Development).

White, L. (1990) *Comforts at Home: Prostitution in Colonial Nairobi* (Chicago: Chicago University Press).

Wienpahl, J. (1984) 'Women's roles in livestock production among the Turkana of Kenya', *Research in Economic Anthropology*, 6, pp. 193–215.

Willis, J.R. (1985) 'The ideology of enslavement in Islam', in Willis, J.R. (ed.) *Slaves and Slavery in Muslim Africa*. Vol. One: *Islam and the Ideology of Slavery* (London: Frank Cass).

Wilson, G.M. (1952) 'The Tatoga of Tanganyika, Part I', *Tanganyika Notes and Records*, 33, pp. 34–47.

Winter, E.H. (1963) 'The enemy within: Amba witchcraft and sociological theory', in Middleton, J. & Winter, E. (eds) *Witchcraft and Sorcery in East Africa* (New York: Praeger).

Winter, E.H. (1964) 'The slaughter of a bull, a study of cosmology and ritual', in Manners, R.A. (ed.), *Process and Pattern in Culture* (Chicago: Aldine).

Winter, E.H. (1966) 'Territorial groupings and religion among the Iraqw', in Banton, M. (ed.) *Anthropological Approaches to the Study of Religion* (London: Tavistock).

Winter, E.H. (1968) 'Some aspects of political organization and land tenure among the Iraqw', *Kyoto University African Studies*, 2, pp. 1–29.

Worby, E. (1988) 'Livestock policy and development in Botswana', in Attwood D. *et al.* (eds) *Power and Poverty: Development and Development Projects in the Third World* (Boulder: Westview).

World Health Organization (1983) *Measuring Change in Nutritional Status: Guidlines for Assessing the Nutritional Impact of Supplementary Feeding Programmes for Vulnerable Groups* (Geneva: WHO).

World Vision (1991) 'Baseline survey of Longido division, Monduli District' (unpublished report).

Yanagisako, S.J. (1979) 'Family and household: the analysis of domestic groups', *Annual Review of Anthropology*, 8, 161–205.

Zaal, F. (1993) 'The cattle market system in Kajiado District, preliminary results of a market information system study' (unpub. paper, University of Amsterdam).

Zoli, C. (1927) *Oltre Giuba: notizie raccolte a cura del commisariato generale nel primo anni di occupazione italiana* (Rome: Sindicato italiano arti grafiche).

Index

abattoirs *see* slaughterhouses
acquired immune deficiency syndrome *see* AIDS
adakars 56
affines 82, 136-7, 200, 204
Africa Inland Church 155
African Land Development Board *see* Kenya
age-mates 110, 116, 200, 204, 207 *see also* friend-ship
age-sets 36-7, 118, 155
agnates 71-2, 81, 97-101, 255
agriculture viii, 23, 32, 149-50, 152, 168-9, 201, 236, 245; Bambara people 154; Datooga and Iraqw peoples 126-8, 137, 143-4; Kenya 172, 181, 185, 246-9; Maasai peoples 29, 40-1, 109, 123, 181, 208, 214-16, 221-4, 232; Pokot people 174-8; Rift Valley 28; Somalis 96; Sonrai people 154; Turkana people 58-61, 63, 76 *see also* name of crop
agropastoralism 91, 126, 128, 151-2, 155, 174, 222-3, 233
aid 9, 15, 64-6, 87, 122, 149-50, 155, 157, 160-2, 170, 172, 177, 182, 205, 240, 245-8, 250-6 *see also* mutual assistance
AIDS 107, 115, 122, 154
Akuj 71
alcoholism 202, 208-10
alienation 75, 78-80, 224-5
Amin, Idi 177
Amolem 246-7
anaemia 152, 159, 161
ancestors 55, 73-4, 140-1, 143
animals *see* name of animal
anthropological approach 7-9, 11, 62
anthropometry 151, 158, 161
Appadurai, A. 62
Arabic language 98
Arabs 111
Ariaal people *see* Rendille people
Arid and Semi-Arid Lands Programme 180
Arusha 112, 121, 123, 215-16
Arusha Chini 28
Arusha people 223-4, 239n
asapan ritual 68
Aseeta 134, 139-40
Athi River 173, 184

Babati 128
Bajuuta people 130
Bambara people 154
Bantu peoples 113
Barabaig *see* Barbayiig
Baragoi 248, 251
Barbayiig subsection (Datooga people) 128-30, 133, 135, 138, 143, 205
bars (drinking) 112
bartering 75-7, 79, 82, 110, 164, 168, 175, 178, 184, 201, 249
Basotho people 92
Bassotu 128

Baudrillard, J. 100
Baydhabo 91
beans 157, 160, 180
beef *see* meat
beer 64, 108, 110-12, 207
beggars 115
Benaadir 94
bilharzia 152
bilis 92-100, 102-3
black market 64-5
blindness, night 151
blood 151-2, 159, 166
blood-wealth 98-9, 207
Boni Forest 105n
Boni people 104n
boon 92-103, 104-5nn
Borana people 149, 154, 168, 200, 205-6, 247
borders 13, 107, 111
bovine cerebral theileriasis 210, 213, 215
boys *see* children
branding and tattooing (livestock) 68, 70-3, 75, 99, 243
breast feeding 156
bride-wealth 6, 16, 60, 65, 68, 72, 76, 80-5, 98-9, 155, 167, 169, 175, 206-7, 209, 249, 255
Britain 26, 39, 61, 142, 224, 235
brucellosis 152
butchers 184, 195

caloric terms of trade *see* food
camels 14-15, 32, 50, 67-8, 73-4, 78, 84, 98-9, 151, 154-5, 161-2, 165, 178
capital 183, 247, 249 *see also* money
capitalism 11, 40
cash *see* money
caste system 92-3 *see also* class, social
Catholic Relief Services 150
Catholics 66, 155, 246, 248
cattle 151-2, 167-8, 165-70, 249, 255; Datooga and Iraqw peoples 126, 132-7; Fulani people 154; Kenya 172; Maasai peoples 21, 24-6, 30-1, 109-11, 122-3, 128, 181-2, 185-94, 199-201, 203-10, 213-14, 216-17, 222-6, 228-31, 233-5; Pokot people 174-80; Rendille people 154-5; Samburu people 32; Turkana people 8, 10, 50, 56-9, 65-87; United States 171 *see also* oxen
censuses 30-1, 33, 46n, 197n, 205, 213, 216-17, 229, 236
cereals *see* grains
ceremonies *see* rituals
Chalbi Desert 154
Cheparaia 180
Chepkobegh 180
Cherangani Mountains 174-5
Chesegon 175, 180
chiefs 93, 97, 251
Chieni, Telelia 27
children viii, 150, 152, 169; Datooga and Iraqw

270

peoples 135, 138; Fulani people 154; illegitimate 136; Kenya 246; Maasai peoples 24, 27, 33, 109, 111, 113, 120-1, 123, 186, 193-4, 201, 207, 209-10, 223, 234; Pokot people 177, 179; Rendille people 14-15, 151, 154, 156-62; Somalis 101, 152; Turkana people 65, 68-9, 81-2, 152
cholera 152
Christian Aid 248
Christianity 28, 136 *see also* name of sect
circumcision 108, 113, 118, 120, 124n, 209, 213, 223
clans 16, 70-2, 76, 81, 91-2, 97, 130-1, 137, 223; meetings 207-8 *see also* mutual assistance
class, social 10-11, 23, 41, 71, 249-50, 256 *see also bilis; boon*; caste system
climate *see* weather
clothes 116-17, 122, 177
cognates 82
colonialism 21, 24, 33-40, 44, 61, 65-6, 77-8, 127-8, 142, 171, 175-6, 224-5, 235, 241-2
commercialization *see* commodity and commoditization
commodity and commoditization 9, 11-12, 15, 18-19, 163-6, 168, 170-1, 241-2, 250; Basotho people 92; Kenya 149, 172, 195-6, 256; Maasai peoples 16, 183-4, 191-2, 223, 225, 244; Pokot people 176-7; Rift Valley 5; Turkana people 62-4, 66-8, 73, 77-8, 81, 87
commoners *see boon*
concubinage 84, 86
conjunctivitis 154
contagious bovine pleuro-pneumonia 181
continuous value register 67
corruption 172, 216
cost of living index 172-3
cotton 64
credit 171, 249
crime 31 *see also* livestock-raiding; theft
culture 9-12, 17, 27, 92, 109, 114, 117, 121-4, 130-1, 138, 143, 167-8, 199-200, 203, 208, 216, 221-2, 225, 233, 248-9
curses 96, 105n, 142
Cushitic peoples 126

Daily News 106, 117
dairying 41, 48n, 68, 174, 235 *see also* milk
Datooga language 144n
Datooga people 12-13, 125-46, 145nn
death 74, 223 *see also* funerary rites; killing; mortality rates
debt 98, 215
deficiency diseases 152
Demenedung 103
Denmark x
depression, economic 66
destitution 6, 23, 25-7, 51, 56, 85, 87-8, 108, 122, 178, 200, 204, 207-9, 211, 213, 217, 241, 245-7, 250-3, 255-6 *see also* poverty
development 16-17, 19, 21-2, 43, 150, 240-56; Datooga and Iraqw peoples 127; Kenya 41, 165, 172, 241-4, 246-56; Maasai peoples 18, 35, 38, 108-9, 115-17, 121-4, 194, 215, 221-2, 224-6, 228-32, 234-6; Rendille people 162; Tanzania, 106, 229; Turkana people 61, 64, 66, 78, 87

DEVRES 230-2, 234
diarrhoea 152, 154, 156, 158, 161
diet *see* food; names of specific foods
Dime people 104n
Dinka people 255
dirtiness, personal 115-18, 121-2
disease (human) *see* health; name of disease
disease (livestock) *see* name of disease
distress sales 176
distress warrants 31
divorce 73, 84, 207, 255
Dizi people 104n
Dorobos 23, 29, 58, 155
droughts viii, 3, 5-6, 42, 168-9, 244-6, 249, 252, 256; Datooga and Iraqw peoples 132; Kenya 172, 175-9, 181-2, 248; Maasai peoples 24, 27, 30, 33, 108, 120, 215, 224, 231; Rendille people, 15, 155, 160; Rift Valley 247; Sahel 149, 250; Somalia 96; Turkana people 50-2, 58-9, 84
drunkenness *see* alcoholism

East Coast fever 181-2, 215, 231
Ebarasit 54-5
education 12-13, 66, 118, 121, 176-7, 221, 225, 229, 236
egalitarianism 3-5, 28, 41, 56
Ekebotonit 53-7
Ekechodon 53, 55-6
Elang'ata Wuas ranch 189
elders 24, 26, 28-9, 33, 35-8, 79, 93, 96-7, 116, 120-1, 127, 131, 140-1, 223, 234, 251
elections 121, 172
élites 121-2, 225
Elongait 53, 55-6
Emali 183-4
embezzlement *see* theft
Emetut 53, 55-6
employment *see* labour
Endabalangda 132
Endagulda 132
Endulen 211, 213-15
engaji 202-5, 207-8
engelata see mutual assistance
engkangs 194
environment 5, 7, 245, 252, 254 *see also* land
epidemics *see* health
epizootics 120
Ethiopia 5, 93, 149, 168, 245, 250
ethnicity 25, 40, 66, 77, 88, 110, 121, 129-30, 134, 137, 143, 154, 195, 223, 225, 239n
ethnography ix, 10-11, 131, 142, 206
European Union 173
Ewaso River 247
ewoloto see mutual assistance
exchange rates 111, 172
exogamy 76
expenditure 64-5, 110, 157, 164, 186, 189, 191-2, 194 *see also* commodity and commoditization; money
exports 34, 41, 64-5, 172, 173, 226, 229

families 23, 25, 27, 41, 43, 53, 65, 97, 157, 200, 204, 207, 209-11, 213, 216-17, 223, 248, 250-2, 254-5; definition of 45n *see also engaji*; households

famine viii, 3, 5, 15, 22, 64, 149
famine relief *see* aid
Fanju Juu terraces 181
farming *see* agriculture
fathers 98-9, 104 *see also* patrilineal system
fats 156, 160-1, 166
febrile diseases 156, 158, 161
feed, animal 170-1
femaleness 100-3
fencing, land 192-3
fertility 74, 82, 116, 126, 139, 143
fines 24, 82
Finland x
firewood *see* wood
fishing 58-61, 63-4, 76, 86, 150
fixed assets 170
food 6, 24, 150-1, 164, 166-8; caloric terms of
    trade 169-70, 173, 177, 179-80, 184-5, 195-6;
    Kenya 175, 178, 190-1, 246, 248, 250; Maasai
    peoples 30, 40, 108-9, 181, 199, 201, 203,
    210, 215, 223-4, 234, 236; Rendille people
    14-15, 156-7, 159-62, 205; seasonality 152;
    Turkana people 52, 58-9, 63, 66 *see also* aid
Food and Agriculture Organization 109, 112,
    246-7
Foqaqoonle subclan 95
friendship 42, 68-9, 94, 170, 175, 178, 200, 204,
    223, 249, 251 *see also* age-mates
fruit 151, 156
Fulani people 151-2, 154
Fulbe people *see* Fulani people
funerary rites 72, 74-5, 80, 139-40

Gabbra people 149, 154
Gafarsa 246-7
Galishu, ole 27, 29, 43
game parks 149
Gassar Gudda clan 97
gathering *see* hunting/gathering
genealogy 70-1, 97, 129
Germany 39, 142, 224, 246
Gidamowsa 142
Gidashiid 140-1
gifts 62, 67-70, 75-6, 82, 98, 167, 190-1, 199-200,
    203-4, 210, 216, 223, 248, 251, 254
girls *see* children
Gisamjanga people 130
goats 151, 167, 249; Datooga and Iraqw peoples
    130-1, 135, 138; Kenya 246, 248, 250-1;
    Maasai peoples 109, 182, 184, 186, 205, 208,
    230, 233; Pokot people 174-8, 179-80;
    Rendille people 155; Somalis 99, 175, 179;
    Turkana people 10, 50, 57-60, 64-5, 67-8,
    73-80, 84-5
gold 177, 179
Goobwiin clan 97
Gourma Fulani people *see* Fulani people
Gourma Tamasheq people see Tuareg
government, central *see* state
grains 76, 151-2, 159, 164, 169-70, 175-8, 180,
    195-6, 201, 249, 251 *see also* name of crop
grazing 22, 34, 39, 134, 137, 177, 181, 185, 189,
    192-3, 224, 226, 228, 230-1, 242-3, 245
Great Britain *see* Britain
guardians 209-10
Gurage people 104n

habash 94
hair 100-1
Ham 96
Hanang 130, 137, 143
hands 97
Harar Mountain 142-3
Hardin, G. 237-8nn
Hartley, J. 128
Hawaadle clan 95
Haydom Lutheran Hospital 140
health 14, 39, 52, 111-12, 115-16, 149-62, 166,
    175-6, 191, 225, 234, 236 *see also* hospitals
Hedaru 122
Hemsted, R. W. 45n
hepatitis 152
herding associations *see adakars*
hides 33, 35, 50, 193-4, 224
hirin 97-9, 103
historical approach 7-9, 20-44
HIV *see* AIDS
Hogg, Richard 247
homesteads *see* households
honey 58, 110, 141
Horn of Africa 149
hospitals 66
households 15, 21, 166-70, 249; Datooga and
    Iraqw peoples 135, 141; definition of 45n;
    Kenya 195, 247; Maasai peoples 16, 18, 24,
    29-33, 35, 37-9, 42, 109, 112, 118, 186-94,
    199, 205-6, 214, 222, 224, 232, 234-5; Pokot
    people 177-9; Rendille people 162; Somalis
    91, 95-6; Turkana people, 69, 77-8, 81-3, 86
    see also engaji, families
housing 193
Hubeer clan 10, 91-105
hunting/gathering 58, 97, 99, 103-4, 104-5nn,
    110, 168, 223
hunting associations *see hirin*
Huxley, Elspeth 17
hyenas 97, 135

Iliffe, John 22-5
ilmurran see murran
Iloikop wars 39, 48n
iltorrobo see Dorobos
immigration *see* migration
immunization 156, 158-9
imports 172-3, 184
income 13, 64, 97, 108, 120, 123, 152, 157, 163,
    171-2, 184, 186, 188-96, 201, 221, 226, 235-
    6, 246, 254-5
inflation 66-7, 84-5, 165, 172
inheritance 10, 33, 36, 42, 64, 70, 81, 95-6, 224
initiation 68, 77, 113
International Bank for Reconstruction and
    Development 226
Iramba people 127, 137
Iraqw people 12-13, 125-46, 145n
Irqwa Da/aw 127-8, 141-2
irrigation 174, 246-8, 250, 252, 255
Isiolo 184
Islam 97, 105n
Iteso 248

Jacobs, Alan 234

Kaisut Desert 154-5

Kalabata 251
Kamba protest 165
Kapenguria-Makutano 175, 180
Kaputei 185
Kaputir 61
Karamojong people 177, 248
Katilu 246-7
Kekarongole 246-7
Kenya 15, 40, 50, 66, 108, 110-11, 120, 149,
    152, 163, 168, 172, 177, 195, 205, 221, 231,
    241-2, 244-6, 256; African Land Develop-
    ment Board 243; Baringo District 14, 28,
    175, 242-4; Central Province 41; Eastern
    Province 243; Garissa District 149; Isiolo Dis-
    trict 247, 250-3, 255; Kajiado District 15-16,
    30, 33, 149, 163-4, 166, 172-3, 181-96, 244;
    Labour Commission – East Africa Protec-
    torate 44-45n; Laikipia District 8, 29, 31, 33,
    35, 181; Machakos District 183, 193, 242-3;
    Mandera District 149; Marsabit District, 149,
    154-5, 168; Ministry of Livestock Develop-
    ment 181; Narok District 149, 181; Northern
    Province 243; Rift Valley Province 184, 243;
    Samburu District 248, 250-1; Trans Nzoia
    District 177; Turkana District 8-10, 12, 61,
    149, 246-7, 250-4; Wajir District 149, 250-1;
    West Pokot District, 163-4, 172, 174-81, 196;
    White Highlands 66
Kenya African Rifles 49n
Kenya Land Commission 45n
Kenya Livestock Development Programme 165
    185
Kenya Meat Commission 173, 184, 195
Kerio 61
Kiboko ranch 189, 193
Kikuyu people 40
killing 128-9
kinship 137, 162, 256
Kisongo people 26, 29
Kituli 247
Kitwai 213
kojakokonit 253
Komolonik Pilot Project 226, 228-30, 232, 234-5
Konso people 104n
Konza 185
Korongoro Integrated People Oriented to Con-
    servation 237n
Korr 14, 155-62
Kumam 248

labour 12, 18, 49n, 169, 171-2; commoditization
    196; Datooga people 13, 143; Kenya 9, 44n,
    165, 167, 196, 243, 246; Maasai peoples 24,
    28-9, 37-8, 42, 108, 120, 186, 190, 193, 243;
    Pokot people 174, 177, 179; Somalis 93-4,
    96; Turkana people 55-6, 60-1, 64-5, 67, 73,
    86-7
Laiser clan 200
Laitayok clan 200, 208-9
land 13, 18, 25-6, 41, 44; alienation 224-5; com-
    moditization 9, 12, 19, 171, 196; Datooga
    and Iraqw peoples 125-8, 131-9, 141, 143-4;
    degradation 226, 242; Kenya 242-4, 246;
    Maasai peoples 28, 34, 40, 108, 123, 183,
    194-5, 224-6, 231, 235-6; Pokot people 177;
    privatization 165, 195, 245; Turkana people

63-4 *see also* grazing; soil conservation
Lelan 180
Lesotho 11
Lewogoso 155-62
lineages 93, 95-6, 99, 125, 130, 137, 139, 144,
    255
lions 135
livestock viii, 3, 5-6, 15, 19, 21-3, 28, 150, 164,
    221, 245, 249-50; and human life cycle 54;
    Borana people 154; cultural significance 10,
    167; Datooga and Iraqw peoples 13; destock-
    ing 126, 246; dipping 230-2, 236; Gabbra
    people 154; growth rates 32-3; Kenya 14, 41,
    149, 165, 173, 195-6, 243; 'large' and 'small'
    distinction 68; livestock units per capita 201-
    5, 216-17; Maasai peoples 16-18, 24, 27, 29,
    33, 40, 108, 112, 115, 118, 183, 196, 202,
    211, 215, 232, 236; raiding and theft 3, 35-
    40, 48n, 51, 80, 85, 128-9, 177, 178, 213,
    245, 248; Rendille people 154, 155, 161-2;
    restocking 205, 215-17, 241-2, 246, 248-56;
    Rift Valley 247; small stock 67, 76, 154, 223-
    4, 233, 252 (*see also* name of animal); Somalis
    11, 97, 100-1, 104; stock friendships/ partner-
    ships *see* friendship; tick-borne diseases 199,
    210, 216 (*see also* name of disease); tropical
    livestock units 175-9, 181-2, 186-8, 190, 196,
    201, 205; Turkana people 9, 51-5, 57, 61-2
    see also camels; cattle; goats; oxen; sheep
loans 167, 199-200, 216, 249, 251, 253-4
Lodwar 66, 78, 84, 87, 251
Loitokitok 40, 173, 181
Loliondo 27
Lomut 180
Longosua ranch 189
Looaa 139
Lukumai clan 200
Luo people 79
Lutherans 248
Luuq 97

Maa Development Organization 237n
Maa language 23, 58, 222-3
Maasai Livestock and Range Management Pro-
    ject 222, 225, 228-30, 232-6
Maasai peoples 7-8, 13, 15-18, 20-44, 106-24,
    127-9, 142, 149, 151-2, 163, 166, 181-96,
    199-217, 221-36, 244, 250
Maasai Range Commission 226, 228, 238n
Maasai Range Project Ranching Associations 227
Mace, Ruth 254-5
Macha Oromo people 104n
Magadi 29
Maghang 142
maize 64, 109, 151, 156-7, 165, 169, 172-5, 179-
    80, 184-5, 193, 196
Makasen clan 200
Makueni 193
malaria 152, 154, 159, 161
maleness 100-2
Mali 149, 151-2, 154
Malka Dakaa 246-7, 250-1, 255
malnutrition *see* food
Mamasita clan 200
Mandera 246
Mang'ati people 130

Mangola 137
Manyoni 132
Marakwet people 174-5
Maral 177, 180
markets and marketing 24, 33-5, 38, 40, 66, 78-9,
     87, 152, 160, 163, 165-6, 168-70, 172-3, 175-
     6; 178-81, 183-4, 195-6, 216; 231, 246 *see also*
     bartering; black market; distress sales; trade
marriage 169, 249, 255; Datooga and Iraqw peo-
     ples 129, 136-7; Maasai peoples 24, 108, 202,
     207-11, 223-4; Somalis 97-9; Turkana people
     52-3, 55, 60-1, 63, 65, 68, 70, 72, 77, 80-6
     see also exogamy; polygamy
Marsabit Mountain 155
Masimba 193
matrifiliation 71
matrilineal system 100-1
Mbalambala 246
Mbulu 138, 143; destocking scheme 126; people
     130
measles 152, 159
meat 151-2, 156, 159-61, 165-8, 170, 173, 183-4,
     189-90, 195, 201, 221, 223, 225-6, 229, 231,
     233-4
medicine *see* health
mediums 139, 141
Melanesia 11
men 152, 170, 255; Datooga and Iraqw peoples
     136; Kenya 246; Maasai peoples 17-18, 33,
     35, 107-8, 112-13, 118-22, 193-4, 200, 202-3,
     207-10, 222-6, 228-30, 233-5, 246; Somalis
     152, 175; Turkana people 65, 84-6, 152 *see
     also* maleness; *murran*
Merifle clans 91, 93-4, 98, 103
Merti 246-7
metaphor and symbolism 9-11, 13, 71, 74, 76, 78,
     87, 97-101, 107, 117, 123, 130-1, 135, 223
Mfereji 226, 228, 230
migration 24, 28, 40, 72, 96, 127, 132, 137, 141,
     168-9, 171, 176, 179, 186, 188, 193
milk 151, 166-70; Datooga and Iraqw peoples
     138; Fulani people 152; Maasai peoples 24,
     33, 35, 183, 184, 188-90, 193-4, 201, 203,
     223-4, 233-5; Pokot people 176, 179-80;
     Rendille people 156-7, 159-62; Somalis 100;
     Turkana people 58, 69, 81 *see also* breast-feed-
     ing; dairying
millet 151, 165, 168, 175, 180, 222
miraa 177
missionaries 49n, 66, 141, 157, 176-7, 248
Mitsubishi Corporation 173-4
modernity 106-7, 119, 121-2, 225
Molellian clan 200, 210
Mombasa 183
Monduli 226, 234
Monduli Juu 214, 230, 232, 235
money 12, 169-71, 255; Kenya 172, 184; Maasai
     peoples 34-5, 111, 115, 117-19, 122, 189-94,
     209, 225; Pokot people 176, 178; Rendille
     people 157; Somalis 99; Turkana people 9-
     10, 59, 64-7, 75, 77-81, 84-5 *see also* capital
morbidity *see* health
Moris, Jon 245
Moroto 176
mortality rates 150, 152, 154, 156
Moshi 114-15, 117

muddo 94
murran 35-8, 48-49n, 110, 223
Muslims *see* Islam
mutual assistance 199-217, 250, 255-6
myths 102-3, 126-7

Nade Bea 141-2
Nairobi 66, 111-12, 120, 183-4, 186
Nakwijit 177-8, 180
Namanga 8, 13, 107, 109-23
Nayobi 211, 213-15
Ndoto Mountains 155
Ngabotok 28
Ngebaren 54
Ngibochoros 58
Ngibosheros 59
Ngikatap see Nkiketak
Ngikebootok 56-61, 76
Ngirionok 58
Ngong 28, 46n, 183-4
Ngong Hills 181
Ngorongoro 16, 26
Ngorongoro Conservation Area 199-217
Ngurunit 155-62
Niger 149
Nigeria 149
Nilotic peoples 126, 255
Nkiketak 59
Noah 96
nobles *see bilis*
non-governmental organizations viii, 66, 150,
     170, 177, 222, 235, 240, 248
NORAD 66
Nordic Africa Institute viii, x
Northern (Maasai) Reserve 31
Norway x, 114
Norwegian-Tanzanian Acquired Immune
     Deficiency Syndrome (AIDS) Project 124n
Nuer people 12
nutrition *see* food
Nyanza 41
Nyaturu people 127

ochre 110
oil 68
Ojayle group 95
Olkarkar ranch 185-95
olkarsis 203
Olkinos ranch 185
Olkonerei Integral Pastoralist Survival
     Programme 237n
Oloirobi 210
Oloirobi-Ilmesigio 208
olparakuoni 203
Ooflawe 91, 93-4, 97
Oromo people 92
Ortum 180
overgrazing *see* grazing; land-degradation
oxen 34, 145n, 248-9
Oxfam 205, 250-6

paddocking 243
parasites 152
parastatals 173
pastoralism viii-ix, 3-44, 240-56 *see also* name of
     people

Pastoralist Network in Tanzania 237n
pathways 10-11, 52, 62-3, 67-8, 70, 72-3, 76-8,
    80-2, 86-8 *see also* roads
patrilineal system 71, 91, 99-101, 104, 200, 206
Perham, Margery 128-9
Poka ranch 189
Pokot people 15-16, 163-4, 166, 168, 174-80, 196
police 113
politics 67, 92-3, 103, 116, 121, 165, 172, 194-6,
    223, 225, 236, 254
pollution, ritual 136
polygamy 16, 69, 83, 135, 194, 202-3, 255
population 168, 175-7, 181-3, 216
porridge 203
potatoes 174
poverty viii-ix, 3-19; conjunctural 7-8, 25-7, 41,
    44, 256; definitions of 23, 53-5, 157; endemic
    23; historical context 20-44; structural 7, 19,
    25-7, 41, 43-4, 256 *see also* destitution; name
    of people
prayers 132, 135-6, 138, 140, 142-3
prices 164-5, 169, 172-3, 179-80, 184-5, 252-3
prison 128-9
privatization 34-5, 39, 64, 108, 164, 192, 195,
    245
productivity 171-2, 195-6, 224-6, 229, 244
property 81, 125-6, 134, 256
prostitution 107-8, 112, 119-20
proverbs 135
Purko people 8, 31

railways 183
rainfall 50, 154, 156, 169, 176, 181-2, 215 *see also*
    droughts
ranching 34, 66, 149-50, 170-1, 177, 183, 185-96,
    226, 228-33, 235-6, 243
'ratchet effect' 7, 27, 249
registration 243-4
rehabilitation 241-5, 248, 250, 252
religion 126, 134, 139, 141, 143 *see also* name of
    religion or sect
Rendille people 14, 32, 149-62, 205
reproduction 71, 73-4
Rer Ma'allin lineage 95
reserves 39-40
resettlement 241, 245-8, 250-3
respiratory diseases 152, 156, 158, 161
Rift Valley 28, 42, 226, 247
rights 134, 224-6, 229, 233, 235-6, 242
rinderpest 27, 43, 65, 181
rituals 68, 70-2, 97-8, 104, 126-8, 131-3, 138-43,
    155, 167, 176, 213, 223 *see also* funerary rites;
    initiation; pollution, ritual; sacrifices
roads 87-8, 183
Roman Catholics *see* Catholics
Rotian Riot 49n
Rumuruti 49n

sacrifices 70, 72, 74, 77, 131, 140
Sahel 149, 250
Salei Plain 202, 204, 209, 213
Sam 96
Samburu language 155
Samburu people 21, 32, 49n, 255
schools *see* education
Scoones, Ian 242

seasonality 18, 152
Sebit 180
sedentarization viii, 14-15, 85, 149-62, 221, 245,
    248
Sekerr Hills 174, 177
seniority 83, 85
sex 107, 111, 115-16, 118-19 *see also* prostitution
sheep 50, 67-8, 73-4, 76, 109, 130-1, 135, 138,
    151, 155, 167, 174-80, 182, 186, 208, 230,
    233, 249-50
Shinianga 216
shuka see clothes
Sierra Leone 11
Sigor 175
Simaga subclan 208-9
simulacra 100
Siyabei 28-9
skins *see* hides
slaughter, ceremonial *see* rituals
slaughterhouses 173-4, 184, 195
slavery 47n, 94, 99
smallpox 181
smell 13, 107, 114, 117-18
smuggling 110-11
soda 29
soil conservation 171
Somali language 91, 104-5nn
Somalia 5, 149, 168, 184
Somalis 10-11, 13, 33, 91-105, 111, 152, 155,
    168, 175, 179, 200
songs 71, 133
Sonrai people 152, 154
sons 98, 104
sorcery *see* witchcraft
sorghum 58-60, 64, 99, 169, 174-80, 222
Soroti Livestock Restocking Programme 248-9
Southern Cushitic peoples 126
Southern Nilotic peoples 126
spirits 13, 74, 134, 138-41, 143-4
starch 160-1
state 32, 44, 170, 245-6; and Datooga and Iraqw
    peoples 128; and Maasai peoples 38, 41, 111,
    113, 116, 122-3, 222, 225-6, 228-9, 231-2,
    235-6, 244; and Pokot people 176-7, 180; and
    Turkana people 64; Kenya 165, 172, 195
statistics 14, 30-2, 47n
stock *see* livestock
structural adjustment 172
Suam River 177
Sudan 5, 66, 149; Bahr el-Ghazal Province 255
sufficiency 24, 30-1, 157, 186
sugar 157, 160-1
Sukuma people 213
Swahili language 113, 122
Swahili people 112-13, 118-21, 130
Sweden x
symbolism *see* metaphor and symbolism
syphilis 152

Talamai 229, 231
Tamasheq people *see* Tuareg
Tanganyika *see* Tanzania
Tanganyika Agricultural Corporation 226
Tanzania 5, 12, 16, 106-25, 173, 183-4, 221, 225-
    9, 231, 235, 242-3; Kiteto District 202, 206;
    Maasai District 224, 226-7, 229, 232; Mbuli

District 128; Monduli District 108, 202, 206, 214; Ngorongoro District 199, 202, 215; Range Management and Development Act (1964) 226; Simanjiro District 202, 204, 206, 213-14
Tanzania Canada Wheat Project 128, 143-4
Tara people *see* Datooga people
Tarosero clan 200
tattooing *see* branding and tattooing
Taveta 26, 28
taxation 21, 24, 34, 44n, 61, 65-6, 77, 176, 224
tea 156, 160, 203
Terat 213
theft 168, 230 *see also* livestock – raiding and theft
Thomson, Joseph 117
Torrobo people 104n
tourism 108, 111, 122, 216
towns *see* urbanization
trachoma 152
trade 15, 28, 34-5, 43, 61, 65, 108, 151, 155, 164, 175-7, 192, 208, 223, 252 *see also* black market; markets and marketing; smuggling
tradition 106, 121-4, 179, 225
trails *see* pathways
training 233-4
Transmara 40
trespass 243
tribalism *see* ethnicity
tropical livestock units *see* livestock
tsetse fly 141, 226
Tswana people 3, 79
Tua Masay 141-2
Tuareg 3, 25, 152, 154
tuberculosis 152
Tugen people 14
Turkana, Lake 59-60
Turkana people 8, 12, 50-88, 149, 151-2, 160, 162, 255
Turkana Rehabilitation Project 250, 252
Turkwell, River 59

Uganda 5, 164, 168, 173, 175-7, 245, 248
United Kingdom *see* Britain
United Nations Development Programme 246-7
United States 171, 234, 238n
United States Agency for International Development 18, 150, 222, 226, 228, 231-4, 236
Upe Pokot people *see* Pokot people
urbanization 61, 87-8, 107, 150, 162, 183 *see also* Namanga

vegetables 151, 157, 160-1, 176

veterinary medicine 30, 176, 191, 193, 199, 216, 221, 224, 229
villagization 106, 235-6

Waanjele group 95
wages 37-8
Wajir 251
Wakwafi people *see* Arusha people
warfare viii, 3, 5-6, 12, 39, 48n, 85, 96, 126-9, 149, 246 *see also* World War I; World War II
Waso Borana people *see* Borana people
water 22, 34, 39, 112, 152, 164, 170-1, 188-9, 193, 216, 221, 224, 226, 228-32, 236, 245 *see also* irrigation
Watta people 104n
wealth 9, 20, 22-3, 27, 32, 42-3, 92, 163, 168, 249; Datooga and Iraqw peoples 125-6; Kenya 174, 184, 251; Laikipia 33; Maasai peoples 20-1, 26, 31, 34, 43-4, 108-9, 113, 186-96, 201-2, 205, 207-8, 223; Pokot people 178; Rendille people. 157; Somalis 98; Turkana people 10, 12, 56, 59, 62, 65, 67-8, 72-4, 76, 78, 80, 85 *see also* blood-wealth; bride-wealth
weaning 156
weapons 176-8
weather 50
weddings *see* marriage
wheat 128, 130, 144
White, Luise 120
widowhood 255-6
wisdom 100, 131
witchcraft 133-5, 146n
women 152, 169-70, 249; Datooga and Iraqw peoples 131, 135-8; Dinka people 255; Kenya 246, 254-5; Maasai peoples 18, 27, 33, 35, 108, 111-12, 118, 120-1, 152, 191, 193-4, 202-3, 207-10, 217, 222-5, 233-6; Marakwet people 175; Namanga 107, 111-12, 115-22; Pokot people 175, 179-80; Rendille people 151, 154, 156-8, 161; Samburu people 255; Somalis 101, 152; Tuareg 152; Turkana people 64-5, 69, 76, 83, 86, 152, 255; widows 255-6 *see also* femaleness
wood 193, 246
World Bank 66, 150, 165, 185, 226
World Food Programme 252
World Health Organization 159-60
World Vision 150, 248
World War I 224
World War II 128, 175